THE EDUC
ROUNDABOUT

GW00373865

To Lis
with love from Anne xx

Launch – "New Orleans", Thames
17 June 2015   £10

THE EDUCATION ROUNDABOUT

by

ANNE JONES

The Memoir Club

© Anne Jones

First published in 2015 by
The Memoir Club
12 Tower Road
Washington Tyne and Wear
NE37 2SH
Tel: 0191 419 2288
Email: memoirclub@msn.com

All rights reserved.
Unauthorised duplication
contravenes existing laws.
British Library Cataloguing in
Publication Data.
A catalogue record for this book
is available from the British Library

Printed by JASPRINT, Washington

I dedicate this book to my children and grandchildren:

Christopher and Sarah Jones, Ben and Alice Jones
Katy and Mike Spencer, Huw and Sarah Spencer
Becky and David Crichton-Miller,
Alex, Harry and Freddie Crichton-Miller

A special tribute to Katy.
From all her family and friends.
Katy will be in our hearts for ever.

In April 2015, I celebrated my birthday with a big family party. My daughter Katy, aged fifty-one, wrote me a lovely card, thanking me for everything. Three weeks later she was dead. She had just received a national award for the pioneer work she had devised and led successfully for the BBC: TEN PIECES. The next day she died of a double brain aneurism, a terrible condition, for which there is no warning and no cure. It was not caused by the incredible amount of work she had done in the service of others. We are all shattered.

My Daughter was a highly successful investigative television journalist who fought all her life for justice and lifelong learning. She began her career at Granada, delivering twenty-five *World in Action* programmes, for example exposing child abuse in Staffordshire. In 1994, she married Mike Spencer, Head of Granada's regional programmes. When their children, Huw and Sarah were young, she also set up 'Child's Eye Media', a highly successful company which made DVDs for Early Years Children, with real children in the leading roles.

In 1996, she worked with Jimmy McGovern to make the Drama-Documentary, *Hillsborough*. This won a BAFTA. Katy's role was as factual Producer. She knew all the families well and ensured that nothing went into the film which would cause them further distress.

In 2010, Katy was appointed to the Hillsborough Independent Panel. Katy continued her meticulous research of the Hillsborough files. The Research panel's report in September 2012, led to the instigation of new investigations. The Hillsborough parents really appreciated Katy's role in all this. A large number of Hillsborough parents attended her funeral and they also sent ninety-six blood red roses to her house.

Over fifteen years, mostly in collaboration with Jimmy McGovern and Nicola Schindler, came many outstanding and award winning films and broadcasts. In 2011 Katy was appointed Executive Producer for the BBC's Learning Zone, making films mainly for schools and children's programmes. In four years, she commissioned over 130 such programmes, winning more than fifty awards, including six BAFTAS. In 2014, Tony Hall, Director-General of the BBC launched the Ten Pieces Project with Katy. He said 'Ten Pieces is the biggest commitment the BBC's ever made to music education'. On her death, he said: 'Katy stood for everything I love about the BBC, its ability to reach everyone, to bring communities and generations together'.

That's certainly true of her. Everybody loved and respected her, her integrity and reliability, her forward looking vision, her sense of humour, determination, inspiration, hard work and affection and beauty.

Katy was delighted that I was writing this book, then she wouldn't have to do it for me! She was very proud of me and vice versa. We were very close.

CONTENTS

LIST OF ILLUSTRATIONS

ACKNOWLEDGEMENTS

It was obvious to me that I would never be able to thank enough the people who have helped me in my life and work. If I started naming people in each chapter, I would be bound to offend others who hadn't been named. I owe a lot to my parents, family and friends. Here are some of the people who helped me do what I have done.

Dame Joyce Bishop gave me a start in counselling and Dame Margaret Miles made it happen, The Kogan twins: Philip printed the second edition of my counselling book and Maurice helped me to get the job at Brunel. The Grubb Institute and particularly John Bazalgette taught me how to define goals and build commitment to ideas with a large or small group and how to lead a team. Charles Handy got me the sabbatical at the London Business School. Tony Watts of CRAC helped my quest for better careers guidance, as did Geoff Cooksey, who also helped me to create community schools and made me laugh. Thomas Calton staff helped me warmly in the transition from grammar school into multi-racial secondary school. Vauxhall Manor staff challenged me at first, then, united, we turned the school around. Cranford was my dream school, which we, (staff, parents, pupils, adult learners, and local employers) transformed together into a really modern innovative community school. The civil service was amazingly tolerant and helpful, considering my sudden arrival to such heights, and we achieved a lot. Brunel was a challenge, but through it, we developed many successful lifelong learning projects. My freelance work, especially the work abroad in Central and Eastern Europe was absolutely thrilling and I was very well looked after. My children, Christopher, Katy and Becky have been loving, supportive and helpful through all this and so have all my friends old and new.

Finally thanks to Lynn Davidson of The Memoir Club for her help in getting this book together

INTRODUCTION

I was first asked to write this book fifteen years ago. In 2013, I finally began. Fortunately I had kept all the key data in the garage so the documentation is authentic. I had no idea how much work I had done; I was so busy doing it. This book could have been a plain academic tome, but I wanted my family and friends to understand better how and why it all happened. So I have included my own commentary and some humour as well. I don't expect my readers to sit down and read it line by line, but to pick out the parts which interest them. My life itself is a story of lifelong learning. My quest to make it more accessible for all continues. Enjoy yourself!

CHAPTER 1: BEGINNINGS

My family background

MY FAMILY LIVED IN COVENTRY. In the nineteenth century my relatives, on both sides, had all been silk weavers, apart from my great-grandfather who was a trumpeter in the army. By the twentieth century, they all worked in local government or in the growing motor industry as office workers, draughtsmen, or skilled or semiskilled operatives. My maternal grandparents still had the 'TOP SHOP' on the third floor where the loom used to be. They had specialised in weaving ribbons for medals. Grandad had turned it into a gym by the time I was there.

My parents, Hilda and Sydney Pickard, were both highly intelligent, the only pupils in their neighbourhood to win scholarships to public (i.e. private) schools. This fact inevitably threw them together and made them 'different' from their home peer group. They both matriculated at fourteen. My father continued his studies at evening college and became a mechanical engineer. My mother took clerical jobs for the local council at which she excelled, but never made the leap she deserved to becoming a senior administrator or her other ambition, a professional actress. In her mid-thirties she took a university diploma in sociology at evening classes and passed with distinction. My father took up the cello and painting in middle age. My mother ran the local drama group. In their old age they did a lot for their lovely village, Bampton, in Oxfordshire, now of Downton fame. Both my parents were true lifelong learners and community volunteers. I have definitely inherited these characteristics!

The war years

I was born and bred in Coventry in 1935. 1940/41 blitz memories of sleepless nights in the air raid shelter, waiting for the bombs to drop, lessons underground, then fifty to a class, back-to-back in the hall. Thrice bombed out, we fled to London, only to be evacuated back to Coventry when the flying bombs started. Lessons interrupted by air

1

raid warnings, rehearsals for victory day parades, jolly singsongs to pass the time, not much 'real' education.

Then peace and I blossomed at my co-ed secondary school. Harrow Weald County was a forward looking co-ed grammar school. I could have gone to North London Collegiate, but my mother thought I was too much of a swot and that it would improve me for the better to mix with boys! My younger brothers, David and Michael later joined me there and my parents were active PTA members. It was a remarkable school: in 1946, the year I arrived, it had already abolished streaming, done away with positions in class and established an effective and democratic School Council, providing genuine pupil power and responsibility. I ended up as Deputy Head girl and Chairman of the debating society.

In 1953, whether or not I should go to university was a question of great debate. My parents had both won scholarships to public schools, but no-one in my family had gone to university before and they were not sure whether a university education was worth it, 'especially for a girl!' Why not a job in the civil service? I resolved to get a state scholarship and worked very hard. Determined to leave the issue in no doubt, I won one (a boy got the only other one) and took up a place at Westfield College, London University in 1953.

Life at university:
Westfield College, London University, 1953-6

In those days only a small percentage, about 5%, mostly boys, went on to higher education, not even everyone who went to grammar school. I won a state scholarship but as my father earned over £1000 a year, my grant only paid for fees and boarding, nothing for me! My parents gave me £3 pocket money a month and I supplemented this by selling sweets at Wembley Stadium on Saturdays for £1 a day and also by joining the University of London Air Squadron which paid for the travel to South Kensington and a small fee.

That was not, in fact, the **only** reason I wanted to join the squadron. It was partly to counteract the fact that Westfield was an all female/all residential college. I was not used to this, having been to a co-ed school. Problem overcome: there were sixty male pilots and twelve female fighter-controllers! I still see some of those pilots to this day! Alan Tipper and Basil Evans are both members of my Club, Phyllis Court in Henley.

Women were not allowed to be pilots in those days. Our job was to 'tell the pilots where to go', that is to direct them from a radar screen into a position where they could shoot down the enemy plane. Scary stuff, especially when we officer cadets went off on summer camps each year to do it for real. I have no idea how I managed to succeed in the maths test we had to pass to get in. I have wonderful memories of my time in the squadron. They wanted me to join up and make it my career, but I had other ideas.

ULAS the University of London Air Squadron on summer camp

The second activity I took up was the University of London Union (ULU) Debating Society. I became clerk of debates. I wish I could track down that minute book! I had debated a lot at school so felt very confident about speaking in Senate House. My colleagues on the committee included two lifelong friends, Jeffrey Thomas, later MP and Terry Boston, later Lord Boston of Faversham, QC. We invited many future politicians and stars to speak, such as Michael Heseltine. Neil Crichton-Miller, then President of the Cambridge Union, was another lifelong friend, whose son David later married my daughter Becky.

The third was being active in college life, including the Debating

Society there. At Easter in the second year, I was elected as President of the Westfield College Students' Union. This was a bit risky, since the last two Presidents had failed their finals and had to take an extra year in order to graduate. That was not a consideration for me. I had already dismissed the idea of a year in France, as I wanted to be independent from my family as soon as possible. I spent my vacations as an au pair girl in France, or at RAF/Air Squadron Camp, or working in seaside Hotels. And I did get my degree in my Presidential year, an upper second in French and Spanish.

Westfield was a small college founded by pioneer women in the late nineteenth century, with about 200 female students in my day. There were strict rules about men. They were not allowed in your room except in the afternoon. Apparently in some colleges you had to wheel your bed into the corridor if you had male guests! If you wanted to be out after 10.30pm, you had to sign a book and sign back in by 11pm. If you wanted to be out until midnight you had to ask permission of the Principal herself. Twice a year you were allowed exeats until 2.30am. When I was President I was allowed to break these rules as I had to go to a lot of Presidents' Balls all over the country!

However, I was also expected to see the Principal every day at 9am just to check that nothing untoward was happening. Those living on the main campus got locked out if they were late, those living in former large private houses could usually get in through a window. Many very sociable students, especially those who had been to boarding school, just stayed out all night and if necessary got someone else to sign them in the next morning. We had to wear our academic gowns for all lectures. Those few girls who became pregnant could easily disguise their condition. The gowns were also useful for warmth and as a kind of pinafore.

One of my achievements as President was to put Westfield on the map. Most London University students had never heard of Westfield, tucked away as it was in leafy Hampstead. We adopted a King Penguin at the zoo as our mascot; we then made a wooden penguin which meant that our mascot could be stolen by other colleges. That gave us publicity in the ULU newsletter! Much later on, Westfield was taken over by

Queen Mary College, London. I became very involved in this in my retirement. More of this later!

Westfield College students adopt a penguin as their mascot, 1955

King's College London 1956-7
Post graduate diploma in education

Anne Pickard, What's My Line? *1956*

I had originally wanted to travel and work in Europe but I settled for doing a PGCE on the grounds that being a teacher would be useful when I had a family and wherever I lived. I was accepted at King's College London. I hardly went to any lectures in the first term!

The reason for this was that just before the academic year started, I had a totally unexpected short spell as a 'celebrity'. I had been suggested by the university as a possible replacement for Barbara Kelly on the

Panel of *What's My Line?* with Eamonn Andrews, Bob Monkhouse Gilbert Harding and Lady Isobel Barnett. To my absolute amazement I was chosen and did a few programs. But it didn't last long. However, to knock up £50 an hour was incredible! The fees helped me to get through the next academic year.

In the summer of 1956, I had been elected Lady Vice President of ULU. The University of London at that time comprised of about 20,000 students and about twenty colleges. In the autumn, the Hungarian Revolution took place and so we spent a lot of time welcoming refugee students, providing food, accommodation, and support. It was hard but very worthwhile. The next initiative I undertook was to set up and run the first ever Student International Festival. We persuaded all the nationalities we could find, and there were many, including some Commonwealth and some European countries, to set up a multi-cultural display and to take part in a multi-cultural concert. It all worked very well and was fun.

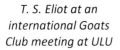

T. S. Eliot at an international Goats Club meeting at ULU

I was also a founder member of the Goats Club which brought the international community of students together for talks from eminent people. Our President was T. S. Eliot. He came and read us some of his poems, in his rather disappointing voice. It was 1953, the year that Hillary and Tenzing conquered Everest and 1954 Roger Bannister ran the first four minute mile.

One of the most exciting events of the year was to meet our Chancellor, Elizabeth the Queen Mother. I had already met her at a ball in Senate House, where we had danced in an Eightsome Reel together… the only way a woman ever gets to dance with a Queen! The next time was at a dinner we, the ULU Officers, were hosting for the Presidents for all the other UK universities. It fell to me to propose the toast for the guests. I remember saying what a pleasure it was to lend OUR River to Oxford and Cambridge for THEIR annual Boat Race, Her Majesty leant over and said: 'My dear that was SPIFFING.'

Anne Pickard, Lady Vice President ULU, 1956-7

During my Vice Presidential year, I was interviewed for the ULU newspaper, *Sennet* by Jean Rook. She included two quotes from me which amaze me now for their accuracy: 'I'm one of those people who always do too much, never have a moment to spare, but enjoy life that way.' Anne intends to take a diploma in education at King's College and to dedicate herself, at least until she marries, (Remember it wasn't long before that that women teachers had to retire upon marriage.) to 'the most worthwhile career' of teaching, with a view to a possible administrative post after part-time study for a further degree in education and psychology, a social science diploma and secretarial qualifications'. Well, that's all accurate too, except for the secretarial skills, which was a big mistake now I have to do all my own word processing!

Teaching at Malvern Girls College, 1957-1958

Surprisingly, in spite of my ULU activities, I did get my teaching diploma. My tutor said she confidently predicted that I would be an educator in the truest sense of the word, whatever that means! So on to my first job as a teacher, a French Mistress as we were called then, at Malvern Girls College. My starting salary was £700pa!

I really didn't enjoy living and eating in an all female staff boarding house. It was worse than college. We weren't allowed men (not even a fiancé) into our rooms at all! I had free afternoons, and then an evening teaching session and we worked Saturday mornings. I most enjoyed visiting a nunnery at the weekends and helping with their garden, singing in the Malvern Choral Society and attending a history of art evening class! The pupils were fine, but they too were over-protected from ever meeting a boy. No wonder my roommate at Westfield, (previously MGC), did very little work in her first year, but partied all the time.

Gareth and I had met and got engaged during the year at King's, so luckily I had a good reason to leave MGC after a year. Apparently all the new young teachers did this. We married in August 1958. I taught altogether for five years, then, on the birth of my son, gave up full-time work until all our three children were in full-time schooling. That took nine years, though I did work one day a week for the last six years.

Touring Czechoslovakia by car in 1958

1958 was the first year that we Brits were allowed to travel in a communist country freely in our own car, in our case a little white A35. In every little village, people clustered around us, as if we had landed from MARS. The men had never seen such a car. The women, in headscarves and aprons, broke off from feeding the chickens or tending the garden. They spoke to us in German, the only language we had in common. Prague was very beautiful but very shabby. We met some students who came and talked to us frankly in our hotel and then were very worried in case the room was bugged. We paid for meals with pre-purchased coupons. These bought the most superior food, such as you got if you were a party official. The food was filling.

Article in *Hermes*, Westfield College magazine, 1959

Last summer, my husband and I spent nine days touring in Czechoslovakia, which of course, was still under Russian control. During the course of our stay in Prague, we visited both the Institute of Pedagogical Research and the Ministry of Education. On both occasions we were received with great cordiality, and were able to ask questions freely about the Czech educational system. I might add that these interviews were conducted in French to my delight, for hitherto my husband had done all the talking, in German, while I stood by, a frustrated onlooker.

We found that the Czechs shared many of our problems and goals: they want to raise the general level of education, expand technical education and provide more teachers and buildings. The difference between us lies in our aims and means. Their aim is not merely to educate each child to the best of his or her aptitude and ability, but also produce a citizen who will work happily and wholeheartedly for the good of the Communist State. The inculcation of Communist doctrine is an integral part of the educational system, rather as Christian doctrine in a Church school here. Centralisation and uniformity of system are the means by which this ideal 'state' servant is produced.

From five to sixteen, all Czech children attend a common co-educational school and are given the same grounding in all basic subjects, including the sciences and Russian at 11-plus. The same textbook and syllabus for each subject are prescribed throughout the whole nation. Schools and classes are kept as small as possible so that a school of over a thousand is regarded with horror as a mere machine. Great stress is laid on creative activity, aesthetic appreciation, health care and physical education.

At sixteen comes selection, based on the child's preference, his school record (academic and political) and an examination. With borderline cases, preference is given to the working class child in order to raise the standards of the nation as a whole. A good political record and membership of the pioneer organisation the political guides and scouts also help. There is no school uniform, but the pioneer outfit, with a red kerchief, is often worn. The best sixteen-year-olds go either to grammar or to technical schools for three more years. Entrance to university is possible from either. At eighteen or nineteen, there is a state examination with compulsory Czech, Russian and mathematics plus four optional subjects, which may include German or English. University entrance is based on this and a report, and again, one's political record. Non-party activities may ruin one's chance of academic success. This was confirmed by two students we met in Prague. The rest of the sixteen-year-olds go to apprentice schools for two or three years. Their training is practical in factories or farms as well as theoretical. These skilled workers may also qualify for university by going to a grammar school for workers in the evenings. Evening schools also provide music and art classes.

The Czechs are anxious to remove the stigma attached to manual labour, and the preference felt for a white collar job. They have legislated that all pupils of fourteen to seventeen must work twelve hours a week in a factory, with the scientific background and theory explained first in school. They believe that this is not exploitation of child labour; it is necessary to give the child a full education. This obviously fits in also with the need of the 'state' for intelligent technicians and skilled workers if the economy is to expand as they wish.

Education is free and grants are available, based on a means test, both for school and university. There is the inevitable shortage of teachers, but despite this, the teachers' training course has been extended from three years to four, and eventually will be five. Non-graduate teachers start their training at sixteen. Graduate teachers do practical and theoretical work on education during their four year degree course.

Teachers' pay is comparable with ours and there is a system of responsibility allowances. Teachers can choose and change their schools as freely as we can. Teaching methods are controlled by the 'state'. The Institute of Pedagogical Research instigates and compares different teaching methods in various areas, then prescribes the most effective for the whole nation. Every syllabus is carefully controlled, and no teacher can do just as he likes when he likes.

Czech educationalists feel that now timetables are overloaded and subjects too examination-bound. They favour practical direct methods, with the full use of films, television, wireless and gramophone. They want to relate all that they teach to real life, and to remove the distinction between physical and mental work.

With nothing left to chance, and with their complete control of every child, the Czechs ought to achieve their aims. It will be interesting to follow the economic expansion of this potentially rich country and to see whether, among this nation of perfectly trained citizens, there are in fact any rebels without a cause.

Postscript
I am fascinated that I wrote this so seriously! I had taken the comparative education option as part of my postgraduate diploma in education, so I was interested already. Little did I know that in 2004 I would be asked by OECD to take part in a study and report on Secondary Education in Bulgaria, Slovenia and Albania! And more, as you will find out later!

Teaching at the Godolphin and Latymer School: 1958-62
This was a wonderful school and I was very happy there. It was an ILEA voluntary-aided grammar school, which meant that there were no fees. We prided ourselves on taking a lot of pupils whose parents would not have been able to afford it otherwise. Sadly, when ILEA went comprehensive, it decided to become an independent fee paying school. G&L raised money to support girls who won scholarships there. Most such schools continue to do so today.

The Headmistress at the time was Dame Joyce Bishop. She was an amazing person, and very much a character. She was unmarried and it was rumoured that she had lost her fiancé in WW1. We all adored her.

11

She ran a very firm but happy school and took great personal interest in both staff and pupils. I must have been twenty-three when I started there. She made me promise to stay for four years at least.

My husband was teaching chemistry at Dulwich College at this stage. Each of us was in charge of the debating society in our respective schools. We were very amused to find our teams in mortal combat in the Finals of the Observer Mace Competition. His team won!

When I was twenty-six, I was made Head of the sixth form. I was amazed, because I was so young and all but a couple of the other staff (mostly unmarried) looked as if they were well over fifty, which of course seemed very old to me then. But then her real motivation dawned on me. She wrote an extraordinary letter to the parents saying that she was worried about the possibility of girls 'getting into trouble' i.e. getting pregnant! She did not put it that way. She offered to 'help them' if necessary. She then asked me to run some group discussions about sex for the sixth form in my lunch hour. This I did with great pleasure. It turned out to be the first step in my future counselling career.

Dame Joyce Bishop, Headmistress of the Godolphin and Latymer School

However, a year later, I went to see her to say that my four years was nearly up so I would be leaving in the autumn to have my first baby.

She looked at me in amazement and said: 'You can't do that, you've been married for over three years and you still haven't got pregnant!' Now I knew why she wanted **me** to do the group work! Gareth and I decided we had better get on with it. I became pregnant straight away which led to some other problems for the school.

Strictly speaking, in those days, pregnant teachers were supposed to give up work eleven weeks before giving birth. We lived in Dulwich at the time, so I had a longish journey. However, we were saving up to get the deposit for a house. In those days you were not allowed to borrow more than 2.5 times your salary. We needed that August cheque. I had two large A-level sets and two O-level classes so it was hard work. I carried on teaching until the exams and then spent the rest of the term knitting a shawl in the staffroom, followed by one week off 'for personal reasons'. Christopher was born in the General Lying-in-Hospital in Southwark, which was overlooked by County Hall who were paying my salary. Luckily all ended well, but I doubt if anyone would get away with that now!

Life at home

The first year at home was grim but very happy. We had no spare money and had bought a huge four storey house in a dilapidated condition, full of potential, but not much actual. We froze and economised and did all our own renovating and decorating. Katy followed immediately after Christopher. Gareth said I was a walking fertility symbol, pricking out seedlings and hanging up nappies in a prolifically flowering garden, earth mother herself. I found it very satisfying.

We lived in Dulwich when the children were young. My husband had taught at Dulwich College, a boys' school, for a while, so they knew me. When I was at home with my first two children, the college asked me to cover for a French teacher who was on a six week sabbatical at Oxford. I ageed slightly reluctantly, as the staff were all men at the time. I found out later that they used to run a bet on what I would wear the next day!

One day, walking along the corridor I overheard two boys

discussing me. 'What a cow. She doesn't half work you hard!' I took this as a compliment. In one lesson a boy drew a cartoon of me. My punishment was to confiscate it. I actually thought it was rather good. Pity about my glasses!

Here is the cartoon I confiscated

After a year of lying completely fallow intellectually, I decided to go out one evening a week to London University extra-mural classes. After four years of part-time study, I took a diploma in sociology with distinction and won a university prize. At the same time I was invited to be a marriage guidance counsellor, in particular to work with the premarried: engaged couples, and teenagers in schools and clubs. I was selected and trained and began as a volunteer. It was through this experience that in 1964, Dame Margaret Miles, Head of Mayfield School a well known comprehensive girls' school in Putney, asked me to set up a counselling service at her school.

School counselling

Our thinking was remarkably similar. I began work one day a week in 1965, having first started further training as a social worker, training which entitled me to some supervision from a psychiatric social worker in an adolescent unit, Mary Kernick. I would not have been able to do the job properly without her professional, but unpaid help and support.

I had made it clear to Dame Margaret that I didn't want to work more than one day a week because of the children. Then in 1966, Becky, my third child was born, so I had a term's leave, then resumed, remaining at one day a week until Becky was five and went to school full time. I used my earnings to buy in some domestic help and I found the combination of the stimulus of the job and the extra help with the chores very important with the three children at such a delightful, but nevertheless, demanding and exhausting stage.

I was asked to write an article about school counselling (*Mental Health,* spring 1967). To my surprise Ward Lock Education then approached me and asked me to write a book about it. ***School Counselling in Practice*** was published in 1970. It seems I was one of the first school counsellors in the country, though one year diplomas in counselling were also starting up around that time. Here is the article.

Personal guidance for school children

Mental Health, spring 1967, Vol 26.11

Editorial comment

School counselling is just beginning in this country. Reading and Keele Universities began courses in educational guidance in October 1965, and other universities and colleges are following suit. Mayfield Comprehensive School for girls at Putney is one of several schools which have started counselling systems of their own and in this article counsellor Anne Jones describes the Mayfield scheme, now in its second year.

In the United States, school counselling is well established. The American counsellor deals with subject choice, vocational guidance, and personal problems, using psychological tests and making referrals to other specialists where necessary. The Keele and Reading courses follow a rather similar pattern. The scheme at Mayfield School, a girls' comprehensive, differs mainly in that we have not as yet included vocational guidance as part of the counsellor's work. We spent a year discussing a frame of reference before beginning our experiment in 1965. We now have two part-time counsellors, each working one full school day. Our aim is to promote positive mental health, to help individuals through temporary crises, to note signs of emotional disturbance in the earliest stages, and make referrals to specialists: in short, not remedial but preventative work.

We decided that it is not a good idea for the counsellor to teach as well, as this makes for conflict of role and relationship. On the other hand, it is important for the counsellor to see pupils functioning normally within their own social group; it is also important for the individuals to know and like the counsellor if they are ever to come for help spontaneously.

We therefore began counselling by seeing the third year girls (who are aged 13-14), in small groups of about a dozen. The group meets the counsellor at least four times and discusses human relationships: within the family, with the opposite sex, at school, and in society. There are many questions about sex: the girls have been taught the facts, but they want to know about feelings. Here is a chance to dispel many an old midwives' tale and to provoke discussion and thought.

In the third session, the girls write an unstructured, autobiographical note which helps the counsellor to know and remember them. In the fourth session, each girl is seen privately. This gives those who are shy of admitting any problem (and this includes the very quiet and the very noisy) a chance to express themselves. Where necessary an appointment is then made for a longer counselling interview.

The relationship established with the counsellor through these group discussions is of vital importance. Already girls seen in groups a year ago are coming spontaneously now a real problem has developed. We shall also see the girls again for another series of discussions in the school-leaving term, to help the transition from school to work.

Girls who come for individual counselling do so in lesson time and with an official appointment. Girls are never asked by their form tutor why they want to come, but we make it clear that girls can make a direct appointment by finding the counsellor in her room: the lunch hour is kept free for this type of interview.

Self-referrals are obviously the most rewarding since the girl has placed her trust and confidence in the counsellor. Staff-referrals include girls who are in trouble with the authorities and sometimes it takes time to make it clear that the counsellor is not a kind of punishment, nor will she repeat what she is told in confidence.

Confidentiality is very important. To reveal what is confidential would not only be unethical but would completely undermine the girls' trust in the counsellor. The staff understood and accepted this. Some feedback to the form tutors is essential, but this can be done in general terms, in a positive way and without breaking confidence.

If the counsellor thinks it would be help the child for the school to be aware of her situation, then she discusses this with the girl and says nothing without the girl's agreement. In an extreme case, if the counsellor thought a girl was in moral or physical danger, yet could not be persuaded to seek official help, the counsellor would take action, but she would tell the girl first what she was going to do and why. It is essential in cases of this kind not to act in haste: so far no such case has arisen.

In certain cases, it is most helpful for the girl if she is referred to specialists. With staff-referrals it is relatively simple to recommend, for example, a visit to the child guidance clinic. With self-referrals it is a more delicate and difficult matter to bring in the right kind of help and involves the cooperation of the parents. This is particularly difficult when the parents themselves are at the source of the problem. There is considerable liaison between the counsellors and the other local agencies, statutory and voluntary in the area: it is certainly most helpful for the counsellor to be able to check, in general terms, a point of law or the implications of a particular course of action.

What kinds of problem does the counsellor come across? In the main, the normal problems of adolescence: worries about menstruation and moodiness, conflicts with parents over going out and having boyfriends, anxieties over appearance, or about the way to behave in a new situation. Some girls feel isolated among their contemporaries; some are not interested in boys yet, but feel somehow this makes them odd. Some have nowhere to go in the evenings and no friends in their neighbourhood. It is often a great relief for the girls to realise just how common these problems are, to understand that people develop at different rates and in different ways, to gain some sense of their own individual worth and values.

Parents sometimes are a problem: too rigid parental control, or none, or inconsistency; sometimes the parents are unhappily married, sometimes they use violence, sometimes there are financial worries, overcrowding or aged grandparents adding to the strain of family relationships. The child's perception of the situation may be distorted or based on fantasy. Are things really as bad as she thinks or is this just the way she perceives them? How much could be altered by changes in her own attitude? Has she ever talked to her parents about her feelings? Lack of communication is an important factor. If a child can come to understand a difficult situation in her family, she can often learn to tolerate it.

Sibling rivalry also causes many hard feelings. A spoilt younger child, unfair distribution of family chores, fighting, a handicapped brother or sister, a twin, a large family spread over twenty years in which no-one seems to have any time for the youngest member, too much responsibility for the first-born. These situations sometimes make for strain.

School problems include worries about school work, strong feelings about unjust punishment or school regulations, perhaps a group problem such as how to handle a troublemaker within the form. The counsellor has to take care not to undermine the authority of the teacher (or parents for that matter) by supporting criticisms; most pupils are extremely reasonable when asked how *they* would handle such a situation. Some of them have unrealistic vocational aims, some do not have any aims at all. The counsellor can help them to think about it.

A girl may feel that nobody loves and respects her, yet it may simply be her own distorted perception that gives her this low opinion of herself. Here the counsellor has an important function as accepting an adult who neither condemns nor criticises, but who listens sympathetically and helps her to come to terms with herself, and her environment, to develop a positive attitude towards herself and those around her.

Traditionally in England, the form teacher has undertaken the pastoral care of her pupils. The counsellor is no way meant to take over this function, but rather to supplement it. However good a relationship a form teacher has with her pupils, her role is necessarily limited by her position of authority. The counsellor does not have to enforce discipline and, because of this special relationship, they hear things which a pupil would never tell even the most sympathetic teacher.

Vocational guidance can most certainly be included as part of the counsellor's work, but of course, there is already provision for this type of guidance within the youth employment and career advisory services. Information and straight forward guidance about careers can be given by the careers mistress; subject choice is better helped by the form tutor who knows the pupil's work over a period of time. The counsellor can help when the vocational problem is really a personal one.

In the States, counsellors spend a lot of time administering tests and keeping records. There is some feeling even in America that the real function of the counsellor, lies in their relationship with the pupil and can be lost in a welter of paperwork. This is not to decry the use of tests, but merely to state that it is personal advice which is really missing from our educational system and which is so much needed when the simple needs of the individual can be so easily overlooked.

Postscript

Mayfield School, Putney, was one of the very first comprehensive girls' schools in the country. The Head, Dame Margaret Miles had invited me to take up the post on the basis of my work with sixth formers at the Godolphin and Latymer School. I had marriage guidance counselling training with emphasis on adolescents and also my sociology diploma and social work training. I was the first school counsellor in the country as far as I know. Dame Margaret and I spoke at an HMI/Heads' Conference and many speaking engagements followed.

After the article in *Mental Health* was published, I was very surprised to be asked by the publishers Ward Lock Educational to write a book about my work at Mayfield. I accepted. In 1966, my Welsh mother-in-law kindly took the children for a week and I wrote day and night alone in our Welsh cottage. The bulk of the writing was finished in a week, all written by hand on narrow feint and margin foolscap. I deliberately took no clocks or radios. I wrote until I dropped, then took a walk or slept! It took quite a while to finish it off, then the nine months it used to take to publish a book in those days. In 1970, it was published by Ward Lock Educational. *The Times* interviewed me shortly after that. Moira Keenan wrote the half-page interview. Here it is.

With permission, THE TIMES, **Wednesday October 7th 1970**
SCHOOL COUNSELLING IN PRACTICE, **Ward Lock, 1970**

Moira Keenan the Women's editor talks to Anne Jones about her new book.

The problems of growing up

- 'I have to be in by eight o'clock every single night. My Dad's very strict – I wanted to go to a party but my Dad wouldn't let me. My Mum won't let me do anything and I get sick and tired of it, but I know it's for my own good but she treats me like a five-year-old.'
- 'My mother can be very nagging if she wants to. I can't stand this and it usually ends with me walking out of the room.'
- 'My parents quite often get on my nerves when they don't understand our modern ways.'
- 'My sister is always causing trouble for me. She will do something and blame it on me. When my mother goes out she will never do a thing I ask her. Every time she passes me she kicks and hits me. But my parents take no notice of what I say.'
- 'I am very shy especially when there are boys about. I go all hot and get butterflies in my tummy, but I do like them.'
- 'I live with my Nan also. I think her moans are dreadful to hear. I am told I do not do enough for my mother. Sometimes I get so wild I stalk out of the room.'
- 'I am fat and I know I am fat. I am very self conscious in the presence of men.'

Anyone who can remember anything about their own adolescence will know exactly how the thirteen and 14-year-old girls talking here feel: shy and self-conscious: mutinous and misunderstood: carrying, they feel, a burden of unfair blame and moving most disconcertingly from moments of extraordinary elation to the very depths of misery when everything seems to be turned against them.

It is all supposed to be so much easier nowadays, the process of growing up. The young do not have instant adulthood thrust upon them: they are an exciting group in their own right with their own kind of clothes and sub-culture: they are a collective voice which gets listened to, a spending force to be reckoned with and a source of envy to older generations who feel they missed out on the fun.

But growing up is still a process beset with problems 'to do with relationships and with their nearest and dearest, with the search for identity and role and with the quest for independence and freedom without total loss of family support' says Anne Jones. Mrs Jones probably sees more than most people of teenage problems because she belongs to a rare new profession which, in this country at least, is still in its pioneering and experimental stage. She is a school counsellor, and what her work is all about she explains in a fascinating book with the formidable title of **School Counselling in Practice** *(Ward Lock Educational).*

It has been estimated, and Anne Jones bears this out from her own experience over the past five years, that about 10% of young people have personal problems. Not problems serious enough for the social worker or psychiatrist, in fact many people might dismiss them as growing pains, but to the sensitive adolescents who have to live with them they are real problems which affect their work, relationships and view of life and which could sometimes grow to more serious proportions. Helping children to work through these problems is the job of the school counsellor, and it is done in school both through group work and through private and confidential sessions with any children who may ask for them.

The idea of counselling in schools is not altogether new in fact Anne Jones says that she herself went to a marvellous co-educational school which did then many things now done in the name of progress, including counselling. What is new is the establishment of the school counsellor as a professional with professional skills.

Mrs Jones herself has been a teacher and a marriage guidance education counsellor, which gives her a flying start. She looks more like a musician or an artist and has the 'calmness... lightness of touch... sense of humour and ability to talk about intimate matters without making them provocative or sweeping them under the carpet', which she herself lists as some of the qualities necessary in a counsellor.

She is married with three children of four-and-a-half, seven, and eight, and says that she believes that if growing up today is an easier process than it used to be, being a parent is more difficult. But, she says 'Parents seem to go to extremes, a great many either seem not to care about their children or when they do care, they start laying down ridiculous rules. Balance is the important thing: I think that if you have got to take a line, then it needs to be a strong line.'

She says her own parents were very helpful and understanding and this combined with the fact she was so happy at school means that she herself grew up very smoothly. 'I didn't have to rebel.' About her own children, two daughters and a son, she says 'I am very open and free. I think they have their own standards and will abide by these. Whether I shall feel the same when they reach adolescence I don't know. I do occasionally think about it and worry.'

Mrs Jones works part-time in a large girls' comprehensive school where she shares the work with another part-time counsellor. The idea for the experiment originally came from the Head, and met with enthusiastic support from the rest of the staff 'which was helpful to me because it would have been terribly difficult to do this kind of work if I had met with any opposition', says Anne Jones. 'I spent a little time getting to know the staff, then I started the group work with 12-15 girls at a time, and of course through the groups I had the perfect way in for anyone who wanted to come and see me privately.'

Everyone comes to the group sessions where they might discuss almost any subject under the sun. Sex and boyfriends are some of them, but are not nearly such a consuming interest as one might think. What the girls are most interested in discussing are the problems which come within their own range of experience: 'The girls enjoy talking about marriage, how they are going to bring up their children, whether they want to plan their families or work when they have children. Sometimes the discussion turns to issues such as racial prejudice or social injustice, or a group problem, such as how to handle a troublemaker within the form.'

The 'clients' as Mrs Jones rather charmingly calls them, who come to her privately come entirely voluntarily and can come as often or seldom as they wish, and Mrs Jones says it is sometimes quite surprising who does come. Sometimes they are girls who seem happy and well integrated and whose form teachers never thought of them as having problems. 'A girl can express herself to a counsellor in a very safe place', Mrs Jones says, 'because the counsellor is not going to condemn her or split on her.' Only rarely, if Mrs Jones thinks it might help to talk to the girl's mother, does she ask the girl permission to do so. She also cannot refer a girl to the child guidance clinic or welfare worker without her agreement.

The majority of the problems involve the family, usually complicated by a lack of communication. 'The counsellor's listening function is very important, but there is more to it than that. If a child is not prepared to work at their problem, then just talking about it is not going to be all that much help. You must try to help them to break the pattern of behaviour, which always produces the same reactions, you have to help them to break the vicious circles of cause and effect'.

The school at which Mrs Jones is a counsellor is large and completely mixed in ability and background. Mrs Jones says 'that the same kinds of problems are fairly evenly spread. I can't say that separation, or divorce or working mothers or anything like that causes any worse problems, and the different backgrounds don't seem to make much difference. Nearly all the girls are articulate and they are all very much individuals.'

To judge from the case histories in her book, Mrs Jones has a high degree of success in her counselling work, but she says that there are some hard cases who don't really want help. 'They usually get it in the end, whether they want it or not, because they end up in court or on probation. It's a pity we can't always help them sooner than that. I occasionally get very dispirited. This work has opened up a whole new world to me. I thought I was just a French teacher, now look what I am doing.'

Postscript

In this interview I was obviously trying not to say anything confidential so my comments were rather guarded. As I only worked one day a week, I spent most of my time looking after my family. However, in addition, I gave quite a few talks about counselling to HMI conferences and some occasional broadcasting such as *You and Yours* and Radio London; I certainly had broadened my horizons!

The transition back to full time work

I had refused to go out to work full time until all my three children were over five and at school full time. So I worked at Mayfield for six years in total, one day a week only. Altogether I was out of full time employment for nine years. It was a happy and fulfilling time.

While I was at home, I gradually became more and more involved with the community. With other young mums, we started a mutual self-help group, providing babysitting, tea and sympathy, pre-nursery activities, pooling, fetching and carrying and bulk buying, I joined the Dulwich and Camberwell Branch of CASE, ended up as Chairman, prodding the divisional inspector with our survey of home/school relations…, see the next page. I also helped set up a community centre in Tulse Hill and found myself acting as local 'ombudsman' on many topics.

It was at this stage I stopped and asked myself whether life might be less hectic if I went to work full time. Then, in 1970 the vacancy for Thomas Calton School came up, near my children's school and with a community vision that I shared, so I applied and I was appointed.

Here's an example of the kind of community work I became involved in. Can you believe now that schools had such minimal links with parents in those days?

Contact between home/school, 1968

A survey of twenty-seven primary schools by Dulwich and Camberwell CASE. (Confederation for the Advancement of State Education)

Factual summary, 1968

This survey was done by a small team of CASE parents, CASE was an organisation set up largely by parents to improve the quality of state education. We were shocked to find that in some primary schools, it was really quite difficult to have a conversation with the Head or the teachers. How things have changed!

Question 1: Does the school have a PTA? (Parent Teacher Association)

Only six had a PTA. Of these, all had meetings to explain teaching methods to parents. This was true of just under one-half of the non-PTA schools, i.e. nine. Of the twenty-one schools without PTAs, three Heads expressed an active dislike of PTAs and another three expressed an interest or a willingness to have a PTA.

Question 2: How often do the parents receive written reports?

Seventeen schools give annual reports and ten give no reports at all. The 'no' report schools had two features in common: they all only interviewed parents when the children first entered and they were all schools with Headmistresses. Seven out of the seventeen schools giving annual reports interviewed parents when their children first entered school.

Question 3: Does the school have any meetings to explain teaching methods to the parents?

Fifteen schools did and twelve did not. Of the twelve that did not hold meetings, none had a PTA.

Question 4: Are there occasions when parents can meet teachers and talk informally?

Twenty schools have an open day each year. Two have an open day each term. Four schools indicated that parents can visit any time. One school Head said, such visits could only be made 'by appointment'. Of the twenty school Heads who said parents could talk informally at the yearly open day, seventeen said it was also possible at any time. The other three Heads said talks were also possible 'by appointment'.

Question 5: Does the school have a systematic arrangement for interviewing parents?

Only three schools had a regular system for interviewing parents, which was an annual event. This is not counting a meeting to explain 11-plus procedures, or a pre-school interview.

CONCLUSION

If we accept having a PTA, issuing a written report, holding meetings to explain teaching methods and encouraging parents and teachers to talk informally as criteria of good parent/school interaction, then we find that there are only four schools which score on all these points. The two infants' schools with PTAs do not issue written reports. Only five more schools not having PTAs score on all remaining criteria and these include the three Heads who would like to form PTA's.

Our main conclusion is therefore that when a school has a PTA, it also seems to have other features which encourage home/school relationships. If the five aspects covered by our survey were obligatory in schools it would leave little room for a permissive approach to home/school communication. Many Heads thought that these arrangements were not necessary and clearly did not recognise the difficulty a majority of parents had in taking an active interest in their children's education.

Postscript

This survey was taken very seriously by the District Inspector, who followed it up with the schools. Today the situation has totally changed for the better. Believe it or not some schools in the sixties even had a line at the gate which said NO PARENTS PAST THIS POINT. Today pupils have detailed reports on their progress in every subject and parental contact with the teachers is now accepted as essential.

Confidentiality provides a basis of trust between the counsellor and girls

CHAPTER 2: THOMAS CALTON SCHOOL

Deputy Head of the Thomas Calton School
Peckham, London 1971-1974

I NOTICED THE ADVERT FOR THIS JOB just as we were going on holiday to France. I was attracted to it because I thought that a community school was exactly what was needed in a community like Peckham: all the services offered in the same place. Before applying, I had made a very conscious decision that when I returned to work, I would teach in a multiracial school in a deprived area. My former pupils didn't really need me. I wanted to work where I could help make a real positive difference to their lives. But would my own children cope if I took on such a job? By Easter, when the job started, all of my three children would be at school full time. At least we would have the same hours and holidays and I was used to working late into the night.

It also helped that the school was very near our home in Dulwich and the route to it went past the infant and junior schools where my children were so I could drop them off en route, though in practice

Katy three, Becky six months, Christopher four

28

they usually walked with friends. I sent in a slightly late application and was called for interview. They phoned the next day to tell me I had got it. I was stunned. I really hadn't expected to get it. I hadn't taught for nine years. I hadn't ever taught in that kind of school. I discussed it all with my husband and we agreed that I should take it. I went back to see the Head and said that I was prepared to accept the job on the condition that I would not stay late after school unless, of course, there was a meeting and if my children were ill I would take time off school! I can't believe I dared to say that, though I did mean it. But the Head agreed and in the event my children were never ill.

Why did I get the job? I suppose the fact that I had done so much during my time at home counted. My first book, *School Counselling in Practice* had just been reviewed in *The Times*. My social science diploma helped, I had continued learning. I was an experienced lecturer on counselling and I had broadcast a few times on programmes like *You and Yours*. I even did *Thought for the day* twice! In the second of these I recounted the story of overhearing my three and 4-year-old children in the bath. 'Do you believe in Father Christmas?' 'Yes' came the reply. 'But I'm not so sure about God.'

The Thomas Calton School was housed in two red brick Victorian primary schools about fifteen minutes apart by car. They had high ceilings and lovely wooden floors, built as a big hall with classrooms off it. In the twenty-first century, many such schools have been turned into luxury flats. But in the 1970s, when they were nearly 100 years old, they seemed rather dark and foreboding. Our roof was crumbling and when a brick fell off and nearly seriously hurt a pupil, we sent the offensive brick to Mrs Thatcher with a letter pleading for a new building.

In fact we were promised a new building and furthermore, it was going to be a community school. I rather doubt that the brick made any difference to that, nor the very depressing news which came later when we were told that ILEA was not going to rebuild the school after all. We were all very disappointed.

The staff made me very welcome, especially when they got to know me. The pupils were of many nationalities and spoke many languages but the majority were Afro-Caribbean. It was a co-ed school, which was another new experience for me as a teacher. Some 30% of the pupils were white and many of those came from the Dog Kennel Hill Estate. You may not know this, but that is where many of the Great Train Robbers came from. One boy in particular was showing signs of being very disturbed. It turned out that his father had been involved in the robbery. The worse thing was that the pupils and even some teachers were afraid of the lad (might he set his father on them?) and this had the inevitable effect of making him even more disturbed. We brought in the School Psychologist (who turned out to be one of my former G&L pupils). She calmed him down and moved him on in a constructive way.

How did I find the teaching? To be honest I found teaching French unbearable. My teaching style was by then completely out of date and included learning verbs and worse still, verb endings! I decided not to struggle to relearn it all, but to move on to my new found subject, social science. Here I was in my element. I found myself teaching sociology, health education and careers guidance, all of which went down very well with the pupils and which I enjoyed. I so enjoyed it that later I turned some of my teaching materials into workbooks designed to help young people think and make decisions for themselves. See the piece about CRAC later. (Chapter 4, page 141.)

My basic job was to manage upper school and take charge of pastoral care, links with other seventies (social services, police and educational psychologists), training and supporting probationer teachers, links with parents and so on. Because of my counselling experience, I made good relationships with parents and pupils. I trained the probationers **not** to write letters like this:

Dear Mrs Smith

You daughter is very late still. If she cannot arrange to come on time we shall have to arrange for a transfer to another school. She is still not wearing school uniform. She must have a regulation white blouse, grey cardigan and grey skirt. She must remember to bring her science overall. Every week she annoys her science teacher by forgetting it and this can't go on. Finally she is being extremely rude and disobedient which is a direct reflection on you and your husband as you must point out to her. She is letting you down and there is no excuse for this. I look for your cooperation in helping to rectify all these matters.

One mother who received a letter similar to this came up and hit the Head of Year concerned with an umbrella. I was not totally surprised!

Michael Rutter of the Maudsley, a very famous psychologist /psychiatrist allowed me to use his social adjustment test. I used it on all the new entrants. I found and was not surprised to find, that nearly 20% of each form, (predominantly boys) were potentially maladjusted. So I also brought into the school a team from the Maudsley Hospital which ran an adolescent unit at that time. We had a monthly meeting with the heads of year and the Maudsley team to discuss serious problem cases.

Later I was approached by the Association of Child Psychologists and Psychiatrists and invited to be the Chairman for the year 1979-8. This meant inviting outstanding relevant speakers for the monthly lecture and dinner. It was thoroughly enjoyable and interesting. I can only think I was asked to do this because of the pioneering work we did at Thomas Calton with the Maudsley staff. Read all about that work in the chapter on the Disruptive Pupil in the Classroom.

In 1979, the ACPP committee and I went to the annual conference in Dublin. I seem to remember that after a grand dinner, a group of us decided to go out to a night club (yes, very adolescent of us I know.) We soon got our comeuppance: they wouldn't let us in because we were too old!

The Grubb Institute

Another organisation I invited to help the school was the Grubb Institute. I had met them in an Inner London Education Authority (ILEA) course for Heads. I had been very impressed about the way they helped people work effectively in large groups and small groups to clarify their goals and remove the blockages to action. I had also followed this up by attending a course run by them at the Tavistock Institute. What I learnt from them stayed with me for the rest of my life. Our divisional inspector and the Head both agreed that we should invite all the staff to go to Folkestone for a weekend led by Bruce Reid and John Bazalgette of the Grubb Institute to work out for ourselves as a group what our goals were. The effect was dramatic and influenced the behaviour of all of us who went in a very positive and beneficial way.

I will come back to this topic later, as thenceforth; the Grubb Institute helped me transform for the better all the organisations I involved them in. I could not have done it without them.

Teaching Southwark kids
Thomas Calton 1972
Supporting probationer teachers

One of my responsibilities as Deputy Head was to support and train the probationers… no NOT teenagers on probation! New teachers recently qualified and/or new to the school. I really enjoyed that. I wrote this especially for them, I think they appreciated it.

So you're ready? You've prepared your lesson, found some chalk, the classroom, a form list, the loo, the teapot. What else? Find out about the children? Children are children aren't they? Different shapes and sizes, colours, accents and aptitudes, but the same underneath? Unwillingly to school, but so rewarding to teach?

Then what are these nagging doubts as you listen to staffroom gossip. 'He swore at me: I don't stand for that' 'Well I prepared this fantastic worksheet, but they turned it into paper darts' 'When I said I wasn't having it, he said his dad would come up and get me' 'Well personally I never have any trouble with that class: they daren't move in my lessons'. 'It wasn't like that on teaching practice: but it was a different kind of area.' 'Can it really make that much difference?'

Fundamentally no, but its worthwhile making time, to find out how the south-east Londoners tick. Strong characters these: salt of the earth, tough, rough, robust, yet incredibly fragile and sensitive underneath, outgoing, essentially optimistic, intolerant of fools and falseness, full of humour and sharp wit, uninhibited, argumentative and unbowed by authority. They have a strong sense of justice and equality.

They object to being pushed around, yet they feel lost if they are left in a totally free vacuum.

They are raucous and rowdy, yet kind and compassionate; generous in a crisis yet infinitely ingenious at teacher-baiting and time spinning; direct and outspoken, full of meaningless four-letter words, funny stories and folk lore; keen to learn but not keen to admit it; intolerant of teacher inefficiency and half-heartededness; liable to lose interest if teacher is late, unprepared and uninterested in his lesson; disturbed and disturbing if teacher fails to set limits and be firm about what he cannot tolerate. They are worldly wise and sophisticated to look at, vulnerable and desperately dependent inside; aggressive and defiant yet so much in need of nurturing, loving and reassuring; restless, energetic, acting out feelings as they come, unable to wait their turn or until tomorrow; occasionally subdued, undernourished, passive and over-controlled but even then, proud and resilient; conservative, resistant to sudden change of room or teacher, loyal to what they know; lacking in persistence, needing constant reassurance, 'could do better'.

Above all they are sensitive to how we feel about then: if we are frightened or despise then, then fearful and despicable they will be. They respond to love, warmth, and respect, they respond to firmness, not to nagging, to authority not force, to stricture not straight jackets, to a sense of purpose, not a sense of despair or futility, to anger born of caring, not rage born of hate, to a genuine desire to help them.

So the problem is how to assert ourselves, not in order to dictate, but to help the class feel secure. The problem is to remain relaxed and secure in ourselves in those first weeks when we may be feeling nervous and worried. The problem is to stimulate and interest all these very differing individuals, to gain their respect, their affection, their cooperation and to harness their energy and their joy.

There are some tricks of the trade which help: well-prepared lessons, preferably with a fund of additional ideas, work sheets and alternatives in case the original lesson does not take well, or to sustain and reward the fast workers. A stock of pens, pencils and paper. Not forgetting the law of diminishing returns. Careful marking of workbooks or projects: children lose interest if we do. A systematic attempt to learn names and make individual contact with class members. A stock of substitution lessons so that you are never faced with a full class and an empty mind. A willingness to scrap worksheets if they prove to be too easy or too difficult. The ability to share ideas, materials and feelings with colleagues.

The children will test us out; they are astute and unrelenting judges of character. They know whether we are genuine or not, whether we accept their way of life as valid and meaningful, whether we mean business or are merely filling time. The children of Southwark are not fools, neither are they easily fooled. They know what life is about: they can teach us a thing or two. Maybe that's where good teaching begins, with being a good learner.

Coping with disruptive pupils in the school situation
Anne Jones Headmistress, Vauxhall Manor School

This is a chapter written by me for Ward Lock Educational and published in 1976. My book called School Counselling in Practice *was also published by them in 1970. I wrote most of this chapter when I was Deputy Head at Thomas Calton School. I have included it because it gives more details of the pioneering work we did there in conjunction with the Maudsley Institute. By the time it was published, I was Head of Vauxhall Manor. I note that I refer mainly to he rather than he or she but in the seventies this was quite normal! Thomas Calton was a mixed school, Vauxhall Manor was girls only.*

My chapter was first published in the following book:
The Disruptive Pupil in the Secondary School 1976 edited by Ronald G. Cave and Clive Jones-Davies published by Ward Lock Educational, the Orion Publishing group.

Teachers are understandably ambivalent about the disruptive pupil, alternately angry and despairing, rejecting and self-denigrating. Nothing divides staffrooms more effectively into two camps than a discussion on how to deal with deviants. Whilst so much emotional polarization is engendered, it is difficult to look rationally at the problem and almost impossible to do anything about it. Few people deny that there is a problem – except those who hope that by so doing it will go away. Some people pander to the problem, indulging in psychological and socio-economic excuse-making and wallowing in a sense of being overwhelmed and impotent. Few really come to grips with what is happening and do something about it.

This is not surprising in an age when schools are very confused about what they are trying to do. It is unfashionable to be authoritarian, rigid, controlling, directive or judgmental. In swinging away from these polarized extremes, in attempting to be child-centred, consumer-orientated, flexible, democratic, non-directive and non-judgmental, we may at times be falling into yet another trap, that of seeming to be without a sense of direction, without powers of judgment, without authority, without anything to teach. Some of our pupils are disruptive because they do not see the point of school: they do not see the point of school because neither their teachers, nor their parents, nor society are really sure what the aims of education should be in this complex and rapidly changing era.

In thinking and talking about the 'disruptive pupil', teachers, parents and the public at large are prone to exaggerate the size of the problem. The media, the local grapevine and the natural desire of the teacher to tell a good tale about the blackboard jungle, all play a part in feeding our fears and fantasies. So the first task for any school which is serious about coping constructively with its disruptive pupils is to find out, as rationally and objectively as possible, the extent, the nature and the cause of the problems. You would think from reading the papers that whole schools were full of professional lesson-wreckers, yet in each class there may be only a minute proportion of disrupters, admittedly very often wielding undue influence on their classmates.

Attempts to quantify the extent of the problem are relatively few. Professor Rutter's study of children in the Isle of Wight showed an overall deviance rate of 10.6%, though not all these pupils were disruptive (Graham and Rutter 1968). A similar study which he carried out in an Inner London Borough showed a deviance rate of 19.1%). The ILEA Literacy Survey (1971) showed a rate of 26.1% for boys, 16.3% for girls. My own research in a London secondary school, also using

Rutter's social adjustment scale, showed a deviance rate of 24% among first year pupils.

However, 37% of these were classified as neurotic and on the whole were not disruptive, if anything rather introverted and withdrawn. Many of this group could best be helped through counselling. Of the rest, labelled 'antisocial', most were not, when systematically assessed and discussed, either delinquent or in need of psychiatric help. They behaved badly at times, not because they were totally depraved or deprived, but for other simple and rational reasons. Maybe they found the transition from primary to secondary school too bewildering, maybe they were experiencing difficulties in reading and writing which led to feelings of frustration and aggression. They had too much physical energy and not enough space to let off steam; they had missed out on various socializing factors; they had not learnt to wait their turn or control themselves; sometimes they were over-controlled at home and broke loose at school; sometimes they were bored, got no sense of achievement out of their work; sometimes they had a weak teacher who did not stimulate them or stretch them sufficiently.

These are all problems, real problems, but they are not insoluble. Many can be settled quite systematically by a series of strategies designed to work at these specific points. What we must not forget is that disruptive children, like teachers and parents, come in many different kinds, each of which might need different handling. Blanket treatment, a polarised, rigid solution, will help only a few. To be effective, diagnosis and treatment need individual assessment. Before we come on to discuss the various strategies which may be used to help the disruptive child and (just as vital) the disrupted teacher, it is important to look at different kinds of disturbance. Nearly all have their roots in the home environment, but some may be exacerbated by the way the school handles its pupils.

Referrals to child guidance

The number of grossly disturbed pupils in normal secondary schools remains relatively low. When I was working as a school counsellor, I estimated (on the basis of six years work) that one or two pupils in every form of thirty would need to see a psychiatrist that is approximately 5% (Jones 1970). Unfortunately those who exhibit the most gross behaviour problems are rarely those whose parents accept the need for child guidance. On the occasions when a school blackmails them into going for treatment (by threatening expulsion if they don't) these children may not respond to the methods used unless they are removed to a special school where their problems can be worked on consistently. The physical lesson-wreckers, those who commit violence and outrage against teacher or school property are by and large not the type to respond to soul-searching. Whilst they may have a need to verbalize the anger which drives them to such outrages, they may not find this easy, even if they are willing. Their parents too may be more used to acting out rather than verbalizing their conflicts. Thus an occasional visit to the child guidance clinic will not have a favourable prognosis in many of the cases which teachers find the most upsetting.

In this kind of case there is a need for the development of new techniques, for example behaviour therapy, which may well be best practised where the problems are actually happening, that is, in the classroom. In one area of London (in fact, Thomas Calton School) where I was Deputy Head, an experiment has been mounted in collaboration with the Institute of Psychiatry to see if ways can be found of helping teachers to deal with serious behavioural problems within the classroom. The project is based on American studies which have demonstrated that the way a teacher responds to a difficult child can dramatically alter that child's behaviour.

A group of teachers has undertaken a ten-week evening course to enable them to apply these principles in the classroom situation. It is too early yet to evaluate the results, but this appears to be one way of helping the teacher to deal with the more intractable problems as they arise. It is understandable but it is also unfortunate that we so often unconsciously reward and encourage disturbing or attention-seeking behaviour amongst our pupils.

We also fail to refer pupils who do need psychiatric help to specialists early enough. A classic syndrome which I have observed in every school I have ever worked in is when a pupil is allowed to make havoc for several terms, even years; when finally the patience of staff and pupils is exhausted, then the child is referred for child guidance with demands that he should immediately be taken off roll and sent to a special school. When it then transpires that there is a six months waiting list at the child guidance clinic, no room at a special school and that the child's parents won't, in any case, go anywhere near a child guidance clinic, the school wrings its hands in despair and says that the psychological support services are no good. In fact the problem may be that the school has made the referral too late. It is as if the teacher in the classroom is afraid to admit his pupils need help, as if this in some way reflects upon his ability to control his class. When he is desperate enough, he brings in the Head of House or Year, who also spends a couple of terms trying to prove he is not going to be 'beaten'. In desperation he finally brings in outside help, by which time the child is well and truly set in a pattern of misbehaviour. The school has colluded with the problem. It should have asked for a specialist opinion right at the beginning: there is no harm in asking, you can only be wrong; there is harm in waiting, for you can leave it too late.

Socio-economic problems

Some of the pupils who disrupt our lessons are not psychologically disturbed, but they may live in very disturbing home circumstances, such as poor housing, overcrowded and broken homes. There is a growing tendency for teachers to want to do something about this; they may even try to act as agents of political and social change. Many will in any case feel sorry for the pupil with a 'difficult' home background and excuse him for his behaviour because of his 'hard life'. There are several fundamental misconceptions here.

First there are limits to what a teacher can and should do to change society. It can be useful for the Head to write a letter in support of a re-housing claim or for the school to call a case conference to get some concerted action about a family whose psychological problems may be rooted in their physical living conditions. But feeling sorry for a child does not help him with his difficulties. It may in fact compound them.

As I have said many times, there may well come into play what I call the 'law of diminishing expectations': 'he can't help it, his family has got problems', or 'Officer Klopsky, I'm really a slob' as the ingenious song in *West Side Story* puts it. This is a way of handicapping further the have-nots: 'He who expecteth nothing shall not be disappointed'. It is good that we should try to understand why our pupils behave as they do, but we must also remember that children are adept at playing up their weaknesses: rewarded for this skill they only become weaker. We must also remember that there is not necessarily any correlation between disturbed behaviour in school and social conditions.

In my present school, Vauxhall Manor a study of truants is currently being undertaken. The factors in their background are being coded and compared with those of a control group of 'normal' pupils. The results will be very interesting whatever they say. All I know from my experience as a counsellor is that many children with absentee or drunken fathers or mothers, with countless brothers and sisters and very little space for living or playing, are nevertheless splendidly resilient mature, resourceful and able to cope with the adversities of life in part because they have 'difficult' home backgrounds. Many a cosseted close-carpeted darling develops no inner strengths, feels unloved in spite of his material well-being and has just as many problems as his 'poor' relations. So it can be misleading and unhelpful to expect a child to have problems.

Counselling

More real, and more amenable to help in school, are the problems of the child, whatever his or her background or intelligence, who feels unloved and rejected. His symptoms vary from angry attention-seeking behaviour to pathetic seeking-after-teacher or withdrawal into mild depression, all of which can be disrupting to the teaching process. This sort of child will respond well to a positive relationship with his teacher, and particularly well to counselling. I will return later to the complexities of establishing a stable and fruitful pupil/form teacher relationship. What the counsellor has to offer the child who feels undervalued is a relationship based on non-possessive warmth, and genuineness. It is (or should not be, in my opinion) a kind of 'feeding on demand' relationship, which is what the teacher may be forced to provide and which may not always help the child because it enables him to manipulate the adults unduly. A counsellor should be able to offer a regular session which the pupil can rely on as his very own. I found when I worked as a counsellor that many very insecure children grew in strength and confidence simply from having a regular session with me. The fact that I was outside the normal classroom provision meant that I had no axe to grind. My positive regard for the pupil was not conditional on his good behaviour in my class and so he was able to be himself. By expressing his true feelings and his own doubts about his behaviour, without having me mock, correct or collude with what he said, he seemed to be able to get himself into perspective, to realize that many of his difficulties in relationships came from the way he behaved. When he was angry he could ventilate his angry feelings; when he was sad he could cry, when he was fed up with others he would say so without being told he mustn't say things like that. Counsellors, like psychiatrists, are not magicians: they cannot achieve the impossible by waving a magic wand.

Some children are not suitable for counselling; these will need alternative forms of treatment. As a counsellor I found that approximately one-third of each class I worked with referred themselves for counselling and of these, (ten in each class of thirty) usually at least two would be suitable for long-term counselling, whilst another two would need referring to specialists. The essence of effective counselling is that the client (in this case the pupil) should want to be helped, should accept counselling as a valid way of being helped and should be prepared to work at his problems. Counselling is no easy way out for the lesson-hopper, for the work is done by the pupil. He has to lay his feelings out before himself and examine them. In a nutshell, as in all learning processes, the pupil must be motivated, otherwise the process is a waste of time.

To describe counselling in full here would take too long, but interested readers should pursue further the literature on counselling, including my own account of my work in a girls' comprehensive school

(Jones 1970). The system I set up was designed to be preventive rather than remedial and was based on self-referrals as far as possible. The objectives were to help the normal adolescent in school in the following ways:

1. to provide support for a child who was experiencing some unusual situational stress (eg parents in hospital, new baby in family, death of a relative)
2. to help pupils with developmental problems to do with the onset of puberty (eg the need to rebel against authority and to establish relationships with the opposite sex)
3. where appropriate, to make referrals to specialists (child guidance, social services, family welfare etc.) at the earliest opportunity
4. to improve communications and understanding within and between the home, the school and the community and the sources serving that community
5. to support and train teachers in their pastoral care functions

All these strategies were helpful in reducing the numbers of disruptive children in the school. But even when I was counselling, it was patently clear to me that counselling was only one way of helping and in some cases was a completely inappropriate method.

Remedial teaching

It is extraordinary that one of the most obvious causes of disruption in the classroom is one which the teacher should above all be equipped to deal with: namely learning difficulties. In a recent experiment in London schools, in which ways of helping children with special difficulties were systematically tried and evaluated, the most clearly consistent success was in the language development and oracy projects. Admittedly these took place in primary schools. Perhaps the secondary teacher, in spite of the overwhelming evidence he faces daily that many of his pupils are poor readers and writers, has not yet adjusted to his remedial role. Many secondary teachers are alarmed when faced with illiteracy and innumeracy, claiming to have no training and no skills for coping with such problems. Yet until the teachers have taught themselves what to do about this situation, their classes will inevitably be full of disruptions. Until secondary pupils can read and write, much of what they are taught will pass them by uncomprehended. No wonder they become restless.

Whatever the virtues of mixed ability teaching (and they are many), it is undeniable that if in fact the ability range is not mixed but grossly skewed towards the less able, unless the teacher is both skilled and confident he may fail to satisfy the intellectual needs of all his pupils. The disrupters may well come from all levels of ability. The bright child may not be stretched at all and may therefore become bored and restless the average child may be under-achieving, aware that he is not dim, yet still not equipped to do the work of which he is capable and therefore frustrated. The less able child may be trying to push himself beyond his capabilities; finding the whole thing too much of a strain, he may well give up and resort to some disturbing activity which gives him a kind of false prestige as a rebel leader. I am not claiming that this is a fair and accurate picture of the average British classroom, but I suspect that most teachers will recognize elements of what they face daily.

The answer is not simple, but it is at least one which calls upon teachers to be teachers, which they are, rather than psychologists, social workers or therapists, which they are not. It certainly points to the need for more in-service training for all secondary teachers, not just remedial teachers, or teachers of English. I feel that if teachers addressed themselves primarily to this problem, which is within their aegis, rather than to socio-economic and psychological problems, which are not, they might find that they would make surprising gains in terms of confidence motivation and positive behaviour of their pupils.

Parents

Whilst some of the learning difficulties faced by pupils may relate to the quality and kind of teaching they get, others may be complicated by pressures from home: not just those of the under-caring parent, but also those of the over-concerned and anxious parent, the parent who has unrealistic ambitions for his child, or who is over-protective, unduly controlling or punitive. I find that these problems are often faced by children of immigrants who have come to Britain seeking enhanced prestige and better job opportunities. When they discover that the system, either in society or in schools, is not as simple as all that, they are bitterly disappointed. Their children may find the school all too permissive and undemanding, and the net result may be frustrating for all.

On the other hand, the kind of parent who appears to his child not to care at all, to have abdicated all responsibility and authority, equally sets up problems for his child which will be reflected in school. So what does the school do about parents? Ever since the *Plowden Report* (1967) so effectively pointed to the importance of parental attitudes to education, teachers have fell burdened with the need to work with parents, as well as with pupils, Plowden was referring to attitudes towards school, but many teachers have gone one step further. Realizing that the parent's attitudes in general need working on, a keen teacher may set off on a home visit, fired with missionary zeal and hoping to change the way parents behave. He may be right in thinking that work with parents on this scale needs to be done, but he is wrong to think that it is his job. Teachers have neither the time nor the training. Nor is it their role to undertake family casework. A school which is particularly convinced of the importance of this kind of approach and which feels that even the best efforts or the welfare and social services are not satisfactory, would be well advised to appoint a trained teacher/social worker who understands the dynamics and limitations of working with families.

I am not saying that schools should not work with parents. I am a strong supporter of the idea that parents should be involved with the education process as much as possible and at as many levels as possible. But the well-meant efforts of the conscientious form teacher to change parents' behaviour may be misplaced and may misfire. If the teacher concentrates on producing a well-taught pupil, then the parents will have less to worry about in the first place.

The antisocial

If we assume that broadly speaking the neurotic child will be best helped by counselling, this still leaves a large group of antisocial children. They may comprise the under-socialized, the undisciplined and the immature. One important way of helping them is to improve the teachers' classroom management techniques. Many of these children simply need firmer handling, not more rigid handling, but more positive, purposeful and constructive handling. When I was doing my 'Rutter' Survey of social adjustment, I was greatly struck by the differences between various classes, differences which undoubtedly related to the way they were taught. Some teachers had almost no difficult children: this I thought was very suspicious! Others appeared to have a whole class full of antisocial children, which seemed equally unlikely. Upon further investigation, I found that the teachers who were themselves unsure and in doubt about what they were trying to do, had the greatest degree of classroom disturbance. In other words the children were catching the mood of the teacher. The minority group of unsettled children will behave badly and lead others to behave badly if they sense that the teacher is worried, unsure, in conflict, tense and not sure what to do next! I am not condemning the teacher who feels like this, merely pleading for greater support all training for the teacher in the classroom situation, in particular for the probationer teacher or the 'returner' teacher.

The immature

Those children who are under-socialized and immature will not always respond readily to firm discipline. They may need to be taken back through very simple socialization procedures step by step. It helps if they have the same teacher for much of the time so that they know what to expect and can build up a pattern of positive behaviour with confidence. In many London junior schools 'nurture' groups have been established in which children are given a kind of 'mothering' in small groups. They are provided with the training, affection, rituals and varied experiences which a mother would normally give her child before the age of five. Cooking, eating, drinking, sharing, going out together, waiting one's turn, cooperating, caring for others: all these experiences provide for the child knowledge of what is expected of him and subsequently a feeling of being a valuable, loved and loving member of a group. As a result he may become more able to cope with the greater stresses of the ordinary classroom situation.

Unfortunately, it seems to me that many of our secondary school children lack 'nurturing' as well and I advocate the provision of similar experience in the secondary school. Many schools do already attempt this through normal teaching procedures, but not with the kind of teacher ratios and equipment that are necessary for the job to be done effectively. For these under-socialized children, the need is neither for talk nor for chalk but for actual first-hand experience of what, for whatever reason they missed out on as young children. The immature child must be brought on gradually from the stage he is at. It is no good calling him a baby and expecting him to become adult in one short step; he has to be weaned through the various stages. He will be able to go more quickly when he is older, but he will not go overnight, neither will his emerging new adult. He is bound to regress at times and move forward unevenly, but if his progress, however slight, is recognized, he will be encouraged to persevere. If it is not, he will sink back into some childish mode of behaviour because this may be more effective in getting him the attention he craves.

The mature

The problem for some of our disruptive children is not that they are immature but that they are in many respects mature beyond their years. For them the strictures and petty regulations of school life may seem childish: indeed I think we should ask ourselves how often our rules and regulations are childish. I can think of several sixteen-year-olds who out-of-school lead what I would describe as 'normal' adult lives. One boy had a Saturday job with tremendous responsibility, good money, a chance to take real decisions and to learn from making real mistakes. On a Saturday night he went to the pub and enjoyed himself like many young adults.

I can think of a pupil who had a baby and returned to school; she looked after her boyfriend and her child, fed them, washed, ironed, shopped, nurtured and loved them in a most responsible manner. Both these young people behaved with great seriousness and achieved efficient success in their out-of-school lives. In school they had to toe the line, follow the dictates of the school bell and only do as they were told. It is not surprising to me at any rate that they kicked against this. They did not need to learn how to live in society the play-way; they knew they could cope with life after school, in some ways more successfully than the teachers who were struggling to teach them. These are only two examples of what must be an increasingly common problem now that the age of majority and the school leaving age are the same. So a school has to ask itself how it will meet the needs of its mature students to be treated as adults. If they are treated like children, they will most certainly rebel and behave childishly; if they don't rebel, then this is also rather disturbing, for it shows an unhealthy degree of passivity.

The socialisers

The last category of disruptive pupil is the 'bored' pupil and the 'social club' pupil. These may share many of the characteristics I have already mentioned. These are the pupils who see no point in school as an educational institution. Lessons are boring, or meaningless, or irrelevant, or they've 'done that before, Miss' and don't want to know. It is a con to think that simply by making the lessons more relevant they will suddenly be inspired to learn and to work. These are the 'passive' rebels; they became 'switched off' long, long ago. They are usually quite harmless unless you try to make them work too hard, then they will make life difficult, so that in the end the teacher and class may well come to an unspoken truce: provided the teacher does not bother them they will not bother him. They come to school all the time, not to learn, but because it is a warm friendly place where if you play your cards right (and sometimes literally your cards) you can chatter with your friends quietly all day long. School in fact is a good social club, much better than hanging about the streets.

This small group of pupils is, I think, as disturbing as the group which actively disrupts. It is disturbing because from it emanates the feeling that it is not the done thing to work in lessons. Those who might want to learn arc under tremendous pressure from the group not to bother. And so many serious students, unless they are exceptionally strong-minded, or conscientious, may be afraid to do themselves justice, in fear of losing their status in the peer group. The teacher faced with this situation has to build up the confidence of the group that wants to work so that in the end it becomes acceptable to work in the lesson. But it is no easy task and the teacher may need extra help in order to do this.

Conclusion

In discussing the various kinds of disturbing pupil (many of which overlap) I have already mentioned many of the practical problems and indicated some ways of dealing with them. The most important point for any school to remember is that adding on ingenious and complicated mechanisms for dealing with misfits will be useless if the main system of the school is not itself as good and consistent as possible. The clearer a school is about what it is trying to do, the more positive will be the response of its pupils, for they will see where they are going to go and what the point of it all is. They will get a much-needed sense of achievement and this in itself will enhance the self-esteem and positive feelings of all. In creating an effective organization in the school, administrators have to watch and make sure the system serves the needs of the pupils. Too often an organization takes on a life of its own, which may well contradict or stultify its stated objectives.

Secondly, it is very important for academic and pastoral objectives to be compatible with each other otherwise they may in fact undermine and contradict each other. This 'double message' may be one of the things which turn a pupil off: the school claims to value and trust him and to care about him, yet he may be locked out at break, locked in the playground at lunchtime and may not even be taught by his form teacher. Secondary schools have a great deal to learn from primary schools about the organization of stable learning groups, with attendant stable teacher/pupil relationships. Do we really have to play musical chairs every thirty-five minutes in secondary schools? Is what we teach our young pupils really so specialised that it must be taught by a specialist? Have we ever been to see how they do it in our feeder primary schools?

A sceptic once remarked that secondary schools appear to be organized in such a way as to prevent pupils and teachers from forming a relationship. What is known fashionably as 'the tyranny of the bell' may simply be a device for disguising poor teaching and poor teacher-pupil relationships. Certainly, the kind of pupils who disrupt our lessons will, by and large, also be those who find it hard to adjust to adults quickly or even to trust a teacher they do not know well. It is noticeable that in London schools new teachers are regarded with suspicion until they have proved that they are really sufficiently interested in their pupils to stay more than a year. If teachers spent more time teaching their own form, they would find it easier to establish a relationship of trust with their pupils. Pupils who feel valued, secure and trusted are less likely to want to destroy their class or their teacher.

The form teacher

It is glib, however, to assume that the job of being form teacher is an easy one, for it is not. It is ironic that many schools which put in a form period to allow their form teachers time with their forms, find that the form teachers at a loss to know what to do with that time. This may not be an argument for abandoning the idea but rather for training and supporting the form teacher in what is expected of him. This is something we need to do far more systematically. When it is done well, the form teacher is likely to be more effective and less distraught, for he will not be perpetually torn with doubts himself about what his role should be. When the form teacher is relaxed confident and calm his form is also likely to be more settled.

The form teacher (and consequently his form) is also likely to be more relaxed if he feels well supported by the school's ancillary services. Teachers are still curiously reluctant to let anyone else help them with their job yet the teacher who is conscientious will find himself overloaded with pastoral follow-up duties, and the teacher who is not will simply ignore what should be followed up. The teacher's prime task is to teach as well as he possibly can; if he is given more ancillary help, either from the clerical staff, or in the classroom, he may find he is able to do his job more effectively, and this in itself will slop his pupils from being so disruptive. If there is a problem at home, then he must get the education welfare officer to visit, not rush round himself. He needs to know what the services on offer to him are, be introduced to the personnel involved. He must not be afraid to ask for help and advice from the relevant agency.

The Thomas Calton School system

In my last school, we had the following provision for pastoral care which we established over three years. We ran integrated studies courses in the first two years so the form teachers taught their own forms for half the week and really got to know them well. Our first year pupils were all systematically tested and screened. They were tested in reading, maths, non-verbal reasoning and the social adjustment scale. I used the results myself as a basis for a discussion with the form teacher. Any pupils who needed specialist help of any kind were referred early. We appointed two teacher/social workers on for lower school and one for upper school. Their job is to work with the Head of Year, form teachers and parents, to coordinate the interventions of other agencies and make a link between home/school. In the lower school we also appointed a counsellor who does group work and individual counselling with all the third years and with younger pupils at their request. In the lower school, we set up a school-based tutorial group, which fulfilled some of the functions of a nurture group, helping children with behavioural problems to work through their feelings by being taught in a small informal group. Children with learning difficulties are given remedial help on a withdrawal basis. In upper school, a further 'home base' class was set up to help the pupils who still had difficulty in following a more academic course. They went to normal lessons as much as possible, but were given extra remedial help in their home room when they and their lessons were incompatible.

Through links with a nearby psychiatric teaching hospital, the Maudsley, a group for difficult adolescents, run by a psychiatrist was set up. Similarly, a support group for staff was established and met once a month; this supplemented the regular year team meetings. Staff attended voluntarily and a psychiatrist, social worker and psychologist, all from a nearby adolescent unit, were also present. It was the kind of meeting in which nothing was done but much was achieved in terms of mutual understanding and trust. In particular we were able to look at ways in which the school handled pupils and set up certain tensions. New teachers and form teachers were given regular support and training, both through the probationer support scheme and through the heads of year. Contact with parents was encouraged, through interviews at school and particularly through the report afternoons and evenings to which all parents were invited to discuss their child's progress. This proved to be a very positive way of making contact with parents. The net result of all this activity was not that there were no disruptive pupils, but that we did at least have a main system and an ancillary system designed to help such pupils as far as possible.

Some of the work we did was a direct result of the 'Children with Special Difficulties' scheme fostered by the ILEA between 1972 and 1975. Under this scheme some six hundred special projects were set up in London schools. Most of the schemes fell into the following categories:

- Sanctuaries or withdrawal groups
- Nurture groups
- Support for teachers
- Diagnostic and screening techniques
- Opportunities classes
- Links between schools
- Links between home/school
- Language programs
- Projects designed to broaden pupils experience
- Pastoral care and arrangements
- Off-site centres for school refusers improvement of school environment

Evaluative research into the effects of the 'Children with Special Difficulties' project to date shows only a marginal improvement in the behaviour and performance of those children who received special help such as we provide. What is salutary to discover is that the secondary control group who received no such help and were initially better adjusted, deteriorated over a period of two years to a point on the scale below those originally picked out for help. This is not an argument for giving up the 'Special Difficulties Scheme' but rather for extending its methods and approaches across the curriculum and to all pupils for reconciling and working at the affective and the intellectual components in education simultaneously not separately.

We must do what we can as well as we can. Schools cannot take on the problems of society as a whole without collapsing under an intolerable burden. It is vital that we recognize the limits of what we can achieve it we are to continue to work vigorously and confidently. If we take on too much, we shall achieve little. We can only do our best within the limits of our task, which is to educate our pupils. If we know what we are trying to do and why, then our disruptive pupils are likely to diminish in number. Given a sense of purpose, of achievement, of stability, of being valued and cared for, they will neither want nor need to disrupt.

References:

DES (1967). *Children and their Primary Schools.* (*Plowden Report*) London HMSO

Graham P & Rutter M. (1968) *British Journal of Psychiatry.* 114, 581

Jones A. (1970) *School Counselling in Practice.* London: Ward Lock Educational

Jones A. (1971) *School Counselling, Trends in Education.* 23 HMSO

The all-purpose all age community school 1972
It's an exciting idea, but not quite as simple as it sounds.

This is an article I was asked to write for the journal, *Youth Review*, Issue 22 spring 1972.

I was already Deputy Head of the Thomas Calton School in Peckham. I saw great potential, especially in such a deprived area as Peckham, in helping the community to work together and for the social and educational services to communicate better with each other. To this day, we are still finding problems in communication and cooperation between services, sometimes with disastrous results.

Trends in the role of youth workers, and teachers

The idea that teachers and youth workers should work more closely together is not at all new. Way back in the late fifties, national conferences were discussing 'closer collaboration in the field and more integrated initial training between teachers, youth workers and social welfare workers of all kinds.'[1] Current developments in all these professions give impetus to turning theory into reality. We already have in our midst examples of teacher/youth workers, teacher/social workers and just a few 'community' schools.

The impending raising of the school leaving age to sixteen, the fundamental changes in school curricula and teaching methods which ROSLA (raising of the school leaving age) has necessitated and the Schools Council inspired, have forced teachers to question their traditional roles as purveyors of knowledge and upholders of the status quo.

Similarly youth workers no longer wish to restrict their activities to the young, the clubbable and the attachable, but propose instead youth and community work, recognising that schools and voluntary agencies should take the main responsibility for the activities of the younger age group.[2] Social workers, thoroughly reshuffled and reorganised in the wake of the Seebohm Report[3], have stopped using their specialist labels and work in multi-disciplinary teams within the community, even occasionally within the clubs and schools. Integration is the keynote.

Yet despite all this ferment of forward thinking, it is true to say that many teachers still do not know the youth workers who may operate in the same building. Similarly the youth worker may never venture into school by day. Thus, through lack of contact there may still develop myths and fantasies about who owns what, which group has damaged the other's property, whose 'things' are taking up much-needed space. Perhaps this box and cox arrangement had its merits: there was always a resident scapegoat to blame for the writing on the lavatory wall. Contact and cooperation lead inevitably to the blinding truth that both professions are broadly in the same business, namely the service of youth.

Furthermore their aims and objectives, in the way they have evolved in the last ten years, are remarkably similar. 'The primary goal of the youth worker is the social education of the young person'.[3] Many teachers would make similar claims. Schools used to mean drilling and disciplining; daily doses of equations and verb endings, parsing and preaching. Youth clubs used to be equally hard task-masters in the pursuit of leisure: activities, team games, basket work and basketball. Now in both professions we have learnt not to despair if our customers sometimes want just to sit and talk, and sometimes just to sit. Learning by doing is supplemented by learning by being.

Having realised our common theoretical ground, the next step was to turn this into reality by making joint youth leader/teacher appointments, even some joint training courses. Then we had the yet broader concept of the community school. Here the unity of the professions is so recognised that they become united under the jurisdiction of the Headmaster who may, as at Countesthorpe College in Leicestershire, be called Warden to denote his wider duties.

Unholy deadlock becomes holy wedlock, and in theory we all live happily ever after. The idea is an attractive one, but if we examine it closely we see that, like any reorganisation scheme, it is not without its snags and limitations.

Direct Lines

The arguments for recognising the central role a school should play in the community are very strong. School is the one place in the community where all young people must go until the age of fifteen, soon sixteen. Therefore through the captive adolescent we have potentially a direct line of communication with all the parents in the neighbourhood. It is uneconomic to equip school buildings and then lock them up at four each evening and for twelve whole weeks besides. Most schools are already used as clubs or evening institutes, but what is ridiculous is that the teachers are so often kept out of their own school in the evenings. And the leaders and instructors rarely operate in the day.

Even if the teacher happens to work as an evening instructor in his own school, little capital may be made out of the links with parents. Schools may often be unable to hold evening meetings for parents and friends because the building is booked by 'other'agencies. There is a good case for staffing a school building all day and all evening with a team of people working for the same organisation. But we also need to ask who should use the community school? If we limit the school to being a centre for all those concerned with young people, are we really providing what is needed?

For some years now, the virtue of providing facilities specifically for one age group has been seriously questioned. Frank Musgrove[4] for example postulated in 1964 that one of the causes of the generation gap was the divisive nature of our facilities for young people: human nature and group dynamics are such that if you split off from the rest of the community, the whole of a peer group (and especially such an explosive, insecure group as the adolescents), then you are asking for trouble. You are rejecting young people, instead of helping them to be initiated and assimilated into an adult style of life. You are telling them to go away and play, you are not helping them share and take adult responsibility in a real situation and you are forcing them to make their own group norms.

So it's not enough to integrate the youth workers with the school: we must involve other professional workers, and we must bring in all age groups. The *Plowden Report* [5] stresses, from a different angle, the importance of involving parents in the life of a school, this being the biggest single factor affecting children's achievement. Changing patterns of employment, of marriage and child bearing, lead to demands for the training and retraining of mature adults, male and female.

So the next logical step is for mums and dads, neighbours and grandparents to come to school and to follow, if they so wish, the same courses as the younger students: the uniting factor could be the content and level of the course (eg English to CSE), not the age of the student – a kind of contemporary version of the old 'standards'. The public library could be on the same site and a crèche to allow young mothers to continue their studies. It would be important to have some resident specialists – perhaps a doctor, a social worker, a careers adviser, and more besides. There wouldn't really need to be a further education college because it would all be happening on one big campus...

Bursting point

But wait a minute. By the time we've integrated all the youth workers, then all the 'service' services; by the time we've got all the young people in and integrated them with the other age groups; by the time we've provided a full range of academic courses (including of course, integrated studies), plus a full range of recreational and social activities, aren't we rather overdoing it? Isn't the building at bursting point and the staff exhausted? Why do we presume that it must be the school that makes this mammoth takeover bid? Why not the college of further education or the community centre? The concept of a community school is a very exciting one, but obviously a great deal of thought must be given to defining objectives realistically and setting some limits: this is something to be worked out according to the needs of each local community, between education, social health, housing and recreational services.

A library and a swimming pool shared between school and public would be ideal, but whether feasible would clearly depend on existing provision, size and location of site. Planning needs to go across sectional committees from the very beginning.

Obviously the school can't do everything, nor should it try. It would be arrogant and unrealistic to imagine that a monopolistic system could serve the needs of the whole community. Youth workers, possibly more than teachers know full well the numbers of dropouts and unclubbables which abound in any neighbourhood[6]. Schools know that a certain proportion of children will always truant and not necessarily because the syllabus is dull: even some of the imaginative ROSLA schemes don't pull in everybody. Some people – and this includes parents and grandparents – shy away from anything which is institutionalised. It doesn't matter how much the institution tries to appear democratic and unbureaucratic, some people prefer to be disorganised and unattached. They prefer the privacy of their own homes, and I use the word privacy advisedly. Anyone who really becomes part of an institution like a school, a church, or a social club, becomes part of the social dynamics, hates and loves, of that institution. Not everybody enjoys this kind of commitment and involvement. Those who do may prefer to choose their institution. Allowing for consumer choice means recognising that some people may prefer to belong to a church youth club, a Boys' Brigade or a working men's club.

Obligation

Others may prefer private enterprise – the coffee bar, the bingo hall, the bowling alley, the pub. The reason why some people prefer private enterprise may be precisely why they object to 'school' functions. When you pay your entrance fee or your coffee bill, you are asserting your status without any kind of moral obligation to that institution; obviously you mustn't break it up, but you don't owe it anything from within yourself. Sometimes that is important to an individual.

So we can't expect a community school to be all things for all sectors of the community. But it would provide the populace with some first rate facilities which rationalised the somewhat arbitrary and often divisive boundaries between schools, youth clubs and evening institutes: furthermore, home/school relationships and adult/adolescent relationships should be improved. It would obviously be helpful if the teachers, youth and social workers in the school shared some basic generic training, but the point must be made that though they may become united, they will not be identical. It is rather like a marriage. We don't expect married partners to lose their individual identities though they will probably share many of the same ideals, and work closely together. So in a community school, whilst we need maximum contact and cooperation between the various workers, and shared philosophy, we still need specialists and specialist skills.

It is unrealistic for every youth worker to try to do everything and it is important to build up a team which includes some real specialists who can serve individuals and also serve as resource points for the staff as a whole. A doctor, counsellor, careers adviser, psychologist and social worker for example. It is vital that the team members should be compatible with each other, for personality clashes can blight the most brilliant of organisations.

The question of who should be in charge of a community campus is highly debatable: the only point which must be made is that no-one can work day and night all the year round. The division of labour between sectional Heads would need to be carefully calculated and defined in operational terms. There would probably need to be a community council to govern the campus representing all sectors of the community, both at the official level (representatives of education, health, housing, social services etc.) and consumers. Industry might usefully be involved too.

There is of course one fundamental difference between a teacher and a youth worker which makes their true unity complicated. Youth workers work with adolescents on a voluntary basis: a young person makes a voluntary contract to join a club or talk to an unattached worker. The teacher has a statutory duty to teach students until they are sixteen.

This compulsory element does in fact conflict with the desire of a community school to give adult status and freedom of choice. Certainly a distinction may need to be made between junior high and senior high students, even if they are housed on the same campus. The older students could be given more freedom to come and go, alongside the adult students. How much further education can be housed on the same campus depends on overall local policy, and space available. But there is another important difference between the teacher and the youth worker. The teacher has a professional duty to teach his students something, though exactly what is currently a debatable point. I doubt if the Duke of Edinburgh's Award exerts such pressure on youth leaders' behaviour, as do GCE and CSE on the average teacher.

Harmful to both

At the moment the teacher is in conflict about how much he should teach; he is searching for a more consumer tailored curriculum, worrying about whether his role is to teach or be a social worker, an instructor or an activator. Ethel Venables[7] makes the point very clearly that total amalgamation of the two professions would be harmful to both. Teachers who give up their teaching function completely risk neglecting the able academically minded. If, on the other hand, youth workers became wholly identified with teachers, then they might neglect the function of caring for those who reject formal education. It is worth reading Ethel Venables's book to realise how very differently teachers and youth workers are perceived by others and by each other.

As teachers we may think of ourselves as very humane, but we may still be perceived as instruments of a system which the individual rejects, or is unable to accept on the terms upon which it is offered. As youth workers we may feel we are functioning as trusted counsellors, but we may still be perceived as 'do-gooders'. The framework within which we work is bound to put its stamp upon us in spite of our individual characteristics.

Perhaps at this point I should state my own interest: I am Deputy Head of a school designated for rebuilding as a community school. Our plan is very exciting, though its execution is somewhat postponed by Mrs Thatcher's cuts in the secondary building program. We are to be rebuilt in the centre of a busy shopping area. In Peckham, so that mums and dads really can drop in for a coffee in the cafeteria, or even breakfast.

We have lots of ideas about what we would like to do, and some of them have been started in spite of our old decaying buildings: for example Boys' Brigade an under-fives club on a Monday. Mothers come for a dressmaking class (arranged through the evening institute) while their infants are looked after and played with by older girls who incorporate this in a child development course. Old people come into school and have their hair set. Students go out and help in local playgroups, or visit old people in their homes, doing odd jobs for them. Our woodwork department is making equipment and games for a nearby old people's hospital.

Extended day

If we had our new building and better facilities we could do so much more: perhaps we could have an extended day to cater for those who find it difficult to study at home. Perhaps we could have a flexible day so that students could choose if they preferred, say, a morning and an evening session, and be free to study or relax wherever they liked the rest of the time. Perhaps teachers and youth workers could work different shifts in a pattern which suits their needs and interests. Perhaps some of our teachers would work principally in an unstructured setting, whilst some youth workers might enjoy some straightforward teaching. Who knows?

References:

1. Bulman, I *Youth Service and Interprofessional Studies.* Pergamon Press 1970
2. Youth Service Development Council. *Youth and Community Work in the 70s.* HMSO 1969
3. *The Seebohm Report: on Local Authority and Allied Personal Social Services.* HMSO 1969
4. F Musgrove. *Youth and the social order.* Routledge and Kegan Paul 1964
5. *Plowden Report: Children and their Primary Schools.* HMSO 1967
6. Goetschius & Tash. *Working with Unattached Youth.* Routledge and KeganPaul 1967
7. Ethel Venables. *Teachers and Youth Workers, a study of their roles;* Evans/Methuen, Educational 1971

Postscript

The editorial said that the article describes the exciting plans for a community school which would bring together the skills of youth and community workers plus other professionals in one building.

'Unfortunately the government's decision to shelve all secondary school improvements apart from the 'roofs over heads' projects is all the more depressing. The ill-fated plans for Thomas Calton, for instance offered a real chance for teachers, youth community workers to work together to test out what can be done in an area of such social deprivation as Peckham.'

Yes, the whole project was cancelled. We did however do what we could without the new building. We employed a full time social worker and worked very closely the local services for young people such as educational psychologists and the careers service. I never gave up on the concept of the community school. My next school was also going to be rebuilt as a community school and then was also cancelled and finally I became Head of one that actually existed. Read on...!

When I wrote this article I had never seen or heard of such a thing as a community school, yet it seemed and still does seem, to be such an excellent and obvious idea. So I come back to this theme many times.

At this point the vacancy for the Headship of Vauxhall Manor School in Brixton arose. I applied and got it. I was sorry to leave Thomas Calton. I had many good friends on the staff and I thank them and the pupils for helping me to adjust to a modern inner-city comprehensive school. I found my role so much more interesting than teaching French all the time. Being Head was going to be even more challenging, difficult and worthwhile. That's an understatement!

Postscript

Only after reading this chapter after I had finished writing this book, did I realise that my original ideas for what makes a community school were nearly all implemented at Cranford Community School later.

CHAPTER 3: VAUXHALL MANOR SCHOOL 1974-1981

AFTER THREE YEARS AT THOMAS CALTON SCHOOL, I decided it was time to move on. I felt ready to be Head of my own school. It wasn't all that easy to be selected and I was turned down several times. The interview experience helped me each time to improve my performance a little, usually by toning it down a bit! The Vauxhall Manor governing body included a staff member, which I didn't mind. The school was well known for its policy of mixed ability teaching. It was situated very near to Vauxhall Bridge, in an area of great deprivation. It was one of the most difficult schools in London. Just what I wanted!

It was, of course, multinational. There were over 100 languages spoken. Afro-Caribbean girls were greatly in the majority, but they came from all over Africa and the West Indies. So they didn't necessarily get on with each other. There was rivalry between some of the West Indian Islands or the various African States, differences in culture and language. 80% of the pupils had no father living at home, many siblings and received free school lunches. Mothers often worked as cleaners in the early morning in the city just across the river, so the oldest daughter looked after the rest of the family. Single mothers were the norm and normal in the original West Indian culture. It was very hard work for them and hard for their daughters to study in peace. Attendance was about 70% when I arrived at the school. We gradually improved it though it was never 100% but in the end the parents responded well to our efforts to help their children succeed academically and hopefully get a good job.

In my first assembly in the Upper School in Kennington near The Oval, the girls all stood up for me when I made my entrance. Alas, then nobody could see me: the girls were so tall. I seated them and said 'let us pray.' A loud voice from the back said 'WHY NOT?' I carried on calmly.

A few weeks after I arrived, the Chief Education Officer kindly came to see me to show his interest and support. While he was there, a girl was knifed by another pupil on the stairs during break. This was a serious matter. After my experience at Thomas Calton, I knew how to deal with it. It did however take a long time to calm down the general hysteria it caused. It never happened again while I was there. The girls soon learnt that I would not accept violence or racism.

Every day there was a long queue outside my door of girls sent to me for some kind of minor misbehaviour. It was one way of getting to know them, which was useful, but after a few weeks. I told the staff that I didn't want to see naughty girls, I only wanted to see good girls. Miracle, I suddenly had a queue of good girls, quite a few of them the same girls! We then introduced a merit card which also acted as an incentive for good behaviour.

The Punitive Vicious Circle 1974

In 1974 I gave a talk to NACRO (the National Association for the Care and Rehabilitation of Offenders) Crime Prevention Conference. Part of it was reprinted in *Residential Care*, the monthly journal of the National Association of Voluntary Hostels and then included in a booklet on *Disruptive and Violent Behaviour in School* compiled by Devon Education Department in 1975. I had no idea it had travelled so far! Later I found out it was the chapter in a book published by Ward Lock Educational in 1976 called *The Disruptive Pupil in the Secondary School* and edited by Ronald G. Cave and Clive Jones-Davies. My chapter in their book was called *Coping with disruptive pupils in the school situation*. I wrote most of this chapter when I was Deputy Head at Thomas Calton School. So I have included it in Chapter 2 because it gives more details of the pioneering work we did there in conjunction with the Maudsley Institute. By the time it was published, I was Head of Vauxhall Manor and found it very helpful myself! My whole chapter was first published in the following book:

The Disruptive Pupil in the Secondary School 1976 ed., Ronald G. Cave and Clive Jones-Davies published by Ward Lock Educational, the Orion Publishing Group. My book called **School Counselling in Practice** was also published by them in 1970.

Vauxhall Manor pupils with the Headmistress

There follows part of my chapter on the punitive vicious circle:

Schools are NOT as almighty, all powerful or as awful as many would have us believe. Their influence upon the pupil is not as great as that of their parents or society; yet parents, society and schools behave at times as if it were. Parents pass over their offspring saying: 'You deal with her. I can't do nuffink with her'. Society has latched on to the fact that schools, in many cases, are more likely to make contact with difficult children and their families than other agencies, and furthermore, not only make contact but keep up that contact. Schools, for their part, flattered by this enhanced role, and as conscientious as ever, thus begin to try to do the work of parents, social workers, or society for them. It sounds good but it isn't good, for many reasons.

First it's an impossible job, and one for which teachers have neither the time the training, nor the necessary skills.

Second, it debilitates and saps both parents and pupils as well as society if school takes over their responsibilities: the aim of the school should be to involve them more.

Third, it splits school off from the rest of society in an unreal 'last bastion' role which means that the school and the community it services become out of touch with each other. Schools bravely battle against the forces of society, seeking to compensate for these deficiencies. Whatever society has failed to do elsewhere, schools are expected to make good. It is an impossible job.

We are faced now with the situation in which teachers are in great conflict: they are not sure what they should teach or how they should teach it. They try to make their lessons more 'relevant', but to the children, they are still 'school' and may still be rejected out of hand. They see the need to work with the 'whole' child. They wonder if they have been in the past too rigid, authoritarian, controlling, directive, or judgemental. They try, therefore, to avoid all that, and endeavour to be child-centred, consumer-orientated, flexible, democratic, non-directive and non-judgemental, whether or not this is appropriate. They find the welfare and social services too remote and too wrapped up in red tape to give their pupils the help they need, so they try to help their pupils themselves, and visit their homes when their parents need sorting out. They know parents are important, but they do not see any difference between what they can do and what a social worker might do if he had the time. Not that they have much free time; but how can they ignore the problems their pupils present them with?

This exaggerated caricature epitomises the dilemma of committed, sensitive teachers who are suffering from confusion: role confusion, identity confusion. They are paid as teacher, they are trained as teachers and that is their main job. If they are pushed by pressures from without and seduced by their own professional pride into attempting to do everything for all their pupils, they will end by teaching badly. They need professional help from other agencies. It may be very desirable for a counsellor to be non-directive, non-judgemental and non-authoritarian, but for teachers to emulate this rigidly can be well-nigh disastrous. They must give directions, they must judge and assess pupils' worth and they must exercise the authority they carry: they do not have to do this in an unpleasant way.

But if they fail to accept their role as teacher, what hope have the class of being pupils? Before we know where we are non-directive becomes 'without a sense of direction'; non-judgemental becomes 'unable to make judgement or decision'; non-authoritarian becomes 'without any authority'. The point of school is not to be a social welfare agency. If we were meant to be social welfare agencies we would not be called schools. Neither would we work with the ridiculous case loads, lack of supervision and constant pressure of lack of time which every school faces daily. So if schools are so overburdened and pressurised by their social problems, why don't they get more help from other agencies?

Many of the blockages to effective communication are, alas, based on ignorance and fantasy. The school feels it has done everything for the child but 'his parents are hopeless and social services never do anything'. Conversely the parents may say that the school is the cause of the problems; social services may say that they're not surprised the child has problems the way the school treats him. Only too rarely do all parties get together, sink their differences and work out what they can each do respectively to help the child. Even case conferences can become a kind of musical parcel game which each party tries to pass the buck on to the other, if only to alleviate themselves of the blame when the problem continues to remain a problem. I exaggerate of course. But there is much more of this kind of thing going on than we can afford.

In particular, social workers and teachers need to have a much clearer idea of the similarities and differences between the way they work. To the social worker, the teacher may appear to be interfering, controlling, manipulative, over-involved, hasty to act, unable to listen properly, blind to obvious cries for help given out by the child, possessive, judgemental and unreasonable. To the teacher, the social worker may appear to be too young and inexperienced, naive, gullible, easily manipulated, slow to act, impossible to contact on the phone, elusive and therefore defensive, ignorant of what the pupil is really like, ineffectual, soft, on the child's side. However much or however little truth there is in these stereotypes, they can only damage and hinder the work which should be going on between the school and the welfare agencies.

But there are other problems which stop schools from making effective use of other agencies. I have already touched upon the professional pride of the teacher. Teachers are curiously reluctant to ask for help or advice, for traditionally the teacher is king of the classroom and soldiers on alone. It is NOT an admission of failure for a teacher to say a pupil has problems. Too often teachers do not admit their doubts about a pupil, as If they feared this somehow reflected upon their teaching ability. A classic syndrome I have observed in nearly every school I've ever worked in is for a pupil to be allowed to disrupt lesson after lesson until it is decided to bring in help from a specialist agency. Alas, the child guidance clinic is not able to wave a magic wand, and so the school decides that child guidance is no good. But the real problem is that the school has not referred the pupil to specialists soon enough.

The trouble is that even when teachers notice and admit a problem in a pupil, very often they do not know who to ask about it. Although in most schools there are now specialists in pastoral care, it would be fair to say that not all these have been trained to recognise a problem which needs referring to someone else. Educational psychologists are so over-worked that they too are hard to catch. School counsellors or school social workers can provide an invaluable service here, but they are still too few. Relatively few schools attempt any systematic screening or diagnosis of their pupils when they are in their first year, in order to identify the pupils who are 'at risk' and may need extra help. Thus most of the children who get help from other agencies do so only at a point of crisis and because they have made a nuisance of themselves. The ones who are not a nuisance are much less likely to get help, which is even more disturbing. Often it is too late to do much, for example, it is very difficult to get a maladjusted child into a maladjusted boarding school over the age of thirteen, yet it may have taken two years for his problems to crystallise. It would have been much easier to help if the school had realised the extent of his difficulties earlier. It is important also to ask why secondary schools do not liaise better with primary schools on this question of early diagnosis.

Another factor which stops school agencies working as closely as they might is the justifiable fear of the agencies, that, if they pass back any information, it will become staff room gossip and handicap the pupil further. Confidentiality is a sore point in most staff rooms, but the line to be drawn between confidential information and gossip is a very fine one and easily broken, Alas, if only social workers knew how much our wickeder pupils had already damaged their reputations and how much staff already knew about their home background. Most discouraging of all for the pupil, who has a good social worker and is willing to try to improve, is the reputation he has already: what I call the vicious punitive circle. It is so hard for teachers to recognise when a child is really trying to make a 'new start' and so, discouraged, the child may give up.

Between the two professionals, there can also be a blockage in terms of language. We hear a lot about the restricted language code in terms of social class: but inter-professionally it can be a barrier too. I remember when I was a counsellor giving a talk to some Heads, I started talking about the 'support' I gave the teachers. One Head who had been looking rather sceptical, reacted visibly at this point and said with great relief; 'Ah, you mean you stand by the teacher through thick and thin and take his side against the pupil.' I did **not** mean that. But no wonder there are misunderstandings when we use language so differently.

Another problem within schools which must cause frustration for other agencies lies in the chain of command. Gone are the days when Heads imagine they can handle all contacts with outside agencies. But it is no healthier for this responsibility to be vested solely in another member of the hierarchy. There is nothing more frustrating and demoralising for an astute and perceptive form teacher than to have to take his 'problem' to someone else, who then proceeds to process it through the organisational machine until eventually a very second hand answer winds its way back. I am sure our form teachers would be less tempted either to go it alone or to deny the problems they face, if they were supported in making contact with agencies themselves. I find, for example, in my position as Head, that it is ludicrous for me to discuss a child I hardly know with a social worker. It's not that I'm not interested, but the interaction needs to be with the person who is most intimately concerned with that child, not only because of the two-way exchange of information but also because that teacher is going to be in a position to help the child. He may discover, for example, that he was colluding with the child's problems and was 'rewarding' his disturbing, attention-seeking behaviour. So often there comes into play these days what I call 'the law of diminishing expectations'. 'Officer Klopsky I'm really a slob'as the song in West Side story puts it. Some of our children are very astute at playing up their problems. Remember:

Blessed is he who expecteth nothing, for he shall not be disappointed.

So what can schools do to help children at risk more effectively? And how can they work more fruitfully with the agencies which service their pupils?

First the schools should concentrate on teachings as whole-heartedly, as passionately, as imaginatively, as inventively and as meaningfully as they can. Of course they must use the resources of the environment, of the community, of the parents, of the pupils, of themselves; but they must not be ashamed to teach the skills that children want and need. Many of our pupils are half-hearted about school because schools are not sure what they are trying to do. When teachers are in conflict and doubt, pupils will be at risk.

Second, the school system must be designed to serve the needs of the pupils, which include being valued, being given responsibility, being trusted, being given room to breathe and grow and make mistakes, being given secure but flexible framework, being given a sense of purpose, being set some limits and being asked to do not as little as possible, but as much as possible. So often the organisation of a school ossifies and begins to contradict its stated objectives at which point both staff and pupils switch off and parents despair. In particular it is vital for the academic and pastoral aspects of the schools to be integrated and not split otherwise the one may unwittingly contradict the other: we trust you but we lock you out in the lunch hour. What is a child to make of that double message?

The pastoral care system needs to be one in which every member of staff feels he can play a part. Senior staff need to support and train younger staff so that they can share actively the responsibility they have and develop their skills. Schools need to make efforts to meet the staff of other agencies; staff need to learn how to write a report for a social worker, how to conduct an interview, how to write a letter to a parent or social worker, how to keep relevant and helpful records.

A school needs to develop the best main system it can: it is disastrous to keep patching up a poor system by adding on extras. Nevertheless, there is, in my opinion, a very good case for employing both a counsellor and a school social worker in a school. One of their main functions is to relieve teachers of problems which press upon them; to support them in the working situation. In my experience, however good the response from the local education welfare office and the social services, they cannot provide in school the depth of breadth of help required. The school social worker is particularly vital in home/school relations. Since Plowden, teachers have tried more and more to penetrate pupils' homes, but not always with great success. Home visiting is a professional job, best done by a specialist and trained member of staff.

Other preventive measures in schools abound: diagnostic and screening systems, nurture groups, opportunity classes, tutorial groups, intensive language programs, sanctuaries, compensatory units and off-site centres for school refusers: all these have their merits but will be ineffectual if the main system of the school is not right.

Agencies serving the pupils of a school need to take much more time and care to feedback to the school much more about what is happening without breaking confidentiality. They will find the school a rich source of help and information which could be harnessed much more effectively in the service of the child at risk. Only by understanding the differences and the limitations of the way they each work will schools and agencies be freed to help each other get on with their particular job. There will always be children 'at risk' but we need to put our energy into getting effective help for these children, not into demarcation disputes and perpetual soul searching. We all need each other because we do different but complementary jobs. Let us admit that need for the sake of the children we serve.

Postscript

I'm not aware of schools being so worried about violent and disruptive pupils at the moment. It's not in the headline news as much as it was in the 70s or even the 80s. Of course, I wrote this when I was working in

Peckham and Brixton, two of the most deprived areas in the country, where even today, tragedies about poor communication between the various social services still occur. But my sense is that teachers now have a much clearer concept of their role, they understand the boundaries to their authority better and are not so *laissez–faire* or anxious to please. But it's hard to generalise: a lot will depend on the tone set by the Head, something, I explored later in my book, *Leadership for Tomorrow's Schools* 1987.

London looks forward
A conference at the Royal Festival Hall, July 1977
In the presence of the Duke of Edinburgh, who also spoke.

Your Royal Highness, Mr Chairman, Ladies and Gentlemen.

I am honoured to be representing **education** at this conference, even though, curiously, this important topic has been relegated to this one slot on the second day and classified as social and cultural. In my view, and clearly in the view of other speakers yesterday, the quality of the education service is crucial to the whole development of London, for it is on our young people that our future depends.

That said may I add that we at Vauxhall Manor School, situated as we are but a stone's throw from here, are delighted that this august event should take place in our local neighbourhood concert hall and so near our local neighbourhood theatre! We do indeed represent that community which goes from this noble Jubilee stretch of the Thames to the midst of Brixton, in other words that part of Lambeth which is known to you all as the subject of many studies, notably the Lambeth Study. I do not need therefore to remind you that this is an area which scores top marks on any statistician's index of social deprivation.

It is an area which has for years been visibly crumbling, losing its indigenous population to the leafy outer city or beyond, and taking under its wing a more shifting population made up of a complex mix of nationalities, colours, customs and creeds. It is now predominantly a vibrant West Indian community. It is an area which alas, offers its people, especially its young people, poor opportunities for work and inadequate facilities for recreation and leisure. The South Bank and The Oval cricket ground, splendid as they are, do not suffice.

Yet in the area as a whole there are now some signs of a Renaissance, a revitalisation of old properties, a rebuilding of desolate demolished sites. This is a new development. Our community also feels more settled. It is no longer an immigrant community, it is a multinational community whose members have settled and become Londoners, who stay, who want and who deserve a voice in what is happening; whose very multi-ethnic qualities enrich and enhance our community. In schools, the tide has also turned. In the early 70s inner-city schools were put under appalling pressures from the society they served. They became the last bastion of practically everything. Schools were expected to be defenders of moral values, protectors of the status quo, soup kitchens and social welfare agencies. All this in an era of acute staff shortages and when one of the main objectives of the school day, was to make sure that each class at least had an adult present.

Under such siege conditions, it was difficult for schools to be outgoing or for the community to penetrate those nineteenth century fortresses called schools. Despite the *Plowden Report* which enabled more and more gross resources to be ploughed into schools in 'social priority' areas, the net results were depressingly undramatic. Schools cannot take on the problems of society without undermining their prime function, which is to be schools, not social welfare agencies.

In the last two years, the situation in London schools has completely changed: we have gone from being overcrowded and understaffed, to being well staffed and less crowded. We have rising standards and falling roles. This makes those of us whose work depends on the very existence of young people, somewhat insecure about our futures: we're not sure where our next pupil is coming from. Predictions for the future are startling. At present our total inner London school population stands at about 360,000. By 1980 it will drop by about a sixth. By 1985 will be about one third less than at present.

These are of course only predictions, which do not allow for the unexpected side effects of an exceptionally happy Jubilee Year. I have already heard that fewer married couples are seeking marriage guidance this year, so perhaps by 1984, a new crop of school children will prove us all wrong. But as things stand, by 1985 there will be 122,000 fewer pupils in our Inner London Schools. It will be of great concern to the community as a whole. What happens to these London schools; whether an educational presence is maintained in each community, whether buildings are closed, pulled down or kept in moth balls awaiting the next baby boom, or whether they become centres for the community to share, to enjoy and to benefit from?

Speakers have already expressed concern about educational standards and facilities: in this falling roles situation, our first, priority must surely be to use the space to give pupils a better deal, to improve pupil-teacher ratios, facilities for sports, technology, science, art, crafts, and recreation and to offer specialist rooms for specialist subjects. Our pupils, that is, our future citizens, parents, workers and rate payers, can and must benefit from this.

The second outcome of the falling roles situation affects the community greatly. In 1973, ILEA produced an inspired and important policy document called *an education service for the whole community*. The vision held by ILEA then and now was that schools could and should open up to and interact with the community as a whole. Education is a life-long process, not something which goes on between 9am and 4pm from the ages of 5-16.

At that time I was Deputy Head of the Thomas Calton School which was to be rebuilt right in the middle of a shopping centre in Peckham, as a community school. We were to have many facilities for joint public and school use: a cafeteria, a library, a sports centre and pool, a crèche, a nursery and facilities for the physically handicapped. The school was to be open to the community for leisure and for learning, during and after school hours, in the evening and in the holidays. We hoped to have a resident psychologist, social worker, community worker, careers officer, welfare officer and counsellor so that the community could share our resources. London wanted community schools but in the foreseeable future, both then and now there is no money for rebuilding secondary schools.

However there will soon be space in many existing schools: here is a wonderful opportunity for schools to develop the kind of community facilities I have just mentioned. My hope would be that such developments would be integrated with, not separated from the work of the schools. It is time the great divide between recreational institutes, play centres, day centres, schools and clubs was well and truly bridged for the benefit of the whole community.

Already schools such as ours send pupils into the community to do voluntary service, to gain work experience, to do social surveys, to take photographs, to paint and to draw. You have evidence of this in the foyer. What they already do shows how much they have to give.

What of our young people in all this? How do they feel? Many of them face problems real problems personal, social, economic and psychological problems, of which they are the victims not the cause. They see their community getting shabbier, their job prospects getting dimmer; they find themselves too easily the scapegoats of society. They deserve better than this. They are better than this.

I would remind you of the law of diminishing expectations:

Blessed is he who expecteth nothing, for he shall not be disappointed.

It is my sincere belief that young people respond very sensitively to adults' expectations of them. If we expect them to be trouble makers, they will be trouble makers. It is no good telling them to go away and play especially if there is nowhere to play. They need us and we need them. Our teenagers are not children. They are young adults, and they need recognition and a positive role in society. They need better facilities and a better chance.

I am sure we are not alone at Vauxhall Manor in finding our pupils full of energy and good will, keen to learn. They respond to having demands made upon them, being trusted and being given responsibility; they are keen to be of service in the community. They are used to carrying responsibility at home and caring for others. They are not all perfect by any means. They need our love, our support, our respect, our encouragement and our care. In their turn they are loving and giving, creative, imaginative, proud of their culture, whatever it may be, full of humour, with a sharp edge to their wit. Our school community bubbles with life with a rich cultural mix: we are proud of our pupils. Whatever

73

their country of origin, they are now Londoners, If they remain Londoners, then indeed London can look forward.

Postscript
Now, in 2015, the falling roles problem has gone away with a vengeance. London and many other regions are currently overwhelmed by the rise in the number of children who are now of school age. There are not enough places in primary schools and temporary buildings are being put up. All this is due to the recently growing influx of immigrants. Many of these bring with them an appreciation of the importance of education, and the determination to succeed. So London LOOKS FORWARD AGAIN.

Shortly after the conference we were told that we were going to become a community school… We were thrilled.

Staff meetings
From time to time I gave a serious talk to the staff. They each received a copy so that they could think about what I had said.

Vauxhall Manor School staff meeting, April 30th, 1979
Pastoral care: myth, mystique, mistake or misunderstanding?
For some time now I have wanted to say something about pastoral care. The way the concept has developed and been interpreted has been causing me and many of you, I know, great concern. I mean, specifically, the splitting that has been going on, not just in this school, but nationwide, between the pastoral and the academic. I'd like to elaborate my thoughts which reflect what I see and hear and I'd like to check out whether this analysis makes sense to you.

I never have liked the term pastoral care. To me it smacks of nymphs and shepherds, Fragonard and Watteau, noble idylls while the peasants are revolting. It smacks of sheep following blindly, being herded, it smacks of do-goodery, missionary deeds among the less-fortunate-than-ourselves. It smacks of smother-love, rather than mother-love. It doesn't have to be any of these things, and very often it isn't, but sometimes this is how it turns out, particularly when it becomes a separate thing in its own right.

To be honest, I don't altogether like the term academic either, which has equal limitations: it smacks of the grammar school, pre 1870 tradition, elitism, Oxbridge, graduate staff, intellectual pretension, exam snobbery and cramming. Again, it doesn't have to be any of these and neither do these terms have to be negative or judgemental. Nevertheless it is an inappropriate term to polarise against 'pastoral.' Both words beg questions and they beg the wrong questions. We need to change the questions and the vocabulary.

Before I attempt this, I'd like to sketch out briefly how it seems to me that we got into this state of affairs. In the last fifteen years or so there has been a tremendous boom in the pastoral care industry. This boom, with its attendant creation of pastoral care posts of responsibility, has made the 'academic' side of the staff and the 'academic' hierarchy feel put out and devalued. Some academics even goes so far as to say that these two ladders reflect the historical split in the teaching profession between the 'sec mod' and the 'grammar', the teacher of pupils and the teacher of subjects. Really I don't think that applies here, but I see what they mean.

The original reasons for setting up, making specific and institut-ionalising pastoral care systems were extremely positive and responded to a real need. When we teach it is nonsense to ignore the emotional needs or the developmental stage of our pupils, it is nonsense to teach at people, to teach history without teaching Jane, it is nonsense to ignore the child's background circumstances if they are having a devastating effect on him. This is of course a caricature, yet with enough truth in it for us to recognise that at the time, some 15-20 years ago, there was a balance to be redressed. But alas, the pendulum swung so far that what began as compensatory became over-compensatory, what started as loving became suffocating, what started as helping and strengthening became weakening: instead of promoting healthy growth and independence, it began to stunt growth and promote an unhealthy kind of over-dependence. Again, a caricature and an injustice too many: but with enough recognisable truth.

Even more devastating, the influence of the pastoral 'caring' spread to the separate concept of learning. And so there seems to have developed the do-it-for-you, rather than 'do-it-yourself' syndrome, epitomised by the ubiquitous worksheet, so often pathetically thin and undemanding, even on those occasions when it is well reproduced. Further to this already unchallenging situation, we have to add socio-economic-psychological excuse making: 'Officer Klopsky, I'm really a slob' as the youths in the musical *West Side Story* said. 'OK, so you can't help it. We can't expect anything. It's all predestined, give up. It's not your fault.'

Fortunately Rutter's key work on secondary schools and their effects on children (*Fifteen Thousand Hours*, published Open Books), has shown that this is just not true. Schools really do make a difference to what happens to pupils. You'll remember I talked a little about this in the September staff meeting. Schools with pupils of comparable backgrounds have completely different effects on the pupils: in other words the ethos of a particular school and the nature of the educational process in that school will change a pupil's life. I find that message challenging and hopeful.

However we are still left with a split which is reflected in most schools in dual academic and pastoral systems, epitomised by the way the points are allocated. When a teacher applies for a post, especially a scale post, he is usually by implication being asked to declare himself either 'academic' or 'pastoral.' There's an implied assumption: are you about social learning or about intellectual learning, as if the two were incompatible goals. And mixed ability teaching which clearly has as part of its original rationale a desire not to split learning in this way, often in practice appears to put social goals before intellectual goals. When this happens it too is unwittingly subscribing to this often consciously unacknowledged chasm in aims and objectives.

When we look at the Scale 1 teacher who is also a form teacher and so hasn't been forced to declare his hand upon entry, we often see even here a terrible conflict within the same person. The same teacher can be seen to behave quite differently according to whether he is in his form teacher role or his subject teacher role. 'I will not have this pupil in my class,' he says as subject teacher. 'How can you reject this pupil who has so many problems and needs' he says as form teacher? It's one aspect of teacher stress: a kind of 'pastoral academic schizophrenia'.

When we look at the form teacher who is still in my opinion the most important teacher for the individual pupil we find him simultaneously asking for more time with his form, then not sure what to do with it and asking for less time. We find him wanting to get to know his pupils individually, but realistically not able to do this, and indeed very unsure how to do it, or what to do if he did! We find the form teacher able perhaps to make a series of relationships with particular individuals or even particular groups (within the class) but often unable to work with the class as a whole except in a rather negative, nagging punitive way. It seems to me that when that happens, it is because he is holding back from his teaching-learning role as form teacher and only trying either to 'care' or to 'shepherd.' On the other hand the subject teacher is trying to 'teach'so he doesn't necessarily see himself as an 'instrument of pastoral care,' neither does he always realise to what extent the pupils model their behaviour on his. And on the whole few of us look very hard at the general overall messages given out by us as a staff, for example in our behaviour between lessons, lunch and break times and in corridors.

So how do schools get out of this syndrome? I've already indicated that I think this is a nationwide disease and in many ways this school is not as deeply into it as some, partly because of mixed ability teaching and partly because we've always prided ourselves on our general tone, quality of relationships, and we've always said we don't support the split. But I know a lot of you are conscious that it exists to some extent, and when I examine carefully various statements of policy and role definition I see the split unconsciously accented in a way I cannot now condone. For example, the definition of the role of the Head of Year says:

- to support the academic function,
- to see that girls are in a fit state to learn

as if the Head of Year were simply a snapper up of unconsidered trifles, a picker up of the pieces so that the class teacher can get on. For example, the constant tension about whether the problem in the lesson is a Head of Department problem or a Head of Year problem with a great deal of passing the parcel going on. And for example in the question of assessment, which is seen as an academic matter with, unconsciously, a revealing split and a missing link with the form teacher. And the pupil is hardly let in on this at all.

So we need to stop and reconceptualise the whole thing. It is all based on a mistaken assumption. It isn't a question of either/or, nor even of both. Everything is total, neither academic nor pastoral, but much more than that, and certainly much more than the mechanical sum of the parts. We are really talking about whole school behaviour, whole staff, whole pupils and whole people.

So how did we get to this point? To recap:

Stage 1: In the beginning school was about academic learning to which you added a bit of pastoral care if necessary.
Stage 2: The social learning became recognised as very important, a kind of implied final goal, for which academic learning was a means. Not all schools have been through stage 2 some are still in stage 1.
Stage 3: Total learning process including creative, social, intellectual, moral, practical, aesthetic and social components.

No doubt we could argue about the categories I have outlined but the points I am trying to make is:

1. the process is a total one, and much more complex than academic/pastoral
2. all the parts are interdependent
3. all the parts are being worked on at once whether we want them to be or not

So in the subject lesson the pupil is learning social skills as well as the subject, but he is also learning everything else as well. He is learning from the content of the lesson but most of all from the total process within the classroom. So the class teacher is not only teaching his subject but also study skills, decision making, coping skills and so on.

In the form room, it also follows that the form teacher's role is not confined to loving or disciplining, he is part of the total learning process. Once we internalise this concept the form teacher is liberated to take a more specific teaching role, for example study skills, making sense of what is happening, moral education, decision making, even teaching a subject like 'health education'. And indeed we've already had considerable discussion about all this in this school.

So if we return to a basic question about what is school for? The answer is that it is about learning. The purpose of school is not 'to be a caring community' though we would hope to be one. The purpose of school is not to love the pupils in the sense of being all forgiving, all embracing, though we would hope to love them and not be afraid to be angry and set limits sometimes as part of that love. The purpose of school is not to see each pupil as an individual with problems we have to solve for him, nor as solely a member of a peer group which may be more of a Prison than a support or stimulus. We need somehow to see the pupils more flexibly, not trapped in an individual group, or even a class, stereotype. And we need to look at the total process not just the separate bits.

As far as our methods go, I am certain that the process at present is too often too undemanding of the pupil's energy. This happens when the teacher does all the work for the pupil; when the teacher rushes round all the tine handing out things, when the teacher pleads for cooperation, waits on the pupil hand and foot: in short when the teacher behaves like a slave, the pupil becomes a bored tyrant. When the teacher is slave, the teacher also becomes stressed and exhausted.

Nobody originally meant the teacher to be a slave and when it happens it is part of the reaction against the other extreme, the teacher as tyrant. But it is also part of a well-meant but often misplaced desire on the part of the teacher to stop the pupil from facing problems or having difficulties a desire to smooth his path so that he can learn more easily. Yet it is precisely the challenge of learning to cope with transitions, with problems, with changes and with difficulties that our pupils need if they are to cope with life after school and indeed if they are going to cope with school itself.

Engaging actively with the learning process includes learning gradually, step by step, how to take responsibility for oneself. Concentrating on pupil comfort, at teacher expense, does not really help the pupil, it merely stresses the teachers. 'Let the teacher take the strain', what about the pupils?

A lot of our strain comes from our desire to protect the pupils, eg. the question of assessment, but maybe they'd feel better (and so would we) if they knew where they stood. In a way this is a part of respecting and valuing the pupils, in being genuine, accepting and emphatic. Honesty doesn't have to be destructive; half-truth can be. Besides, pupils are not fools nor are they easily fooled. Further the pupils infinitely prefer it, and learn more if we are able to take adult roles and use our authority. And especially if we can be secure enough to recognise our adulthood as well as their childishness.

In this paper I am trying to articulate something which is not altogether clear, but which is emerging from within us. I regard this year as a very important year for the school. There is less overt change, but a lot of growth and development in us as a staff. I feel the energy of the whole staff coming together in a more coherent and constructive way. I feel an atmosphere of trust, of openness, and a corporate moving forward which is quite profound. I hope we can continue to share our experiences and keep working on this issue.

Anne Jones, Headmistress

COMMENT

This sounds rather top down to me now, but curiously the staff seemed to enjoy it, partly because I faced up to a few issues, for example I think it made it clear that I wanted the staff to be honest in their assessment of pupils' work. We also took the staff away for another weekend in Worthing, led by the Grubb Institute, and it did have the same effect on all of us as it had at Thomas Calton. We were clearer about our goals and more honest, trusting and open.

When I became a Head, I had originally had to learn to be more directive since as counsellor I had been as non-directive as possible! When I finally got myself into the right balance between these two extremes and was giving genuine leadership, the staff gave me a much treasured picture. The Head of Art had done a hand-drawn copy of the Delacroix picture of *Liberty Leading the People*. All the people were caricatures of the staff, with me as Liberty! And on the back, there was a long row of pin men, all in a line. And each pin man had the signature of a member of staff. The message was that they were all behind me in fighting the same fight!

Membership of government bodies

Over a long period of time, I found myself participating in various Bodies set up to advise the government on a variety of matters. Here are a few examples:

Home Office: Member, Advisory Council on the Misuse of Drugs 1977-83

In 1977, I received an invitation from Merlyn Rees, later Lord Merlyn-Rees, (changed surname to Merlyn-Rees by deed poll 1992) who was Secretary of State for the Home Office at the time, to join this Council. Merlyn had been my economics teacher at school. He was a great teacher. He used to invite sixth formers round to his house for supper and debate. I was delighted that he remembered me and I knew he would have chosen me on my merit, not our connection. I served in the Council for two sessions, each of three years.

The Council was full of very learned medical experts and it was a very serious subject. I had dealt with some drug issues in my counselling job and had advised the Head how important it was to educate all the pupils about drugs and the serious dangers they brought. The Council pressed for better drugs education in schools. A few Council members wanted to relax the rules about cannabis but it didn't get through.

I had a cannabis scare once. I had let out a flat to some students. In the long vacation it looked as if one of them was trying to squat. I went in and to my horror found that they were growing cannabis under lights in the coal cellar... At least I supposed it was cannabis, since I had never seen any my whole life. I took it into the local police station. The Officer said: 'Ah, you think that's cannabis don't you... OH, it is!' We went back to the house and found that the squatter had fled. That was the end of that problem.

I knew that in law, the person owning the property, where cannabis was grown or found, was legally to blame. It would have been very unfortunate for a Member of the Council to be not only in possession of drugs, but also propagating them. We hastily dug up the ones they had planted in the garden and re-carpeted the flat to get rid of the smell!

Home Office: Policy Advisory Committee on Sexual Offences 1981-84

I must have been invited to be on this one because of my counselling skills and guidance to teenagers about sex and drugs. It was very interesting. We interviewed a leader of the Prostitutes Union, who was very sensible. We recommended that men who tried to pick up women by stopping their car should have their name and addresses published in the newspaper. We viewed some very disturbing pornographic films, and realised how difficult it was to censor such films and prevent them being distributed. It appears that many of them had rather misleading titles such as *Snow White and the Seven Dwarfs*: the mind boggles!

Our report was purely advisory so we had no say in what finally became law, but we felt confident that our advice had been considered.

Department of Education and Science:
West Indian Study Group: Assessment of Performance unit 1978-80

This was important, as it revealed that West Indian boys performed worse in school than West Indian girls. My experience at Vauxhall Manor was useful here: we had shown that WI girls could do very well and go to university with encouragement and support. It was thought that the WI boys problem was in part because they often lacked a male role model, and gangs they joined were sometimes far more important to them than school. Most West Indian women remained single, as was customary in those days. That will have changed by now. But even today there is some evidence that the WI males still under-achieve a little.

An example of disturbing behaviour comes from my own experience. I was working late one evening. My room overlooked Vauxhall Park. I looked out and saw a gang of boys pestering some of my girls. I stomped out without a thought for safety. Suddenly, I found myself in the midst of the crowd. A boy was standing in front of me, about to hit me on the head with a broken bottle. I remembered (where did I get this from?) that with tigers you look them right in the eye and do NOT look afraid. This I did. He put his arm down. The crowd dispersed. I talked to the girls about it and the staff told me off for taking such a risk.

At home with the flu, I once found two young West Indian boys prising open my french windows with a spade. I strode rapidly towards them and told them fiercely to F*** Off. They immediately ran away. On another occasion I found a young West Indian in my sitting room looking as if he was about to steal my TV set. 'OH no' he said, 'my friend stole it and I'm bringing it back!' 'Thank you', I said and he calmly left.

Department of Education and Science: Educational and vocational experiences of young people from ethnic minority groups 1982-1985
Of course, this working group covered the whole spectrum of nationalities. In all the schools where I was Head, there were over 100 nationalities and it is hard to generalise. In general the Asian children were very well supported in their studies by their parents who are also ambitious for them in terms of their careers. But even as I write, I know that this is not necessarily true, but depends on the background of the parents and indeed very many other factors. In the West Indian community, boys tended to be less successful than the girls. Some thought this was because of the lack of a good male role model. This is less true nowadays. It was however very good to know that the DES was being very sensitive and thoughtful about this issue. Good educational and vocational advice is very important for people who don't know or understand the English system very well.

The single-parent child in the inner-city school concern no 2: Focus on one parent families, summer 1976
This article was written by me at the request of **The National Children's Bureau**. *It describes Vauxhall Manor School, Lambeth, just south of the Thames at Vauxhall Bridge, where I was Head from 1974-1981. It was*

one of the most deprived schools in a very deprived area, with 80%
pupils of Caribbean or African origin. Most of them came from large
single-parent families, and were brought up by their mother. The West
Indian tradition then was not to marry. The children were named after
their actual father. If we can break through, then we shall really be
doing something significant towards meeting the real needs of the
adolescent in transition to adulthood.

How can a school compensate for an unstable home background, and
provide the essential support to a child from a one-parent family,
without at the same time 'labelling' and stigmatising them? Vauxhall
Manor, a girl's comprehensive school in south London in the Vauxhall
and Brixton area, has organised its structure to meet this challenge. But
it was a real challenge and took time to achieve.

Imagine a typical inner-city school: nineteenth century buildings,
holding out bastion like in a visibly crumbling area, gradually losing its
indigenous population to the outer-city ring or beyond, taking under its
wing a more immigrant population, a complex mix of nationalities,
customs and creeds, serving a populace which scores above average on
any statistician's index of social deprivation. This is a pattern we see in
any large inner-city conurbation. The problem for those of us who
work in schools in such areas, is to recognise and cater for the nature of
our intake without pandering to its problems, without labelling and
without lowering our expectations: blessed is he who expecteth nothing
for he shall not be disappointed.

At Vauxhall Manor we do not single out one-parent pupils for
special attention. We accept the one-parent family as a feature of
society which is normal in some cultures (eg West Indian) and
increasingly normal in Britain as a whole, with one in five marriages
ending in divorce and a growing acceptance of unmarried motherhood
by society. We also recognise that two-parent pupils can be deprived
and stressed, as indeed can pupils from affluent homes. We notice that
many pupils cope admirably with seemingly 'difficult' home circumstances, developing tremendous qualities of character and practical
skills. So we do not label, either by background or by ability. We teach
our pupils in mixed ability classes and we expect them to do their best.

All our pupils need to feel loved, valued and respected; they also need to work within a secure framework, a structure rather than a stricture, which gives them sufficient freedom to be able to develop their own particular strengths and talents. In seeking to provide this, we clearly supplement and complement their home lives. We make special efforts to help new pupils settle into the school and to identify with it to help them get maximum benefit from the education provided. We try to do this in a number of ways.

1. Easing the transition from primary to secondary school

We recognise that the transition from primary to secondary school can come as a rude shock to any pupil, insecure or otherwise, a crisis point which merits extra attention. So we have appointed a teacher in charge of 'primary links'. She works closely with neighbouring primary schools, arranging for both pupils and teachers two-way visits, shared projects and even joint lessons. As a result, communication, interaction and understanding between us and our neighbours have greatly improved. More importantly, many of our new 11-year-old pupils already know the school and some of its teachers before they come. Furthermore, their primary teachers are able to be more reassuring and confident about the transfer because they, too, have a clearer idea of what we are about.

2. Continuity and stability in teacher/pupil relationships

Most junior schools work on a system in which the pupils spend the greater part of their day in their own classroom, taught a variety of subjects by their own teacher. A strong feeling of 'home' can develop in the classroom. On transfer to secondary school, the pupil may have suddenly to adjust to a number of different teachers and changes of subject/classroom and teacher at regular intervals: a kind of musical chairs dictated by the tyranny of the bell. We have tried to cut down this movement. As far as possible 'first years' (i.e. eleven-year-olds,) are taught in their own form room for several subjects, if possible by their own form teacher. It is also easier for them to take a pride in their form rooms – where they may be for up to half the week – and to put their work and pictures on display.

We also offer double lessons (1 hour 10 minutes) or even 'half days' with the same teacher when the subject allows. All this has done a great deal to help the pupils feel more secure and able to develop their work in greater depth. We give the 'first years' special priority in this, but throughout the lower school the basic teaching unit is the form. Thus girls do not constantly having to readjust to a new peer group. Continuity of subject teacher is given priority where possible, so that at the beginning of the academic year, the class does not waste time and energy readjusting to a new teacher. The heads of years who are responsible for the 240 pupils in each school year move up with their pupils for several years so they can build up their knowledge of the girls and their families. All this is designed not only to increase learning opportunities, but to give pupils consistency in their relationships with adults and continuity of care. This is always important, but particularly so if pupils lack this at home.

3. Curriculum and teaching methods

Our teaching methods, based on mixed ability classes, use the small group within the classroom situation, as a further way of integrating academic and pastoral objectives, and developing the total resources of the pupil. The groups provide opportunities for learning how to cooperate, how to share, how to help others, how to solve a group task, how to take and share leadership and responsibility, how to discuss and reach a group decision. We aim to give the pupils as much responsibility as possible for the management of their own learning, either in groups or as individuals. We teach them where to find information, how to study, evaluate, assess, organise, and make decisions or judgements. We do not always succeed, but our methods do help to increase their self-confidence and resourcefulness.

4. Preventative work

We recognise that though teachers can do a great deal to help pupils 'at risk' by the way they teach, by providing a 'model' of adult behaviour, by listening to and supporting the pupil, there is a need for specialist help to be brought in at the earliest opportunity if an effective *preventative* (rather than remedial) service is to be provided. Attached to the first year (age 11-12) we have a school-based social worker seconded full time from social services, working closely with the Head of Year, form tutor and education welfare officer. For the upper school, we have appointed our own part-time counsellor and social worker. Not only are the pupils helped directly through these services, but the teachers too can get 'instant' advice and support. Teachers are less tempted to get out of role, yet their skills are not lost, but rather, enhanced. The boundaries between the professions are not blurred, yet the amount of direct help to the pupil is increased, and referrals to specialists can be made early enough to be effective.

We also have two 'compensatory' units, one in lower school to help pupils with learning difficulties, particularly immigrants needing extra help with English; the other in upper school to provide a secure base for truants returning, who need a 'halfway house' between home/school, or for pupils going through a particularly unsettled phase. Both these are organised on a sessional basis with the aim of getting the pupil back into normal lessons as soon as possible. Our provision here is minimal, and on-site because we believe that to proliferate Off-site centres eventually undermines the mainstream work of the school. All this extra provision of support in school has required back up from extra secretarial staff and extra interviewing rooms, made from converting under-used cloakrooms. The counselling and social work services are already working to full capacity. The benefit to the pupils is obvious.

5. Enriched facilities

Luckily the school has recently been redecorated and refurnished; we have more wall displays, and a garden; the girls have also started to paint the walls with murals. But what about that arid time of day between school and when parents come in from work? We have set up an 'end-on club' which meets three evenings a week from 3.30-5.30pm in lower school. This provides a wide range of educational and recreational activities from drama to gymnastics; attendance is voluntary and the club is well supported.

Many of our pupils have never been away from their parents for a holiday some have never travelled much, not even in London. We build into our normal lessons a full program of visits, excursions and school journeys: the half-day session is particularly useful for this. Visiting a museum or gallery not only expands intellectual horizons, it also gives the girls the confidence to go again, or to try others. We now as a matter of policy offer all first years a full week's residential course, for which they obtain a grant if necessary. Half this year's first year accepted the invitation; the other half were given a special week's program of outings and excursions based on London.

6. Increasing contacts with parents

We make a great deal of effort to get to know whoever is responsible for our pupils at home, because we know how important it is to get maximum cooperation, understanding and support between home/ school. In junior schools, parents have easy access to the class teacher. In secondary schools it can be more difficult for parents to gain informal access. We try to get round this by offering an interview before the pupils come, by making it clear that parents are welcome at any time and particularly by our system of giving out reports. We do not send out reports, but instead invite parents up to read and discuss what the teachers have said.

In lower school some 80% of parents come up. The benefits of this are enormous. It is too easy for parents to be sent for only when their children are in trouble. This method provides an opportunity for a positive interchange. When parents come, particularly parents on their own, they often confide in us their own personal difficulties. We listen and then put them in touch with the agency that can most help them. Our social work staff follow-up this liaison work. When a girl seems to be unsettled and disturbed, we ask the parents to come up as early as possible. We find our parents relieved to know that we care, and that we will not tolerate antisocial behaviour. Together we discuss what best might be done to help the pupil benefit more from her education.

A small minority of our girls are absent from school, sometimes permanently. We do what we can, through the education welfare and social services, to get these girls into school. Sometimes they are away because they are needed to look after a sick parent or child. Sometimes they are chronically ill. Sometimes they are over-dependent on their parent(s) and cannot leave home and sometimes they are just bored or antisocial and do not like school. The attendance in our lower school, particularly in the first year, has improved greatly since we set in motion the measures I have outlined. This gives great hope for what schools can do, though some pupils will never come whatever the school is like.

In the last few years many schools have felt overwhelmed by the social problems surrounding them. It is easy in these circumstances either to give up teaching and concentrate on trying to solve social problems – in fact, to become a kind of social work agency – or alternatively to cling Canute-like to teaching methods and standards which worked in the past but do not work now. It is clear to us at Vauxhall Manor that we have to be sensitive and adapt to the changing needs of our pupils, but that the best way of helping them is to do the very best job we can as a school.

Postscript

This took a long time to achieve. The staff were marvellous. You had to be dedicated to work in a school like ours. They were very suspicious of me at first and challenged me hard. I eventually challenged them back and once we really understood our roles and how we could all contribute to the girls futures, we really made progress. The biggest fight I ever had with them was to try to get them to accept that we should be offering more O-levels. Most pupils only did CSEs. This handicapped their chances of going to university. On the day of the staff meeting to decide this, I stomped round the school picking up crisp bags. Coming up from under a fire extinguisher, I severely banged the back of my head on it. Despite feeling strange, I took the staff meeting and the vote for O-levels was carried and then implemented. When I got home my children sent me to A&E to check whether I had fractured my skull. I hadn't, but my brain was really shaken up. In the end I had to take six weeks off, while it settled down again.

The number of university entrants per year began to go up dramatically after this point, to six, including Marcia Smith, who went to Cambridge.

EITB: The Girl Technician Scholarship Scheme. 1976-1981

I was very keen to support equal opportunities actively. The

Engineering Industry Training Board invited me to join the Board that set up the Girl Technician Scholarship Scheme and monitored the progress of the girls. The aim of the project was to encourage young women to enter the engineering industry as technicians. Very few girls train to be engineering technicians. For equal opportunities, something needed to be done to change the situation. I was very keen to support such a good cause.

Fifty scholarships were offered each year. Part of the training was done in an Engineering Training Centre and part in a local college of FE. In their second year, the girls undertook three placements with three different companies, each of which provided specific training in different technician work. The girls were placed in groups of two or three. This was helpful. It meant that they were not the only women in training: technician training was mostly taken up by men. The other problem, which the girls confided in me, was to do with the toilets. Often there was only one female toilet in the engineering company (presumably for the secretary). It was less embarrassing if you were not the only woman!

At the end of the second year, the EITB helped them to get a job in a reputable engineering company. That was very encouraging. However, there were difficulties initially in recruiting the girls via schools. So they approached the parents and girls directly. The problem then evaporated. The calibre of the girls turned out to be remarkably high. Entry requirements were O-level English, maths and a science preferably physics, a higher level than demanded for the NTI (new training initiative). I was thrilled to be involved in this successful and important project.

Vauxhall Manor School: Staff meeting September 3rd 1979

This was a meeting in which I distributed this list about 'the climate' of an organisation and its importance getting it right if an organisation is to thrive. The ideas come from a Volvo publication. The ideas/concepts were discussed in small groups and generally applauded. The ideas apply both to the classroom and also the school as a whole.

The Importance of the Climate of an organisation

Field studies have shown that specific features of an organisational climate can block or enable organisational learning and the utilisation of human potential. The following characteristics of climate are prerequisites for the release of motivation, energy and competences in an organisation. The staff were asked to think about these statements and discuss.

Anne Jones Headmistress of Vauxhall Manor School

Organisational values and attitudes needed for growth

1. Organic view of the interdependent and interactive nature of its policies, value systems, functions, processes, systems procedures, and behaviours/attitudes of employees at all levels

2. Optimistic assumptions about the needs and capabilities of staff at all levels

3. Relationships of trust between individuals, groups, grades and functions

4. Awareness and respect for individual differences between people

5. Readiness to take risks, to experiment, to turn mistakes into learning opportunities

6. Acceptance that people need for intrinsic satisfactions are as

important as extrinsic rewards

7. Perceiving technical, social and person problems as opportunities
8. Having confidence in the successful outcome of change and the determination to achieve it

Postscript

We had already worked our way through some difficult times when we hadn't always all agreed, as I have already explained. We were all working together very well at this stage! So well, that I took a terms sabbatical in the autumn of 1980. That meant that I trusted them.

My term at St Peter's College, Oxford, autumn 1980

I had applied and won a term as a school mistress scholar at St Peter's College, Oxford. I was treated as a member of the Senior Common Room. It was there that I began working on my next book, *Leadership for Tomorrow's Schools*, which actually didn't come out until 1986. My colleagues there were very helpful. When I left they made me an honorary member of the Senior Common Room. This meant that I could continue to dine there, a privilege I greatly enjoyed for several years. I went back to my school refreshed and invigorated. The school, staff and pupils had coped well.

All in the mind:

This article first appeared in *The Guardian* Jan 6th 1981

Anne Jones is Headmistress of Vauxhall Manor School. She is currently Schoolmistress Scholar at St Peter's College, Oxford. The views expressed in this article are her own and not necessarily those of her school or Authority. This article is adapted from a chapter by the author (Anne Jones) in Out of School *by L Hersov and I Berg published by John Wiley and Sons in 1980.*

Since the *Plowden Report*, there has been an implicit assumption that if you give schools more resources, their pupils learn more. Now, there is considerable doubt as to whether the net results justify the gross expenditure. In the present economic gloom, we could perhaps take some cold comfort in realising the possible relevance of Herzberg's theory of motivation to the present dissatisfaction with pupil outcomes: improving hygienic conditions only brings temporary relief, the important factors being those which motivate.

So although, of course, we need adequate resources, to some extent the fault, dear masters, lies in ourselves that we have under-achievers. Fault perhaps is too negative a word, for our problem has not been in our unwillingness to school, so much as our over-enthusiasm, our over-conscientiousness, and our over-work.

We in schools have not known where to draw the line: we have been snappers-up of unconsidered trifles, trying to be all things to all pupils: an uncomfortable amalgam of amusement arcade, prison-house, soup-kitchen and sanctuary. As a result we have suffered from role confusion, role diffusion, nervous exhaustion and self-doubt. Much has been written about teacher attitude to pupils: but what about pupil attitude to teachers? Pupils respond extremely sensitively to teachers' self-rating and to the overall ethos and sense of identity of their school. What we think we are, we are.

If I am right, and some of our problems are 'in our own minds', then ironically, some of the answers to them are also in our own hands. They are closely connected with our attitudes, our self-esteem and our job satisfaction. You can't really have higher teacher expectation until you have higher teacher morale.

Yet teachers constantly underestimate the value of what they do. So the first essential for higher pupil standards is greater recognition by teachers and by society of the value of their work.

The second is to have a clearer shared understanding of what their task is and what it is not. And the third is to get the pupils themselves to do more of the work.

In the last ten years, society has been particularly ambivalent about schools, on the one hand querying whether teachers serve any useful purpose, except ineffectual childminding. On the other hand expecting too much in terms of learning and in instilling standards of behaviour. It is time for schools to reaffirm their belief in their value and purpose. Schools need to be clear about their main task, to concentrate on doing that well, to say 'no' when asked to do something for which they have neither the training nor the time. Many pupils will be helped to overcome their socio-economic or personal problems if they are really well taught.

When schools feel a sense of purpose, of identity, of value, then they are not afraid to make demands on pupils. These demands actually increase the pupil's esteem for the school and their desire to be associated with it. They also help the pupils to engage actively in the learning process, to use their energy in a constructive way and to grow in confidence. The compulsory nature of schooling to sixteen has put schools in a supplicant role: the more we plead with our pupils to come, the less they want to. When the school is recognized as a valuable experience, few pupils stay away.

The real point is that too often current teaching methods do not sufficiently engage the pupils in the challenge of learning. The prevailing culture is too often 'do-it-for-you' instead of do-it-yourself. Schools may have developed into more of a passive dependent culture than they did in the 'bad old days'.

I suspect that in too many schools, we do not demand enough of our pupils; we do not allow them to make mistakes and learn from them. We over–organise and over-rule them and we discourage them by not sufficiently recognizing their differences, their maturity, their ability to take responsibility.

Let the pupils take the strain! When teachers believe in themselves, when schools have am overall ethos which is positive, challenging and geared towards learning, the pupils are only too willing and ready to learn.

The Regeneration Game: Education for greater leisure:

An after dinner speech delivered by me to Division 10 of the Secondary Heads Association at 8pm on Saturday 22nd September, 1979 at St Hilda's College, Oxford.

An example of what Heads get up to when they are off duty!

It gives me great pleasure to be here in Oxford, where the grass really is greener. I am delighted that you have decided to give the after-dinner slot to a woman. I had to ask myself, before accepting, whether this was the best way of spending my Saturday night and Sunday morning leisure. I found myself saying 'yes', not absolutely convinced that I was right, but nevertheless challenged and tempted – and like Oscar Wilde,

I can resist anything but temptation.

So here I am.

However the very fact that we are all here gathered together does raise for me at any rate, my first fundamental question: what are we all doing, giving up our leisure to be here? It reminds me of the famous remark made by Mrs Kinsey when her husband produced his notorious report on the sexual behaviour of young people: 'It really is quite a problem. I haven't seen much of my husband since he became so interested in sex'. So, *quis custodiet?*

If we are to become the great exponents of leisure, we must also look to put our own house in order. Teachers serve as models and Heads as supermodels. If we want to be serious about relaxing, we have to be seen to be what we say. We need action, not words otherwise we are simply 'talking Heads.'

I always feel nervous when I address a group of colleagues. When I was young and new to Headship such presumptions used to cause me to question my right to 'try to teach my grandma to suck eggs'.

Now, with the experience that comes with age and the age that comes with experience, I find myself still nevertheless, bloody, bold and resolute, but in addition, more philosophical and even sometimes cynical. In the twenty-six years since I first became a teacher, I have seen the merry-go-round of educational fashion swing the full circle at least once, if not twice.

As a cynic once said:

If you stay put in education and refuse to change your ideas, you eventually become avant-garde.

I think that may well be true of the last twenty-five years: *Plus ça change, plus c'est la même chose.* The role of the Head over this period as a change agent or agent of change was mainly confined to reorganisation and endless curriculum development. Whilst I would not wish to imply that these were easy tasks, they were at least working on the same set of basic premises, largely inspired by the 1944 Education Act, the welfare state by the population bulge and increased affluence in the classroom.

At this point, many of the teaching profession began to protest against 'curriculum development' which produced such a state of perpetual flux that no scheme of work ever lasted. The fact is that the burden of lesson preparation became intolerable. People within and without the profession began seriously to doubt whether pouring money into projects and classrooms had any effect and whether the gross effort justified the net results. These are not the points we have to face now.

The changes and development most of us have faced were in a certain set of circumstances, particularly economic circumstances, a boom. Now the cliché that that most of us have been coming out with for years, about preparing for a life of change, about learning to cope with a future which is uncertain and unpredictable, becomes unnervingly true. We move from prediction of a life of change to reality about a change of life, and as we all know, this menopausal state in both men and women can be uncomfortable and requires a lot of adjustments.

The baby boom is over, despite a significant rise in the birth rate in Jubilee Year. The economic boom is over. The electronics revolution is with us and henceforth there will certainly be chips with everything. I find it significant that top of the pops for months was The Boomtown Rats song, *I Don't Like Mondays*, which began 'the silicon chip inside her head' and explored very bluntly the depressing effects on the young person in transition from school to work, of economic depression and uncertainty. Many of them, as in the song, prefer to stay in bed.

So back to the future. As you know, in our lifetime, in the next few years, we face total transformation of the pattern of work and leisure. My very serious hope is that we will use this transformation scene like the good fairy in the pantomime, to create something better and more beautiful. For example the ghost of unemployment is one I would vanquish. To do this would probably mean job-sharing, accepting three day working weeks, with a probable cut in income and a gain in leisure. Any takers?

I personally can think of nothing more delightful. There most definitely comes a moment when money is worth nothing and time everything. To quote Oscar Wilde again:

In a choice between the price of everything and the value of nothing, or vice-versa, I know where I stand.

I suspect however that not everyone would feel like this! I can hear even now the revolutionary cry 'Workaholics of the world unite'. One of the problems is that, without meaning to, our profession, particularly Heads, is one of the most workaholic I have ever met. We need to give up our drug dependency and remember the old Chinese proverb:

Abstenth makes the heart grow fonder.

I will come back to this in a moment. First, I want to concentrate on the positive benefits of far greater leisure, increased unemployment and the silicon chip revolution for the teaching profession. Far from being done out of a job in all this, it seems to me that we are going to be in greater demand than ever, provided we can change **our** ways to adapt to this new scenario. The boom is going to come in particular in the adult and further education sector, and most obviously in recreational activities. All these things are already expanding, but when the community at large has more time, then eventually they are going to want to do something with that time outside the home, even if only to escape from the wife or husband. There should be a greater demand for family activities. There should be a greater demand for retraining for new skills and many of those will be to do with technical/electronic skills, some to do with interpersonal skills, personal growth and development. There will be an increased demand for guidance and counselling of all kinds.

In all this, schools could be left out, left behind, if they keep narrowly to an 11-18 or 11-16 role. So in my mind, the concept of the community school becomes not just a pleasant idea, but a necessity. Part of the reason for this is selfish: professional survival, partly positive and developmental. I have never supported the idea of a teenage ghetto:

one of the greatest losses to society and cause of problems is the creation of this awful teenage impotence. For many complex reasons related to threat, jealousy and economics, we sometimes castrate our teenagers at their most potent/creative/idealistic stage. Schools still have a kind of custodial role on behalf of society and as we all know, the pupils who don't like it, opt out and stay in bed or on the streets. It's an old problem. Autolycus (in *The Winter's Tale*) cried:

I would there were no age between sixteen and three-and-twenty, or that youth would sleep out the rest.

I don't think we can do away with it, but I think we could recognise it and use that teenage frustration and energy more constructively. Adults and young people can learn from each other, what is important is the mix and the method, as in cement or cakemaking, and the timing as in making love.

So we have to beware of being defensive about these developments. Schools have a tendency to put up invisible if not actual walls and we have for too long had to take a last bastion role, with the 3Rs being replaced by the 3Vs: Violence, Vandalism and inVasion by intruders. Heads have been tempted even goaded to pull up the drawbridge and defend their fortresses, but rather like the eminent philosopher, who said that his greatest kick in life was lying in the bath, pulling out the plug and battling against the tide. This is a silly and unreal game. The regeneration game is a development to be taken seriously and includes learning to laugh at ourselves.

I think we can take up these points further in discussion. In the last part of this talk I would like to address my remarks to the work-alcoholics of the teaching profession. Because this is a Head's Conference, I am going to concentrate on Heads rather than teaching staff, though much of what I have to say will apply to both. Most of the discussion one hears is about teacher stress and teacher comfort. Head stress is rarely considered. Yet in various subtle ways, many Heads, far from being autocratic and privileged have become the servant of their staff and not the master. It is part of the self-centred to soft-centred swing which followed from the child-centred phase in education… You do everything you can to make the pupils and staff comfortable and free of problems and then they will work better, do their jobs properly. Would that it were as simple as that!

Postscript

Alas the last page of this handwritten speech has disappeared and I can't remember what I said! Please note that the baby boom had just ended so Heads then were very worried about falling rolls. Quite the opposite of now! I wonder what I said next?

Improving job prospects for Vauxhall Manor School leavers

A pioneer scheme for preparing pupils for the world of work and helping them to get a job or a place at college or university

Attendance was about 70% when I arrived at Vauxhall Manor, but we gradually improved it. Our ultimate goal was to help every girl to get a job or a place at college or university when they left. It took seven years to achieve this. We had an excellent careers teacher and we developed an extensive program of support for getting a job. The local careers service worked very closely with us. We arranged for mock interviews with real employers and also at Ovalhouse, both with feedback to the girls. In 1977, we followed up the girls who had left school and then we helped further the ones who still hadn't found a job. We continued this every year. This was the key to our success in getting all the girls into jobs, training or further education. Our 'output' figures improved every year.

With the help of the Training Services Division of the MSC (Manpower Services Commission), we also arranged for the sixth form some real work placements. In our pilot, a link was set up between the school and a group of employers: Londex, GEC-Marconi, Westminster Hospital Catering Division, and a branch of Marks & Spencer. Of the fourteen girls, each spent a week with each firm, beginning with a simulated job interview and going on to the week's work experience at various aspects of the job in question and ending with an evaluation from the employer.

The girls received help from the school both at the start and the finish of their weeks of work experience. Before starting, they were briefed on what to look out for when preparing for and taking the interview and the various ways their routine differs from that of the school routine. At the end they returned to school, discussed their experience and worked on all the things they have learned from them.

This experience also provided them with something else of immediate value. Their tutor noted that the whole experience had expanded their horizons in different ways. Firstly, it widened their views on jobs they could take other than the traditional retail/clerical rut. It also provided something of much more direct value. Throughout their school career, these girls had moved in a very limited orbit: home/school/home again. Some of them had never even crossed the River Thames, even though it was only a short walk away from our school. The firms participating in the scheme were some distance from the girl's home neighbourhood. The girls had to make their own way every morning to their job for the week. This helped them to attain a sense of self-sufficiency and independence. We found that employers do realise that, for some jobs, not many qualifications are needed, but personal qualities are. O-levels don't necessarily prove that you are reliable, capable, have the right personality and have potential for growth.

By 1979, only five girls out of our 184 school leavers were still unemployed in September at a time when there were 918 other young people on the local unemployment register. 40% decided to stay on at school for the sixth form for more school education. 7% of the sixth form leavers went on to further education for more vocational education and training or a degree. This figure includes six girls with admission to university, including Cambridge. And one became an Engineer. What an achievement for them all!

For the last few years, I had taken a group of girls, nearly all West Indian to Oxford one year and Cambridge the next, just to widen their horizons. In the end it paid off, though it was hard to find a girl who had the confidence to accept an offer. I have finally tracked down the details of the first of our pupils to do this: Marcia Smith.

New Hall, Cambridge (*now* Murray Edwards College) had a scheme to encourage applicants from inner-city comprehensives. Marcia really liked it. I followed this up. New Hall were so impressed by Marcia that they, quite rightly, offered her a place, provided she got two A-levels, which she did. Marcia was a very intelligent pupil who was very concerned to help other pupils do their best. She wanted to go to New Hall because, she said, it had a completely different atmosphere from the other Cambridge colleges: it was prepared to believe in your potential.

Vauxhall Manor girls in a production of The Match Girls

Marcia was also an outstanding drama student who took a large part in the play called *Wicked Women*, about the persecution of witches in the fifteenth century. The girls had written the play themselves through a series of drama workshops run by their brilliant teacher, Elyse Dodgson. The play was so good that it was performed not only at the Ovalhouse in Kennington but also for one night at The Cottesloe Theatre at the National Theatre! Our girls were very talented, given a chance and some encouragement. Elyse and Marcia later worked together on a second script called *Motherland*. This was also performed at the Ovalhouse and was a great success, so when Marcia went up to Cambridge, she was already a writer!

Postscript

I hadn't realised how pioneering we were in our idea of following up whether the girls had employment or a place at college or university after they left school. That is how we got such a high employment or continuing education record for our pupils. The pupils did it, but they needed our help and support in following what became of them after they left school. A few years s later in 1983, TVEI took up the same idea and then I took over TVEI in 1987. Not all schools follow-up their former students in the way we did. It really did help them.

My broadcasting 'career': like Topsy, 'it just happened.'

I had done quite a lot of broadcasting when I was working as a school counsellor: Radio London and BBC 4 occasionally involved me for programs like *You and Yours*. I also wrote some scripts for a schools TV drama about teenagers. From 1978-1984 I was a member of the Schools Broadcasting Council first with Harry Judge as Chairman then Ted Wragg. While I was still at Vauxhall Manor, I was asked by BBC Radio 3, to write a series of about twelve programs for the radio about *Child Development from Birth to Adulthood*. Various famous child development experts were interviewed by someone else, then cut and linked into coherent discussion by me. I also had to present the series myself. Apparently the series was repeated the next year and one or two of the staff had come across them, and even congratulated me, which for me was praise indeed.

During my time at Vauxhall Manor I was involved in a number of BBC productions. *The Education Debate* was a series of four programmes, which were filmed at Vauxhall Manor and included interviews with some pupils and staff. They took up some of my major themes at the time, namely that pastoral care had gone soft and not enough demands were made on the pupils. Whilst schools had needed to soften the rather over-strict school regimes of earlier times, we had now swung back to the other extreme. This was not helping the pupils.

Yorkshire TV did a long interview with me in a program called *Heart to Heart*. I think I would now find it rather cringe-making! My first appearance on the panel of *Question Time* was in 1981 and included Viscount Whitelaw. Believe it or not, I had never watched that program before, mainly because I didn't have time in the evening, when I normally kept up with my work after the children had gone to bed! It went well and I was asked again several times.

In *The Guardian* newspaper, I had a weekly column for a while in which I answered parents questions. One reader decided to explore enrolling her daughter with us. She took one look at the West Indian and African faces and backed off. We did have very few white pupils, less than 10%. It was a pity from all points of view.

Vauxhall Manor to become a community school

In 1980, it was decided by ILEA/County Hall, that Vauxhall Manor was to be rebuilt as a genuine integrated community school. Not just a new building to replace our two nineteenth century school board buildings but a school for the community as well! We were all delighted and took this as a vote of confidence in our school as well as a much-needed benefit to the whole community we served.

We set about preparing ourselves. I had already visited and reviewed half a dozen community schools elsewhere in the country and reported back to ILEA and the staff. We then trained the staff to understand the benefits of community schools, helped greatly by Geoff Cooksey, Head of a highly successful, newly built community school called Stantonbury Campus in Milton Keynes. He invited the whole of my staff to join his staff for a day in his school, followed by a weekend conference. It was a great success. On the Saturday evening, he put on a dance for us and he even played the piano in the eight-piece staff jazz band. We began the planning of the actual building. Hours were spent consulting architects and staff, looking at possible layouts and deciding where the various departments should be placed.

Then suddenly there came another period of financial cuts and the whole project was stopped. It was at this point that I applied, in 1981, to be the Head of Cranford Community School in Hounslow, a community school which already existed and was as near to my vision as possible. I had done seven years at Vauxhall Manor and between us, we had transformed the school. By then, when our pupils left school, they very nearly all got a job, or place at college or at university. I felt able to move on. Remember, I had already had one disappointment like this. I had applied to be Deputy Head of the Thomas Calton School Peckham because it was also going to be rebuilt by ILEA as a community school. This was also cancelled. So I decided that I had better go for a community school that actually existed.

So, after seven years as Head, I moved on in 1981 to become Head of Cranford Community School, in Hounslow, a school which had everything I was looking for. I persuaded myself also that, in any case, a change of school was good for the school and for me so that I did not become stale or complacent. I was sad to leave the staff and the pupils, but thrilled with the progress we had made together during my time there. It showed that it is possible to turn a school round if you all work together with shared goals and mutual help and understanding. It is impossible to mention any names without offending some people, but my gratitude for and pride in what the staff and pupils achieved together is with me still.

The evening of my leaving party turned out to be the evening of the Brixton Riots. The girls were not allowed out to sing and dance for me that memorable evening, the area was in flames and people fighting.

Since then, Vauxhall Manor Upper School building, a fine example of mid-Victorian architecture, has been turned into a block of expensive flats. With the lovely wooden floors, high ceilings and tall windows, they must be delightful. And so near to the South Bank with all its amenities: Royal Festival Hall, the National Theatre and much more. And near The Oval cricket ground too. Once upon a time I had persuaded The Oval to let our girls use the outfield for hockey practice! Can you visualise that?

A few years after I left, Vauxhall Manor was combined with a boys school, Beaufoy, to become the Lilian Baylis School, I gather that it had a completely different culture from us and there were some transitional difficulties. In October 2013, I read that Lilian Baylis was still a school in an area of great social deprivation and was receiving extra funding from government to help with the problems. Today in 2015 it is now the Lillian Baylis Technology School and in 2013 was graded outstanding in an HMI inspection.

Plus ça change plus c'est la même chose

A VOICE FOR ANNE by James Berry

We were very lucky at Vauxhall Manor to have for year a poet in residence, James Berry, who was from Jamaica, in fact an early immigrant. He was already a famous and well-established poet and story-teller. The girls adored him. Here was a West Indian man whom they could respect and obey. He was able to demonstrate to them that he had a great sense of humour, but also could be very strict. He told us that we were too soft with the girls. When we tightened up a little, the girls responded well and told us they preferred it. A lesson there for all of us.

Being too kind does not really help.

Wha man dohn know is good to know: **A Caribbean proverb**

James Berry our poet in residence with a poem for Anne

James Berry was born and brought up in Jamaica, and now divides his time between Jamaica and the UK. He is a distinguished writer and has published poems and short stories in the USA, UK and the Caribbean. In 1987 he was the Grand Prix Winner of the Smarties Prize for his collection of short stories, *A Thief in the Village*, and in 1989 he received the Signal Poetry Award for his collection of poems, *When I Dance*. In 1991 he won the Cholmondeley Award for Poetry given by The Society of Authors. James Berry has a special interest in education as a means to cross different cultures and backgrounds, and is very active in encouraging children to express themselves in writing.

In 1990 he was awarded the OBE for his services to poetry.

At my leaving party, Brixton was in flames: it was the night of the Brixton riots. The girls were going to sing and dance for me. Quite rightly, the girls were not allowed out, so we had a more modest event James Berry gave me a poem which he had written especially for me. All too true!

A VOICE FOR ANNE

Like a seed the wind planted
She found
No-one at home pushed her
To want to touch the sun
It was the inner echo
of intellect and instinct
That interchanged in her
A warrior
And a male and female god
Looking like a female
So when the world did not see her
Either as Venus or Zeus
They saw
An ordinary human
Never resting on what has been done
And being restless
Once the drive of the travel is over
She moves
To arrive again
Peace and love. James Berry, 13 April 1981

CHAPTER 4: CRANFORD COMMUNITY SCHOOL 1981-1987

I WAS OVERJOYED TO BE HEAD of a real community school at last. It was purpose built, located in Hounslow, very close to London Airport with air conditioning and double-glazing to keep out the noise of the aeroplanes passing overhead. There were eleven acres of playing fields, all well used by us and the whole community. The students, boys and girls, were approximately 40% Asian and 60% other. There were over 100 languages spoken by our students, so it is hard to generalise about nationality or race. At last, a chance to build an integrated multiracial community? I soon found it was already one.

The Asian families were very supportive of the school and of their children: they were keen for them to be well-educated and to get professional jobs. There were a large number of Sikhs. The young boys wore their turbans in school colours and the older Sikh boys sometimes grew moustaches. There was already a good atmosphere and an excellent staff.

However, there were some bad moments. Soon after I arrived there, the senior Deputy Head came in to tell me there was a 'spot of trouble' in the playground. I went outside and found a line of rather tough-looking English boys moving forward to meet an approaching line of Asian boys. Without hesitating, I went into the middle, between them and said firmly STOP. They stopped. Then I said to my Deputy; 'Call an immediate assembly for the whole school.'

The assembly was short and to the point. I made it very clear that there was to be no violence and no racism in our school. Anyone so involved would be excluded. The reaction of the students was remarkably positive. I often wandered around the grounds, so that they could talk to me if they wanted to. Lots of them came up and thanked me for taking such immediate and forceful action. 'It was racism Miss wasn't it, they wouldn't call it racism and they said we were naughty, but it wasn't naughty, it was racism Miss, wasn't it?' The moral of that is that students like straight talking and being treated as sensible adults.

It turns out that following on from the riots in Brixton, the young

Asian males in Southall felt that they should also be asserting their rights otherwise they might be regarded as weak. These riots didn't last long. We did sometimes have little feuds between families of the same nationality. Two boys would fall out and an uncle or a big brother was said to be coming to 'sort out' the name-caller and would be waiting in their car at the gate at the end of the school day. If I heard about it, I would go to the gate early, charmingly disarm the conflict makers and send them on their way.

Later on, three girls came and asked me what my religion was. We sat down in my study and had a lovely chat. There we were: a Muslim, a Sikh, a Buddhist and a Christian and all happy together. Once I was established in the school, I invited the leaders of all the local religious leaders to meet me, including Catholics and Jews, to see if we could cooperate in any way with each other. It didn't get much further than this but at least we had made a connection.

The pupils were on the whole very well-behaved. However, shortly after I arrived a Head of Year came to see me to tell me that there were twenty boys in his year who were both disruptive and disobedient. They should go! I thanked him for telling me and asked to see them one by one. They each arrived looking terrified but I said that I just wanted to have a chat with them. In fact it was the reverse: I just asked them to tell me about themselves and how they were getting on. They all told me about their families and what kind of trouble they were getting into in class. We unravelled how these situations developed. 'Sir annoys me so much that I lose my temper and start to swear at him'. Having established that such behaviour was totally unacceptable, we had to think of ways of avoiding it. I asked them to come and see me if trouble was brewing. Thenceforth from time to time, there would be a knock at the door. One or other came in and let off steam. 'I can't stand Mr X. If he says that again I will swear at him etc. etc.' When they had calmed down, I simply said 'Feel better now?' It appears that after that there was no more serious trouble from these boys. I never told the staff about my pact but it seemed to work.

I was pleased a few years later to be visited by a former pupil, a girl, who had committed a lot of minor offences... make up, loitering in the toilets etc. 'Miss, why was you so nice to me when I was here?, I was AWFUL'. 'Well, I rather liked you' I said. In both these situations, I had listened to them but had not condoned their bad behaviour. I think I had got them to take responsibility for dealing with their own problem. This shows something about the way my counselling skills affected my ways of dealing with pupils. 'I hear you, how are **you** going to solve the problem?' I tried to avoid reverting to being a counsellor but that training had given me a lot of insight into people young and old. When I first arrived I also had a one-on-one chat with each member of staff. Again I just listened, but it made such a difference to the staff (and me!). From time to time staff having classroom problems would come and see me and say 'I can't go on teaching.' Sometimes they then decided to move on. I had listened to them and they had made their own decision to change their lives for the better.

Passage to India

This Article was originally printed in *Education* 19-26 December, 1986

Hounslow Schools have a large number of Indian pupils. The Education Authority decided to send a group of its Heads to find out what it was like to live and to be educated there. We were very privileged to do this and it was very helpful to us. A brilliant idea! Later we also visited Denmark. Here is the article about India.

NO! I didnt fall off

110

A party of English Heads, Deputies, Advisers and Education Officers marching in a solemn crocodile line up a narrow bazaar street on our way to visit a Maharaja's Palace somewhere in the middle of India. As usual, we are the only English people in sight and we cause quite a stir: not only are we white, but we are a motley collection of shapes and sizes, M&S and Next, elegant panama hats and squidgy English porkpie hats.

The people point at us and laugh. We stare at them, equally amused and bemused. Cattle wander along the street, mixed up with the open drains, mopeds and motorised scooters. Urchins and shopkeepers try to lure us in to buy their wares: silk paintings, puppets, saris, wooden toys and marble trinkets. The air is suffocatingly hot and dusty. What on earth are we doing? Why should a party of Hounslow teachers take on the role of a minority ethnic group in an overwhelmingly different new culture?

The reasons are simple and obvious. In Hounslow so many of our pupils are Indian in origin that it seemed a good idea for us to stop talking about multi-cultural education in theory, something almost rosy and romantic, and to put our money where our mouths were: namely to visit and to experience at first-hand something of the rich inheritance of our pupils. Others had gone before us, but this time the Borough made a real effort to get school leaders to go, on the grounds that both as policy-makers and as front-line community linkers, we needed to know, understand and do more about the Indian culture at first hand.

Our first 'discovery' was, of course, that there is not an Indian culture, but a series of cultures: sixteen in fact. It had never occurred to me that there would be a problem about multi-cultural education in India! Yet when we visited the National Centre for Cultural Propagation in Delhi, we found that there was a systematic 'Cascade' Program to train the teachers, designed both to ensure that they know the cultural traditions (music, art, drama, dance, costume, stories) of all their regions and that Indian culture is not taught only in the expressive arts subjects, but across the whole curriculum. 'You can teach Indian culture through maths. Well, yes: we've been trying too. But how salutary to find it a problem there as well as here.

The motives of the Indian government in promoting this multi-cultural approach in their own system are several. In part they are obviously an attempt to free up and make more expressive and practical a system which is in caricature rather rigid and formal. But also try to 'build India' without losing the rich diversity of its component parts. On the wall of a girls' High School in Delhi, the words of **Indira Gandhi** strike home:

Let us build India

- Where no caste or tribe experiences injustice or indignity and are equal in reality
- Where women, half the nation, get their full share of power and responsibility
- Where knowledge, courage and self restraint will all grow to find a new balance
- Yet let us build a strong dynamic India in which the individuals think not of religion, language, or promise, but of India

I made friends with this family, we had a little dance together

The girls' school in Delhi where these words were displayed was fascinating. Despite Mrs Gandhi's policy of 'equal opportunities', the curriculum appeared to emphasise 'female' subjects: arts and crafts, cooking, dancing and singing. 'Hard' academic subjects were for a small minority. Facilities (eg for teaching science) were very limited. The pupils were absolutely delightful: well-behaved and motivated, yet not in any sense regimented or subdued. It reminded me of a first class secondary modern school of the sixties.

It was interesting to note that the state system was so stretched that the buildings were used by two completely different schools. In the morning, the turquoise and white 'Shalwar Khameez' pupils with their own teachers and in the afternoon, the pupils in blue and white, with their own teachers. Hutted classroom accommodation was flexible and cheap to erect in a way which would have pleased the Audit Commission: open air tents.

By contrast, the Army school in Delhi was entrepreneurial, elitist and well equipped. Rated as one of the best schools in Delhi, it has 5000 pupils, all boys, all fee paying. No falling rolls here. To extend the buildings and improve the facilities, the school is playing the numbers game as hard as it can, packing sixty rather than forty-five into a class, in order to make more money from fees collected. The next step is to raise academic standards and improve the exam pass rate further. It sounds arid but it is not. Unfortunately, during our visit there were very few pupils around, only those taking practical exams.

Please note, 'negotiators of conditions of service', that in India, when the teachers are marking end of year exams, the pupils stay at home so that the teachers can do their job properly! Those pupils we did meet seemed confident, articulate and poised. There were a lot of out-of-school activities, keenly supported. There was also an excellent track record for students leaving. In this school, science and other technical facilities were good. The curriculum was that of a traditional grammar school, in the best sense of that phrase. Motivation of the pupils was good and there were few discipline problems. In both the state and the independent schools, there is now an activity called 'socially useful productive work', which I would equate with our prevocational work. It includes voluntary work.

The positive attitude to education we found everywhere reflects, of course the fact that in India, education is by no means taken for granted. In the village communities many children hardly go to school and, of those who do, many leave as soon as possible because their parents need their help economically. Parents have to pay a small fee each term even at a state school. This somehow emphasises the fact that education is positively valued, though of course in some cases, parents are put off by this system. In one rural area, a convent school offers free tuition in basic skills and school dinners for pupils who are prepared to work at carpet making in the morning. By contrast, a small prep school, attached to a prestigious hotel, has uniformed five-year-olds writing immaculately and neatly on the English model of the 1940s.

In Bombay, now called Mumbai, I was privileged to visit the JB Petit High School which has a deserved reputation for being progressive as well as having high academic standards. Here I found an admirable Head and staff, dedicated to active learning methods, making students think for themselves and become capable as well as intellectual. It is worth noting that this school, fully subscribed and highly popular with the intelligent middle class parents, had, by comparison with almost any comprehensive school in England, very poor facilities. In the library, lovingly cared for by a volunteer helper, the books were exceedingly well-thumbed. In the classrooms, rows of traditional school desks and strict school uniform give the feel of the fifties. Yet also in the classrooms, there were masses of work displayed and the same kind of creative writing to be seen as in an English junior school: projects, pieces about 'myself', solar systems, hobbies, surveys and imaginative paintings. This school was a joy to visit.

We travelled a great deal and in almost every possible mode: by camel, elephant, horse, bicycle, rickshaw, motorised rickshaw, canoe, coach and overnight express train. We only saw a little of this vast country, but we understand now so much more about our pupils. For me, the journey raised questions about what we were doing at all, apparently trying to adapt this wonderful culture to our western culture. Is it really so much better a life in Britain, even if you get a reasonable job? Certainly, the more we can show that we value the culture our pupils bring with them and use it across the whole curriculum, the more we shall show the respect that this wonderful nation deserves. And the education we offer will be enhanced.

Postcript

My brother Michael and his family were working and living in Karachi, Pakistan at that time so I went on to visit them, the country and the people there. To me it was important and I was very lucky to have this opportunity. It was not so very different from India.

Later on, back home, I was invited to a dinner in Hounslow, by the Pakistan Welfare Association. I took one of my male deputies as my companion. I was welcomed as the guest of honour. However, just before dinner, they realised that, as I was a woman, I should not be on the top table. All the men went out. After a long discussion, they came back and asked me to sit with the wives, all along one side of the table. My deputy sat on the top table, but I was still formally welcomed as the guest of honour. I had a great time talking to the women who were very bright and positive. They said they actually ruled the roost at home!

Working together: an unusual staff consultation:
Motivating staff, students, parents and the community by helping them define and share the school goals

This was the first time I hadn't invited the Grubb Institute to come and help me to get the school to move forward. I must have felt more confident in my role. We did it ourselves. It should not come as a surprise to anyone that when I moved to Cranford at Easter 1981 that the first things I did were:

- To ask the staff what skills, knowledge and values they thought the pupils should have when they left school
- To ask the pupils what they thought of the school now and what they thought it should be doing next
- To set up a school-to-work course in the lower sixth

In the staff meeting held in June 1981, from 3.40pm-5.15pm, we divided into small groups, then each group reported to the whole staff and I collated their responses into a list. This was then discussed and agreed at the next staff meeting. What was so interesting about the list is that it had nothing specific to do with subjects, exams or content. It went right across the curriculum and the way we all behaved. I was very encouraged. Here is the list:

1. AREAS OF KNOWLEDGE

- Numeracy
- Literacy
- Linguistic skills: fluency and confidence; presentation of argument; selection and organization of materials; sensitivity to 'tone', listening skills; ability to communicate orally as well as in writing
- Logic: how to question, criticize; how to make rational decisions based on information; how to use resources/environment/facts in this; how to make choices; how to learn by discovery and how to solve problems
- Creativity: artistic sensitivity; divergent thinking; imagination; aesthetic appreciation
- Scientific literacy: including manual dexterity and technological competence
- Physical: how to take care of selves and others; exercise, diet, health and sex
- Political and social: knowledge of current affairs; ability to accept change but also to participate and contribute to changes in society; how to be good citizens, politically aware
- Moral and spiritual: awareness of different cultures and beliefs; ability to tolerate and respect differences; sense of social responsibility; not restricted by gender differences

2. SOCIAL AND PERSONAL SKILLS

To be able
- to communicate and develop relationships
- to work with other individuals in groups; in an authority/work setting

- to cope with the demands of life
- to present self well

To develop
- Self-confidence; self-awareness;
- Awareness of own potential; interviewing skills
- Independence and personal autonomy
- Independence and mutuality
- Reliability
- Tolerance of differences and respect for others

To accept and adapt to change
- to be willing to broaden horizons;
- to be willing to take risks; adaptability;
- to be able to work on own initiative
- to relate to adults/those in authority as well as peers
- to be balanced persons, coordinated

3. LIFE AFTER SCHOOL
- Awareness of the relevance of school life to working life
- Awareness that education and learning is a life-long process
- Awareness that learning continues at work
- Appreciation of the value and possibilities of leisure
- Aware of career opportunities
- Prepared for life, work, leisure, unemployment, parenthood and citizenship

My response to the staff, after first congratulating them was: 'No doubt we could refine or add to these categories. The next question is: If this is what we are trying to do - and we might want to check that out, add or subtract a few more things then consider how we-can-do-it within the framework of our curriculum?'

There then followed a curriculum review and an extensive program of **staff development** to integrate these ideas with the curriculum and the teaching methods we used.

At the end of the second meeting, I suggested that we should now put the same questions to the students. There great consternation at this idea, but I managed to persuade the staff that they could do it. I allocated a double lesson slot to the task. The staff came back with their form's ideas and very excited at their responses. Some of them were in fact messages to the staff about their behaviour and the improved amenities needed by the pupils. Here are a few examples:

4. THE STUDENTS' SUGGESTIONS:

- **The image of the school** Need for better publicity, better contacts with primary schools, less litter and stop ice cream vans
- **Amenities and appearance of the school:** improved signposting, more displays of pupil work, more litter bins in the playground, build a bicycle shed, a book and stationery shop, benches in the concourse, swimming pool, vigilance about smoking and violence
- **Staff behaviour:** NO denim, (jeans or skirts), smart appearance, polite language, stick to homework timetable, more teacher presence needed in breaks
- **Lunch hour** more things to do needed: clubs, homework room and library access
- **Uniform:** allow the girls to wear trousers in the winter. If uniform exists enforce it, otherwise abolish it
- **After school:** Access to the community activities for pupils
- **Educational:** more of the outside world coming into the school more work experience, voluntary work, first three years not purposeful enough, careers talks before the options chosen, more solid preparation for external exams

Most of these points are very sensible and we took note and action. The pupils told me that they appreciated being asked for their views and I think the staff took them very seriously. The goal was to get us all to define and work to our goals and values with new vigour and rigour. We took the results of our various discussions to the governing body, the Community Council and also to the parents. Everybody had a chance to make an input. The end product was that we had a broad overarching agreement about our mission and thenceforth we moved forward together and improved step by step.

There had been some feeling that the success of the community activities had been detracting from the school itself. I think this was more imagined than real. But on all sides we strove to improve all aspects of our activities. The community activities and the school-to-work course are explained later.

On the academic side, we decided to raise the bar: we needed to do more about the middle achievers, who could and would do better with stimulus, and support. They needed to be more ambitious, to aim higher. Numbers going on to higher education improved year on year. The outstandingly clever ones needed extra encouragement and confidence boosting to make them apply for the best universities.

One such student was Tien Xuan Doe. When it was suggested he should apply for Oxbridge, he shrugged and said no, not possible. Finally he took my advice. He ended up at King's College, Cambridge and gained a first class degree. We have kept in touch, and when I visited him and his delightful family in Singapore, he thanked me for my confidence in him. He said he would never have been appointed to the high powered job he held in the Singapore Investment Fund Management Firm without his track record.

Tien Xuan Doe and family

119

My work for the RSA, (the Royal Society of Arts) founded 1754

When I was invited to become a member of the RSA in 1981 I was immediately co-opted on to Council and remained there until 1992. The Council were an amazing group of delightful and highly intelligent people. The Capability Campaign was started by RSA members such as John Tomlinson and gathered much support nationally. The next step was to run the Capability Award Scheme. More about this later!

On Council, the biggest decision was to agree to Professor Charles Handy's suggestion that we opened up the vaults and turned them into a restaurant to be used for light meals and refreshments and for certain events. It became a beautiful space with room for exhibitions and small conferences. It was also useful for dropping in for a light meal.

The annual lecture program was always first class. There were also many smaller conferences with themes. At one education conference, the speaker referred endlessly to Headmasters. In exasperation, I stood up and said: 'speaking as a Headmaster'. It brought the house down.

I was asked to speak very many times. The most prestigious lecture was the Cantor Lecture, 1983, which is much too long to include in this book. The theme was 'Tomorrow's schools open or closed?' It used some of the data from my book, *Leadership for Tomorrow's Schools*, 1987.

The Duke of Edinburgh was our President and that meant that he came to a dinner for eight once a year. I was asked to go to three of them, since there weren't many women on Council! The Duke was a delightful dinner companion with a great sense of humour.

From 1992-95, I chaired a small working group on Parents in a Learning Society. The idea was to encourage parents to take a more proactive role in bringing up their children, helping them to be more capable of managing their own lives, and to show initiative and confidence.

Here is an example of one of my RSA lectures:

Royal Society of Arts Conference: Education for what? 6ᵗʰ July 1982. The classroom: constraints and challenges
Mrs Anne Jones, Head, Cranford Community School

In this lecture, I elaborate on the way we implemented our goals at Cranford and raised standards of achievements.

Mr Chairman, Ladies and Gentlemen

I rise with enthusiasm and some trepidation to join this debate. My task is both awe-inspiring and awe-some, but alas I can't resist a challenge, so here I am.

In such a distinguished audience, I will not presume too much. My intention is not to 'try to teach my grandma to suck eggs' but rather to try to articulate on behalf of many of those here present some of the current thoughts shared by those of us responsible for the future patterns and provision of education, particularly in schools, I know from public and private debate with many of you here, that there is a growing consensus amongst us about an 'agenda for action'. I know that amongst us, there is not only hope but light, not only idealism but many practical examples of ways forward, ways which meet our needs as a nation to view and use education in a new way without, throwing out the best of our traditions. Indeed, perhaps new is the wrong word: as one distinguished HMI now retired, once said:

In education, there are swings and roundabouts, and if you stay put for long enough, you eventually become avant garde!'

I am however assuming that most of us here share the basic principles of the Education for Capability movement: the big C's, developing competences (that is both skills and knowledge), developing coping skills, creativity and cooperation. Of course we respect intellectual development, but set in context as one of many aspects of man and woman which need to be developed to the full, along with moral, spiritual, social and political, creative, aesthetic, practical, physical and personal development.

Montaigne, the great French philosopher, said:

Life is a preparation for death.

By analogy, school is a preparation for life after school: life in every sense of the word, at home, at leisure, in the community, in society, in the world, in the context of today. That means life in which there is stress, uncertainty and rapid change in day-to-day matters; it means a life in which personal confidence, self-esteem, and mutual support become of paramount importance. That means a life in which our certainty comes more from our philosophy and our relationships than from our circumstances. Oscar Wilde once described a cynic as:

A person, who knows the price of everything and the value of nothing.

In this uncertain and turbulent age it becomes increasingly important to reassert a framework of values and beliefs within which we can then cope in a flexible way with whatever life may bring.

We have moved suddenly from prophetic predictions about a life of change, to a reality about a change of life, and as we well know, this menopausal state can be uncomfortable for both women and men. It is, however, my belief that we have the skills, the competencies, and the strength to cope, both as a nation and as a teaching profession.

My brief is to look at the constraints and challenges of the classroom. Let me say straight away that the greatest possible constraint is to view education as something which takes place only in a classroom, the old view of the classroom as a kind of magic box in which 'information passes mysteriously (and somewhat patchily) from the teacher, to the blackboard, to the exercise book and finally to the exam paper without touching the mind of the 'learner'.

Learning experiences are everywhere: what we often miss out of education at the moment is the opportunity to make the connection between what we have experienced, in or out of school, and what we have learnt from that experience. Classroom learning is certainly not enough: my greatest moment of triumph in my last school was when one of the senior Inspectors decided to make a surprise visit to see how the pupils really behaved and arrived to find absolutely nobody in school but me. The entire pupil and staff population was spending the day out on projects in the community and beyond, learning from life outside school.

It has been fashionable, ever since the Ruskin speech and the great debate, to knock schools. This was not all that helpful to us: in the late 70s we were pushed and pulled by equal and opposite forces and many of us began to feel immobilised. Hadn't we been coping with changes for years? What more could we possibly do without collapsing with total exhaustion? More and more money had been pushed into curriculum development and special, provisions and even we were beginning to ask whether the gross efforts justified the net results.

What we did not perceive then as clearly as we may do now, was that the changes over the last twenty-five years were to do first of all more with structure (comprehensive reorganisation and expansion), then with content (curriculum development) and then with structure again (falling rolls and amalgamations). What did not change significantly during that time was the style and processes.

Essentially, despite the comprehensive movement, it was the mixture as before, fundamentally an 'academic' education for all rather than, as we had hoped, a 'comprehensive' education for all. So what was needed and still is needed, despite notable exceptions, was and is a new way of working with pupils, a way which uses and develops their many talents, a way which makes them feel valued and valuable, a way which makes them grow in stature, status and esteem. In a curious way, the more we have tried to help our pupils and do things for them, the more passive and dependent, and lacking in resources they have become, and the less they have mobilised their creativity, their competency, their coping skills and their cooperation.

The problem seems to be connected with ethos, attitudes, teaching styles and processes rather than with structure or content. Making the curriculum more 'relevant' makes no difference if the ideology and the methodology are misplaced. As the pupil said 'It's still, a bloody school.' The fact is that, it is sad, but true, to say that there is nothing like adversity, or even dare I say adversaries, for sharpening the mind.

We are now on the brink of a revolution in our approach to education. The main impetus for this change of attitude has been falling rolls, diminishing resources and youth unemployment. The question now is how to achieve a bloodless evolution so that our highly skilled teaching force can make the transition in teaching style with dignity and pride.

The evidence I have so far and others will bear me out is that where teachers have been supported in this transition, they have found the experience stimulating, exciting and motivating. There is no lack of goodwill, energy or skill among the teaching profession: what is needed is examples of good practice and a clear philosophical lead. When teachers have themselves had to cope with uncertainty, and make transitions, they are in a much better position to help prepare their pupils for life. However uncomfortable it may have been at the time, they will have had to look at their own basic assumptions, their own values and attitudes, the kind of messages they were unwittingly transmitting, to the pupils, for example about work, about exams, about promotion.

As teachers, if we are really to respect and value all our pupils, we have to come off the one dimensional 'wanting to be, top' ethic, the valuing of people for their position, in society rather than for themselves. The fact is that many people will be unemployed for part of their lives, very few will get to the top, but that all of us will be capable, in various, ways and styles, of leading satisfying lives. The old criteria for 'success', will not do.

In schools, because we are fundamentally conscientious, we have allowed ourselves to be weighed down by the albatross of ancient history, with its deep split between the academic and the vocational, between middle class and working class, between examinations and life. We have been trapped in the present system. It is our duty to help our pupils pass as many exams as possible, yet we know

1. that they impose an intolerable burden on our pupils, even the intelligent ones,
2. that they tell you more about what students cannot do than what they can do,
3. that they have doubtful currency for employment in the present climate even for the haves,
4. for the 40% of the have-nots, they promote feelings of rejection,

stigmatisation, alienation and potential revolt.

Even the phrase 'terminal examination' makes the whole thing sound like a cancer, rather than as it should be, a milestone, a marker at the beginning of a life of learning experiences. There is no doubt that exams have been a powerful motivating and controlling mechanism for up to 60% of the pupil population, but it is my prediction that, unless the system alters radically, this will not continue to be the case. Neither do the employers particularly want O-levels. What they want is a form of assessment which gives an all-round picture of a pupil's development, attainment potential and capability.

To return to the challenge to the classroom teacher. To my mind the constraints, dear Chairman, lie in ourselves, not in our stars. Of course, more resources would help, and in particular, time for us to work in teams to share and reflect upon what we have learnt from what we are trying to do.

But there are some small ways forward which I can speak about with confidence since we have tried them at Cranford Community School. First, we have sat down together and tried to make explicit our basic assumptions, our philosophy and values and to make explicit the skills, knowledge and values which we hope to develop in our pupils. The process of doing this has in itself been, valuable. We have realised that we often actually do the opposite of what we say we are trying to do. We are reviewing our methods and procedures in the light of this.

We are doing a lot of team building between the staff, developing more co-operative methods of teaching, planning and reviewing. We are taking some risks, trying out new courses, adjusting them in the light of experience, making some mistakes and learning from them. We are finding more and more that it pays to listen to what the pupils have to say, to negotiate with them certain aspects of the curriculum, to let them in on their own assessment, to allow them to manage certain aspects of school life and of their own learning and to involve them actively in the learning process.

In the near future, we are suspending the timetable for a week to enable the pupils to participate with other members of the community in a community festival. In February, the whole of the fifth year, including the most able, went on work experience. In the sixth form, all pupils follow an expressive arts course which is essentially practical and experiential. Also in the sixth form we have experimented with a new 'school to work' course, which has been particularly exciting for pupils and staff. Through it, we have learnt to cope with such terrifying concepts as social and life skills, cross modular projects, profiling and pupil self assessment, reflecting upon experience, negotiating the curriculum, and listening and acting upon pupil criticisms of our teaching styles.

We have learnt enormously from these experiences as have the pupils. Our joint motivation, commitment, enthusiasm, growth and development are wondrous to behold. We have developed a small concrete example of 'new style' teaching and we find colleagues wanting us to extend what we have learnt to themselves and other parts of the curriculum. We are also lucky in that we are a community school, catering from pre-cradle to the grave and thus embodying a belief in continuing education, and a belief that it helps young people not to be hived off into an adolescent ghetto for those uncomfortable 'years between'.

So, in sum

1. The constraints in education are mainly in our own attitudes. Teachers are unduly modest. We do have the skills needed if only we can raise the courage to begin. Our experience is that it is worth the risk and the discomfort. We feel exhilarated. The main challenge is from young people themselves, but we need not be afraid of their challenge. They need us to support them in their growth but not to do it for them. Schools need to be pupil centred rather than organisation centred. As Moliere said:

   Il faut manger pour vivre et non pas vivre pour manger!

2. In 1948, CM Fleming, author of *Adolescence and its social psychology*, who specialised in adolescent psychology made an invaluable list of what adolescents need: Acceptance; to give and receive: to learn new things: to experience new adventures;

understanding; responsibility. Teachers can satisfy these needs if they will let go a little their desire to control and protect and trust the pupils to have a say in the negotiation of the curriculum, in their own assessment and in the running of the school, eg School Councils. They need to be heard more than seen.

3. Teachers and pupils need to value the processes of education as much if not more than the product 'It ain't what you do but the way that you do it' as the song puts it. It is worthwhile giving time to reflection upon learning, to making the connections between activities and learning. As far as possible, pupils need active experiential learning methods in which they can take responsibility for the management of their own learning.

4. Fundamentally, all these points are to do with trust, with openness, with mutuality, with growth and development, rather than power and control, and with positive expectations, and reciprocity.

5. So with pupils, as with teachers. It is very important for Heads to demonstrate their belief in their staff, in their competences, coping skills, creativity and cooperation. Only then will the pupils really be able to share in these processes.

6. It would be false and naive to make it sound as if these transformations are easy. Teachers brought up in the 'dependent' mode of teaching need support and time to make a gradual transition to more 'self-reliant' modes of teaching. But I see this only as a change of emphasis, not of fundamentals. I believe that we-can-do-it: On this I pin my faith, my hope and my belief.

Postscript

The principles outlined here still hold good. The Education for Capability movement which I mentioned was an important one at that time with support from all the most distinguished Educators of that day. Here is the statement put out by the Royal Society of Arts in 1982 as part of the Education for Capability Recognition Scheme and signed by over a hundred distinguished people, mostly, but not all, Educators.

Education for Capability 1982

CRANFORD was one of the first schools to receive the Capability Award.

The Manifesto

'There is a serious imbalance in Britain today in the full process which is described by the two words 'education' and 'training'. The idea of the 'educated person' is that of a scholarly individual who has been neither educated nor trained to exercise useful skills; who is able to understand but not to act. Young people in secondary or higher education increasingly specialise and do so too often in ways which mean that they are taught to practise only the skills of scholarship and science. They acquire knowledge of particular subjects, but are not equipped to use knowledge in ways that are relevant to the world outside the education system.'

COMMENT

Too true, the movement did influence a lot of schools. Alas the message is still needed today. Let us hope that the point will be taken up again. The coalition government is on to it.

I once heard a university Dean of Faculty say: 'Universities don't teach students how to DO anything. We just tell them about it.' No wonder we don't have enough highly skilled graduates! That is one reason while later on the Enterprise in Higher Education (EHE) Project was launched... by me!

Pastoral care and guidance

This is part of an article for the NUT Secondary Education Journal Oct 1982 Vol 2 no 3. It is based on my work at Vauxhall Manor and at Cranford Community School

In a strange way, the pastoral care and guidance systems of the last decade or so have contributed to under-achievement among pupils. This is not because either concept was intrinsically wrong but because in practice they became inappropriately used. Pastoral care, originally introduced some twenty years ago to combat the over-academic emphasis and the size of the new comprehensive schools, became *in extremis* split off from the academic system, over-protective, based on low expectations, and in fact inimical to learning. Guidance has not really properly begun until recently: what little exists has tended to be directive and concerned with 'option choices' and timetabling conven-ience. A pupil once said to me: 'is this a choice Miss or can we do what we like?' So the form teacher, standing on the side-lines and simply trying to do a good job, can be forgiven for feeling somewhat unsure of what his or her pastoral role is supposed to be now.

Split

Yet in the beginning, when comprehensives were created on the 'academic' model and found lacking, there was a tremendous boom in the pastoral care industry. Scale 4 heads of year or House were suddenly invented, making the 'academic' side of the staff feel curiously devalued. Many of these pastoral posts went to the old 'secondary modern' staff, thus reinforcing the unfortunate historical split between the secondary modern and the grammar school teacher, the teacher of pupils and the teacher of subjects. Yet at the time, in the early 60s, it was vital to try to get teachers to be more conscious of the emotional and developmental needs of the pupils they were trying to teach. It is nonsense to teach history without also teaching Jane.

Unfortunately, the pastoral system began to develop a life of its own, so that in many schools there were eventually two systems, the pastoral and the academic, each with its own code, expectations, rewards, punishments and ethos, and often unconsciously contradictory and divisory, Therefore stressful for staff and pupils who found themselves split – what I call pastoral-academic-schizophrenia. The 'caring' part of pastoral care also suffered a sea change. Often the chief carer (the Head of Year or House) would become the ogre/witch figure, the chief disciplinarian, whilst the form teacher would try to compensate by being over caring, positively protective. Sometimes these roles were reversed. They were often gender-linked. They reflect the roles parents often take up, and children soon learn to manipulate.

So sometimes what started as compensatory became over-compensatory, what started as loving became suffocating, what started as strengthening and helping became weakening; instead of promoting healthy growth and independence. It began to stunt growth and promote an unhealthy kind of over-dependence.

Fortunately, Rutter[1] (among others) came along. Rutter's message in particular was well heard by teachers. Schools *do* make a difference: the *ethos* of a particular school, the *nature* of the total educational process will change the pupil's life to some extent. In this the hidden curriculum is as important as the actual curriculum: punctuality (staff and pupils), appearance (staff and pupils), participation (staff and pupils) and amenities (staff and pupils). It was particularly good to note in this research the importance of the way pupils are treated, respected, involved and challenged.

But by then we were stuck with a points system which labelled teachers, from Deputy Head down, as either pastoral or academic, though in fact everybody is both. Those with 'pastoral care' posts began to say apologetically that their job was not pastoral, but to 'support the academic function', i.e. see that the pupil was in a fit state to learn. Those pupils who were not in a fit state became hived off into 'special units' sometimes called (significantly) 'disruptive units'. For every problem an 'extra' solution was added on until it became clear that what we really needed to do was to take another look at the *main* system – integration rather than gradual disintegration. Then the Warnock Report[2] arrived with its proposals for 'mainstreaming' everybody, warts and all. This coincided with a growing cry for 'whole school policies', 'whole school curriculum' and a 'pastoral curriculum'; for examining the learning experiences offered by a school, rather than single subjects;[3] for preparation for adult and working life;[4] and finally for counselling, guidance and personal development for all.[5] The quest for knowledge has been supplemented by a new stress on skills, qualities of 'mind, body, spirit, feeling and imagination', on understanding and self respect.[6] *Plus ca change:* that's what we really meant by pastoral care in the first place!

Response

So the message is not to give up caring in order to be more academic. The message is not about being soft or being hard: either extreme behaviour can be detrimental. Most important of all is finding an *appropriate* response to a pupil's needs, and to try to meet the needs in a way which helps the pupils to learn how to cope for themselves, with our help if necessary. As adults, we need to learn how to be sensitive without being sentimental, strong without being overpowering, flexible without being flaccid, loving without being over-involved, gentle without being rigid, tolerant without being silly. These are not easy skills to manage, and most of us need help in developing them. Maybe one of the problems for teachers is that too much energy has gone into devising systems for dealing with pupils and not enough energy has gone into our helping each other develop these skills, into giving each other support, so that we too strengthen our self-esteem and inner confidence. This is just as important for the teacher as it is for the pupil. It is when we are feeling personally insecure that we convey the wrong message, draw the line in the wrong place, put up with that which we should not allow, or jump too hard on the wrong issue.

So where are we now? Do we need pastoral care in secondary schools? Does it help us to combat under-achievement? The answer to both questions is clearly yes, but depends totally on the nature of the pastoral care, the way it is provided and the basic assumptions which are behind whatever system exists. Guidance I take to be a **part** of a good pastoral care system. It might help if I put down some of the basic assumptions I hold. Yours may be totally different.

- Pupils learn from their **total** experience of the school – not just in lessons. They learn as much from observing the way teachers treat them, each other, the building, as they do from the actual lessons. They also learn from each other and from other adults.
- Pupils are never fooled, whatever their ability: they respond to *genuine* care and concern which will include setting limits, having positive expectations, valuing each person, and not putting up with nonsense.
- Pupils need teachers to support them in their personal growth and

131

learning, but **not** to do it for them.

- Pupils need acceptance but not condonance; they need to be able to give as well as receive, to show that they can take responsibility, initiate ideas.
- Pupils learn as much from the processes in the classroom as they do from the content.
- Pupils need to be involved in assessing their own progress, development, strengths and weaknesses.
- All pupils need guidance from the age of eleven: this to include real opportunities for making decisions, choices and mistakes; for making contact with people other than teachers, and for visits and outings outside school; for voluntary service and experience of work.
- Pupils need opportunities to learn to work together in pairs, in groups, in classes, as a whole school – as well as to develop their individual qualities.
- Pupils need a system of organisation which they understand as well as the teachers, and which has their learning as its objective, not the convenience of the system.

Implications

If a school holds basic assumptions such as these, how do they affect under-achievement, and what are their implications for organisation? Under-achievers are usually pupils who have switched off for various reasons. The main principle behind the assumptions is to engage the pupils actively in their own learning, and not to write anyone off; to avoid negative labelling, to hold positive expectations, never to give up but always to challenge and make demands, to support and be honest: in a word, to care. Organisationally none of this works unless the same system of trust, shared responsibility, respect, with opportunities for initiative, self-assessment, mutual support, and creativity, applies to teachers. If the senior staff cannot work as a team, or the house or year tutors, then how can the pupils learn this? If teachers are not considerate, honest, reliable, supportive and punctual, how can the pupils be so? If there is no real delegation – or conversely there is total relegation or abdication – from senior to junior staff, then there will not be much from staff to pupil. If teachers are not able to express their views, it is very unlikely that the pupils' views will be heard.

In such a scheme then, the form tutor is ascendant[7] a member of a team, given leadership and support from the Head of Year or House. He or she works within a clear philosophical framework and structure, which gives guidelines on matters of principle, but is not a constraint. Pupils who do have serious personal problems get help at the earliest opportunity. There is good contact with parents. There is special 'provision' but this is designed to support mainstream work, not to take over from it. The amount of administrative paperwork is kept to a minimum and time is spent on contact between people rather than between pieces of paper. There is, however, a system of evaluation in which team members participate.

All very bland and fine you may say. What about actual practice? Is it like that at your school, Cranford, for example? The honest answer is not altogether: not yet and probably not ever. 'A man's reach must exceed his grasp or what's a heaven for.' Human imperfection and the constant evolution of circumstances, mean that in schools we never achieve the perfect system – or if we ever did, then school would be dead. We have to learn to live with imperfections. What is important is that we have the most appropriate system (i.e. suitable for the needs, skills and talents of pupils and staff) that we can have for the moment. This is something to be checked out constantly.

Strategies at Cranford

At Cranford we are conscious of the under-achievement of our 'middle' pupils in particular. We haven't yet succeeded in getting the best out of both ends and the middle simultaneously. This may well reflect the fact that we have only just gone fully mixed ability in lower school, and that we may formerly have been subconsciously labelling pupils. Our pastoral care system is set up recognisably on the 1974 model (very similar to the one I established as Head of another school at the same period), with all the trappings of the 'school as a caring community' which was the fashionable phrase much used at the time. We have a year system, ascendant form tutors, a counsellor, a careers teacher, a special unit, an 'ESL' unit (English as a second language) as well as a remedial unit, and a gipsies unit (there is an official gipsies site very near the school. We have close contacts with the educational psychologist, the EWO (Education Welfare Officer) and social workers; we have excellent support from parents, both at parents' evenings and individual interviews. And we are a community school. All these aspects of the school we value enormously and will guard zealously. But what we have found ourselves doing recently is to look at the way everything works and to make some important operational shifts. It remains to be seen what difference these make to pupils' achievement in the long term, but in the short-term they have had notable (and positive) effects on staff motivation and morale.

We have begun by working together to try to define whole school philosophy and policy more clearly. In this, what is important is not so much the piece of paper produced at the end, but the process of sharing ideas, differences of perception and emphasis. In the senior staff team in particular, we are spending a lot of time building a sense of team. It is gratifying now to see to what extent each member of the team speaks for his or her patch but with total consistency in terms of overall philosophy. The same processes are also beginning to happen at year team and departmental team level.

Second, we have looked at our extra provision and have decided that, excellent as it is, it needs pulling together, coordinating and reintegrating with the main stream work. The ESL unit no longer has a prime function of 'total immersion' but there is much work to be done in the classroom alongside other teachers: collaborative team teaching, as well as some withdrawal. Significantly the remedial unit and the gipsies unit have moved from an isolated hut in the playground to the main building so that their teachers can work in a more flexible way with a wider range of pupils and teachers. The special unit is reviewing the question of whether pupils who go there stay too long! It would be a strain to have a more flexible membership but it might help these pupils more. The counsellor has developed the role of advising senior staff on referrals, without losing her special role with the pupils; she has also run a superb counselling course for staff, which means she herself acts as a training resource and support for form tutors. The 'extra provisions' have now joined together to form the Department of Special Needs, or SEND as we affectionately call it.

Third, we have looked at the amount of support and training we give our teachers 'on the ground'. Significant in this respect is the creation of a new senior staff post: the Director of Development. This curiously contradictory title is meant to indicate that we believe in staff development but we do not think it should be left to chance: it needs leadership, direction and planning. Following the success of our 'counselling' course we are this term mounting a six-week course in 'group-work skills in the classroom', to be run by our youth leader. We are also increasing using department and year team meetings for development and support of staff's work rather than purely administrative matters. We have devised a 'devolved' network for year teams, with two team leaders in each year taking extra responsibility and initiative within their mini team. Further staff development and support is provided by the Heads of school (lower, middle and upper) who are 'not in charge of pastoral care': they are responsible for the 'overall learning and development of the pupils in their care'. They are in fact mini-Heads. Their brief includes the coordination of the overall assessment of the work of pupils in their care, and of their guidance program.

It is also a significant fact, contributing enormously to staff morale and mutual cooperativeness, that staff join in many out-of-school activities together: for example (last year) a yoga group, regular football, rounders and hockey matches, badminton and squash leagues, a staff Music Hall Performance to the whole school and several staff social events and outings (eg to France, to a restaurant). This is not to say that schools should be run on a 'social club' model, but there is no doubt that such activities increase our trust, confidence in, and affection for each other, and decrease any 'labelling' or stereotyping which might go on between us. We are not afraid to get to know each other as people and this helps us to be more confident and less defensive with pupils and parents. Being a community school means that we are, all of us, including the pupils, already less defensive about 'outsiders' on the premises than we might be.

Finally, but not least, the guidance program for pupils. This is something we have not been satisfied with in the past. Too much has fallen on the lone careers master and not enough on the team of form teachers. Careers guidance and health education have had too little timetabled time. Options choices have been unduly constricted by the pooling arrangements. All these matters are now in hand. The common core for years four and five has been extended. Thanks to a computer and the skill of the Deputy Head using it, most pupils have their chosen subjects in the fourth year. What we are embarking on now is the detailed development of the tutorial program from year one. We are also endeavouring to teach social and life skills through the whole curriculum as well as specifically in our new 16-plus courses.

Pupils' participation

It is interesting that when we conducted a full-scale survey of pupils' views last year, they put in a plea for careers guidance from year one, for 'more contact with the outside world in lower school, not just in years four and five', and for 'better preparation for options choices'. Which brings me back to one of my basic premises: the participation of the pupils in negotiating their own program. We are making strenuous efforts to take the views of the school council more seriously in future, to the extent that the school council meetings have been calendared as part of the consultation and participation procedures. School Councils need to be heard, not simply seen.

We do not claim to be doing anything original or to be doing it to perfection. But we do have a strong sense of commitment, exuberance and enjoyment. Our hope and our aim is that the net result will be greater learning for all our pupils, whatever their ability, gender, race or class.

References

1   *Fifteen Thousand Hours: Secondary schools and their effects on children*: M. Rutter et al (Open Books 1979).

2   *Special Educational Needs*: Warnock Report into the education of handicapped children and young people (HMSO 1978)

3   *Curriculum 11-16*: Working Papers by HMI (HMSO 1977)

4   *A Framework for the School Curriculum* (DES/Welsh Office

January 1980)

5 *17-plus: A New Qualification* (DES/Welsh Office May 1982)

6 *The Practical Curriculum*: Schools Council Working Paper 70 (Methuen Educational 1981)

7 P*astoral Care: organising the care and guidance of the individual pupil in a comprehensive school*: M. Marland (Heinemann 1974)

Neil Kinnock addressing Cranford's speech day, 1983

CRAC: Careers Research Advice and Consultancy

CRAC has made a substantial contribution to careers education and guidance nationally and internationally and not only in schools. Here is an after dinner talk by me which includes some of its history.

CRAC, 21st Anniversary dinner Merchant Taylors' Hall, April 1985

Secretary of State, Ladies and Gentlemen,

I am both privileged and honoured to have been asked to propose the toast to such a remarkable assemblage of distinguished and disparate persons. I have to begin with confessions of a Headmistress namely to say that in some curious way. I regard myself as having been, as it were, in at the conception of this remarkable and now fully mature organisation.

My association with CRAC began some twenty-one years ago, when Adrian Bridgwater and myself, surrounded by our families, (which included at the time a collection of very young children) sat in the grounds of his house, excitedly discussing the crucial importance of providing better careers education for our young people, the need for improved careers literature, which, spoke directly to young people and the enormous possibilities of that new skill called counselling, which at that stage had not been developed much in Great Britain. We recognised even then the vital importance of forging real and practical links between Education and Industry, of preparing our young people better for the world of work, both for their sakes and the sake of the economy and our national prosperity, and the importance of trying to relate the curriculum of schools more to the realities of life in a practical way. We have been working to this end ever since and if we have not completely succeeded it has not been for the want of trying.

Although our CEO David Blandford has said elsewhere that nobody would ever have guessed twenty-one years ago the ways that CRAC would develop, I personally know for a fact that the seeds of everything which has happened, were there in the beginning in that remarkable partnership between the founders, Adrian Bridgewater and Tony Watts. In the beginning these were words, but they are now words made flesh. The organisation has remained flexible and responsive to new ideas, but the principles upon which it works have remained constant.

I have been lucky in being associated with CRAC as a working partner all these years as a lecturer, as a counsellor, as a co-author with Tony Watts for Hobsons, as a group leader and as a member of Council. But that is not the real reason I was asked to make this toast: I have to confess that the real reason is that Lady Platt and myself found ourselves at our last Council meeting having to speak up rather firmly for equal opportunities for women. So that if CRAC wants any suggestions for further worlds to conquer, might we gently but firmly suggest that in this area of equal opportunity, both with regard to gender and I suspect to race, there is still more to be done. That, of course, reflects the situation still in society as a whole.

But enough of that! My purpose in speaking is to welcome our guests. When I was thinking about what to say this evening, I took out a very large piece of paper and tried to do one of those sorting exercises, which our children do at primary school, to see what categories of person we have here. It was quite a staggering experience, for it made me face up to the fact that we have here assembled a most unlikely set of bed persons. It is CRAC's genius that it has actually not only itself made links with everybody here, but has also got everybody to work together in one way or another.

In categorising our guests, I was of course forced to put our Guest of Honour, Sir Keith Joseph, our Secretary of State for Education, in a class of his own. May I say, Sir Keith, on behalf of us all, how delighted we are that you have honoured us not only with your presence but also your penetrating and pithy comments. Likewise Sir Peter Swinnerton Dwyer, who will reply to this speech in a few moments, if only I would sit down!

Of the other guests, I must begin by expressing our thanks to the Master of the Merchant Taylors' Company for allowing us to use this magnificent Hall for such a notable occasion. As a Londoner, I am delighted and not a bit surprised that a provincial Cambridge organisation thought fit to come to this splendiferous location, rather than hide away in some rural Cambridgeshire dining hall. We congratulate CRAC on this choice of venue, a sure mark that it has come of age. We are, of course, used to this Oxbridge dependency on London for any event of any importance: we do, after all, lend you our river for your annual Boat Race!

After the principal guests, the categories become easier to define but are impressively diverse. We have representatives of schools, both the private and the state sectors (not quite enough and alas I am the only woman), representatives of universities, and polytechnics, and of these I must make special mention of Hatfield Polytechnic, which has for ten years now hosted, NICEC, the National Institute of Careers Education and Counselling.

And then the employers. We have a most impressive collection of employers of all shapes and sizes, from retail, to consultancy, to nationalised industries, (assuming they stay that way), Insurance, Banking and Manufacturing. We welcome you Sirs and Mesdames. All the household names are here. Then we have a motley collection people who are, in various ways, encouraging links between industry and education – UBI, understanding industry, careers officers and education for industry: industrial society, enterprise, business links, microelectronics, technology, economics projects, industry year, enterprise, engineering and so on. Please do not feel offended if I have not mentioned you by name.

And finally we seem to have succeeded in getting into the same room and hopefully, by now, communicating fluidly with each other, representatives of the DES, MSC, HMI, FEU, DTI, TVEI, SEO, SATRO, IMS, BBC, SSCR, SERC, NEC, RI and so on. Please note that there are no extra marks or drinks for those who understand what all these initials mean!

Having by now, I hope, thoroughly deciphered the list and totally unciphered your good selves, it only remains for me to say, on behalf of CRAC how much we value and esteem, not only your presence this evening, but also the enormous goodwill, practical support and positive help you give our organisation. We are very honoured by your presence. I propose the toast to the Guests!

Postscript

This is a good example of making a speech (which went down very well), apparently about nothing, but in fact it reveals how much the School-to-Work 'Industry' had developed over the twenty-one years since CRAC was founded. Little did I know then that three years later I would become the Senior Civil Servant in charge of 'School-to-Work' initiatives nationally.

The Living Choices Workbooks

The reference to Hobsons the publisher is interesting. Tony Watts, Jan Marsh and I wrote three workbooks for pupils which were published by Hobsons in the 70s. They were workbooks for classroom use, without answers, only questions, designed to make the pupils think for themselves. *Male and Female,* aims to help young people to overcome gender stereotyping at work and at home. *Living Choices* aims to get young people to think about the lifestyles that go with their future careers and home lives and *Time to Spare* aims to help them to think about the kind of spouse, partner, friends, home, interests, and activities they want and whether these will fit with their work. The three workbooks sold very well in secondary schools over a long time. I started writing these books when I was teaching at Thomas Calton School. They are based partly on my teaching notes!

Tea with Prime Minister Margaret Thatcher

In October 1985, Margaret Thatcher invited about fifty educationalists to tea. She had chosen a good mix of people. She had a plan of who we all were at the Lectern, so that she could invite people to comment or immediately mention their name if they spoke first. She was completely in control at the same time as listening very carefully. There was a teachers' strike on at the time so I had had walk through the picket line to get in! Soon after that I wrote to her to make sure she remembered what I had said, and more importantly so that my staff could see what I said: I put I on the staff notice board Here it is.

Dear Prime Minister

8th October 1985

Dear Prime Minister,

Thank you for inviting me to 10 Downing Street for a seminar on Education.

Thank you for the splendid reception. I thought it might be helpful if I summarised the points I made in writing.

1. Education is a priority for the future prosperity, stability and health of the nation; it therefore must be given priority funding if we are to maintain and raise standards, and move forward.

2. Speakers at the seminar seriously underestimated the profession-alism and good sense of the teaching profession as a whole. I do not share Mr. McIntosh's view of the current situation and it is not like that where I am in Hounslow, ten miles from the centre of London. Surely, no school is NOT is promoting anti-racist, anti-sexist policies? The question is not whether, but how.

3. Resourcing is not of itself sufficient. We need at the same time to change the culture of schools so that they encourage our pupils to develop their initiative, resourcefulness, autonomy, creativeness, enterprise and initiative. Both parents and students have far more common sense than we give them credit for. Mobilising pupils' energy is vital: our greatest untapped national resource is the energy of young people themselves.

4. As far as schools and vocational education are concerned, we need to rationalise the 14-18 provision. The unnecessary divide between 'academic' and 'vocational', the lack of flexibility between sectors, the tangle of examinations, and the apparent competition between providers, is divisive, wasteful of resources, offers young people unbalanced and lopsided learning opportunities, and wastes precious human energy and national resources.

5. To overcome this we need to consider the setting up of a Department of Education and Training which would rationalise this situation, create greater flexibility of provision for young people and for adults. At local level there would need to be representative groups, something like Area Manpower Boards' extended and reconstituted which could respond sensitively to local need.

6. This greater flexibility could also extend to higher education which needs in future to give more open access to those who, for whatever reason, could not take advantage of it earlier. This more open access, with 'modular courses' could extend to adults who

needed retraining and upskilling, as well as re-educating. Again, the rigid distinction between sectors needs to be overcome.

The following is my RSA Cantor Lecture which expands my views in more detail.

Yours sincerely

Anne Jones
Head, Cranford Community School

Postscript

I was amazed to get a charming letter from her a few days later thanking me, saying she had read my letter and was grateful for this expansion of my comments. She added that she hoped I had found the seminar as useful as she had. Whoops! I hadn't actually said that. She said she had read the Cantor Lecture with great interest. About a year later, I had a very polite note from her Private Secretary apologizing for the fact that the PM hadn't replied to my letter! On the contrary, it looks as if she had replied 'by return' and my letter had become detached from the rest of her mail on the subject of the seminar!

Later in that year Sir Keith Joseph, Secretary of State for Education invited me to tea in the Houses of Parliament and we had a lively discussion. He wrote afterwards to thank me for meeting him and saying how much he enjoyed the papers I had given him, I have only just made the possible connection between the two events!

Schools Council Conference, Leeds May 1983
Curriculum Issues 14-19
Integration and Differentiation

When I was invited to give this speech I had been doing a lot of thinking about the 14-16 curriculum both in my own school and also as an active Council member of the Secondary Head Association, part-author of the SHA Paper, *The View from Bridge*

It is always extremely daunting to speak among such a gathering of experts. However with the experience that comes from age, and the age that comes from experience, I speak in the spirit of a practitioner wrestling with these issues in my school at this very moment, having set up a 14-19 Working Group. So I speak in the spirit of one who is sharing thoughts, concerns and concepts with colleagues who are I know equally concerned and perplexed.

The blame for the title of this talk is entirely mine: I suggested it. It was a book by Lawrence and Lorsch called *Organisation and Environment* which put me on to the importance in any large organisation of managing simultaneously the concepts of integration and differentiation, of managing the whole as a unified concern and concept, at the same time as recognising and indeed, using differentiation in tasks and differences in the needs of individuals and groups. When as a nation we went comprehensive and eventually mixed ability as well, we appeared, superficially at last, to be going for total integration, everything in one large unified undifferentiated equal blob.

We were no longer tripartite; therefore everybody must do/be the same. But it didn't work like this. That offended our sense of individuality. This was the age of the individualistic society characterised by the self-seeking aims of self-autonomy, self-direction, self-actualisation, selfishness some would say. Pupils had to choose what subjects they wanted to do: 'free choice' (so called) was equated with freedom. I remember vividly a pupil coming up to me and saying: is this a choice or can we do what we like? So we had the irony of comprehensive schools with a cafeteria options system. Integration was sacrificed for differentiation but both of the wrong kind. What we ended up with was a totally incoherent system in which it was difficult for young people to make sense of the whole, and in which any sense of corporate identity or corporate goals was lost in the cult of the individual. If we add to this the fact that during the last twenty-five years most of the changes in secondary schools have been to do with structure (comprehensive reorganisation), then with content (curriculum development) and then with structure again and amalgamations, we have to admit that though we changed from a tripartite to a comprehensive system, what we did not change significantly was the style of our teaching, or indeed its hidden and overt objectives. Despite the comprehensive movement, we had the mixture as before, fundamentally an 'academic' education for all instead, as we had hoped, a comprehensive education for all.

Major stress was still on individual academic achievement, with relatively little emphasis on physical, practical, creative, expressive, social, political and moral skills. There was no guaranteeing a comprehensive curriculum for each pupil who might have either a totally biased academic curriculum, or one comprising a selection of ingenious 'Mode 3s' ranging from motor vehicle studies, child care, typing to 'underwater knitting'! And even with this exciting deal some pupils still stayed away! This must surely have been because of the built in sense of failure of those also knew that in spite of being comprehensive, they were not going to pass any exams.

But then I had another staggering realisation. Not only were comprehensives on the grammar school model, inappropriate for all but the top 20%, but they also reflected the deep split in British society between the academic/intellectual and the technical/vocational. The comprehensive curriculum was neglecting the world of work, and in particular neglecting technology and all its skills, both ancient and modern. Ironically schools themselves, fundamentally about information, seem to be the last place to be let in on information technology. So yet again, schools are not as integrated as we might expect. The attempts of the NTVEI scheme to redress this particular imbalance should not be scorned, but used to help pupils of all abilities to master the techniques of the technology of the future. What we want are opportunities for a technological education appropriate to a technological age for a comprehensive range of pupils.

No sooner have we grasped this point than we are forced to face another. Our examination system has for years, despite the intolerable burden it puts on young people, served as a powerful motivating and controlling force for some 60% of our secondary pupils. It made the remaining 40% feel rejected and rebellious, but it did just about hold down the majority. If the exam system did not exist would it be necessary to invent it? 'Your must work had and pass your exams and then you will get a good job'. No longer will teachers get by with this threat: work and qualifications do not necessarily go together. So what does that do to the system?

In spite of our best efforts, in most of the country, our comprehensive system is not comprehensive. By and large we offer an incoherent fragmented individualistic and random set of separate subjects which neither guarantees a coherent set of learning experiences for all nor differentiates constructively between the different learning needs of pupils. Our system is based on a set of assumptions which are out of date and inappropriate, even assuming they were ever right.

The HMI Survey 'Aspects of Secondary Education' reveals a secondary system still based on the value of academic qualifications, knowledge and rather than experiences and skills, intellect rather than the whole person, with particular neglect of interpersonal skills, study skills, the development of creativity and coping skills, or the ability to work co-operatively. Technological education and preparation for adult and working life are too often reserved for the 'non-academic'. Pupils are given relatively little responsibility for the management of their own learning, for using initiative, for negotiating their own curriculum.

A further worry is that the moment schools began to take seriously the question of preparation for working life for all abilities: work itself receded into the distance. When work was a reality we ignored it; now it is a mirage, we teach it. What does this do for our credibility with our pupils?

It would be very easy at this point to give up and say that in schools we have an impossible task, an impossible dream. Whatever we do, 'they' are against us: the exam system, the economy, parents employers, politicians, the time-tablers and even the pupils. It is easy at this point to wallow in delusions of paranoia and to give up. My belief is quite the opposite that we have the power, the skills and the opportunities to turn the secondary system around in a most significant way. The Prophets of doom and gloom plus the very forces of despair such as economic recession, falling rolls and diminishing resources all sadly in fact give a cutting edge to our deliberations and a new impetus for action. So what can we do?

First, we who work in schools should set out our basic assumptions quite clearly, instead of having the assumptions of others put upon us. We need to set limits to our task. We need to say what we think we can and what we cannot properly and effectively do.

We should face up to the diminishing effectiveness of the work ethic as a motivator.

We need to check out our own assumptions: how much are we ourselves prejudiced in our values and attitude? To what extent are we genuinely non-racist, non-sexist and so on? How non-judgemental are we about other people's misfortunes?

If we believe in the comprehensive principle, then we must see that it works all ways, for example so that intellectuals are not deprived of a whole range of learning experiences. The secondary curriculum should nurture in all pupils of whatever ability, a whole range of skills: creative, practical, physical, social, aesthetic, expressive, intellectual, moral and personal.

There needs to be a common core of experiences in secondary schools with choice within areas. It should not be left totally to the vagaries of geography or the options system whether a pupil has a balanced curriculum. Education needs to be affective as well as cognitive. Head hands and heart are all important. Too often feelings are neglected.

Areas of learning experience are highly debatable, but the comprehensive curriculum 14-19 is likely to include, for all:

- Communication and language
- Numeracy and maths
- Science and technology
- Expressive arts
- Social and environmental studies
- Moral and spiritual development
- Vocational and recreational studies
- Interpersonal skills
- Physical education
- and skills for learning

In addition, the following important points need to be considered:

- The timing of the school day and the school year need not be the straight jacket they so often are. We need to build in more flexibility, more of a modular system which takes into account pupils' developmental learning needs.
- Formal education needs to be seen as a beginning not as an end in itself: we should be building systems which encourage adults to continue their education and training throughout life.
- Pupils need more say in their curriculum, in negotiating methods of working: this so that they their skills, and move from passive dependency to autonomy and interdependency.
- Methods of assessment need to be changed to involve the pupil more.
- The split between education and training needs to be removed. Prevocational studies are appropriate for pupils of all abilities and as a way of extending skills, self-confidence and choice in life.
- We need to take much more note of Adolescent developmental needs, to build confidence, self-esteem and a sense of belonging to a group or a community. We need to develop more tolerance and understanding of the differences between each other: gender, race, age, social class and so on.
- In terms of the curriculum 14-19, many now argue that pre-vocational work should be left to the sixth form otherwise we shall 'run out' of syllabi. My view is that if we putting more emphasis on processes, skills, values and attitudes, then to tag this on at sixth form stage is too little and too late. The whole curriculum needs to be permeated by this approach.

I see no problem in making, for example, the curriculum framework of the City and Guilds 365 the common core curriculum within which pupils take O-levels if appropriate as well as a City and Guilds diploma. What may then come about is that we build in:

- A coherent course framework instead of a set of unrelated subjects.
- More active pupil self assessment methods
- A bridge between school and life outside school which helps give meaning to experiences in school: 'only connect'

- Greater self-esteem for all pupils
- Pupils with better all-round development, whether or not they are going to work or to college.

In the lower sixth it is possible to build similar course frameworks such as BEC (Business Education Certificate), TEC (Technical Education Certificate) and various City and Guild courses - which in many cases obviate the necessity for pupils to suffer the indignity of O-level, yet still leaves for them a route to higher education, if and when they want to use it. Many people will prefer to continue their education when they are much, much older, and as a nation we should do more to make this possible.

In the Cranford model (my school) for 14-16 as at present there are three 'free options' left. We see no objection to specialisation in these options provided we are satisfied (as we are) that the rest of our core gives all our pupils a sufficiently comprehensive set of experiences to give meaning to the work of the school as a whole and yet also recognise individual differences and needs.

However, as I have already said, we are still not satisfied that we have got it right and are working now to reconsider our curriculum framework. That sounds like the really difficult part, but the real crunch will be to change our teaching styles to ones which take more account of processes skills and values at the same time as retaining academic' excellence. We have some signs of success in this at sixth form level. We are moving now to 14-16. But perhaps we really should begin at eleven or do I mean five?

Postscript:

Schools Council Conference in Leeds 1987: the whole curriculum

Ironically, three years later, in 1987, I found myself speaking at the same conference but this time as the newly appointed Director of Education Programmes for the Manpower Services Commission. There were several problems for me. It was my first big speech in my very new job, the latest version of the National Curriculum had just been announced and teachers didn't like it. However, the speech went surprising well. I survived the Q & A session. I explained the ways the National Curriculum and TVEI could complement each other. Two significant facts: in 1987 only 12-14% of our young people went on to higher education. Most of the UK's managers had gone straight to work from school and had very little higher education or management training. How things have changed! See Chapter 5 for the 1987 speech in full.

Cranford Community School receives first ever Curriculum Award, 1984

In 1984, Cranford was awarded one of the first ever Curriculum Awards for being an outstanding school. The award was given on a national basis and judged over a two year period. Only 100 schools nationally were commended for this honour. Here is the report on it.

The awards were designed by the Society of Education Officers in partnership with the magazine *Education* 'to publicise good schools and to increase public awareness of what makes a school good.' (*The Times Educational Supplement*, September 28th 1984). The panel of expert assessors were looking for schools which both drew from and contributed to the local community and environment in its work with pupils. A special presentation was later made to the school at the Institute of Education.

The Head chatting with pupils in the lunch break

It was noted that at Cranford it was possible for someone to use the school from the cradle to the grave: starting with the antenatal clinic, then the creche or nursery while his/her parents went to daytime classes, later using the sports facilities while the pupil was at infant school, then secondary education, followed by evening classes and/or sports as an adult, and finishing with the pensioners' lunchtime club and health clinic!

The facilities and staffing levels are very good. The Head explains that they can afford six extra staff because of the money earned from providing training and education for nearby large international companies, including British Airways. Managing 1200 pupils, 1,500 regular users of the sports facilities and over 1000 adult students during the day and the evening, plus countless others using the clinic, the playgroup, and attending the clubs and societies is a tough task, and clearly one that is well done. But the award is above all recognition of the quality of the curriculum of the school and the way it is inextricably linked to the community it serves, a community which includes Heathrow, and a large number of bilingual pupils from all over the world. Reciprocity is a very important part of the School's philosophy, the idea of both giving to and receiving from the community. The Head believes that by being open to the community rather than being a closed community, the students learn more, and are better prepared for work and for life. The school is more able to move forward with the times rather than be locked into a kind of adolescent ghetto.

Postscript

Yes it certainly was a big task. But how was it that we managed it without any serious incidents and in harmony? It says a lot for the behaviour of the staff and the students that there were no serious incidents. We had a code of mutual respect which we all followed, but somehow the other people coming to the site felt and also obeyed. There were several occasions when this trust was put to the test... More of this later!

Cranford is visited by Her Majesty's Inspectors 1985 Reported 1986

An article written by me for the Community Education Association newsletter

Her Majesty's Inspectors visited Cranford Community School in Hounslow in 1985 and their report appeared at the beginning of the summer 1986. We asked Anne Jones, the Headteacher, for her evaluation of the Inspectors' performance. Here are her comments.

HMI came to Cranford in January 1985: Twenty-nine of them for a week. They published over a year later: 1st May '86. And we were not damned. The limbo period coincided almost entirely with the teachers' action. We waited in mild trepidation and eager anticipation. Would we go the way of other community schools: misunderstood, misinterpreted and misjudged? Would I have to resign? Would we find a critical assessment of what we were doing which would stimulate us to further endeavour and *pour encourager les autres?*

The answer is no to all three questions. The truth is that I had to read the report twice before I realised that it was actually very positive. HMI language, worth a study in itself, seems to be carefully neutralised, and factual in perplexing way. For example: 'the heads of year are all men'. So! Is that an accolade, a criticism or merely a statement of fact? Faint praise or civil leer! More interesting would have been a comment on the fact that that the heads of science and maths were all women! No matter. The real problem of their communication is not so much the language, for that can be learnt, but the fact that the approach and methodology of HMI does not really fit a community school.

Actually, it did not totally suit a comprehensive school with integrated subjects either: Integrated science and combined humanities were recognised, but expressive arts (art, drama, music, dance and creative writing) fitted very uncomfortably into the single subject specialist approach. Nor did equal opportunities fare any better. Gender and anti-sexist strategies did not even appear to be on the Agenda, but multi-cultural education and anti-racist strategies did. These however were not picked out by HMI as part of our main philosophy. We moved to English support some time ago, but in any case we do not particularly locate our multi-cultural efforts there. As for community aspects of the school, this section revealed further confusion in HMI's own minds about what it was they were actually trying to look at.

Further confusion

There did in fact appear to be twenty-nine views about what was going on: Twenty-nine snapshots of several planets in orbit, each taken from a different angle, a different viewpoint, and a different attitude to community schools. Some HMI appeared to be examining a Secondary school, some a Comprehensive school with community bits added on, and some a community school in a multiracial context. The format of the report reveals this. The really pithy section on the community school is relegated to paragraph twenty-four, when it should have come near the beginning, 'community studies' is for some reason, tagged on after that, when in fact it is part of our main curriculum. The 'concluding' paragraph 12-9 shows considerable confusion. Neither, does it make the report useful or helpful for it to be a year late in appearing. Nearly everything has changed since the visitation. The youth club, for example, then with a membership of 300, and justifiably praised, went almost immediately into one of those phases where everybody grew up and left. And so we started again.

Feedback

Was the immediate feedback helpful? Not as much as we hoped. The school was at a rather delicate stage of transition, moving it seemed to us, at last through 'the sound barrier' to become a real community school. We had also been working hard on the curriculum and teaching styles. Preparing for and dealing with the inspection took a lot of time and caused us to back track rather than move forward. We were actually trying to produce butterflies, but as we were at the chrysalis stage, it was rather difficult to judge what was happening. HMI still seemed to us, to be counting caterpillar legs.

Since the visitation, some of the potential butterflies have begun to emerge. We now have 7,000 adults a week coming through the campus, more adult use of the building in the day than ever before, more staff teaching adults as well as children. Staff are demanding more training for teaching adults and more help with building a 'community curriculum', hence our plans to appoint before October, a senior teacher to stimulate, support and coordinate the community curriculum.

Effective evaluation

Are we being fair in expecting HMI to evaluate community schools effectively? Not only are their individual tools and yard sticks not altogether appropriate but also maybe they need more help from the advocates of community schooling in building up common framework of understanding by which to make any assessment at all. The problems are that community schools are continuously dynamic and changing and very difficult to 'group'. They are different from each other. The 'snapshot' technique, with an overview, only produces a set of phenomenological views which do not reveal a coherent 'whole picture'.

So maybe the CEA (Community Education Association) itself should come to the aid of HMI by helping them to define some national criteria for community schools. These could then provide a national framework, no doubt locally interpreted, which might help HMI complete their formidable task. And it might in the end help the idea of community schools to spread more effectively. What we need is more dialogue with HMI.

Postscript

I noticed later that the Inspectors were not in the least impressed by the fact that Cranford was one of the first Schools to receive a Capability Award AND one of the hundred SEO Curriculum Awards!

Shortly after my CEA article the Chief HMI, Eric Bolton invited me to meet him and some of his colleagues and we had a lively and productive discussion. Some ideas were heeded.

One point I did not mention in my piece for the CEA was about discipline. One inspector was heard to say that there was 'no discipline, but the pupils behaved perfectly!' YES! That's what real discipline is, when the students have learnt to behave well and don't need nagging or marshalling all the time that is something we had worked on and YES it had worked!

The biggest test of this was when the teacher strikes were on. I called an assembly. I explained that I would be almost the only member of staff on duty over the lunch time.

I was willing to keep the pupils on-site then, provided they behaved themselves. Any trouble and they would have been locked out. There was no trouble and no mishaps. They behaved very well. They were rather challenging to the staff when the strike was over, but not for long!

During the strike, I also asked the pupils to report to the dining room if there was no teacher for a lesson and to bring a book to read as well as working on their homework. This also worked well. The teaching staff did not in any way take it out on me for having kept the school going. They were a wonderful staff, highly talented and professional. We liked and respected each other.

Why teachers need to be brave
Article in *The Guardian* November 13th 1984

A kind of educational schizophrenia has set in between the academic and the practical. It is not the route but how teachers travel it, says Anne Jones.

You would think that teachers would be feeling pleased with the Secretary of State for Education, Sir Keith Joseph's progress at the moment: a black mark for the Green Paper on parental power, a double question mark by AS levels, but the Sheffield speech, the impending integrated 16-plus exam system, the development of records of achievement, the Certificate of Prevocational Education and the new curriculum guidelines on the organisation and content of the 5-16 curriculum, these should give new impetus for action in taking schools forward into the twenty-first century.

So why is it then that the prophets of doom and gloom are still muttering in their corners? From Sir Keith's pronouncements you would deduct that he is very concerned about the bottom 40%, that he wants schools to relate their work more closely to life, work and economic reality, that he wants pupils to succeed rather than fail, and further that he wants their 'records of achievement' to include more than 'academic prowess'. What more could we ask? Some of us have been pressing for these changes for years. Those who are still uncomfortable articulate different reasons for so being.

First, and most common, is a fear of central control: the natural British resistance to a nationalised system. We are particularly suspicious at the moment because we are not sure what the government's underlying inexplicit intentions are.

Second, there are those who fear that Sir Keith's ambition of raising academic standards is incompatible with his aim of relating school life more closely to real life. Those people think that 'academic standards' mean the old knowledge based O or A-level routine, a hoop-jumping exercise designed for some 20% of the population and of not much more use, except as a passport to higher education. They may or may not be right much depends on the format of the new examinations. But the fear is that the nature of what is being examined will take us no further forward than we are now and that the 'academic' tradition will still dominate the curriculum. This idea persists in spite of the fact that teachers themselves will have a large part in the composition of such examinations.

Third, set of reasons for concern has much to do with the nature of teachers themselves, and the changes in learning and teaching styles now demanded. Teachers' natural resistance to change was undoubtedly reinforced by the low morale brought on by a long hot summer, industrial action (by no means resolved) and cuts in staffing and other resources. In an atmosphere of retrenchment rather than growth, it is more difficult to get teachers to change their ways fundamentally. Curiously teachers are not as confident as they deserve to be that they are capable of change, and it is this nagging doubt which can undermine even the most forward looking of teachers.

Fourth, set of arguments is about the nature of the curriculum and how much can be fitted into a school week. The 5-16 curriculum document makes a big point of doing away with clutter, by which it means outdated, irrelevant knowledge, or undue repetition. Curiously, the entitlement curriculum suggested by the guidelines gives only scant and oblique attention to one of Sir Keith's pet areas of concern, economic literacy, which I would take to include money sense, consumer education and the world of work. Health and careers education, and computer studies (surely they mean information technology?) get a mention, but it is not clear how they are to be fitted into the curriculum. If you put subjects like careers/health in, what do you take out?

Which 'academic' subjects do you drop? Some people would question whether it is necessary to teach these 'skills for living'. Pure educationists would say that a good education will teach people to discover, analyse, evaluate and decide for themselves on almost any issue. The context is unimportant. What is important is the scientific method. Would that this were so in practice! In so many schools the emphasis in the curriculum is still on content rather than on process.

The underlying tensions beneath all these arguments seem to be about the nature of education itself. On this we appear to be a divided nation. We need not be. The present polarisation appears to be between those who see education in terms of knowledge (knowing that) and those who see it in terms of skills (knowing how). So when Sir Keith proclaims his intention of raising academic standards and relating the work of schools more closely to life, people raise their hands in horror and say it cannot be done. He must mean one or the other, and as he is patently more interested in AS levels than the CPVE (the Certificate of Pre-vocational Education) he must favour traditional education.

It is important to try to understand this apparent split in educational thinking and practice. Education is at a crossroads, but the dilemma is not whether to go left or right, or even uphill or downhill, but rather whether to go forwards or backwards. Over the last decade or so, there has been discernible progress in educational thinking. More and more people have been articulating the importance of process rather than content, active rather than passive learning, the development of self-reliance rather than over-dependency, and team work rather than individual competition, of the ability to take wise decisions in the context of reality, rather than to receive others' judgments on tablets of stone.

What we are after is not the accumulation of knowledge, but the wisdom and skill to use knowledge appropriately. Yet suddenly, polarisation sets in, a kind of educational schizophrenia, between the academic and the practical, education and training, usefulness and enjoyment, knowledge and feeling. Are we going up the old academic ladder or down the new CPVE slippery slope?

The reason it is hard to grasp is because it invites and demands new teaching and learning styles which are simultaneously exciting and frightening. And this is a challenge which we need to take up if our teaching is to be at all useful in the future.

The concern expressed by some people, that in spite of everything, the new examination system at 16-plus will reinforce traditional academic values is underlined when we come across examinations in new subjects such as 'social and life skills'! 'What happens', as one redoubtable Head said to me 'if you fail?' With our preoccupation with measuring and assessing everything that moves, we do seem to have got ourselves into a terrible tangle. We strike a blow for freedom from exam domination then discover that the new curriculum is all being boxed up, measured *reductio ad absurdam*. When you realise that employers look more closely at the actual person than the qualifications, then you have swung the full circle.

Is there a way out of this? Only by healing our splits (largely more imagined than real,) by returning to first principles, and by having a clearer and more integrated understanding of what it is we are actually trying to do in schools. Each school/teacher has to work at this question in its own way. One definition would be to produce well educated people who have had the opportunity of developing as far as possible, a wide range of skills.

These skills should be not merely intellectual and cognitive but also creative, practical, physical, aesthetic, social, spiritual, and moral;

people who are self-confident capable, autonomous, as well as interdependent, able to make decisions, cope with uncertainty, solve problems, be flexible and resourceful.

There is nothing in the curriculum guidelines for 5-16 to stop this. Teachers have it in their power to develop teaching methods and learning strategies which harness the pupils' energy, involves them actively in negotiating and managing their own learning, empower them to use the skills they have acquired in other contexts, help them to make connections between school and life and to want to go on learning all their lives.

School Management Training; can business help? 1984

I wrote this next piece in 1984 when I was seconded to the London Business School to do some research for my book 'Leadership for Tomorrow's Schools' which finally came out in 1987. I was also exploring whether Headteachers would benefit from management training. I was one of a growing number of Heads who thought that this was needed. Some years later, such an organisation was set up as I explain later.

Here is my report on my sabbatical:

A one term sabbatical at the London Business School has given me an excellent opportunity, not only to work on my own research into Heads' training needs, but also to ponder on ways in which places like the Business School could help with Heads' management training. The concept of 'transferable' generic skills, much used and abused in terms of Youth Training Schemes, has obvious application here. The knowledge, skills and understanding needed for management are broadly speaking the same, whatever the context. It could be helpful to Heads, normally confined to adolescent ghettos, to rub shoulders and exchange ideas with the would-be captains of industry, particularly from the point of view of extending Heads' understanding of the importance of industry, wealth creation and economics. So what 'generic' courses does the London Business School offer, which Heads could use? My own research points up motivating staff, team building, conflict resolution, strategic planning, staff appraisal and keeping up with what is happening nationally as key concerns. A glance at the Business School brochures reveals aims and objectives very similar to our own.

To take but one example, the London Business School Executive Program (a one term course) aims to help participants:

- Increase their understanding of what is going on around them
- Develop their analytic problem solving and decision-making skills
- Improve their effectiveness in working with other people
- Build on their existing methods of dealing with their environment
- Gain new perspectives on themselves and their jobs
- Obtain an introduction to areas of the business world with which they may have had little contact
- Explore different ways of learning and to find methods which will be helpful to them in their future careers.

The emphasis and context of such a course is obviously on business and commerce, but the methods are primarily active experiential learning and discussion. My research shows clearly the need for Heads to work precisely on the aims outlined above.

Other short courses for which Heads have said they need include:

- managing in multi-cultural situation
- information technology
- interpersonal skills for general managers

This later one week course has three components

- the employment process the whole business of selecting and appointing
- the control process, including appraisal and accountability
- the interactive process including managing working relationships, groups
- Resource management in uncertain times.

Business schools do of course include Public Policy sector work, and Heads would for their part have a valuable and realistic perspective to contribute to this sector. There is no question about the need, nor about the supply. The snag however is the cost. The London Executive Program costs £6,500 for a term, short courses around £850 a week. It could be argued that other universities could put on similar courses more cheaply. And so they could. However I doubt if they would have the cutting edge which I find so stimulating in the ethos of the London Business School, where the academics legitimately keep one foot in industry and practice what they preach.

At the very least, I would have thought that

- The DES could consider sponsoring a few places on some select courses and evaluate their relevance and effectiveness for Headteachers in training or indeed trainers of Headteachers in training.
- The Business School itself could set up in the first place some very short training modules specifically for Heads in the first instance, and later perhaps for mixed clientele.
- Headteacher trainers in the education section should talk with Business schools to discover in what ways they might pool, share and enrich their resources and experience.
- It would also be valuable for there to be a permanent if rotating Education Fellow at the Business School to make sure that the needs and the contribution of the managers of education are not overlooked.

I was very fortunate that Professor Charles Handy was able to get me this opportunity at the London Business School, a real 'space' for research and reflection which greatly helped me with my book, *Leadership for Tomorrow's Schools*, Blackwell 1997. By then the term School Leadership had largely replaced the term School Management.

Postscript

What happened to my School while I was away? The Leadership Team did very well and it was a good opportunity for them to develop and extend their skills and understanding.

It's worth mentioning at this point that I never appointed anyone a Deputy Headteacher unless I judged that they would become a Head within five years, I then gave them a lot of responsibility, in some cases, the chance to mastermind some new idea. This gave them a terrific incentive to do their very best and to be innovative. Candidates of very high calibre were attracted to the school as they knew they would get on- the-job-training for the next step. Including of course, what NOT to do!

What happened later? A National College for the Training of Heads was set up in the late 80s. The National College for School Leadership joined with the Teacher Academy in 2014 to become the National College for Teaching and Leadership. To become a Head you have to pass three modules:

1. Leading and Improving teaching
2. Leading an effective school
3. Succeeding in Headship. It is an NVQ structure for better or for worse

The Royal Society of Arts: The Cantor Lecture 1985

I was honoured to be asked to give this very prestigous annual lecture at the RSA. Here are a few paragraphs, as the lecture is much too long for this book. I have chosen paragraphs which come near the end of the speech and which make the title of the lecture a little clearer. Some other parts of it are found in other articles or speeches.

TOMORROW'S SCHOOLS: CLOSED OR OPEN?

By ANNE JONES, BA Head, Cranford Community School, delivered to the Society on Monday 11ᵗʰ February 1985, with Peter Gorb, MA, MBA, a member of the Society's Education for Capability Committee, in the Chair.

THE CHAIRMAN: This is the second lecture in our series 'Educating for Tomorrow'. The three Chairmen are all members of the Education for Capability Committee and so too is Anne Jones. I was privileged to meet her for the first time when as a member of that committee I visited her remarkable school.

She has recently spent some time as a visiting Research Fellow at the London Business School, working on a book about the management of schools. Her school itself has won not only an Education for Capability Award but also the Schools' Curriculum Award.

Management styles

As far as management styles go, it does seem to me to be vital that school leaders should look carefully to see whether their way of doing things supports or cancels out their own aims. There is a fine balance to be kept in any leader's repertoire, between pulling, pushing and just waiting. The real skill is knowing when to do which. What does seem clear to me both from my readings in the literature of management, and from the experiences of others, including myself, is that a primarily autocratic or a primarily bureaucratic approach is not the most fruitful at this stage to the development of schools. Neither is an anarchic, laissez-faire style of leadership and management. The mode which I find most fruitful at the moment is one which emphasizes teamwork, partnership, tasks and trust, professionalism and creativity. What is clear to me is that the 1944 Education Act has it all wrong and now needs to be rewritten.

To make the Head responsible for the internal management of the school is to lock the Head into the middle of the organization and to diminish opportunities for working with the reality of life outside school. With the increase in the numbers of Deputies (I have three and am about to have four) it seems to me that team management replaces the Head as one-person band. This makes it easier for the Head to work on the boundary of the school, to see that the school is an open rather than a closed system. It is a vital part of the Head's task to enable people and things to come into the school or go out from school so that the experiences of the pupils are realistically enriched; equally, to help staff and pupils relate what goes on inside school to what goes on outside.

In this scenario a crucial skill of leadership is the ability to manage integration and differentiation, to acknowledge and recognize rather than deny the differences between people as well as using them creatively to formulate a set of overarching goals which give a framework, a meaning, a sense of community to what is otherwise a potentially meaningless society. The Head does not do this alone, but through a team of people, through developing a capacity to receive and to respond to the message of the people on whose behalf he or she works, by developing a capacity to articulate this corporate response.

Schools are not closed systems, or else they would close or be closed; my plea, however, is that schools need to work towards being more open than they normally are. Schools need to be open to new ideas, open to parents, employers, members of the local community; open to new experiences, risks and uncertainties; open to constructive comment from their members and neighbours; open to anybody who wants to go on learning; open at times which suit the public at large; open and honest in word, thought and deed. My thesis is that unless schools open up, unless schools begin to adapt the model upon which they traditionally work, they will cease to be useful or relevant and eventually may well have to close.

I speak these words knowing that I have the backing of my professional Association, the Secondary Heads Association, whose paper, *A View from the Bridge*, touches on many of the points I have made (not surprising as I helped write it!). Many of us would like to change the way schools work, and what we need, as Headteachers and teachers, is your support and public approval. If society in general, the Royal Society of Arts in particular, would help to make legitimate more kinds of trends and developments such as those I have outlined, then it would give schools the courage to change their ways, to become less closed, and through becoming more open, to stay open.

Postscript

For my book *Leadership for Tomorrow's Schools*, Basil Blackwell, 1987 I did a detailed survey of 550 Headteachers. I was amazed to find that so many of them were feeling completely exhausted and disillusioned. One point became clear: a large number of them were taking the burden of everything that was happening in their school, upon themselves. They were not delegating enough, nor working through their senior management team or their staff. They were becoming trapped inside their schools and were not moving forward with the times. Many were struggling to preserve the old values and standards and others were too radical for their long established staff, Most had not learnt to manage the boundary of the school in an open and welcoming way. The evidence of my research was compelling and needed to be heard.

The London Illustrated News, September 1985

This is another extract from my Cantor Lecture. I didn't know it had been done!

The London Illustrated News *included the following paragraphs and a photo of me in their September 1985 edition.*

*Anne Jones, Head of Cranford
Community School aged fifty*

Education is at a crossroads. The dilemma is not about going left or right, uphill or downhill, but about whether to go forwards or backwards. The role of schools in society must change. I envisage a time when information technology will make it possible for pupils to do much of their learning at home. Schools would then become places where people of all ages went for mutual support, for a sense of community and for guidance and support from teachers.

We wouldn't put pupils into classrooms with thirty places, where they learn single subjects for set amounts of time. Teaching would start from where the student is; he or she would have more say in planning what to learn and in assessing it. There would be greater emphasis on cooperation, caring and practical coping, rather than on just individual success or academic achievement. There would be more learning outside the classroom: school journeys, outward bound courses, work experience, voluntary service.

All this should encourage people to go on learning throughout life, to see education as something that helps them to develop. At present the system judges and grades them like eggs. The difficulty is to persuade people to make changes. In my very worst moments, I wonder whether society has some investment in an education service that does not succeed. Schools can then remain a convenient whipping post for the failures of society.

Postscript

I'm not sure I completely agree with that now! The take-up of IT as teaching tool has been slower than expected. The web has helped many students to research facts but this can lead to other problems, for example plagiarism which is a crime if used in a public examination and can also lead to the collection of inaccurate or biased data. Government had pledged in the early 1990s to maintain an online record of achievement for life for each student, but this has proved difficult, Private companies have not had much commercial success in this either. And then there is the custodial role of schools, the bottom line of keeping young people off the streets, something which gets harder as the age of compulsory education goes up. The new coalition government proposals for traineeships and apprenticeships, designed **with** employers, will help enormously particularly if they can lead on to higher qualifications, vocational, professional and /or academic throughout life.

School to work. What now?
THE NEW TRAINING INITIATIVE 1981
Coping with Youth Unemployment in Hounslow
Anne Jones suggests Hounslow pilots a scheme to help avoid Youth Unemployment

Hounslow has a positive program for schools-industry liaison: understanding industry schemes, Project Trident, the code of practice for work experience, the directory of opportunities, secondments, curriculum developments, these all point to an existing awareness of the importance of 'school-to-work programs in schools. But what happens when there is no work to provide for? The employment situation in Hounslow is worsening rapidly, even though this is an area where the new technologies such as micro-electronics, computer applications, communications systems, are likely to burgeon. The employment situation for young people is not as desperate as it is in other parts of the country, but nevertheless it is urgent that action is taken to avert the depressing and alienating effects of youth unemployment already felt in other parts of England. In a multi-cultural society, the problem is further exacerbated. A positive program of action all the more important.

By taking the initiative, rather than waiting for the moment of crisis, Hounslow has an opportunity to make plans based on sound principles, rather than expedience, planned over time, rather than suddenly tacked on. The current review of the curriculum, instigated by the Director of Education, gives schools an opportunity to build new thinking and new strategies into their policies. In government documents 'the School Curriculum', 'the Practical Curriculum', and 'a Basis for Choice', the importance of preparation for adult life and process skills are greatly stressed.

The consultative document, produced by the Manpower Services (MSC), 'A New Training Initiative', goes further and moves toward to a position where all young people under the age of eighteen have the opportunity either of continuing in full time education OR of entering training OR a period of planned work experience, combining work related training and practical experience.

In terms of a philosophy of education, it would seem important for all pupils to be prepared for adult and working life, not simply the less able. It would also seem important for this process to begin both within the comprehensive school and in combination with FE. The great divide between school and life after school needs to be bridged in a planned and systematic way. The hope is that all pupils would be both better and more realistically educated and that pupils of all abilities would be better motivated as well as understanding better the relevance of school life to adult life.

The 14-plus curriculum

It follows that the conscious building of a bridging program for all pupils should be an integral part of the curriculum from the age 13-14. This would include not only structured experiences outside the school, but also making the vocational relevance of what they are taught in school clearer. In particular the importance of process skills, transferable skills and a flexible co-operative attitude need stressing.

The 16-plus Curriculum

At 16-plus pupils are more likely to take different routes. Some would want to take courses designed in conjunction with Training Boards and employers, thus giving them specific, yet also generic and transferable skills. Courses which contained a considerable proportion of 'on-the-job' training would also help. It would be important for the funding of such initiatives to be joint, reflecting the commitment of the education and employment sectors and of industry to making such initiatives work. Good will and mutual understanding are essential prerequisites for such action, but to be effective, initiatives need to be made in genuine partnership.

Implications for the training and retraining of adults

The changing pattern of work and employment (redeployment, early retirement, the shorter working week, retraining, unemployment etc.), make it likely that schools, particularly community schools, will have an opportunity to offer the chance of both learning and teaching to a wide range of adults over the age of sixteen. The young and middle aged unemployed, the retired or part-time workers could find themselves engaged in learning activities within a school, a kind of learning exchange in which sometimes they are sharing their skills with young people, sometimes learning with them or from them, sometimes taking up their hobbies and activities, sometimes creating new events and ideas. Whilst we must start with the needs of the 16-19s, we need also to be open to the idea of mutually enriching developments. Community schools are ideally placed to develop on these lines.

A possible pilot program

We propose that meetings are set up between representatives of Education, including the careers service, employers, employment agencies plus the MSC Local Training Boards and trade unions, to see whether we can achieve agreement on objectives and begin to take action. In the meantime, a 'pre-pilot scheme', with some funding from the MSC and Industry, could begin this September. The time is ripe and the need for action urgent. Cranford is willing to test out these ideas in a pre-pilot.

Why Cranford?

Cranford already has a well established Community Studies course. All year ten and eleven students do voluntary work in the community and work experience through project Trident and the careers service. Cranford is a community school very near Heathrow with excellent links with the local community and active links with many world class businesses.

A new 'school to work' course is already planned to start in September (1981.)
It comprises

- It comprises three days work experience and two days life, social and basic skills
- Work experience in a variety of settings
- A basic clerical skill course
- A new technologies course
- Existing staff positive, motivated and exceptionally skilled
- Commitment of British Airways to be a full partner agreed
- Further support and advice from the Air Transport and Traffic Training Board

The actual pilot course went ahead at Cranford

In the first year pilot 81-82, there were eighteen students of mixed race, gender and ability who worked mostly in two groups. There was a two week induction course. This was followed by five weeks of work experience and a one week outward bound course. The pattern was repeated with one group in for six weeks and one group out. The 'in school' curriculum covered communication skills, social and life skills, numeracy, literacy, social, economic and environmental studies, vocational studies, individual and group guidance and counselling. The work experience at British Airways was mainly manual and clerical, but with some catering and welfare. They also followed the City and Guilds 365 course successfully.

BTEC and BEC

In the second year 82-83, we added a BEC course in conjunction with our local FE College and a City and Guilds engineering course. In 83-84, we added a TEC course (science) and a City and Guilds Retail and Distribution course. The teaching staff also became off-the-job trainers for a new training initiative managed by BA!

These students taking part were not ready for work at the beginning of the course. They could have done O-level repeats, but not necessarily successfully. By the end of their school-to-work course they had matured beyond recognition and were confident and ready to take on the responsibility of a real job. We thought this was much better for them and so did they! The teaching staff also learnt a great deal and much appreciated the new skills and knowledge they had gained from this experience.

COMMENT

I don't recall getting a reply to this proposal or to getting any extra funding from Hounslow, but we were allowed to go ahead. A brilliant and appropriately skilled existing staff member took charge. British Airways provided a range of excellent, varied work placements, and two graduate trainees at British Airways looked after the students when they were working at BA. The MSC gave us a small grant towards extras, such as an Outward Bound Course. By 1987 we had established and delivered a highly successful course. The BBC made a film about it which was televised. The trainees all did well after they had left.

In my book *Counselling Adolescents in School and After*, a second updated and extended edition of the original counselling book, was published by Kogan Page in 1984. Chapter 8 describes the course in detail and Chapter 9 the students' reactions to it. Hounslow did NOT take the idea on across the Borough. One reason that it worked was through the calibre of the staff running it, the positive ethos of the school, plus the mature and responsible behaviour of the students.

Anne Jones, Chairman of the West London Area Manpower Board shows Richard Branson a Community Programme Project

Postscript

But the good news is that it does sound like the present coalition government is about to do something very like this across the country. Announcements about traineeships and apprenticeships propose a similar model to ours. Let us hope that they continue after the next election.

The Manpower Services Commission: I should add at this point that from 1983-1987, I was Chairman of the West London Area Manpower Board for the Manpower Services Commission. The Board consisted of representatives of education, employers and the trade unions. It was very satisfying to bring this Triumvirate into constructive harmony and also to check the progress of NTI and other local initiatives. Little did I know then that would be joining the MSC full time in 1987.

Community schools and the New Training Initiative 1987

I wrote this as I was about to leave for my new job as a Director, of the Manpower Services Commission, a Senior Civil Servant post as an Under-Secretary in the Employment Department. The article was published in Transition *in November 1987. I still wanted the idea of community school to go forward, and I still do now!*

Since the New Training Initiative was launched, as long ago now as 1981,there has been growing recognition of the importance of linking education and training, of offering continuing education and training to adults, and of connecting the work of secondary schools more closely to the world of work.

The economic imperative is written clearly on the wall: we need to invest in education and training at all ages and stages if our supply of man and woman power is to be adequate in quality and qualifications to meet our economic needs for survival, let alone growth on an international scale.

A further part of this growing recognition concerns the education sector and in particular the work of schools. The argument run thus: the process needs to begin at school and continue throughout people's lives, in short, a lifelong process from cradle to the grave. How to achieve this? Various policies and strategies have been thought up, but one obvious one has been almost totally overlooked, namely the potential of the community school or college for helping to implement these very important aims and objectives. Community colleges are not a new idea, yet their potential does not seem to have been recognised on a national scale.

The reasons for this are twofold. The concepts behind the idea of community schools challenge many traditional assumptions about the nature of learning. They are not easy to grasp, they are sometimes uncomfortable to absorb and therefore easy to dismiss. Community school were, in original concept, ahead of their time, an obvious vehicle for implementing NTI objectives before they were even articulated. Because they were ahead of their time, many community schools have now become caught, like so many traditional aspects of education, in a time warp of their own creation, on a model which itself needs a radical rethink in the light of current needs and concerns.

The original community colleges, dreamt up and created by Henry Morris in the 1920s in Cambridgeshire, embodied the notion that schools should be the focal point for further and continuing learning opportunities for the whole local community, regardless of age. Later, other LEAs, such as Leicestershire, Nottinghamshire and Coventry, followed suite. Today, over the whole country there is a patchy, but nevertheless persistent provision of community schools. In some areas, there is a coherent LEA policy for all secondary schools, in others a series of one-offs. Currently many LEAs are thinking through the idea, but waiting to decide when they know how other national initiatives are going to work out, for example 16-plus education, that is both 16-19 and 19-plus.

What is a community school or college? What are the ideas behind them which make them worth considering so seriously at this moment in time? Their advantages are considerable and some should particularly please those who seek value for money and economic use of resources.

The first argument is economic, a telling one at the moment, to do with rational and economic use of plant, buildings, teachers, learning resources of all kinds. Traditional school are closed between 4 pm and 9 am and for eleven weeks of the school year. A community college, unlike a school, is always open. Community schools are open the whole year, day and evening. Mine was open 7am-11pm!

The second argument is to do with making schools more realistic, more in touch with the demands of real life and the world of work. Teachers in community schools have the opportunity of teaching adult as well as pupils. This can have a significant effect on teaching and learning styles, as well as the economic and flexible use of precious teacher hours. The secondary pupils benefit too. They are no longer closeted in 'adolescent ghettos'. Both pupils and teachers have more contact with adult life and the world of work and are thus better prepared for preparing students for both.

The third argument concerns the role of the school or college as a learning resource for the whole community, responsive to local needs, with an important role of bringing a sense of dignity and pride, of membership and mutual support to that community through providing learning opportunities for a wide range of people of all ages. Growth rather than decay, development rather than destruction, hope rather than despair. These arguments, put together sound compelling, economic good sense, investment in human resource development, a sense of community and self-help, so, why has the idea not been taken on more widely?

First, community colleges themselves have not recognised and articulated their potential in terms of current national needs. Too many are working on an outdated model which could easily, without much extra cost, be transformed into something totally apposite for tomorrow's world. Second, the government, teachers and the public at large often think of schools in a very narrow way as 'providers of pure education' (whatever that may mean) and a useful childminding service. In the past vocational education and training has been conceived as separate from secondary education, as something which should come later and preferably as far away as possible from schools. This situation is now changing, particularly with the advent of TVEI, but nevertheless the concept of prevocational education, in its best generic sense, is ill-understood both within and without the education system.

Not only that, many community schools are themselves prisoners of their own former good practice. Too often adult education is totally separate from the school in which it is housed. Furthermore, it may be trapped in a 'leisure and crafts' mould which, worthy as it is, does not help to equip adults with more marketable skills, confidence, new expertise or new job prospects.

What can community schools do to help implement the NTI? Here are some examples of what we have done at Cranford Community School in Hounslow, west London under my leadership when I was Head there, 1981-7.

On our eleven acre site we managed to include all of the following:

- A fully fledged and high achieving 11-18 Comprehensive School with ever improving academic success
- Extensive provision of adult education and training
- Sports and recreation facilities: Eleven acres of sports fields, squash courts, tennis, gymnasium and weight lifting
- Youth Club and other youth activities
- A creche and a playgroup
- A 'Pub' (Bar and Lounge). I was the Licensee!
- Old people's Club and chiropodist
- Open from 7am to 11pm, fifty-two weeks a year
- Off-the job training for Youth Training Schemes
- Adult training courses, mainly for women returners and ethnic minorities
- A Community Programme which provides a print shop
- Off the job training for the new JTS scheme
- Managing Agent for all the off-the-job training in the area
- A locally supported self-study agency
- Access courses for the Open University
- Developing Open Learning Systems as far as resources allowed
- Tailor-made courses for local employers
- Employer participation in our three week work experience scheme for all pupils.
- A Curriculum for all the pupils which includes economic awareness, computer literacy, information technology, enterprise, science and technology for all until age sixteen.

We also earned quite a lot of money from these various activities. That meant that we could buy at least five extra teachers, which benefitted the pupils enormously. I believe that the pupils' learning was also enriched by the fact that our teachers understood the context in which they were working, the local and national labour market needs and the value of a curriculum which was broad, balanced, coherent and relevant. At the same time we still catered for more traditional clubs and classes. Interestingly the academic success of our comprehensive pupils improved by leaps and bounds.

It was not ever thus. In order to turn ourselves from a 'traditional' community school, we had to look at ourselves differently. This change in our self-perception and attitude was itself significant in bringing about the developments which occurred between 1981 and 1987. We began by working on our location. We no longer saw ourselves as an outpost of an outer London Borough. We were at the centre of a world market, namely the busy international business community which surrounds Heathrow Airport. We no longer offered a set program to a reluctant local community; we found out what was needed, we negotiated according to the needs and requirements of the learners. We responded to requests from local industry, we put on courses at very short notice for people when they needed them and at times which suited them.

Anne Jones, Cranford Community School and Tony Shillington HR Director Hoechst UK, finalising their programme of joint education industry activities

We became more flexible in our use of staffing, yet at the same time found that we used our staffing more fully, never a wasted hour, the kind of tight–loose properties encouraged by Peters and Waterman (*In search of Excellence*, Harper and Row). We made great demands on our staff and at the same time build their self-respect, and their skills. We expected our staff to understand the world of work, be capable of teaching adults, to deliver their program with rigour as well as energy. We supported our staff by providing for their in-service training, work experience with local employers, work-shadowing and better resources for learning, which we were able to buy from the money generated by the extra classes we put on. The net result has been that, not only the school community but also the school pupils themselves have benefitted. We have also attracted a lot of outstanding staff to apply for jobs at Cranford, as the word got around that it was a stimulating demanding, rewarding place to work.

Our philosophy is simple: striving for excellence, collaborative learning, learning aims and objectives negotiated with students. We view learning as a lifelong process and coming best from experience and reflecting on that experience. We particularly stress mutual respect and the importance of valuing each person's contribution to the whole. We have built up the adult education and training to the extent that there are now more adult part-time day and evening students, than our 1,200 full time pupils. Including the sports and club users as well as the pupils, students and trainees, upwards of 6000 people, use the school each week. What is also remarkable about this is the fact that the various client groups blend harmoniously at the same time as keeping their own identity. And the pupils themselves are not fazed by all this, neither are they any trouble. We are a harmonious multiracial community of all age and stages of development.

At Cranford, we took the concept of traditional adult education and extended it from the concept of 'leisure-time occupation' to the idea of opening up for students' new horizons, giving them a better chance in life. Many of our adults' courses are now designed for adults who are unemployed, under-employed, under-qualified or qualified inappropriately. Such students are prepared to travel to reach us and their pride in their achievements is gratifying as well as useful. The fact that we provide a crèche has been immensely important in opening up access to women returners in particular.

What are the implications of this kind of development nationally? It is tempting for employers to think of adult education and training as best provided at the work place, through training agencies or college of

Further Education. Yet at the same time there is general concern about the problems of the inner-city, about the breakdown of local communities, about economic use of expensive resources, about flexible and localised training and retraining opportunities for adults, all of which problems the community college can help to overcome. There is room for many models. The advantage of the community college idea is that it can provide a truly local response, economically and flexibly at the same time as enriching the way that school pupil learn and behave, Then the objectives of 'Better Schools' as well as those of the NTI are met simultaneously. The employers who have worked with us at Cranford, notably British Airways, Hoecht, United Biscuits, Thorne EMI, Beechams and IBM, have been both surprised and thrilled at what they have found. If we are eventually to build a coordinated system of education and training for people over the age of eighteen, it is certainly worth considering and using the contribution that community schools can make to this process.

Postscript

Unfortunately community schools, even adult education classes, declined later over the years and schools concentrated on exam results and league tables. Adults and schools lost out. But, wonder of wonders, the coordinated system of education and training I had visualised could be about to happen again. The coalition government is reintroducing the idea of of traineeships for some 14-18 year-olds followed by apprenticeships, largely designed by specific businesses or trades. Let us hope that this movement survives after the next election. But yet more joy: this is not a question of either training or education. English and maths continues until students have reached a high standard. We could be back to the future with ideas conceptualised in the 1990s.

It was during the Blair era, under the Banner of Education Education - Education, that the School-to-Work measures introduced by the Conservative party gradually faded, without the standards of education improving as much as expected as we now know. More of this later!

Networking, influencing and learning

I was lucky to be invited to join many prestigious groups of thinkers over the years: for example with business leaders and senior civil servants with the aim of promoting better mutual understanding between them This was before I became a civil servant myself! It meant that I was learning all the time and I was sharing my ideas with people who might even take some notice of what I said. A seriously enjoyable experience was the conferences held in Windsor Castle.

Weekend conferences at St George's House Windsor

These were really serious discussions on a range of practical topics, with attendance by distinguished relevant experts. We were housed inside the Castle grounds, and attended Sunday morning service in the Chapel, where many English Kings are buried: a strange feeling to look down on their graves as we sang hymns. It was both stimulating and refreshing to take part in such events. And a great privilege to be in such historic surroundings.

Princess Diana

I was privileged to meet Princess Diana once only, at a very worthy cause. She had invited a large group of distinguished women to lunch in Malborough House, to help support and to raise money for the National Rubella Council and to celebrate the World Health Day, She spoke to each of us and later we each received a lovely photo of the attendees. Unfortunately she herself was not in the photo. She did a superb job for this excellent cause.

Prince Charles

The first time I met Prince Charles was at London Airport. I was meeting him with reference to my capacity as Chairman of the West London Area Manpower Board. On the evening before, I had been a panel Member on BBC *Question Time.* The other members of the Panel were Ken Clarke, Tony Benn and David Steele.

Prince Charles arrived and I was preparing to curtsy, when he suddenly said: 'I saw you on the telly'. As it happened, someone took a photo as he was saying this, one of my treasures. He then proceeded to discuss the content of the program and was very interested in the discussion about drugs. I was a member of the Advisory Council on the Misuse of Drugs at that time, so I did know something about the topic. That didn't stop me saying I had three points to make and then forgetting the third point! I was still a Headmistress at this stage.

Meeting Prince Charles the morning after appearing on BBC Question Time

The second time was dinner at his country home, Highgrove, in December 1979. This time the topic was the serious decrease in the numbers of pupils in secondary schools learning modern languages. There were eight of us at table and I guess I was asked because I was a senior civil servant who had also been a French teacher and who now was responsible for TVEI, which was impacting on the National Curriculum. We had an excellent discussion and also a delicious meal.

HRH was a wonderful host. He was very proud of the fact that all the food came from his garden: lamb, new potatoes, beans, peas and raspberries. He shared our concerns about languages and I believe he spoke at a CBI conference about it later, as indeed I also did at a conference run by the Association for Language Learning. We came up with some first rate ideas, but I never heard what happened next. Not surprising, there is currently great concern in the UK still on the same topic. In 2015, the coalition is taking steps to change the situation as fast as possible. In 2001, 29% of secondary education pupils were learning modern languages. In 2010, the number went up to 43%. In 2015 it is 43% and rising. Financial Incentives that is Bursaries, to get languages graduates to teach are also in operation.

Queen Mary, University of London

In the eighties many London university colleges amalgamated, particularly if they were small and not really sustainable. Women's colleges were particularly vulnerable: They were generally turning co-ed, even in Oxford and Cambridge. Westfield, based in Hampstead, went co-ed in 1964 and had long since set up a Science block. After long negotiations, Westfield finally joined with Queen Mary College in the East End on the Mile End Road, which itself was and is famous for its street markets and its former Music Hall, the People's Palace which is part of the Queen Mary site. The Palace was restored to its `former glory in 2006. In 2014 the magnificent organ was also restored and relaunched.The Palace and the organ open for both college and public events.

Before Westfield and Queen Mary amalgamated, the contrast between the two sites was striking. Westfield was small, mainly residential with a lovely central house plus a chapel and beautiful gardens. It was established by a small group of women in 1882. Over time the college had also bought up many large houses in this leafy and up-market area, not far from Hampstead Heath. In my day, the fifties, with only 250 students, we could all live in. Later when it expanded, this was not possible. But it was an elegant calm place to study.

Queen Mary, by contrast was in a very tough multi-cultural area. The college had limited space and was non-residential. When I was a student, I went there once to a Saturday 'Hop' as we used to call a Dance. The atmosphere was a total contrast to Westfield and the area a little rough and scary.

In 1992, I was absolutely thrilled to hear that Queen Mary had decided to make me a Fellow, which is their equivalent of an honorary degree. I have a stunning gold orange and blue gown which, alas, I now hardy ever have occasion to wear! I was very pleased that my mother was able to come to the presentation event. I was also pleased that my former Spanish Lecturer John Varey had become the last Principal of Westfield. He was crucial in leading the amalgamation which finally took place in 1989. Alas he died in 1994. He had been very wise and diligent in guiding Westfield to join QM.

With my mother and senior staff at the Fellowship ceremony

From 1992, I became more and more involved with the college. I was a member of Council and served two terms of office, 1992-2002. I was also asked to Chair the Career Committee. Later I became a member of the new Principal Adrian Smith's Strategy Committee. He is now (2014) the Vice Chancellor of the University of London.

I was also a member of the Westfield Trust from 1992 until it was wound up in 2009. The Trust did a marvellous job with the Westfield money. Some of the Westfield site was sold to King's College London, the Westfield site was worth millions, and we spent the money very carefully over a long period. We built a crèche/nursery for staff and students' use, a flat for visiting academics, a garden in a derelict courtyard, bought a new organ, funded new curriculum developments, set up scholarships for students, bought pictures and funded sculpture for the grounds, everything to help make the college more aesthetically pleasing and welcoming. We were in fact adding a feminine touch to the rather harsh bare atmosphere.

In the meantime, from 1992 onwards, the college was transformed on all counts. Student numbers and quality were high, brilliant new Professors were recruited, the research ratings went up and up and the college joined the Russell group, a small cluster of the very top University of London Colleges, no mean achievement. New money and land was acquired and new department blocks built. And best of all, the Westfield Village was built on the land between the college and the canal.

Princess Anne, who succeeded her grandmother Elizabeth the Queen Mother as Chancellor of the University of London, came to open the buildings in 2004. There were 2000 student rooms with en suites. Westfield has left its mark on this thriving academic community. Once again residential areas, huge this time, in a buzzy area, yet also very close to the City, and named the Westfield village. What a brilliant combination. Westfield will not be forgotten. QM was called Queen Mary and Westfield College when we first amalgamated. By the time the two colleges were well and truly joined together, we were very happy to become Queen Mary, University of London.

University College London

I was also a Council member of university College London from 1977-81. When you visit it is always strange to see Jeremy Bentham on display. Their Principal then was a delightfully eccentric man, who swam around the island battling again the tides and measuring their strength. The college was highly academic and very successful then and now.

The Secondary Heads Association

I joined this when I became a Head and rapidly became a Council Member and Member of the Executive Committee from 1979-87. It was a very worthwhile organisation and very useful, because it meant that you always kept up with what was happening in Education in general and also in government policies and important research. It was also good to meet a lot of other Heads, exchange views, have a laugh or discuss a problem.

In 1983 a small group of us wrote a short paper called *A View from the Bridge*. It was an attempt to say what SHA thought the curriculum should be and why. It was also only two sides of A4 for clarity and ease of recall, though admittedly it was in very small print! When I became a civil servant, I learnt that Ministers and Businessmen would never read anything longer than one side of A4. Wish I'd have known that sooner! In 1983, The Schools Council then invited me to talk at their September conference in Leeds on the 14-18 curriculum.

Surprisingly our Head colleagues liked *A View from the Bridge*. Hopefully, it helped clarify their own ideas, even if they didn't always agree with it. In 1987, we wrote a second paper called Future Imperative, a view of 14-18 and beyond. It put the case very strongly for a coordinated system of education and training which begins at fourteen and continues to eighteen and beyond an also a coordinated system of Education and training for people over the ages of eighteen. The coalition government seems to be developing ideas rather like this again at last!

I had agreed to stand for SHA Chairman before Christmas 1986 and before the job advert and interviews for the MSC job had come out. At our Easter conference in 1987, I was duly elected National Chairman of the SHA. This was very embarrassing. By then I had had the interview for the MSC post, but I had no idea whether I had got it and apparently there were 500 candidates so I was not allowed by government to tell anybody that I had even been a candidate. The press were hounding me for an answer, but answer was there none. Worse than that, the process of checking my credentials and clearance by MI5 took a long time, so I was not allowed to mention it to my staff at my school either.

Leaving Cranford

Finally, one evening, I heard the amazing news. It was going to be announced in the Press the next day, so I would be able to tell the staff then. The next morning at 4am the phone rang. It was the School

Caretaker. 'Sorry to bother you Mrs Jones, but the school is on fire!' I drove rapidly to school, put on the wellington boots I kept in the boot of the car and walked in. It was not a hoax!

The fire was soon put under control. The damage could have been worse but it was still very disturbing especially as some of the students lost their practical GCSE work which was stored in the damaged building. We sent all the children home and the staff all gathered in the dining room. When they were all there, I went in. After agreeing the next action steps for the school, I announced that I was leaving at Easter, and why. I had no choice because it was going to be all over the papers the next day. I felt terrible. What a way to go!

I was very sad to leave, I had been very happy there and I really loved the school, the staff, and the students. I felt very proud of them and also of the great progress we had made together over my six years there. It had been a joy to work with such a talented staff. I also felt very sad and guilty to have to give up being Chairman of the Secondary Heads Association and at short notice. I consoled myself a little, since it sounded as if I was going to be able to influence policy and some of the changes SHA had been seeking.

But of course it is not as simple as that: Ministers decide civil servants just carry out their wishes... Well, it's not exactly as simple as that either. I was fortunate to be able in my time as a civil servant to initiate and implement a whole series of initiatives which still fitted my beliefs. As you will see in the next chapter!

CHAPTER 5: FROM HEADTEACHER TO UNDER-SECRETARY 1987-1991

Innovation and implementation

WHEN I GOT THE JOB, I didn't know just how senior it was. If I had, I would have been even more terrified. Now, looking back over my various writings as a Head, I see no clash between my ideas and beliefs and the job I was now being asked to do. All the ideas I had been promulgating were my genuine ideas and beliefs. Yet they fitted perfectly with the new job. This was very important for me. I have always worked passionately and whole-heartedly for what I believe in. I would not take a job which compromised my beliefs.

Nevertheless, it was quite a shock to be appointed to a post as an Under-Secretary straight from being a Head. I hadn't the slightest idea of the hierarchy of the various posts in advance. I soon found out when I got there! What I did know was that it was an organisation which was aiming to do what I believed in and that I had been working hard to implement for years. The match was perfect. The school-to-work courses I had initiated both at Vauxhall Manor and at Cranford had caught the attention of the MSC. They invited me to join a group which wrote two important and useful booklets: *Making Experience Work*, 1979 and *Opportunities for Girls and Women*, 1980. I spoke at several conferences on the New Training Initiative in 1981. In 1983, I was made Chairman of the West London Area Manpower Board. The Board had a tripartite membership, like the MSC itself, with representatives from Education, Business and trade unions. We became a very constructive body which worked together well. From this, I learnt a lot about the way the Manpower Services Commission worked.

The MSC was a non-departmental body of the Department of Employment with the role of coordinating employment and training schemes in the UK. It was part of, yet a separate body, from the main Employment Department, with responsibility for getting the bodies represented by the ten Commissioners (industry, trade unions, education and local authorities) to work together.

My initial appointment was as one of the eight Directors of this organisation. The MSC was staffed by civil servants, but we had quite lot of freedom of manoeuvre, something which appeared at times to annoy the main Department. I was the Director of Education Programmes, which at that stage consisted only of one progamme, the new high profile TVEI initiative, which had started as a pilot in 1983, plus some Further Education work-related funding. After I took up my post in 1987, TVEI was extended to become a ten year project with a budget of £1 billion. This is when I came in!

However, there were some snags about taking up my post. I was to work mainly in Sheffield at Moorfoot, which is where the MSC offices were. I was asked to live in Sheffield. However, I also had a central London Office. So I kept my London flat. First I rented a flat in Sheffield, and then bought my own. But in fact I was up and down to Sheffield or vice versa like a yo-yo. The worst thing was if you were seeing the Secretary of State or a Minister: The 07.20 train from Sheffield got you to Whitehall just in time for a 9.30 meeting. Later we started doing occasional videophoning.

In fact, I travelled all over the country all the time, visiting TVEI and other projects in England Wales and Scotland, often for a meeting, or a conference, dinner and a speech to deliver. So basically, it was a working life, with little or no time for recreation. I was used to working every evening. That part was just like being a Head, but with more travel and fewer holidays. However there were some advantages, I loved the Derbyshire countryside: wonderful hill walks and scenery, delightful pubs, and some good friends to see, weekends only.

There was one other snag. No longer was I allowed to be on *Question Time* or have a regular column in *The Guardian*, or write articles telling government what I thought they should do about education. I was particularly sorry about losing *Question Time*. The last time I did it, with Tony Benn, Ken Clarke David Steele was particularly successful. Unknown to me, later, the Producer, Barbara Maxwell, had followed my boss to a CBI conference to ask if an exception could be made in my case. NO came the answer: civil servants are not allowed to broadcast their views or appear to be competing with their Minister or Secretary of State. So yes Minister! What a pity! That was the end of my Media Career. Just like that!

The culture of the organisation was very male and there was only one other female Grade 3 Director in Sheffield at that time. The language was quite masculine: cricket terms like 'close of play' were frequent. The first time I attended a Commission meeting, I arrived early. A Commissioner arrived and asked me to get him a set of papers. I said 'My PA will be here soon and HE will find you some'. I smiled and took my named seat.

When I began work in Sheffield, my first big speech was the School Council Conference, held in Leeds on The Whole Curriculum: 14-19 provision. This is exactly the same conference that I spoke at in 1983, when the title was Curriculum14-19: Integration and Differentiation!

I was anxious, not only because it was my first MSC speech, but also because teachers were at that moment very hostile to the new National curriculum. AND very unsure about TVEI, not only as a concept, but also because they could not see how it would fit or could be used within the national curriculum framework. I was expecting some very difficult questions. In the event it went very well.

I wrote my speech myself. Later on most of my speeches were written for me, and sometimes given to me to read out, practically at the last minute. This is the normal process. I found this quite difficult at times and eventually learnt how to liven them up without straying too much from the given text. However, I haven't included any such texts in this book. So for my first MSC speech READ ON!

Schools Council Conference Leeds September 25 1987 THE WHOLE CURRICULUM 14-19 PROVISION

Paper by Anne Jones, Director of Education Programmes, MSC
It is certainly difficult to follow three such outstanding speakers, and I do so with some trepidation, partly because this is my first public appearance in my new role. First, let me say how pleased I am to be

with so many old friends and colleagues. It is extraordinary to recall that I gave a paper on the 14-18 curriculum at the Schools Council Conference here four years ago: may I make it clear that any link between my appearance and the future of SCDC is purely coincidental!

As Director of Education Programmes for the MSC with a remit to be the 'bridge' between education and training at school. Further and higher education levels, my job is to help to see that as a nation, we have a supply of well-educated and trained man and woman power. Note the stress on **educated**. It is more and more apparent that our workforce needs continuous opportunities for continuing education and training throughout life. Education and training needs to be recognised and rewarded by the provision of a system of educational and vocational qualifications which starts at fourteen, and which student-trainees can build up, over their life time, module by module, to suit both their own needs for personal satisfaction, and their own job satisfaction and prospects in the market place.

This need for continuing education and training is no longer a frill, no longer the idealistic vision of a minority. It is an economic imperative if this country is to survive in the world economy. We have a mere 12-14% of our young people in higher education, and if we look at the Handy Report on the Making of Managers, we find that too many of this country's managers left the education system young, straight after school, and have had relatively little higher education or management training. The pool of ability which the Robbins Report talked about in the 60s (he postulated a higher education entry of 20%) is still largely untapped, particularly if we add to the diminishing cohort of 16-19 year-olds all those people who were denied access to higher education when they were that age: those who missed out the first time around, especially women, ethnic minorities, the handicapped, those with special needs, and those who were educated and trained inappropriately. With the changes now taking place on the nature of work and in the kinds of qualities and skills needed at work, it seems probably that most people will need further opportunities for education and training throughout their lives.

Particularly important is the building up of each individual's dossier of qualifications: they need to include personal development, and validation of experience both on and off the job, as well as appropriate tests and examinations. Investing in Human Resource Development is crucial to the future economic survival of Great Britain. It is the major untapped resource which we have left. Therefore the role of the teacher in the future is going to become more important than ever. With the advent of open and distanced learning systems that role will change, but it is vital to the nation's success.

With all the current debate about the National Curriculum, it is easy to forget that the government has already put out a White Paper on this subject: 'Working Together', July 1986, jointly signed by the Secretaries of State for the Department of Employment, the DES (supported by Scotland and Wales), the Department of Trade and Industry and the Paymaster General, clearly set an agenda based on the following objectives:

- greater opportunities in vocational education and training and better qualities at all levels
- greater responsiveness to labour market needs
- a greater variety of learning environments
- access to vocational education and training which starts in schools and continues throughout working life
- recognition of competencies and achievements
- a structure of recognised qualifications
- a good quality supply of vocational education and training;
- value for money;
- a system which employers and employees understand, respect and use to the full, with a major increase in their investment in training.

What, may you ask, has all this to do with the whole school curriculum and in particular 14-19 provision? A very great deal! It is too easy to think of 14-19 as an adjunct to the original 5-14 curriculum, instead of thinking of it as the first stepping stone in the agenda for 'working together' which I have just recalled, and which specifically states that access to vocational education and training starts in the schools and continues throughout life. It is very easy within the education system to lose sight of what it is all for, to become engrossed with the finer points of educational academic debate, to work within a closed rather than an open system, disregard the contexts of learning and its long-term purposes. Making the connections between education and adult and working life makes education in its purest sense more vital, more enjoyable and more obviously useful to its consumers.

The Technical and Vocational Education Initiative, which began in 1983 and for which I am soon to be responsible, was set up specifically to help the Education service make exactly these connections. Its brief was and is to help find ways of organising and managing the education of 14-18 year-olds in order to:

- seek qualifications/skills which will be of direct value to them at work
- become better-equipped to enter the world of employment
- more directly appreciate the practical applications of their qualifications
- use skills and knowledge to solve real world problems
- develop initiative, motivation, enterprise problem solving skills and aspects of personal development
- cross the bridge between education and training, schools, further education and higher education by direct contact with local employers (for example through work experience).
- learn through collaboration at local level between LEAs, industry and the public sector

The extension of TVEI, announced in 1986 in *Working Together*, both underlines the importance of this agenda, and the importance of providing criteria, resources, teacher support and training for managing the far reaching changes in teaching and learning styles that these developments bring in their wake. I am pleased to announce that every LEA in the country is now engaged in bidding to join in the TVEI scheme, including, may I add, this very city Leeds, which only two days ago took the decision to make such a bid. The effectiveness of TVEI, I would submit, comes from the fact that it does not have a purely or solely educational base. I will elaborate that point later.

The kinds of skills that the TVEI initiative is trying to develop in pupils are not exclusive to TVEI. Such skills as the ability to analyse and evaluate, to think critically, to solve problems, to find and organise information, to synthesise, to transfer knowledge and use it in different contexts, to think creatively, to make decisions, and to communicate effectively and clearly that these are not the prerogative of TVEI, but essential parts of any effective school curriculum, a kind of woof against which the weft of the various subjects fits to make a 'whole curriculum.'

It is for that reason that the National Curriculum does not present the kind of insuperable barrier or obstacle to the objectives of TVEI, which I know is something many of you here fear. The document itself acknowledges both the need for many of the learning objectives I have already identified to go across the whole curriculum. It also acknowledges the role that TVEI will have in 'helping LEAs in the development and the establishment of the National Curriculum particularly in the areas of science and technology and also in enhancing the curriculum's relevance to adult and working life'.

I am pleased to note that the new red book also takes pains to stress, very many times, the importance of formative assessment, the need for schools to have flexibility about the ways they organise their teaching, the need for 'space to accommodate the enterprise of teachers', for teachers to have the flexibility to adapt what they teach to the needs of the individual pupil, to try out and develop new approaches, and to develop in pupils their personal qualities. Paragraph sixty-eight states that the role of the working groups will be 'to ensure that the context and teaching of their subject brings out its relevance to and links with the pupils own experience and practical applications; and that the program of work contribute to the development in young people of personal qualities and competence, such as self-reliance, self-discipline, an enterprising approach and the ability to solve practical real world problems'.

For many schools, the National Curriculum merely affirms what they are already doing: for example, the school where I was Head until recently, has a large common core already, including integrated science, integrated humanities, technology and expressive arts, all to age sixteen for all pupils. We had already worked out the importance of the entitlement curriculum, particularly in respect of equal opportunities connected with gender and race. Very many schools have done the same.

However the effectiveness of the National Curriculum, particularly in terms of its relevance and significance in relationship to adult and working life, will depend not so much on the overall framework but in the way the learning objectives and criteria for each subject area are defined.

Ultimately the effectiveness of the whole curriculum depends upon the ability of the professional teachers to use their creativity, imagination and ingenuity to match overarching goals of the framework to local contexts and individual learning needs. The success or otherwise of the National Curriculum depends totally on the skill of the teaching profession.

This is of course where TVEI comes in again. The contribution of the MSC's TVEI unit to staff development and the management of change in the 14-18 curriculum is now generally acknowledged to be both substantial and helpful. Furthermore, TVEI spans the 14-18 curriculum, whereas HMI curriculum papers, as well as the National Curriculum, do not: their remit is 5-16. This watching brief over the learning programs of 14-18 year-olds, is very important, particularly in terms of ensuring progression, continuity and coherence. It is all the more important since in many local authorities organisational solutions to the 14-18 curriculum have made a break at sixteen more common. It would be good in the long-term to try to find solutions to these problems of transition which were learner centred rather than institution centred.

Not only does TVEI span 14-18. Its second strength is that it is Department of Employment/MSC based, yet retains the strongest possible links with the DES, HMI, LEAs, and indeed with the DTI. It therefore brings with it not only a background of understanding labour market needs in their broadest interpretation, but real experience of vocational education and training throughout links with employers. This interface between the world of employment and education is vital if we are to begin to overcome the divide between education and training and between the academic and the vocational.

Third, TVEI has now developed a system of delivery which effectively combines the systems management skills of civil servants with responsiveness and sensitivity to the needs of teachers and pupils. Though most LEAs did not welcome TVEI initially, it is now the case that not only do they all want to join in; most now appreciate the impetus TVEI has given to genuine curriculum development particularly in the management of change, the provision of effective in-service training and the development of new teaching and learning styles.

Fourth, TVEI has done much to promote cooperative working between institutions, and this is particularly significant in terms of 16-18 provision. TVEI has been encouraging the development and use of open learning systems and self-supported study. It has also been encouraging the development of a modular curriculum, not only in the 14-16 age range but also in A-level courses where the importance of work experience, residential experience and personal development is also recognised.

I would therefore submit that the TVEI experience

- might encourage and hearten those of you who now have doubts about the National Curriculum;
- might be very helpful in the implementation of the National Curriculum in a way which is consistent with the aims of *Working Together*, and indeed much recent educational thinking.

In conclusion, 14-19 needs to be seen not as an end, nor even as an end in itself, but as a beginning, the first phase in a lifelong period of education and training. We need to inspire our young people to want to go on learning all their lives, and to build up their own bank of credits and qualifications. We need to be less concerned about institutions and more concerned about the quality of young people's learning. We need to encourage more young people and older people to go on to higher education and we need to make alternative conditions of access for those who missed out on qualifications the first time around. We need to include in our thinking the possibility of developing more community colleges, where adults could retrain and relearn as well as young people. We need to ensure that the school curriculum, by whatever name, really does make that link between education and adult and working life in the fullest sense of those words.

Postscript

This lecture resonates with the kind of thinking the coalition government is promoting now, twenty-seven years later, The Education Roundabout is still turning! I survived my first talk in my new job and I wrote my own speech! Later someone usually wrote them for me. In my view, reading a text doesn't communicate as well as speaking.

Imtec International Conference
Aspen Colorado USA October 4-6 1988
School Year 20:20 New Schools

Amongst others, my Directorate undertook to sponsor and promote this huge conference. It was amazing. Our task was to prepare ourselves for the future. 2020 seemed a long way ahead then and our 20:20 vision a bit blurred. But we all had a great time and came home very inspired. I was one of the keynote speakers on the first day. I had managed to get to the Grand Canyon on the way over. Waiting for a change of plane, I became completely absorbed by the book I was reading and missed my plane. I had to stay over and the next day the only available plane got me to Aspen less than an hour before my speech. I just about made it to the platform on time. However the speech went very well, because my title was Under-Secretary, many Americans thought I was a senior politician with lots of money to throw around, so I was much sought after! No, sorry folks!

An International Vision for the Future of Education

I am both delighted and honoured to be here. A risk taker like me can resist anything except temptation and this conference was an overwhelming temptation. We do all need a vision for 20:20 which, however imperfect, will inspire and steer our future actions. I speak now as an Under-Secretary in the UK Department of Employment. My title is Director of Education Programmes and my main responsibility is to ensure that the Education sector and the Employment sector work closely together at all levels: schools, further education, higher education, adult and continuing education. I am responsible for a key set of programs, all designed to connect Education and the world of work. Currently I am responsible for a budget of £300 million... and growing. Our government is taking this question very seriously.

I speak also as the former Head-teacher – you would say Principal – of two inner-city multi-racial secondary schools and in particular, as the former Head of a community school which was actively involved in the education and training of young people and adults, with over

Under-Secretary the Department of Employment, UK

1,200 pupils and some 700 adults passing through each week.

In addition, I was also a pioneer of the guidance and counselling system in British schools and in 1965 became its first school counsellor. And finally I speak as a practising theoretician on school leadership and the management of change. My recent book *Leadership for Tomorrow's Schools* (published Blackwell's Oxford 1997) sums up my research and my vision on this.

I now have a dauntingly key role in the UK government, I am in a position to influence the education system and in particular to get it to adapt to the future. At the moment, too much of the education system in the UK is, as elsewhere, on what I call the dinosaur model. My message to the education world is stark: dinosaurs are out. It is time to adapt or die.

On my way through Phoenix, I happened to pick up a copy of the latest Tom Peter's book. *Thriving On Chaos, Handbook for a Management Revolution* (Knopf, 1987). In it, I found a wonderful quotation from Barbara Tuchman. She identifies three outstanding attitudes as persistent aspects of FOLLY i.e. indicators that an organisation is at risk and needs to take action to re-energise itself:

1. Obliviousness to the growing disaffection of constituents
2. The primacy of self aggrandisement
3. The illusion of invulnerable status

Has education got this message, or is it suffering from a kind of ostrich-like 'head in the sand,' turtle-clad protective shell, a kind of *folie de grandeur*?

My view is that education has not got the message, though the writing has been on the wall for some time. It's too late now for an evolution in the way schools work. We need a revolution and we need a revolution now. No longer can we make vague generalisations about preparation for a future which will be uncertain and unpredictable. The future is NOW. Predictability is a thing of the past. How are we going to equip ourselves and our young people to cope with this degree of turbulence, so that it becomes exhilarating rather than exhausting?

Before I tell you about how we are setting about this in the UK. I think it might be helpful to draw up the framework of values and beliefs which lie behind my words. I am conscious of speaking to an expert audience and I guess that though we may have different practices in each of our constituent parts, there may well be a 'global framework' of ideals underpinning our common overall goals. I put ours before you for you to check this out.

1. **The importance of relating education to the world of work.** This is not, as some people think a narrowing of education, but rather a broadening or enhancing of education. This gives it a context, which makes it realistic and meaningful. Without this context, education is in a sealed vacuum, disconnected from the world. Relating education to the world of work motivates the learner. It also helps to equip people in such a way that when they do go to work, far from being factory fodder, they are in a position to call the shots.

2. Education for Capability: If we accept that education is not something abstract and disconnected from the realities of life, then it follows that, to be of any use, it should not only help people to know and to understand but also to **do**. Education should result in capability.

3. Head, hands and heart are equally important. Too often schools concentrate on the intellect, for some reason, restrict practical skills to the less able and neglect the education of the emotions and the development of interpersonal skills. We need all three legs of this stool, otherwise we get lop-sided people.

Experience + reflection = learning: The best kind of learning comes from direct first-hand experience and opportunities to reflect on that experience and to realise what has been learnt. Too often education offers abstract learning, unrelated to experience and the reflective stage is missed out altogether.

Learning is lifelong process: The accreditation of learning at school leaving age is not a terminal point, but a milestone at the beginning of a lifetime's learning.

Learning comes from the interaction of experience and knowledge. Therefore people who have been at work are likely to have increased and accelerated their educational aptitude at a later stage if they are given an opportunity to return to learning.

Learning delivered in a lump say from 9am-5pm. from age 5-16 or 18-21 is not necessarily the best way to learn. It does not suit everybody's patterns of learning; neither does it recognise the way most people develop over time or the way most people learn. Many people have bursts of learning. Their learning curve is not neat or incremental. It does not fit into the school day or the university term. It certainly cannot be measured out in coffee spoons. The forty-five minute lesson is a sort of institutionalised musical chairs. This is the best way of avoiding true learning that schools ever invented.

4. People have an infinite capacity for growth and development. Too often education appears to discourage rather than encourage learning. We need to make it easier, not harder for people to continue their education and training. We need to create opportunities and remove blockages.

We need to empower the learner and to give people responsibility for managing their own learning. They can do it. Too often teachers act upon the assumption that they can't.

We therefore need to change the role of the teacher from controller and director to facilitator and enabler. We need to help the learner have measurable and attainable goals. The bottom line is that learners need a feeling of achievement to inspire their further learning.

5. The leadership, management and organisation of schools. This is crucial to the achievement of these points. The style and quality of the leadership, management and organisation will have serious effects on the outcomes for the learner. An authoritarian school will not produce independent learners. Most schools do NOT promote active learning, though TVEI, for which I am responsible, is doing a great deal to change this state of affairs in the UK.

We need to face the fact that most schools in their present form are inappropriate for their task. We not only have to change classroom practice, but also the way schools are managed. Unless there is a good enough match between the stated aims of the school and the way the system as a whole works, then attempts at classroom level to get pupils to manage their own learning, to take initiative, to work in teams, show originality, determination and even rigour will be cancelled out by the tyranny of the bell, an overly hierarchical management structure, a competitive individualistic approach to learning and a concentration on learning by rote and working to rule.

6. Competence and competition. In this important report (NEDO/MSC 1984) it was stated that employers want their employees to be able to:

- Use acquired skills in changed circumstances
- Perform multi-task operations
- Cross operational boundaries and work in multi-occupational teams

- Act and help manage an integrated system with an understanding of its wider purpose
- Diagnose relevant problems and opportunities and take action to bring about results

Now, if we agree that these are the qualities needed in the labour force today and work back to the way schools manage pupils' learning. I think we have to agree that we would not have started from here.

7. **Exploiting the advantages of open learning**. This is something schools have not yet begun to do, with notable exceptions, of course. In the UK, we are developing a form of open and flexible learning in schools. Eventually this will enable students to get regular examinations and qualifications from a program of study which is largely self-directed, but with support from the teacher, the peer group and the school/college/community itself. The idea is to help young people learn to learn in this way with the support of the school community. The hope is that they will carry on learning in this way after they have left school. However, introducing Open Learning into schools in a major way is not just a question of technical equipment, important as that is. It is more to do with attitudes, particularly teacher attitudes. Open learning is not isolated learning, nor should it be so open that you fall down the big O, like *Alice in Wonderland* down a tunnel.

Above all, Open Learning requires especially well-trained and skilled teachers. One of its merits is that it can and should harness the peer group itself and also adults other than teachers to assist the learning process. It offers learning possibilities for the whole community; it is not age, place or time bound. Most importantly, the students manage their own learning at a pace which suits both their ability and the way they learn. We have to make sure that computers are used in this way and not merely as rather expensive work sheets or workbooks.

8. **Schools are not sufficiently open**. In 1983, I was privileged to give a Cantor Lecture at the Royal Society of Arts, London, entitled 'Tomorrow's Schools, Open or Closed?'I addressed three concepts, the open school, open access to learning and open learning itself. I quote:

Schools are not closed systems or else they would be closed. Schools need to be open to new ideas, to parents, employers, members of the local community, open to new experiences, open to constructive criticism from members or neighbours; open to everyone who wants go on learning; open at times which suit the public at large, open and honest in thought, word or deed. Some are not very open at all. Yet unless schools open up, unless schools begin to adapt the model upon which they traditionally work, they will cease to be relevant or useful and may well close.

There speaks the Head of a community school. In modern society, such schools are needed as a focus for community life to bring a sense of 'community'where otherwise there might be anomie, alienation and anarchy.

9. School leaders too often behave as if they are running closed systems

My evidence for this comes from my own research into the views of 500 secondary school leaders. My book, *Leadership for Tomorrow's Schools,* published by Blackwell in 1987, tells the whole story. The majority of the Heads I studied were on an 'outside–in' rather than an 'inside-out' model. That is to say that they put all their emphasis on running a tight ship, a well-ordered system where everything was in the right place at the right time.

Relatively few looked at the outside context of the school or used it to enrich the learning of those inside the school. Most were reactive rather than proactive. Their use of time was fragmented, mostly spent dealing with staff problems. Conflicts were not resolved, often denied rather than used constructively to enhance learning. This applies particularly to racial conflict.

From this, I conclude that if we want schools to change fundamentally, our main energy has to go into helping school leaders and teachers to feel confident in the face of change, to be able to manage change, to understand strategic management, to give proactive rather than reactive leadership.

Ansoff, *Implanting Strategic Management,* Prentice Hall, London 1984) has defined strategic management as 'a systematic approach to the positioning and relating of the organisation to its environment in a way that will assure its continued success and make it free from surprises.' Managing discontinuous change in an extremely turbulent and variable environment is, once you have learnt how to do it, as exciting as sailing a boat. You change tack according to the external conditions, but you know where you are going and you get there.

10. **Supporting classroom teachers.** The most crucial skill in building schools for the future is of course, helping the classroom teacher to feel confident in the face of overwhelming changes, particularly if these involve a fundamental change of teaching style. Teachers are very nervous of giving up their 'control' of their class or pupils. This factor, more than any other, can stop the pupils from managing their own learning.

One problem about teaching and learning styles is that they have a tendency to oscillate from one extreme to another. When I was a school counsellor in the mid sixties, I was trying to get the school system and teachers to be less authoritarian, less directive and less judgmental. But then in the early 70s, 'non-authoritarian' in its extreme form became 'unable to use authority', non-directive became 'without a sense of direction,' non-judgemental became 'unable to use judgment'. The truth is that extremism doesn't really work.It is not 'either-or'. It is both. So we need knowledge and process, control and growth, integration and differentiation, academic and_vocational. In fact we need a contingency approach to school and classroom management, with the freedom to use the appropriate balance and method for any particular situation. To do this requires great teacher confidence, calm and skill.

11. **The way forward for 20:20.** So the vision I hold for 20:20 is based on the framework of beliefs and values that I have outlined. To steer a course forward, we need a flexible framework of principles, rather than a prescriptive set of rules. Then and only then can each member of the community, take decisions and act confidently in moving into the future forwards.

12. **Schooling and work.** If we turn now more specifically to the question of schooling and work, I have to say that in the UK (probably more than many countries), there has been some professional teacher

opposition to the idea of vocational education. We still have a split system in which approximately half our pupils go on to work and training at sixteen (including our own Youth Training Scheme) and half stay on in full-time education. This split between academic and vocational, intellectual and practical, is deep in our culture and reflects a system which goes back to the middle ages. I need hardly add that whatever its intentions, by and large, it not only still reflects the 'elitism' of the old grammar school system but is, unwittingly sexist and ethnocentric. The UK does not yet appear to have come to terms with 1992 and the single European market, let alone a global view. I suspect that we are not alone in this.

13. **TVEI: The Technical and Vocational Education Initiative.** WHY was this needed? In the UK, serious doubts about the effectiveness of education and statements about of its lack of connection with the world of work were expressed, notably by Prime Minister Callaghan in his famous Ruskin Speech, as early as 1976, when youth unemployment began to bite.

In 1983, TVEI was announced. Its aims are, broadly speaking, to ensure that young people 14-18 in full time education have the kinds of learning opportunities which equip them for the demands of working life in a rapidly changing society. Great emphasis is put on problem solving skills, initiative, enterprise and creativity. TVEI is not a narrow vocational program. The overarching aim of TVEI is to equip young people with learning opportunities which will, prepare them for the demands of working life in the information society and a rapidly changing world. These are the kinds of skills and competences needed in tomorrow's and today's world of work. TVEI began as a pilot, in a few schools for some of the pupils and part of the curriculum. By 1992, all being well, all students in full-time education in the UK should be influenced by TVEI an across the whole curriculum. This is a massive, sustained and planned program of educational change, spanning altogether fourteen years at a cost of £1 billion.

It is now government policy in the UK that all pupils should undertake work experience in their last year at school. Furthermore, teachers are being encouraged to take up work shadowing or work experience placements. A National Curriculum is now being introduced. It gives relatively little choice to the pupils. A feature of this curriculum is that it makes science, technology (including information technology) and modern languages compulsory for all pupils, to help with the problems of general competence and of supply in these particular areas. The National Curriculum is being developed by the DES (Department of Education and Science). The Employment Department, which includes the Training Agency, (formerly the MSC) manages TVEI and is developing the necessary process skills across the curriculum, action plans and records of achievement for all pupils. The two departments liaise regularly.

TVEI, the Technical Vocational Education Initiative: Its aims

This Initiative was set up by Margaret Thatcher and her government in 1983 as a pilot and extended in 1987, just after I was appointed Director of Education Programmes within the Employment Department. When I took over, there was much confusion about its goals so we have just restated clarified and published them as follows:

The overarching aim of TVEI is to equip young people with learning opportunities which will equip them for the demands of working life in the information society and a rapidly changing world by

- Ensuring that the curriculum uses every opportunity to relate education to the world of work
- Ensuring that young people get the knowledge, competences and qualifications they need in a highly technological society which itself part of Europe and the world economy
- Ensuring that young people themselves get direct opportunities to learn about the nature of the economy and the world of work through work experience, work shadowing and projects in the community and so on
- Ensuring that young people learn how to be effective people, solve problems, work in teams, be enterprising and creative through the way they are taught
- Ensuring that young people have access to initial guidance,

counselling and training and opportunities for progression throughout their lives

This is very tall order. But I hope you will recognise within it many of the 20:20 ideas which most of us here espouse. TVEI is important because it is a national initiative, planned over time. That should give you some hope that these changes will eventually have impact on schools and the pupils and reach all corners of the UK.

The Training Agency Education Directorate 1988

In 1987, I inherited TVEI with great pleasure and then introduced other initiatives to cover other sectors of the education and training system. So I am now responsible for:

1. TVEI: all secondary schools over time, a £1 billion project from 1983-1995

2. Further Education: funding FE College projects designed to make FE more responsive to the needs of employers

3. Higher Education: Access to HE: Measures to help more people, young and old to have access to higher education.

4. The Enterprise in Higher Education Initiative: (EHE). This new initiative aims to help HE students (and staff) become more enterprising through an enterprise curriculum. Competitive bidding from the universities will eventually, over time, enable all 100 Higher Education Institutes each to implement a £1 million program over four years. The model is similar to TVEI.

5. Compacts: another new initiative: Our newest initiative really does need a word of explanation. They relate to the demographic changes caused by falling rolls in schools now taking place in the UK. We are moving now from a problem of youth unemployment to a problem of youth scarcity. The number of 16-18 year-olds drop by nearly a third by 1994. The danger of this situation is that young people will be tempted by employers paying high wages, to take jobs without training, dead-end jobs, jobs without prospects. Yet if we look at the distribution of the population over the next few years, we see that we shall no longer be able to count on young people to carry our economy, We need to bring back older people, particularly women, who may have missed out in the past and to retrain and re-educate them. Good news for women I think! There is so much wasted and hidden talent there.

But if we look at the shifts predicted in the distribution of occupations and especially the more specific shifts, it becomes a clear as crystal that people who are unskilled, unqualified and unprepared for the future will be out of work. This despite the growth of highly skilled jobs at professional, managerial and particularly technical jobs. So we need to raise the skill base of our whole nation at every age, stage and level of ability. And I for one believe that we have that capacity. Our main effort needs to focus on the development of that capacity and competence, for the good of our people and our economy.

As far as young people are concerned, this means that we should not encourage them to go to work young, but rather that we should invest in their education and training to make sure that they have the best possible opportunities to work at these future more demanding levels. In the UK we are thinking hard about how to achieve a more integrated and flexible system of education and training which brings together the best in youth training. We have not yet come up with a solution, but our first step is our latest initiative, the establishment of compacts.

Compacts are based on partnerships between employers, educators and the local community. The deal is that the employers in the local community offer jobs with training leading to a job for those young people leaving full-time education, whether at sixteen, seventeen, eighteen, or twenty-one or over, who have met targets agreed between the young person, the school and the employer. A feature of this new initiative is that it is both top-down and bottom-up. The national guidelines leave maximum room for local initiatives and developments, according to the needs and features of the local situation. The idea of COMPACTS was launched in March 1988 as part of the Prime Minister Margaret Thatcher's inner-city initiative. The response to the initiative was so positive that in August, the then Secretary of State for Employment. Norman Fowler announced not twenty-five COMPACTS

206

as originally planned but thirty. Business in the community, the CBI (Confederation of Industries) and the Chambers of Commerce are now publicly supporting partnerships. We have take off.

I predict that the extension of the education/employer/community partnerships, whereby the partners work closely together on the quality, nature and outcomes of education and training at school, further and higher levels will prove to be a way of revitalising local communities, of giving our people, particularly young people, the best possible opportunities at the same time as strengthening the economy. To be effective, these initiatives need to build on the models of learning we, in our various ways, are developing here. We shall do our best to see that these principles are not lost in practice.

Any questions? Yes lots!

Postscript

This speech went down very well indeed to a huge audience and was followed up with many spontaneous discussions with the international members. I did not reveal on that platform that the COMPACT initiative was developed by me, very quickly. The PM was looking for a further proposal to help her inner-city initiatives. Luckily I had been thinking about what to do next. I worked out the proposal on the back of an envelope on the train from Sheffield to Whitehall on the Thursday and it was announced and funded the next Tuesday. Treasury didn't like being bounced into this commitment. Fortunately it was a very successful proposal.

The TVEI Team work together to clarify and commit to the aims of TVEI

Back in the UK, we realised that there was still a great deal of confusion in the UK about what TVEI was trying to do and why. We decided to reaffirm its aims and disseminate them so that we could focus our efforts better; in fact we called it the Focus Statement.

We set up a conference for the whole TVEI team and I invited the Grubb Institute who had helped previously to turn my schools around, to join us. We all participated in working out the key aims of the project and together, we came up with what became known as the 'Focus Statement.' This worked well because we all had taken an active part in the process. It was not hierarchical, it was genuine participation. This method completely re-energised and motivated the team. I guess this was a new way of working within the civil service. The Grubb Institute methodology worked again. Having written the Focus Statement, we needed to make sure the education world understood it as well.

Author thinking!

The Real Aims of TVEI

This article was first published in *Education* on April 14 1987

Anne Jones signals a change of emphasis in the TVEI program to focus it more closely on the world of work.

Moving goalposts is a frequent accusation levelled at government initiatives. This year's guidelines to LEAs for TVEI, just out, reveal what I prefer to call a change of tack but not of direction. TVEI has now been up and running for six years, nearly half of its lifetime; by 1992 all

British school students 14-18, some £2 million, or more if the staying on rate goes up, will be directly influenced by TVEI.

The model of TVEI changed in 1987 when it went from pilot to extension. But the core aims of TVEI remain substantially as they were in the beginning, that is, to equip young people with the knowledge, skills, competencies, qualifications, and attitudes which they will need at work in a rapidly changing highly technological society.

As a nation we are desperately short of people with professional, managerial and technical skills, and oversupplied with unskilled workers. We need to raise the levels of achievement of all our students if they are to find work, and if we as a nation are to survive economically. This is not an idealistic or remote *Cri de Coeur* but a realistic statement of facts.

In the UK, some 14% of eighteen-year-olds go on to higher education, whilst in Japan and the USA the figure is 38%, 36% in France and over 20% in Germany. Countries like Singapore, Taiwan and South Korea are already way ahead of Great Britain in their investment in higher-level education and training, and therefore in highly skilled man and woman power. We cannot afford to waste the potential of any of our young people, especially with the demographic time-bomb ticking. With the dramatic one third drop in their numbers by 1992, young people are like gold dust. Neither do we want our young people to waste their time or their talents going into dead-end jobs where there is little prospect of promotion, progression, continuing education or training. We need our young people to raise their sights and their expectations, their levels of confidence and level of achievements.

The most important qualities young people need to develop today are leadership, initiative, and the ability to think, to adapt to change, be flexible, to transfer their skills from one context to another, to work in teams, to be technically competent and proficient, to be able to solve problems, and to apply their knowledge, skills and competencies in any context. These requirements apply to jobs at every level. In today's world, this includes not only the ability to change employers, but also to change jobs completely. It also means being prepared to work in or

209

with other countries, not only Europe, but worldwide. The most important saleable qualities organizations will need are what Charles Handy calls the 'triple I's: intelligence, ideas and information.'

We need all our young people to develop their potential as far as they can throughout their lives. We need to equip them so that they can call the shots. We need to empower them so that they can cope with the turbulent and ever changing world environment in which we now live. These are and always have been fundamental aims of TVEI. Factory fodder was never on the TVEI agenda. It has always been about increasing young people's capability.

By the summer of 1988 we in the TVEI Unit felt the time had come to refocus the aims of TVEI and to target them more specifically. As our remit now goes across the whole curriculum for all students 14-18, and by 1992 in all schools and colleges, we need now to focus our resources where they are most needed. Employer-education links are the key.

TVEI was in many ways a pioneer, though not the sole pioneer, in this field. It needs to be said that TVEI's task has been helped enormously by other recent educational developments, notably the national curriculum and all its works, GCSE, the growing demand for records of achievement and individual action plans, and the recognition of the importance of the whole curriculum, not just those parts which are statutory.

However, such has been the success of TVEI in stimulating diverse innovative and creative teacher and curriculum development that by the summer of 1988, we in the TVEI Unit felt the time had come to refocus the aims of TVEI and to target them more specifically. As our remit now goes across the whole curriculum for all students 14-18 and by 1992 in all schools and colleges, we need now to focus our resources where they are most needed. Employer-Education links are the key.

The Focus statement begins thus:

TVEI aims to ensure that the education of 14-18 year-olds provides young people with learning opportunities which will equip them for the demands of working life in a rapidly changing society.

TVEI was in many ways a pioneer, though not the sole pioneer, in this field. It needs to be said that TVEI's task has been helped enormously by other educational developments, notably the national curriculum and all its works, GCSE, the growing demand for records of achievement and individual action plans, and the recognition of the importance of the whole curriculum, not just those parts which are statutory.

In the beginning, TVEI spent less energy on industry-education links. It had to spend a lot of time ensuring that schools'curriculum plans were broad and balanced, and in particular contained science, technology, and information technology to sixteen for all. Research evidence suggests that TVEI's impact on the take-up of science and technology to sixteen has been considerable and particularly in terms of gaining access for girls and ethnic minorities. So far so good! But now the National Curriculum framework takes up the legal side of this particular battle, TVEI energy is released to ensure that the whole curriculum is related to the world of work. This applies not merely to those subjects which have obvious vocational connections, but to every subject, and for that matter, to everything that happens to a young person whilst in full-time education – the whole curriculum in the real meaning of the phrase.

- **By making sure the curriculum uses every opportunity to relate education to the world of work, by using concrete/real examples if possible.**

  Far from giving up its claims to the curriculum as a whole (*Education* 10 March), TVEI has now spread across the whole curriculum. There is no subject, or activity which is not enhanced by being set in a real context, with real examples, provided if possible by adults other than teachers. This applies as much to the expressive arts or PSE as to science and technology.

- **By making sure that young people get the knowledge, competencies and qualifications they need in a highly technological society which is part of Europe and the world economy.**

  This aim relates to learning outcomes. It is over-simplistic and naïve to think of the national curriculum as being about knowledge and

TVEI about the learning processes, and even more so to think of these as conflicting. It certainly is not a question of either a knowledge-based curriculum *or* a process-based curriculum. Both are needed, and not for their own sake, but in order to arrive at an outcome which is a capable confident young person, technologically competent and worldly-wise, aware of the global situation.

- **By making sure that young people themselves get direct opportunities to learn about the nature of the economy and the world of work – through work experience, work shadowing, projects in the community and so on.**

  But it is no good young people hearing about life at second hand, being told about working life or the economy. If they are going to be able to use their judgement, they need first-hand experience, which preferably is built into the curriculum and properly assessed and reflected upon.

- By making sure that young people learn how to be effective people, solve problems, work in teams and be enterprising and creative through the way they are taught.

  This one is about teaching and learning styles and applies to any subject, whether or not it makes any explicit connection with the world of work. The aim is to encourage pupils to take responsibility for their own learning, to manage their own learning, to know how to learn, to take decisions, evaluate evidence and work in teams in an enterprising and creative way.

- **By making sure that young people have access to initial guidance and counselling, and then continuing education and training, and opportunities for progression throughout their lives.**

  This is something which needs to be built into the way young people are helped to assess their progress towards attainable goals, to set themselves long-term broad aims and short-term specific goals. It means looking at education, even education 14-18, as merely a stepping stone, not as a terminal exit point. It means giving young people open-ended unprejudiced guidance (and counselling too if need be), so that whatever choices they make, they realise that these are only first choices not final choices.

Taken together, it is clear that the aims of the Focus Statement, which are included in this year's TVEI guidance, make demands which should result in students emerging as confident, capable young people who are aware of their new-found purchase on the education and training system. Hopefully, these young people will realise the opportunities they have if they do not give up learning at the earliest opportunity, but rather if, whichever route they take at sixteen, they make sure they keep their options for a better job and a better lifestyle as open as possible.

Michael Howard Secretary of State, the Employment Department 1990-92, admiring this TVEI project. He is now the Baron of Lympe. Anne Jones is in the challenge cart

In 1990, the Rover Group generously developed and provided the Rover Challenge Cart, shown above. As part of the their GCSE in craft, design and technology, some 5000 TVEI pupils had to assemble the go-cart then transform the spartan chassis into a smart single-seater, capable of

35mph. A truly enterprising and imaginative project!

Employers are, as they have already shown through their support for Compacts and Education–Business Partnerships, increasingly willing and enthusiastic about helping young people get the most out of their education before and after they go to work.

The Focus Statement is not a response to Training and Enterprise Councils (TECS). It was formulated way before TECS were invented in an attempt to get a clearer message out about TVEI's real aims. But through this clearer message, it does give LEAs a remit to work closely with TECS in building Business Education Partnerships which benefit the young people themselves, the quality of their learning, the future prosperity of the local community and the nation as a whole. Working with and through TECS will be crucial to these goals.

The Times in January 1988 referred to TVEI as 'one of the most positive advances in secondary schooling since the 1944 Education Act: 'the initiative has captured the imagination and application of teachers and pupils alike'. It has great potential to redirect schooling towards the world of work. It does not fall into the trap of training for specific jobs or the acquisition of narrow skills. It lays the foundation for craft and technician skills to be acquired'.

So be it. With only seven more years to go of planned and managed change, TVEI has a responsible and urgent task to fulfil, not only to give young people the best possible start in working life, but also to help meet the desperate skills shortages which are upon us. TVEI works and only works, like any other education initiative, through the skill of the teaching profession. It is to be hoped that the profession will realise that investing in our young people's skills is neither a frill nor a piece of political indoctrination, but their entitlement. On them our nation's future depends.

Postscript

It is hard to measure the legacy, though there is no doubt in my head about its impact at the time. However, over the years, the pressures on schools have changed. We wanted more of our pupils to stay on and to go to university. Schools became ranked by their position in the league tables. Preparation for public exams took over, and preparation for working life faded. Huge numbers of pupils repeated their subject exams several times until they got the desired grades. So even for those teachers who today still espouse the TVEI aims and objectives, it has become difficult for them to implement them.

However, the new coalition government plans for careers guidance, vocational education, traineeships and apprenticeships plus the changes in curriculum and the examination system may begin to change the situation again. **The Educational Roundabout** starts up again. A lot depends on which party wins the next election. I have always maintained that academic and vocational preparation are both essential and that both go across the whole curriculum. I am really looking forward to this next phase.

Harnessing the female resource
The Queen Elizabeth Hall, London, July 1989
A report of a speech I made to the Women's Education Conference. At that time there were very few women in 'top jobs'. There was only one other grade three female in the Training Agency with me.

'Our economy can no longer manage without women. This is not a temporary phenomenon, as in the war, but a permanent feature of our future workforce'. Anne Jones, Director of Education Programmes, Department of Employment Training Agency, spoke up in praise of older women, the key to our future economic prosperity.

'The nature of work is changing radically: more home-working, contracting out, flexible hours, and several changes of job over a lifetime. Women have many skills which are particularly suited to the needs of the emerging job market. Women are good at managing change, multi-skilling, working in teams, networking, sharing and co-operating, working at several levels simultaneously, thinking creatively and strategically as well as getting things done and attending to detail. Women network and look after each other. Women think holistically and at the same time pay attention to detail. Women are sensitive and strong. We have a lot to offer.

The Training Agency puts great emphasis in all its programs on

215

equal opportunities. TVEI in particular is building up the confidence, competence and capability of younger women. In FE and HE, it is promoting courses which give access to high level skills and qualifications to women. The Higher Education Branch is currently sponsoring forty-two '**women only**' high level courses in science, engineering and management, with a throughput of 670 women a year. In ten years' time, today's discussion will seem very odd: women will be managing the economy equally with men and the economy won't manage without them.'

Postscript

It's nearly twenty-five years later and, by Jove, I was right. Women are now in top jobs as well as middle management, and many men are happy for them to be the main breadwinners. There are now more women than men going to university, so now we have the qualifications to prove our capability. Yes, there still aren't enough women on the boards of companies. But it is a completely different scenario from the old days when so very few women reached 'the top!' And there's no going back!

Looking back now, I recently came across a book published in 1992 by the Industrial Society in which they interviewed twenty Inspirational Leaders/Managers and compiled a book called *Leaders, the Learning Curve of Achievement.* But there were only four women leaders named and sixteen men: typical! Their theme was that the most effective leaders never stop learning. The four women included Dame Stephanie Shirley and myself. She and I now meet again as members of the Phyllis Court Club in Henley. Yes, we are both strong on lifelong learning!

Revealed, the fifty most important women in Britain today!

In April 1988, *Woman* magazine printed an edition listing their choices. It was preposterous: Princess Diana was 14th I was 15th and Edwina Currie was 16th! **This is what it said about me:**

The 56-year-old Head, who landed the country's biggest educational job as Director of Education Programmes for the Manpower Services

Commission. With an annual budget of more than £500 million p. a. she has to persuade schools, colleges and universities to give education a more vocational slant.

A very serious press office photo

The press office sent a very serious photo of me. The magazine was ridiculous but it still makes me laugh!

Imtec 2020, Oxford, September 1990
Future Agenda: What now?
Anne Jones, Hon President, Imtec UK, Director of Education Programmes, the Department of Employment, UK

This is a follow-up to the 1988 '2020' conference in Aspen, as originally planned. This was my final summing up and looking forward speech

A changing world
The Millennium is about to arrive: we are not preparing for a life of change it is a life of change: a change of life for all. We are not preparing for the future, the future is NOW, it is happening.

1990 has heralded in not a series of 'step changes' but a whole set of 'sea changes' which are global, coming in waves across first one Continent, then another. These changes, like the ebb and flow of the tide which comes in and wipes out the shape of the beach, are total and continuous. They are not just economic and political but also social and physical, affecting people everywhere. Overnight, changes occur in standards and ways of living, economies and national boundaries. In this unpredictable climate of changing fortunes rags to riches and riches to rags it is no longer a question of preparing for one change at a time; change is discontinuous and unexpected. This is what we have to learn to live with.

All this is something which I believe those of us here understand, intuitively perhaps, because you cannot codify and classify such changes: you have to learn to go with the changes, to develop the capacity to create opportunities out of chaos, above all to support each other in developing the capacity not only to cope, but, to use to Tom Peter's phrase 'to thrive on chaos.'

A small world

Simultaneously we have two compatible yet contrary-sounding trends being global and being local. We have never been more conscious of the interdependency of the human race, nor the importance of a local response to a local need. Decentralization combined with a sense of being a world citizen. The experiences of this week, the sharing of experiences of people of so many nationalities, the real experience we all now have of instant communication on a global scale, through the new technologies, these experiences bring home the reality which is with us now. We already have mechanisms, not only for communicating, genuine communicating on a world scale. We also have mechanisms for teaching and learning on a world basis. To give but one example 'The treasures of the Smithsonian', as *The Independent* reported on September 3rd, can be explored genuinely explored in the comfort of your own home, at relatively little cost, and no doubt at less cost in the future.

The Information Society: an agenda for action

So in this incredible information society which we are no longer predicting will happen, but which has happened, if only we knew how to use it and if only we all had access to it, what are we actually going to do about our global and our local education systems?

The first point to make is that those of us who are lucky enough to have some understanding and some experience of what is already happening need now to be less modest about what has been achieved so far and what needs to be done next. One of the major outcomes of a week such as this must be the confidence and the courage to think bigger, speak more clearly and to act more positively to make things happen. In thought, word and deed, we all know now that we are not alone. Although we may be at completely different stages of development, we share a common agenda, and we know that it works: it is not just pie in the sky (or satellite in the sky). Our feet are on the ground thinking about the needs of local people, at the same time as our Heads are in the stratosphere, thinking and communicating globally.

The second point to make is that the agenda we appear to share is about:

1. Changing teaching into learning
2. Opening up the education system so that it is more flexible in the way it helps people to learn
3. Getting access to learning for all people throughout life
4. Providing learning opportunities at a pace, place and time which helps people to develop their potential to the full
5. Encouraging learners to manage their own learning, to take responsibility for themselves, supported rather than controlled by teachers
6. Empowering and motivating the learners by giving them opportunities for setting goals, deciding how they want to learn and achieving success

We need a culture of success not of failure

The third point is that the new technologies are crucial to these developments, and we need to help young people use them wisely and well so that they are their masters and mistresses not their slaves. There is a problem about resourcing such technologies on the scale now required, but they are becoming cheaper every day. Further there is a growing sense of urgency from major employers about the need to take action. ICL, our sponsor is one outstanding example. My observation is that, in spite of their need to compete with each other, major companies are so concerned about the quality of the workforce, present and future, that they are prepared to work cooperatively with each other to get something done.

Partnership

Therefore, as I predicted confidently in Aspen in 1988, partnership between educators and employers and government at a local, national and international level, is going to be crucial to the future success of this movement and more importantly to the future success and well-being of the people of this world. I think we should now set up international partnerships between government, employers and teachers. Already as I predicted, in the UK at least, such concepts have grown and developed like wildfire over the last two years. I am quite certain that in the UK not only will there be Training and Enterprise Councils in every locality in the UK by 1991, but that in each of those TEC communities there will be an active Business Education Partnership linking the TEC world to the education world. These partnerships will be the cornerstones of the activity which help the people in our local communities develop to their full potential.

Then, if we now understand the need to learn to live with change; if we now have teachers with vision and skill to convert these ideas into reality; if we now have employers who want to help with speeding up this process; what is the problem about getting the 'sea change' to happen inside schools as well as in our minds? This I know is the question that's in your minds: we have a vision we share, the problem is to make it a reality.

Of course the solution is partly about getting more resources, partly about changing national priorities and prejudices, partly about changing traditional values and attitudes. But what I know you feel, indeed as I feel, is that we now have to go from the rhetoric of vision to the practicalities of implementation. And my message to you is that you, we, can do it. Not alone, but together in the knowledge that you are part of a movement which in an amazing way, is worldwide. Yes, we will all fight to adapt national policies where necessary, get more resources, but we know that these are finite and that the most valuable resource is ourselves, that is the human resource, the teachers.

Making our vision reality

So supporting teachers to give them the confidence and the courage, not only to try new things, to do them well and to succeed, becomes a priority task. Helping teachers to change their role so that they are less controlling and more enabling becomes a key task. Sharing successful experience becomes a key mechanism for breeding more success. In all of this Networking is vital and I know that you are going to build on and extend the networks established here.

Of key importance is the East-West link. It has been very exciting to include representatives of fifteen countries at this conference, and in particular, we welcome our Russian colleagues and their proposals for a mini-conference in Moscow next year. The next full conference of Imtec will be in Berlin in two years time and this will be a tremendously exciting development. I know that most of you will be keen to exchange addresses, information, resources and set up visits and so on when possible across the global community we represent.

I have not come here to tell you about the UK programs, though I understand that TVEI in particular has been recognised and applauded for its strategic role in building up a quality workforce for the UK. The agenda we have in the UK mirrors the agenda each country has:

- giving more young people opportunities to continue in further and higher education
- ensuring that all young people are equipped to cope with change
- increasing the number of people who are successful learners and want therefore to go on learning throughout life; bridging the academic-vocational divide
- Building a more flexible and responsive education system
- Using modern technologies in the classroom so that they more readily mirror the realities of life after school

Finally, I know that I have not said one thing which you did not know already, I have attempted to play back to you what you have said and to say 'you can do it'. Now is the time for deeds not words. Together I genuinely believe we can make it happen. The task is urgent, the time is ripe, go forth and make it happen.

Anne Jones Hon President, Imtec UK

Postscript
This was a final rallying call after a week's conference. We had an excellent week. The highlight was an amazing Dinner and Ball at Blenheim Palace.

Study trip to the USA and Far Eastern Countries 1990
I was fortunate to go on this study trip for the Department to find out what was happening in other parts of the world in education and training for the new technologies. Here is a summary of the message I brought back with me, and shared with my senior colleagues.

International Competition:
Visit to the United States, Canada, Japan, Korea and Singapore 1990
Are we keeping up with the rest of the world?

We tend to think of the Pacific Rim countries as behind us in some ways, too much counting and not enough interpersonal skills? Their high achievement rates in compulsory and post-compulsory education put great emphasis on knowledge, but it is not always acknowledged that their students are also capable and good with people. In the UK we need to keep head, hands and heart in better balance. In most cases, this now means putting more emphasis on 'head'. Knowledge workers will be almost the only workers of the future. We need every ounce of brainpower we can develop if we are to remain 'world class' and competitive as a nation. How do we compare with other countries?

In 1990, I was privileged to visit the United States, Canada, Japan, Korea and Singapore on behalf of the Department of Employment and with the aim of investigating what effects the revolution of information and communication technologies was having on working practices. More importantly, I looked at the implications for the education system: what kind of education would be needed to equip people for this kind of global, instant, real-time economy? I came back convinced that we had got it wrong in the UK. We now had too little emphasis on knowledge, precision, attention to detail, rigorous methodology, delivery on time. My comments upon my return follow:

1. In terms of competitive advantage, the UK is way behind these other countries. We have not begun to grasp in reality the order of magnitude that these technological changes bring about. It is like going into a new dimension where everything is on a different plane. It is not a step change but a sea change into something new and strange. We are not prepared.

2. We know intellectually that we are going to need more highly skilled people and fewer unskilled people but will these highly skilled people be able to think in 3D rather than 2D? Will they be able to work in teams to solve impossible highly technological problems? Will they be able to be self-motivating and self-managing? How will they react to a paperless world, in which there are virtually no supervisors, no secretaries and no middle people? A world in which the technologically illiterate might as well be deaf and dumb? Yet this is what we saw in Pratt and Whitney, Nova Scotia, Canada.

3. We know intellectually that training is a 'good thing', yet in every country we visited our questions about training were regarded as 'odd'. Without exception, training was built into the workplace system, very often in cooperation with the local community college which delivered more effectively and cheaply than private providers. Most companies had their own learning 'businesses'with sophisticated learning systems, fully accredited by the local college, with virtually continuous training built into the job. In Seattle, USA, the Boeing Company has a motto on its wall: 'an engineer has to be retrained every two years.'

4. We may think intellectually that Japan is merely a copycat nation, simply replicating other nations' high-tech inventions. We may think that the Japanese are uncreative thinkers, low on innovation and poor at people considerations. How wrong can we be! Major

223

companies invested nearly all their profit in research and development (R & D) with hardly any going to the shareholders, and innovation is the most highly prized quality in an employee. Qualities looked for in the employees (lifelong employees with lifelong training) were: 'bright, positive, dynamic, optimistic, balanced and in harmony, able to make a positive contribution. 'The competition is there but it is achieved through teamwork and cooperation,4 to achieve the success as a global cooperation we believe that mutually rewarding co-existence must be the guiding principle of all our actions'. (Canon, Japan)

5. We may think intellectually that because few companies have fully integrated computer manufacturing systems, that there is not much to worry about: 'No, they are not fully integrated, they have a few islands of integration', we say reassuringly to ourselves. But the global companies in the East and the West are preparing now for a fully integrated system; preparing their staff, their markets and their products. Cutting down on staff? No way, the aim is increased productivity. A Sapporo Beer plant in Tokyo runs on thirty people but has quadrupled its productivity. Computers mean you can employ more people because you can produce more, and increase your share of the world market. Making people redundant is alien to the Japanese culture, though even they may not be able to keep this up for ever.

6. We may think intellectually that countries like Korea must be way behind third world countries making spare parts for Japan? Not any more! Korea seems to have thrived on adversity, with war followed by oil crises, because it has invested massively in technology. Hyundai Electrics was only set up in 1983 and is now the largest conglomerate in Korea. It naturally has its own state of the art resource/training facilities. All employees take courses in management, salesmanship, computers and foreign languages. In Korean primary schools, all pupils are taught basic skills using computer learning programs. In secondary schools all pupils are computer literate, able to word process and use modern technology. 94% of the pupils now go to high school, which ends at eighteen.

7. We may think intellectually that Singapore is too small a country to be much of a threat internationally. Do not be mistaken! Here again, strategy and action were as one: a program of computer assisted learning in primary schools; IT skills in secondary schools; 100% IT training program for the whole workforce, up to senior manager level with a government subsidy for employers; forward investment in people and in R & D to keep at the leading edge of technology; and getting other bigger countries with more space to do the big manufacturing jobs for them.

8. Surprisingly, Japan did not appear to have a work-related curriculum, nor to teach computer skills in schools. No need to when the pupils are taught to work in teams for long hours, and deliver to targets from the age of six. Work habits learnt at school matched those needed in work. This includes looking after those with learning problems.

9. The good news is that TVEI still holds up as a bold national strategy with all the right components. Maybe we should be even bolder about stressing the importance of achieving high standards of success in exams, especially maths, science, technology, IT and languages. But we are absolutely right to stress as well as much as we do the 'person'and 'task management' skills. None of the other countries put as much stress as we do neither on these, nor on links with industry. So these additional factors could be our trump card. If we could pull off the trick of continuing to achieve an increased participation rate in post-16 (relevant and appropriate) education, and better exam results, we could still rule the world.

10. But this will not happen if working practices in industry do not change. TVEI pupils will want to go to work in places where their skills and capabilities are used, otherwise they will become disaffected and frustrated. We are preparing our future workforce but are we preparing our workplaces?

11. The 'future shock'is fundamental not cosmetic, in most cases a change of organizational culture, management styles, working practices, education and training provision, value systems and human relationships. Incremental changes will not be sufficient.

Only those companies that take a strategic view which they follow-up with action will survive in the competitive global economy which is already with us. In other countries, companies are tackling these issues with a precision and determination. If they have not done so already, islands of integration will suddenly snap into fully integrated systems. What are we going to do, now, to overcome our apparent competitive disadvantage in the world market?

12. Looking back it seems to me that we had taught our pupils about the information technology revolution but we had not systematically taught them how to take part in it. That may be because we, the adults, were not then sufficiently confident at using these new technologies ourselves. Most of our young people have taught themselves and now surpass their elders in competence and capability. Nevertheless, the fact remains that our targets for school leavers still do not include explicit competence in Information and Communication Technologies (ICT). Contrast this with, the example of Singapore, admittedly a small country, but one where all school leavers are technically proficient in ICT, and where a program of adult IT literacy ensures, at government expense, that all managers are ICT trained.

What was also disturbing to note from this visit was that there was a marked difference in approach to education and economic success between the West and the Pacific Rim countries. In the United States and the UK in particular there was, and still is, a great emphasis on education-business partnerships: a great deal of energy and time spent on getting the two 'sides' to talk to each other and understand each other better.

In the Pacific Rim this was deemed to be unnecessary. The pervading culture included an agreed implicit assumption that economic survival depended on being competitive on a world scale. There was no need to muddle up and confuse the roles of education and industry; everybody accepted that economic success depended absolutely on each sector developing the potential of its people to the utmost. As Pascale and Athos, (1985) put it:

The core of management is precisely this art of mobilizing and pulling together the intelligent resources of all employees in the firm.

With the Principal of a major Institute of Technology in Korea

And this task has been ruthlessly pursued with a great deal of apparent success. We might feel that all-round development has been neglected at the expense of high-tech performance, but we may be wrong even about that. If we do not take this competition seriously we are in danger of deluding ourselves. It used to be said that the USA fostered individual brilliance and collective mediocrity, whereas Japan fostered individual mediocrity and collective brilliance. Whatever the truth of this, in the UK we certainly need to target both individual and collective brilliance.

The fact remains that the Pacific Rim countries are pushing, and successfully, for ever higher standards of academic achievement, albeit on rather narrower indices than we have been pursuing in the West. This fact is reflected in the numbers now staying in education to eighteen and/or completing higher education. This would not in itself constitute such a threat to the UK economy if it were not combined with other factors. In the UK we have a rapidly ageing workforce, and in Europe in the year 2,000 more people will retire than will join the labour market. We also have an expensive and relatively unskilled workforce. In the Pacific Rim countries, conversely, there is a growth in numbers of young people, who themselves are well educated and highly skilled. These countries therefore have a growing number of highly competent skilled workers, who are relatively cheap to employ. So, in thinking about the curriculum for a changing world and uncertain future, we have to take account of the international competition, and to do this on a number of dimensions. To maintain and re-secure our leading edge, we need to think and act very fast. And we certainly cannot afford to waste the talent locked up and under-developed in our existing workforce.

Postscript

When I got back to England I reported all this to my colleagues in the senior management team of the Training Agency as we were then called. We had for some time been aware that we were lagging behind many nations in terms of highly qualified manpower. We were all aware of the problem, but what went wrong? We have woken up too late. But in the years between 1990 and 2012, the nature of secondary education changed and not for the better.

In 2013, I was annoyed to find so much criticism of the UK education system in the press. We scored very low on the PISA Scale My warning had not either not been heard or had melted away. So I wrote to *The Times* and repeated my warning note! Here is an abridged version of my original report about Japan, Korea, and Singapore with a different conclusion.

The Times   **Thursday 5ᵗʰ December 2013**

Japan Korea and Singapore were pushing for ever higher standards of academic achievement, reflected by the huge numbers now staying in education to eighteen and/or completing higher education. This would not in itself constitute such a threat to the UK economy if it were not combined with other factors. We have an expensive and relatively unskilled workforce. They have a growing number of young people, who themselves are well educated and highly skilled, thus providing a more highly competent skilled workers, who are relatively cheap to employ.

The UK has fallen down the International league tables, especially in basic skills such as numeracy and literacy. We are weak in maths, science, technology and engineering. And in the last fifteen years, work-related skills have also dropped out of the curriculum, enterprise education has crumbled again despite a short 'Enterprise in Schools Project'. Instead, schools have put enormous energy into raising GCSE grades to improve their position in the league tables. And they have chosen the 'easier' subjects so that more pupils get better GCSE's. Not enough pupils have studied science and maths, technology or engineering or languages to a high level. Not enough students get high grades in the basic subjects English and maths. We now have too little emphasis on knowledge, precision, attention to detail, rigorous methodology, delivery on time.

Prof Anne Jones, Henley-on-Thames

So, in thinking about the curriculum for a changing world and uncertain future, we have to take account of the international competition, on a number of dimensions. To maintain and re-secure our leading edge, we need to think and act very fast. And we certainly cannot afford to waste the talent locked up and under-developed in our existing workforce.

It looks as if the coalition government has begun to catch up with all this again and to take measures to improve our position are being put in place. Let us hope that they continue in the future. I hope isn't too late, the skills needed are all there and just need releasing: hard work, commitment and determination.

Postscript
Better news about improving our PISA scores: Top marks on problem solving.

In April 2014, I was very heartened to read in *The Times* that an international study has found that 'our' teenagers are better at practical problem solving tasks than in academic subjects. They scored well above the average across forty-four countries when asked to undertake real life challenges such as operating an MP3 player, setting a thermostat and calculating a route between destinations. I call that the

TVEI effect, Now we have to get our pupils to practise the PISA tests as well so that next time, we also come high on the academic tests as well and show the world that we are a bright and talented as the Shanghai students who came first in the academic tests after a lot of rote learning. OECD experts couldn't work out why it was that our students scored top marks in problem solving? Answer: The TVEI influence is still there after all these years - that's why! 'Good problem–solving skills give young people the edge in the world of work', Here here!

I have never understood why rote learning is so often regarded as a 'bad thing.'Why does every thing have to be 'either/or? Combined with many other ways of learning, it can be very helpful. Those of us who took the dreaded 11-plus exam quickly found that our scores improved rapidly if we practised. I suspect that our students today would find the same if we did some teaching, preparatory testing and learning the Eastern way as well as the TVEI way. Precision, accuracy under stress and quick thinking are needed in our workforce as well as imagination and creativity.

Reviewing Quality Education Service for the 1990s. 4 March 1992, The Hague

Quality in higher education: Achievements in Enterprise in Higher Education (EHE) and the EC perspective

Professor Anne Jones, Head of Continuing Education, Brunel University and former Under-Secretary, the Employment Department, and Director of Education Programmes

Soon after I retired from the civil service, I was asked to take part in a conference in the Hague at which I was able to review the EHE project five years after we had launched it. The Europeans, OECD in particular were very interested in the Enterprise in Higher Education Project; Was this a model to copy? EHE was launched in 1997, so this report is five years later. It was also helpful that I had been working in a university which had taken part in the first tranche of this project.

It is extremely enterprising of the Southern Region Enterprise Directors to organise this event in advance of the ratification of the Treaty of Maastricht: a pre-emptive strike. It gives me particular pleasure to see how far the Enterprise in Higher Education Programme in the UK has come, metaphorically as well as literally, since it was launched in December 1987. Not all of you will be aware, as I am acutely aware, that in September 1987, when I joined the Department of Employment, EHE did not exist and it had to be invented. Indeed, Higher Education Branch did not exist either. My first task as a new and rather nervous Under-Secretary was to set up the Branch, and then to read the runes, that is the minutes of various very high powered discussions, to ascertain what were the expectations of Ministers (Lord Young and Kenneth Baker at the time) and to work out how to get these to spark off a response from a reluctant higher education world. I well remember addressing 100 Vice Chancellors (all men!) in Senate House, London University and being surprisingly well received. At the time it was pretty amazing that the Department of Employment had been invited in to 'do something' about higher education. Higher education itself had been well protected up to then from the interventions of the then crusading and swash-buckling advances of the Manpower Services Commission (MSC), as this part of the Employment Department then was.

The original concept of Enterprise in Higher Education (EHE) was, it has to be said, less sophisticated than the present version, but born of the genuine and I think, well-based concern, that our young graduates emerging from the system, were not sufficiently enterprising, or capable, or aware of the needs of industry and business. My own crude caricature at the time was to talk about the 'egghead' who couldn't boil an egg. The original think tank, which included representatives of CVCP, UFC and NAB, had in mind the strengthening of small and medium enterprises, providing advice to undergraduates about self employment, secondments and work placements. They envisaged some employer-led initiatives (ERTEC is the nearest approach to this) and even a role for Continuing Education/ Lifelong Learning, very advanced thinking this, as I now realise! The read-across from TVEI was recognised, but the net effect was rather bolt-on, as indeed TVEI also was at the time.

What we actually came up with included most of these elements, but crucially got the change culture into the bloodstream of the whole system: an integrated approach. TVEI also began to develop in this way, which is why I think the effect of both initiatives will eventually be to have changed considerably the nature of learning in both the schools and the HE sectors. Both initiatives are now unstoppable, even if the money dries up, as it now has for new EHE projects.

The anarchic dinosaur culture of the Higher Education (HE) System has moved itself forward, with a little help from EHE, to the stage when it is just about ready for the slings and arrows of the new HE Funding and Quality Audit Regime. Without EHE, the HE system would not have progressed as systematically and competently as it now has towards strategic plans, development plans, annual targets and performance indicators. Whether or not we like this Brave New World, HE needs to be prepared for it. And it is. It is worth noting that the pressure for change in HE is not only top-down, but also bottom-up.

In 1992 the first eleven LEAs in TVEI extension will be sending TVEI graduates to HE, and in growing numbers. The staying on rate at 16 has improved dramatically since TVEI extension began in 1984, when it was 47%, to 60% in 1992. It will be interesting to see whether or not TVEI undergraduates will be already more enterprising, confident and demanding than their predecessors. It is just as well for HE to be prepared for students who are likely to be critical if they find a wholly top down, passive, rote approach to learning, and furthermore who are likely to say so. If the judgement of quality is to be, in part, in the hands of the learner, then the results could be very interesting. Let us hope that the quality of mercy is not strained.

The real outcomes of EHE are extremely difficult to judge accurately. The kinds of head-counting activities required by Treasury tell you a lot about the width but not much about the quality. Rather like BS 5750 as opposed to TQM, there can be merit in seeing that things have been done in a systematic way, but the really important measure, that is the quality of learning of the students, and the extent to which EHE has helped them to be more confident, enterprising, capable and effective in their future lives, is not going to be easy to measure, or to disentangle from other variables.

No matter. The most dramatic and obvious outcome of EHE so far is the effect on HE institutions themselves and their staff. Like a pebble in a pool, or yeast in a mix, EHE has rippled and bubbled so that the effects are far greater than the sum of the parts. Demand for institutional change now comes bottom up, as a result of the growing awareness of the EHE providers of the context in which they now work. This awareness has been released and articulated as HE teachers/lectures have themselves become more confident and capable. Like school teachers, HE teachers too often regard themselves as 'useless': 'I have been here for twenty years and I can't do anything else'.

Not true. The emphasis given to staff development by EHE has helped release the talent of those HE academics who were not natural entrepreneurs. It has also helped them to understand the learning needs of their students better, to motivate their students more and to give their students more responsibility for the management of their own learning.

Charles Handy, in his book *The Gods of Management* classifies higher education as a 'collection of individual stars', what I call an anarchic culture, a collection of robber barons all doing their own thing. The demands of the new HE for a more corporate approach run counter to this deep culture. Yet a degree of institutional corporate mission becomes essential for survival in the growing competitive and underfunded regime of the new Higher Education Funding Council (HEFCE).

The organisational trick here is what Lawrence and Lorsch have called 'integration and differentiation' that is, building an integrated whole system which nevertheless recognises the unique and different contribution of each part. To achieve this requires institutional leadership of a new order.

EHE itself is a precursor of the new Quality Assurance Unit by helping HE to build institutional development plans with annual reviews, to develop its staff more systematically and to emphasise the quality of teaching and learning, may have done more than is recognised to help prepare HE for this sea change. Vice Chancellors, with a new role thrust upon them, may find that their EHE colleagues have paved the way. Those Higher Education Institutions (HEIs) which are not in EHE (there are currently sixty-four contracts for sixty-nine institutions) may find that through networking, they can reach those parts of the system that EHE core funding has not yet reached. However, there are some danger points to be noted. There is no doubt that modern thinking both at UK and at European level, is looking for the 'value-added factor'. Has EHE helped improve the 'productivity'of the education system? What difference has EHE made to capability of students graduating and getting into work? Will EHE graduates contribute more to the success of GB Ltd. and to Europe Limited than non-EHE graduates?

It is very easy for the enthusiasts to get carried away with the pleasure of experiential learning, and to reject or conveniently forget, the economic imperative which makes it essential for both the UK and Europe as a whole to have a highly skilled and capable workforce if they are to retain any competitive advantage whatsoever internationally. Remember, *il faut manger pour vivre et non pas vivre pour manger.*

There is no longer, even if there ever were, any such thing as a free meal. Nor in the future will government money flow for new initiatives. In a tightening financial regime, more UK students will have to earn their way through HE, as they do in other parts of the world. Work-based learning combined with part-time flexible HE may well become the norm. It certainly should be. Lifelong Learning is essential to the health and well-being of both individuals and organisations if we are to keep up with the rest of the world.

The EC is well aware of this. The 'Memorandum on Higher Education in the European Community' not only stresses this trend but also brings home the need for the internal market having people who have the capability to operate across national and cultural boundaries. 'Given the pace of technological changes, a new balance between initial and continuing education becomes an absolute requirement for the future'. 'A comprehensive European policy at institutional level' is essential, as are staff exchanges and extending the European experience of students.

EEC has an aging and declining population which is under-qualified at the higher levels of knowledge and skill. With knowledge depreciating at least the rate of 7% a year, and competition from the Pacific Rim intensifying, the EC has to move fast. I congratulate the organisers of this conference on recognising the importance of the 'European dimension' and doing something about it. I trust that, in the plethora of activities which follow, that the quality of the students own learning will not be overlooked. Quality and capability: that's the EHE effect.

References

Charles Handy: *The Gods of Management* 1978 Pan Books.

P R Lawrence & J W Lorsch: *Organisation and Environment: Managing Integration & Differentiation.* 1967 Harvard University Press.

Commission of the European Communities: *Memorandum on Higher Education in the European Community.* 1990 Task Force Human Resources Education Training & Youth.

Postscript

Eventually about 100 HEIs took part in the EHE initiative and hopefully became more enterprising. There is plenty of evidence that the majority of lecturers and students took part and both groups learnt from it. That's hard enough to assess, but the real test of its value is how long the EHE effect lasts, both in individuals but also in the HE system. I regret to say that I can't help you on that. I can only imagine that in the following decades, HEIs became overwhelmed with the task of expanding numbers of students to meet the new national target of getting 50% of school leavers into Higher education. Let's hope that their enterprise skills helped them to cope better!

From Education Programmes to the Training Agency's Education Directorate

After nearly five years in the Employment Department, under my leadership, the Education Programmes Directorate had not only developed five major Programmes, but was also respected and recognised within and without the department as having a coherent policy which was having the intended effect on the Education system and the links with Business and with other government departments. Education was really punching its weight.

It had always been difficult to measure the outputs of any of the schemes. TVEI was particularly difficult, though it did get considerable praise after an early audit.

The Education Division of the Training Agency (EDTA)
THE TRAINING AGENCY'S ROLE IN EDUCATION

The Training Agency's fundamental role is to ensure that the workforce is equipped with the competencies needed in a high productivity, high skill, and high technology economy. The demographic downturn, the skills mismatch, the need for higher level skills at all ages and stages makes the role of education in helping deliver these high level competences more, crucial. Left to itself the Education system does not work to deliver the skills needed in the world economy of today and tomorrow. Thus the Training Agency's influence is crucial to the harnessing of the education system to the economic needs of our society and the training needs of our people.

The Education Programmes Directorate therefore seeks to build partnerships between government, employers and the Education system (that is schools, further education colleges, higher education and adult and continuing education) with the aim of ensuring that the capacity of the workforce is developed to its full potential.

WHAT
It does this by helping education to be:
- Relevant to the world of work:
- Responsive to the needs of employers;

236

- Accessible to adults at any age or stage;
- Practical and enterprising as well as academic;
- More flexible in delivery;
- Courses tailored to meet the needs of the individual;
- Training accredited by qualifications or records of achievement;
- Effective in raising standards of achievement.

HOW

It does this by a series of interventions and programs which have the following elements:

- Involvement of employers directly in education, through governor-ships, steering
- Committees and commitment in cash or kind.
- Involvement of students in the world of work directly through work experience, work shadowing or doing projects in the real economy;
- The development of Teaching and Learning Strategies which develop enterprise initiative and capability in the students.
- Involvement of employers in the curriculum to make it more real, relevant and motivating and work related eg case studies, problem solving, team working.
- A guidance and counselling strategy which encourages individuals and employers to make individual action plans with achievable goals.
- Include a record of achievement.

Some evidence about impact

The work was divided between five branches or teams. It was good to see below some of the evidence of some of the action and impact they were having or planning to have on the systems.

EDTA 1
TVEI: The Technical and Vocational Education Initiative

- is a long-term strategy 1987-97
- equips young people 14-18 for the demands of working life by providing them with more relevant and useful curriculum which is

responsive to employers' needs
- more qualified students, particularly in hi-tech skills such as science and technology,
- information technology and modern languages
- work experience, work shadowing and projects in the real economy for students\
- development of enterprise initiative and capability in students
- Records of achievement which employers want

TVEI Further extension 1997-99
- Will influence all 14-18 year-olds in full time education. Already 26% are involved in 3000 schools/colleges. Overall costs £900m: 1989-90 £117m

Achievements
- Doubled numbers taking science to 16 (from 36% to 64%)
- Doubled numbers taking technology to 16 (30% to 55%)
- Doubled numbers of girls taking technology
- Improved GCSE exam results and staying on rates (47% to 52%. 1987-90)
- 89% of employers are satisfied with TVEI graduates Students
- 84% TVEI graduates have learnt to work with others: work experience particularly valuable
- 72% teachers recognise how TVEI has changed their teaching styles that make the students more capable

EPD2
COMPACTS IN INNER URBAN AREAS
- Based on local partnerships between business and education
- A bargain between young people, employers, schools/colleges/ training providers.
- Young people agree to work towards locally negotiated and agreed goals in return for
- a job with training, or training leading to a job

Progress so far:

- **Twenty-nine** Compacts fully operational and twenty-one in preparation. All urban priority areas will be covered by 1991.
- **17,000** jobs with training guaranteed **3,800** employers/training providers involved **255** schools
- **38,000** young people involved in year 1. Early evaluation shows (London)
- Increase in staying on rates from 37% to 52%
- Improvement in exam results (English 72% to 78%
- **Maths** 52% to 62%)

EPD3

Work Related Further Education (WRFE)

- Incentives for further education colleges to respond more rapidly to the changing needs of employers and individuals.

Achievements

- A 20% increase in FE courses tailor-made for employers in 1989-90
- 100% of LEAs with strategic plans
- 65% of LEAs have redesigned course provision
- 65% LEAs recognise the need for staff training for vocational qualification
- Ninety-two of 113 LEAs say that without Training Agency involvement, improvements would not have taken place or would take longer.

Changes between academic years 1984/85 and 1988/89

- **LEAs** holding discussions with employers about future needs, increased from 33% to 76.1%
- **LEAs** with planned marketing strategy increased from 4% to 61%
- **LEAs** recording first destination of student leavers increased from 10% to 86%
- **LEAs** undertaking surveys of employer perceptions of colleges increased from 7% to 71%

EPD4
Higher education
- Encourages HE to be relevant to working life, responsive and accessible.

Achievements
- Enterprise in Higher Education (£8m 1990/91)
- Develops enterprising students. First year eleven institutions begin their projects
- 180 courses changed, 2,800 staff trained, employer contributions 90% of TA spend

High Technology National Training (£20 million 1990/91)
- High level provision, national shortages
- 25% long-term unemployed 1000 training places
- 400 courses, employer partnership best courses, 100% trainees find jobs

EPD5
Careers service Taken over in 1990
- Remit of offering guidance to all school leavers. Involved in Credits.

Achievements
- Over a million individual career interviews and over 83,000 group sessions carried out 1989
- 174,000 employers and training providers visited in 1989
- 134,000 vacancies notified to Service
- 78,000 placings into jobs
- 184,000 placings into YTS
- The Education Programmes Directorate therefore seeks to build partnerships between government
- Practical and enterprising as well as academic
- More flexible in delivery
- Courses tailored to meet the needs of the individual
- Training accredited by qualifications or records of achievement
- Effective in raising standards of achievement

Who does what?
The Programmes which deliver these elements are:

1. **TVEI extension 1987-99** which will influence all 14-18-year-olds in full-time Education. Without TVEI's influence secondary education would be purely academic, and students less capable.

2. **WRFE: Work Related Further Education.** Further Education Colleges deliver 70% of the training in the country (Funding Study). Without TA's influence it would not be sufficiently flexible or responsive to the needs of employers and individuals.

3. **Enterprise in Higher Education** is making undergraduates more enterprising and effective when they finally go to work. Without EHE, higher education is regarded as too 'academic' and graduates insufficiently useful and practical at work.

4. **HE Branch** is also encouraging employers to give access to Higher Level skills and qualifications to the employed through the HE system.

5. **Compacts and education/business partnerships.** These are taking much further the close working relationship between employers and schools/colleges with the aim that all those leaving full-time education get jobs which guarantee training and continuing education. Before the Training Agency's intervention, education/business partnerships did not have clear goals which improved training.

Without the Training Agency's active intervention none of this would have happened. There is still a great deal more to do before all our people reach their full potential at work. Education and 'training' need to work together to get the best possible results. This partnership is essential to get the higher level skills the economy. Over time, this is what gradually happened.

Comment
The question is what has happened to all this in the last twenty-five years and WHY. As far as I can see, most of what we were doing in the late eighties has disappeared. The record of achievement was abandoned largely because it was too difficult to design suitable robust

computer systems. The careers service in its old version was abolished, then various versions came and went, though there is an emerging realisation that more is needed and earlier, to support young people and adults in preparing for work and getting jobs. TVEI is long completed, and I do sometimes meet teachers who are still imbued with the philosophy and practice, but it is a dying breed. The new apprentice-ships look very promising, especially if the employers and FE colleges work closely together and the course design teaches the skill needed for the jobs. A short-lived Enterprise Education Project in secondary schools in the early 2,000s had some good ideas but was not supported long enough to have much impact.

In the last decade or so, overall secondary schools have become driven by the need to score highly in the league tables and the necessity to get everybody to get high grades and to go to university. This has not been healthy, especially when students have chosen the 'easy' subjects both at school and at university, That means that there are still not enough students proficient in the subjects still needed for our economy AND that those students may not be very employable.

As for the education–business partnerships, systems have changed several times and the situation is patchy.

I am however delighted that there are many new positive ideas brewing: the coalition government has been working hard to reform the education and training system. I trust that these excellent ideas will not get lost in the future.

On retiring from the civil service

In 1990, government was very keen to cut down on the number of civil servants. Not surprisingly the Employment Department was targeted again. In our department there had been, as elsewhere, creeping growth, with occasional 'culls' each time our budget was cut. So pretty well everybody was given the opportunity to take early retirement. I had never even considered the idea. In a routine way I sent off to see what the offer was. I had already transferred my teacher's pension across to the civil service, even though it was not worth all that much against the civil service scale. However, it turned out that the offer included a lump sum which might help towards up-grading my small flat in Hammersmith. I began to consider it seriously.

There were no real reasons to get out. I was enjoying my job, in spite of the long hours, the continuous travel, the huge responsibilities (shared by my senior colleagues) for over 500 people and projects of various kinds all over the country, projects which had to be visited and encouraged, speeches to be made, many on behalf of the Employment Department at big national conference events. When I considered the difficulty of managing homes in the north and in the south and caring for my mother, now widowed, or seeing my children, now fully adult and independent, but all in different places. I began to think about it more deeply.

There were some changes in the air and the department was in transition. Our leader, the Secretary, Sir Geoffrey Holland had moved to become Secretary of the Work and Pensions Department. We really missed his positive, inspiring and dynamic leadership. My immediate boss, Ian Johnston, who had mentored and supervised me when I began, had moved to head another part of the department. The TECs (Training and Enterprise Councils) were just being set up across the country and it was not at all clear how they would relate to the work of EDTA (the Education Division of the Training Agency,) as my programs were now called. Among the various ideas discussed was the idea that each of us in the senior management team should look after a specific area of the TECs, in my case the South East.

I guessed I could have handled that, despite yet more travel, but what about new initiatives? I had enjoyed the challenges we had overcome, especially now we seemed to be winning. I decided to review the situation and I was feeling very happy at what had been achieved in my patch in less than five years. My budget increased from £200 million p.a. to approx £500 million p.a. What had been achieved during my time?

1. **TVEI**: the establishment and further planned development of TVEI extension until 2009

2. **Enterprise in Higher Education 1988**: a completely new initiative we had designed, marketed and developed. The 100 universities were all eagerly awaiting their turn

3. **Compacts:** a completely new initiative 1988

4. **Education Business Partnerships: a** completely new initiative 1988

5. **Further Education:** revision and improvement of the funding methodologies

6. **Careers service:** Taken over by us

7. **Teacher Placement Service**: relocated with us from the DTI

8. **National Record of Achievement:** agreement with Education and DTI with us leading.

9. **Infinitely better communication and cooperation with and between us, the DES and the DTI, and ourselves** something I had had on my own sub agenda and had worked at quietly. No doubt so had others.

During my first four years, there were opportunities to initiate, develop and sustain some important initiatives. But would I have that opportunity in the future? I had detected just a little resentment at my expanding empire. Did I want to have to go on fighting for my corner? Would my projects miss me? No, I had great confidence in the civil service's professional ability to maintain momentum and find the right person to deliver what was required. Was I too young to retire? Fifty-six sounds too young, but then I could do consultancy work? Or even relax more? Or write a book? Or even take on some more work?

After a lot of thought, I said yes. After that was a horrible period. In order to be 'sterilised', staff give up their responsibilities three months before they leave and their replacement takes over. That means that no confidential ideas are leaked in any way in advance of their approval by their Secretary of State, Treasury and government.

I let it be known that I was leaving. Four very reputable universities offered me part-time posts on their staff. I had already been made a visiting Professor at the University of Sheffield. I was also offered Professorships at Sheffield Polytechnic, Keele University and at

Brunel University. I already had good friends and connections at each of these places. I was very tempted to stay north because I had a lovely flat there and also new friends. I loved the Derbyshire Dales and my daughter Katy was nearby in Manchester, working for Granada as a Producer of *World in Action*. And Becky had studied for her degree at Manchester.

Left to right: Katy, Becky and Christopher in the early 1990s

In the end, I chose to go south to Brunel University. I bought a five-bedroomed house in Hammersmith. It was situated only ten minutes from the tube stations and just round the corner from the Godolphin and Latymer School in Hammersmith, where I had taught previously. Not only did my three children come to see me much more, Becky came to live with me for a while, Christopher had completed his Oxford degree. Katy was married and still in Manchester. Gareth and I had split up amically over ten years before and then divorced so that he could remarry. It felt much better to be nearer to my family again. In addition, my brother David and his wife Sue were working in Singapore running the headquarters of the Overseas Missionary Fellowship, so their son Matt came to stay during the long vacations while he was a student. Hammersmith was an ideal location. It didn't take long to get to my island weekend cottage in Henley-on-Thames, or to Bampton-in-the-Bush where my mother still lived, alone, and rather house bound. I definitely needed to stay with her more often. I retired!

I took a long break, which included a two month tour in a motor caravan. We went to the Alps, camped at the foot of Mont Blanc, the Matterhorn, the Jungfrau, and travelled around the whole area. The campsites were excellent, clean and with stunning views. Then finally, I began work at Brunel.

CHAPTER 6: BRUNEL UNIVERSITY

Professor at Brunel University 1990-2001
Director of the Centre for Lifelong Learning from 1995

BRUNEL WAS NEAR TO CRANFORD AND HEATHROW and easy for me to reach both from Hammersmith and from Henley-on-Thames. I was already aware of its philosophy and admired it. The Vice Chancellor and the Secretary General been told about me by Professor Maurice Kogan, Head of the Social Sciences Faculty and the twin brother of Philip Kogan who published the second edition of my counselling book. After an interview, they immediately asked me to join them as Professor of Continuing Education. I had been made visiting Professor of Continuing Education at Sheffield University when I was working in Sheffield, so it was easy to keep the title of Professor of Continuing Education. After much thought, I took the Brunel offer, particularly as it brought me closer to my family, especially my mother who now needed more help. And I would be able to go to my weekend island cottage in Henley again. It had been very difficult to maintain or even use it during the five years I worked in the north.

Brunel, were very keen to get me and were in a race with Keele, Sheffield and Sheffield Polytechnic. I said I wanted flexible hours and I didn't want to work full time. They agreed, so I said yes. That didn't last long! It soon became clear why they needed me. There were only two members of department: an administrator and a secretary. The department hardly existed. My job was to build it almost from scratch.

There was also a well-established program of courses for businesses, called the Brunel Management Programme (BMP), which was managed by an independent unit. There was no Continuing Education in the traditional sense of extra-mural classes for adults. Brunel did not really want any. That did not make my task easy.

In the first place, I was to work 2-3 days a week, with some flexibility and to earn my salary by bringing in continuing education grants which Brunel was largely missing out on. I consulted all the Heads of Department. They were charming and courteous, it was important to get to know them all. But they just didn't want to know about Continuing Education. I soon discovered that there was no appetite for traditional adult classes anywhere. The academic staff already felt overworked. Their priority was to increase and improve their research funding and academic reputation. I could understand their point of view.

Brunel had from its very beginning an admirable philosophy. Wednesday afternoons were left free to enable other activities to take place: sports, cultural, artistic and creative. In addition, most of the students also took a year out in the middle of their degree course to do two six month work placements with a company. This was carefully managed and the students did a real job of work, sometimes including a project which linked with their degree course. In all cases, the students ended up with a much better appreciation and understanding of the world of work. They were very employable and Brunel usually came very high on the HE Employability Scale. All this fitted very well with my own philosophy of education.

Later on departments and students were allowed to opt out of the work placements and many departments encouraged this. The students gradually lost their top position in the Employability league tables. This was a great pity. However, I know that it has re-established its reputation for excellence in employability and has very close relationships with local SMEs. That's very good news.

I soon went full-time as Head of Continuing Education. I couldn't resist the challenge! So I was back to working full-time and in the evenings. We appointed further members of the team and we managed to survive and cover our costs. I succeeded in winning most of the bids I put in, so I paid for my own salary and that of all the people in my team. We were all on temporary contracts! We eventually took over the Brunel Management Programme which had been brilliant but which now was not attracting enough business customers to be viable. Sadly, eventually we had to close it down.

We had several attempts at setting up online courses and flexible part-time degrees. This was not easy, nor helped by the fact that it was not part of Brunel's strategy at first. Woolworths approached me, through a contact with a former member of the Thomas Calton staff who was now seconded to Woolworths, to find out more about the way businesses work. (A continuing legacy of the Teacher Placement Scheme!) Woolworths wanted to ensure that all their store managers had management qualifications. They bought into an online management course which was later taken over appropriately by the newly established Management Department. Likewise, the very forward-looking and ahead-of-its-time Environmental Studies Masters course, developed by the Brunel Management Programmes staff, was successfully established and then absorbed into the mainstream science faculty. It was one of the very first Environmental Management courses in the country and in both cases I was pleased to penetrate the Brunel culture: part of my agenda.

In 1992, I won a contract from the Employment Department, which had run for a long time a scheme called the TPS, the Teacher Placement Service. When I joined the Employment Department, in 1997, Lord Young, who had been our Secretary of State moved across to the DTI (Department of Trade and Industry) and took the TPS with him. We, the Employment Department, were very sad about this: it gave teachers a chance to find out what it was like to work in a business, and it would have been very helpful for the TVEI extension.

But what the Employment Department had never done was a reverse version, a scheme to get business people a placement in schools so that they understood schools better and could also advise them on what businesses were looking for in an employee. I bid for this contract and got it for Brunel. It ran from 1992-4. Regretfully, it did not take off with a bang. Business people did not see it as a priority. It was most useful in Compacts or EBPs (Education Business Partnerships), but even then it was still not a priority for business. It was quite useful in finding retired business people who wanted to 'give something back' and help schools understand industry better. The good news is that as I was leaving the Employment Department, the DTI gave the Teacher Placement Service back to us in Employment!

While I was at Brunel, I frequently got invited to make major talks at various events connected with my previous role. Brunel did not mind this because it helped with their profile. I knew pretty well most of the Vice Chancellors because I had addressed a hundred of them (all men at that time!) in Senate House, London University, when I was launching the Enterprise in Higher Education Project in 1988. They often told my Vice Chancellor they knew me and all the work I had done for government, especially, of course, Enterprise in Higher Education which eventually virtually every Higher Education Institute took part in! Most of the Brunel staff had no idea that it was me who instigated the Enterprise in Higher Education Program, in which Brunel had already participated: a £1 million EHE grant was worth having, and did make a difference.

Here is an example of an 'extra Brunel' talk.

Living with Technology, Attitudes and Energy
The Royal Society, January 22nd 1992

Attitudes of the Young to Energy: Professor Anne Jones
The seminar was organised by the Foundation for Science and Technology, part of a series on Technological Innovation and Society.

My role this evening is to comment on attitudes to energy, particularly the attitudes of the young. My expertise rests not at all upon my technological capability, but on my long experience as an educator in close contact with the young and the young in mind. Not only are the young more confident and competent than their elders when it comes to using the new technologies in the home and at work, they have also thought deeply about energy, its use and misuse.

They have thought about it in part because, in the modern school curriculum, energy, the environment and environmental health are issues which appear regularly on the timetable for pupils aged 5-16. Indeed, they may well be more popular than other recurring topics such as the ubiquitous dinosaur, and sex! They will have been encouraged to think about the issues, and to understand the science behind them. This knowledge and experience will have been reinforced and extended by the media: newspapers, periodicals and above all TV, which constantly shows, in close detail, the benefits and the disasters of new energy policies across the world. Further, even if they are not specifically religious, most young people are of an age when idealism and a questioning of the apparent values of modern society are both natural and healthy.

In a fascinating book *MILLENNIUM 2000: Towards Tomorrow's Society*, the author, Francis Kinsman, researches the views of young people. He discovered three sets of basic attitudes: 29% were 'sustenance driven', that is with a concern for security above all else; 35% were 'outer-directed', that is more concerned about their own esteem and status above all else; 36% were inner-directed, the 'self-actualised' who were little concerned about materialism, and very concerned about 'world issues' to do with people. This group, which it appears is a growing group, is particularly concerned about energy. The majority of young people do care.

Their actual behaviour sometimes belies their words. They are against squandering energy but they leave the lights on all over the house. They are against using up natural resources, but they drive about a lot. Generally they eat, drink and are merry more than us at their age or at least they did before the present recession. But they are very concerned about environmental issues relating to energy and its consumption. They can talk, and do so with authority, about the greenhouse effect, global warming, rain forests, poverty, flood and famine.

They are well informed about ways of saving energy (quoting the Centre for Alternative Technology in Wales): wind turbines, waterpower, solar energy, windmills, wave power, water power, methane gas power and insulation. They know about healthy and energy saving and energy giving food: organic, vegetarian, herb teas, no smoking. They get frustrated when their surveys showing that school dinners are unhealthy are not heeded. They insist on energy saving/environment friendly household equipment. They are scathing in the extreme if their elders happen to buy sprays which are not ozone-friendly and toilet paper and washing powder which is not 'ecological'. And light bulbs must be long life.

As for nuclear fuel, they welcome it cautiously, but are very aware of the risks, potential or actual. They have seen too many TV programs about Chernobyl, Windscale/Sellafield to be reassured by the reassurance. They worry about other sources of fuel running out, about nuclear disaster, whether caused by war or simple human error.

In terms of education, whether initial or continuing, what can be done to prepare for this brave new world? Most important of all is that young people leave full-time education equipped with the ability to think scientifically and to use their brains. Scientific knowledge and hands-on experience of scientific experimentation are vital to create this kind of enquiring mind which is neither overwhelmed nor frightened by the new technologies. Lateral thinking needs to be encouraged to release that creativity which is the hallmark of a thinking person. Positive attitudes to energy conservation and environmental health need to be fostered.

Continuous improvement through continuing education becomes essential if we are to enjoy and exploit the advantages of modern advances in science and technology. Currently, knowledge depreciates at the rate of 7% per year. In that climate, confidence, positive attitudes and the ability to go on learning become of prime importance.

COMMENT

There followed questions, discussion and supper, I attended many of these evenings and spoke again at several others in the beautiful and historic surrounding of the Royal Society. They were very worthwhile events. Some continuing education for me! And very interesting company.

Brunel: The ongoing quest for Continuing Education/ Lifelong Learning contracts

In the mid 90s, we won a contract from BAE Systems for teaching a part-time Management course for all its young managers. This was very successful. It was taught partly on their premises and partly through distance learning. We had a great presentation event at BAE and it was well publicised. BAE were pleased. We were also accredited by the CMI

251

(Chartered Management Institute) as a training centre, but this displeased the Brunel hierarchy, so it was cancelled. This was a backward step. There was huge demand for that kind of learning. NVQ's (National Vocational Qualifications) were catching on fast as possible for many professions and trades. But at Brunel, we were not allowed to run NVQ courses, not even NVQs at Management level. What a lost opportunity for the university and the local businesses. Our experience was that SMEs would no longer pay for a chalk and talk lecture, but vocational qualifications were seen as worth paying for. And sometimes the employees would help pay for the costs themselves! A missed opportunity for Brunel.

My saddest example of this lost opportunity is about the man who had saved up and taken time out to do a master's degree at Brunel in order to get a better job. He qualified, but found he was still unemployable at the level he was seeking: a master's degree does not guarantee a promotion. At the time, I was running a short online course, in conjunction with the local TEC (Training and Enterprise Council). The course included the European Driving Licence. This has nothing to do with driving at all. It was an NVQ which took you through all the basic computer programmes. He qualified and immediately got the lob he was looking for. Later on we were able to use this online training course in our ADAPT project.

We had also worked with the FE colleges nearby to consider pre-university courses especially in the sciences, to ease the transition to university and to attract better prepared students. We had even run a trial short evening class in physics in order to boost the number of applications to read physics. It was not very well attended, but it wasn't encouraging for those would-be students to navigate the way into the lecture room in the evening when everything else was closed. But at that stage, Brunel did not approve of running or being involved in courses which were below degree standard. 'We were a university not a college'.

Brunel had forgotten that we used to be a technical college. Perhaps that's why it was a touchy subject. Sadly, a few years later, the Physics Department was abolished through lack of numbers. What ever would the great Brunel himself have said about that? Much later on, the whole situation changed as the university expanded the central site and physics lived again.

In our next initiative, we worked with a Professor from Lowell College near Boston USA. Together we had run a conference on Plastics at Brunel. At his invitation, I then went over to Boston to find out more about the community colleges there. (Yes, I have never given up on that cause!). I found the colleges admirable, catering as they did for all levels of learning from basic skills, job-related skills and university level modules which could be built up over time until a degree could be awarded. Lowell College was thriving in this we-can–do-it culture in which lifelong learning could be a reality for those who chose to better themselves without having to give up their jobs. Neither did they have to take all the courses within a time frame. You could progress slowly or fast according to your commitments and your needs.

Even more interesting was my visit to the Harvard Continuing Education Department. Mainstream Harvard had realised that there was a huge market around for Adult Education at every level, including part-time degrees. Many people had retired young and had time on their hands and money. They wanted to spend it constructively, filling gaps in their knowledge, getting that degree or further degree that they were too busy or too poor to get before.

Harvard's adult education classes were so successful and financially rewarding that they were able to build from the profits a huge Tower Block building exclusively for adult learners. And then of course, it flourished even more. No squeezing into an old school classroom with shabby furniture and a caretaker standing at the door ready to lock up as soon as you got out of the way. Instead, good lecturers and well furnished rooms, coffee bars and restaurants.

I was very excited. Here is something we could do with at Brunel. We needed to set up a part-time version of the university, running a second session of courses in the evenings, obviously with the appointment of extra staff, to provide access to those many people who have never had a chance to get a degree. For example, that generation of people who could not go to university because in their day the universities were still highly selective, with only a 12-14% intake. These people could now be in the annoying situation that they were being managed by young whipper-snappers with degrees. What did these youngsters know about the real world? Other potential learners might have retired young with huge pensions and really keen to show that their brains were as good as anybody else's... or better!

It would be an enormous project, but could be done gradually. It could include some online learning and webcasting and summer residentials, like the Open University. It could do so much to raise the quality of the UK's skills and knowledge. It would do a great deal to enhance Brunel's prestige, desirability and financial stability, assuming it was well managed. It could help us in the UK to hold our own in the emerging world market. And Brunel would have done something innovative, socially and economically useful and profitable for Brunel, something I thought Brunel himself would have been proud to have done.

When I got back, I went to see a very senior member of the administrative staff. I was not well received. This was not because of sensible things Iike the need to do market research, about whether there was in fact a market for this idea, whether it would make a profit, or whether the staff would wear it.

It was a NO, a resounding NO, 'Brunel is a university for 18-21 year-olds to study full-time for three years'...or words to that effect. I was flabbergasted and very nearly resigned on the spot. In my opinion, if the university was not going to move forward to meet the needs of the time, it would not survive for very long. I was wrong about that, thank goodness, in fact Brunel is thriving, partly because it has reasserted its links with businesses in a professional way.

Postscript

In 2014, at a conference run by UALL (the Universities' Association for Lifelong Learning), it was stated that, even now, many universities hang on to that outdated model. This is a serious blockage to progress. Adults need to have opportunities to extend their academic and vocational learning and to get recognition for it throughout their lives. Without it, our economy shrinks and our people suffer.

And to be fair to Brunel, the model, I wanted has still not really taken off in the UK. There are some examples of good links between universities and their local FE Colleges. But I was talking about proper university courses, delivered in a flexible way, Now that Massive Open Online Courses (MOOCs) are coming, perhaps this idea will take off at HE level. MOOCS are world Class lectures given by the best academic lecturers the world over, shared with other universities, accessed online and watched by all who want to use them. A brilliant idea, (and obvious common sense) which has taken a long time to happen.

However, I heard the Vice Chancellor of the Open University putting the case for them and I know he has done a lot to make this happen. One problem is academics not wanting to share their intellectual capital. The other may be, but is never mentioned, is the fact that world class academics don't all present very well! At the conference I mentioned,, I unfortunately heard that some HE academics are already saying it's a problem to fit MOOCs into the higher education structure. Precisely, that reveals that the system still needs to change and become yet more flexible. You can still have a separate discussion group about the lecture online, at any time to suit or even in the flesh. The freedom of open learning is that you don't all have to watch them in room together and at the same time.

After my idea was turned down without even any discussion, I thought about retiring again. I finally decided to stay a bit longer. It was clear by then that I really still liked working full time, by which I mean all day and a good part of the evening as well. The weekend was my recreational time. I really didn't want to retire, I had begun to make an impact on Brunel and I wanted to finish the job. I was still not ready for a life of leisure.

However, within Brunel, in the nineties, various mini-reorganisations began to take place, one which slightly elevated me, then collapsed through internal politics. Before that, Brunel had started taking over other nearby colleges. One of them was the West London Institute of Higher Education. I had been a member of their Council since 1991. I had worked closely with them when I ran Cranford, so they knew me well and trusted me. I had a slightly uncomfortable spell with dual loyalties, when I was on their Council and Brunel decided to take them over. The negotiations took some time. In the end both sides were content and the merger took place in 1995.

One interesting point I noticed was Brunel's initial attitude to some of the disciplines which the West London Institute brought with it. It had built up over years an absolutely magnificent PE Department. It also had an excellent Health Education Department which included a large contract for training nurses.

Some Brunel members were somewhat sceptical about these two subjects: they were not **real** academic subjects, with high academic standing …like physics! However, once these faculties arrived at Brunel they were recognised for their true value and indeed their Research potential. Brunel's sports activities now rate amongst the highest in Britain. Now people like Usain Bolt spend time there.

After the success of taking over the West London Institute, Brunel moved students out of the other three sites that it had taken over, sold the sites for a fortune, upgraded the Brunel site and built many excellent buildings, both residential and academic. At last Brunel has the buildings and grounds it deserves and is doing well on all counts. Now it even has a female Vice Chancellor!

The Centre for Lifelong Learning. Our projects 1995-2000:

Instead of retiring. I decided to change my title and to change tack. Brunel clearly did not want any continuing education. So I set up the Centre for Lifelong Learning in 1995. I had decided the Head of Continuing Education was a very out of date title and that a better one would be Professor of Lifelong Learning. No-one in Brunel objected!

I announced that I was the Director of the Centre of Lifelong Learning! As far as I know, I was one of the very first Professors of Lifelong Learning in the UK, just as I was one of the first school counsellors in 1970.

The title never went through Senate. Nobody said a word. But the Centre thrived from thenceforth. We had found our mission and no-one ever queried anything we did from then on. We were loosely based in the Social Science Faculty and linked with the now flourishing management department who were very supportive and positive if needed.

Dr Philip Blackburn, Prof Michael Stirling, Prof Anne Jones, Dr D Sargent, Peter Hutchings, Ian Green and Tom Alderson

Fortunately I have kept some of the facts and figures about the Projects we did in this period, so I can be very accurate about what happened. They were very varied but all did something towards our goals which were the support and encouragement of Lifelong Learning. And we began to bring enormous amounts of money into Brunel.

All the money in the projects I ran was spent entirely on the projects, no bonuses for me. By 1995, we had a good spread of projects to support all our running costs. Here are some examples of what we did.

1. Widening Provision and Access for HEFCE (the Higher Education and Funding Council) September 1995-99

£480,000 i.e. £120,000 per year for four years.
AIM: To help HE become more accessible to people at work and in the community, to develop more flexible provision, more use of ICT and to

help develop the Brunel Lifelong Learning project, for which we had already developed some software to further develop the key skills which will be used in the Lifelong Learning System.

This grant underpinned our work and as it lasted for four years, it enabled us to appoint staff with some confidence, but always with temporary contracts of course. Including me!

2. BRUNEL LINK: DFEE September 96-August 99
Three overlapping projects linking graduates to SMEs

1. **Pathways to a good start in working life: DFEE and ESF (European social fund), £91.000.** Piloting a system for placing graduates in SMEs. Opens up the SME job market and provides support to graduates in their first job.

2. **Support and training for unemployed graduates, £ 69,094.** This project strengthened Brunel Link by enabling us to offer online training and support to the unemployed graduates seeking employment in a SME.

3. **Accessing higher level skills and graduates: Closing the loop, March 1998 GOL (Government Office for London) June 97–Mar 98, £20,000.** Links with Brunel link, building a database of SMEs who take graduates and providing the SMEs with the support of a trainee.

Spreading the word

The following article by me was first published in a Brunel internal magazine then the *DFEE* used it in one of theirs! It is a light-hearted yet serious account of the ways we got employers in SME's (Small and medium enterprises) to take on new graduates in a placement and then take them on as full-time employees.

I liked this because it was something we recognised was needed when we were setting up Education-Business Partnerships in the Training Agency!

HEBP: NETWORK NEWS November 1997
Brunel Link: Paradoxes & Paradigm Shifts

The DFEE, Department for Education and Employment (as it was then called), published this article by me in their Higher Education Business Partnership newsletter. It was apparent that small businesses were reluctant to employ new graduates, partly because most SME owners were not graduates and felt that they might overwhelm them. They also felt they could not afford them. Some of the best undergraduates did of course set up their own nimble and largely successful businesses. However, SMEs did not always realise at this stage that new graduates were not necessarily 'work-ready'. I put in a bid for a grant. We had to place fifty graduates in SMEs.

Ten graduate placements in jobs for starters, followed by two batches of twenty, total fifty: sounds easy, particularly when your university already has good links with SMEs and an existing HE-Employer-TEC-Business-Link Partnership. In practice, it has proved hard to achieve our first ten against our self-imposed time deadlines. We will just about do it, though there's no knowing whether or when our carefully nurtured link will suddenly break down at the last minute because our graduate has become tired of waiting for the employer to clinch the deal and has gone and got another job all by him or herself!

Horror: shouldn't we be pleased? Wasn't one of the aims of the project to help graduates improve their job-search, job-interview skills, develop more initiative, take responsibility for the management of their own career paths, learn the skills of management including that most important of skills, managing your boss? Success or failure? And what about the graduate who had been out of work for a year, took a placement he didn't enjoy, claimed it hadn't helped him all that much and then promptly found and got the job of his dreams? Success or failure? Do the apparent outcomes tell the whole story?

Of course, number crunching is important. Without targets; we might all have wasted time thinking about what to do instead of testing out our ideas. But the real proof of the pudding will be whether we actually helped improve the employability of our graduates and whether or not we helped to penetrate the defences of SMEs. At the end of all our projects, will more SMEs be willing to employ young graduates? Will more graduates be prepared to work in SMEs?

We have some interim impressions from our action research so far.

It would be interesting to compare them with the experiences of others. In our experience so far, SMEs often say that they would like to take a graduate placement but their follow-up action does not bear this out. They are often slow to define the job or task on offer, even with skilful prompting. They may take a long while to interview the candidates and then to come to a decision. Yet at the same time, they want a graduate NOW and are impatient if we don't have the right one on our books. Their expectations of graduates are unrealistically high, as if to say, well if I'm going to take one of these, they'd better be really good value for money! Very few see the merits of taking a general management trainee unless they have decided to take one on their permanent staff for themselves; in this case, they sometimes prefer to run the whole process themselves, rather than involve the university. However, in fact their skills in interviewing and job defining are often limited. They too need some training and development but they are not going to admit it or make time for it. Time is a major factor. Very few see the merit of employing a non-high-flying graduate as a general office junior. Alternatively, they are often 'in awe' of this supposedly brilliant young person.

Our experience is that the graduates themselves are a very mixed bunch. Some of them lack core skills and basic skills, as well as the skills of holding down a job: timekeeping, team-working, enthusiasm, courtesy and appropriate initiative. Those who have already done work-placements, and this applies to most Brunel graduates, are already infinitely more employable than their inexperienced counterparts. This shows in their ability to secure and keep a job. We have spent time trying to get the graduates to see the merits of the experience of several jobs if they really want to build up their skills for employability. We offer an opportunity to develop self-knowledge, a real context in which to find out about, to test and to develop those skills which will help to build inner security in the face of total uncertainty in the job market. Oh yes? Not all of them have received the message, let alone heard and understood it. In our minds, getting a 'proper job' might not be the best outcome for the new graduate. How to get this paradoxical message across? How to achieve the paradigm shift?

Telling people about it certainly doesn't seem to work: they have to work it out for themselves. But that doesn't mean that pamphlets, publicity and propaganda have no place. The opportunity to meet up, to reflect on their experience, to record learning outcomes, yes, that should do it. But what happens if they don't come, some because they have 'failed' some because they have succeeded in getting a job? Success or failure for the project!

Do professionals in the field behave differently? I was once at a meeting of personnel managers who were asked, at the end of a management development meeting, to review and record their learning for the session. Nobody offered to join in. Does that mean that they didn't learn anything? Not at all! Does learning only count if you write it down, or tell someone else about it? We all believe that this helps, but do we do it ourselves? No? Do we fill in our travel expenses every time we go out? Do we respond instantly to requests for annual reviews, job descriptions? Do we always give feedback to others? Do we keep immaculate records of our own learning or even records of any kind? Are we any different from the SMEs?

So, is it realistic to expect graduates and SMEs to follow our schemes as we would wish? A further question: in this free market economy of skills development, is it possible to measure accurately and fairly what difference we have made? Are our measures of success appropriate? Who deserves the credit/blame for what happens next?

What of the partnerships in all this? It has become fashionable and expedient for partnerships to be set up. They are particularly useful for people making bids in a hurry (and bids are almost always done in a hurry, not only because they were announced late, but also because, just like records of learning, people so often put them off until the last minute). But how well do partnerships stand up under pressure? Is enough time spent building a genuine working relationship, ensuring that partners really do share the same goals? Are partners willing to help each other, give up some autonomy and some resources to make a win-win outcome? Partnerships are rather like marriages: so often it is only after the papers have been signed that the true nature of the relationship comes out, for better or for worse.

We're still optimistic, merely conscious of the fact that it's all much more complex than it sounds. Our next big idea is to take the learning straight into and out of the SMEs through an electronic link. We'll let you know next time whether or not it worked.

BRUNEL LINK PROJECT: MISSION ACCOMPLISHED

Brunel Link: Two years later in 1999, I was able to send the following report and recommendations to the DFEE

For the last two years, the Centre for Lifelong Learning, in the School of Business and Management, has been responsible for a DFEE project which set out to encourage small and medium enterprises (SMEs) to employ graduates and to encourage graduates to work in SMEs. With 98% of organisations now small and medium in size rather than large, graduates need encouragement to take up opportunities in SMEs, now often a prerequisite of getting a job in a larger company. SMEs are sometimes reluctant to employ graduates, often expecting too little or too much of them.

Thus it was that the project team set about finding work placements in SMEs. By the end of the project, fifty graduates were successfully placed the targets had been met, but more importantly, a great deal had been learnt about how to broker the graduate/SME market.

IMPACT AND RECOMMENDATIONS

1. The need for an SME/HE brokerage service

SMEs do not feel they have access to Higher Education Institutions and HEIs do not necessarily seek out SMEs because it is not cost-effective for them. This is an important factor for HEIs to take on board. A brokerage service is needed, but the question of who pays is more complex. It became apparent from the research/project that prior to working in an SME, many graduates considered this a second best option. Working with undergraduates on the changing nature of work and of the job-market, including the significance of the growing SME job market, would help them assess their career opportunities.

2. Training issues
- It is clear that SMEs
- do not always recognise how much learning/training they provide already
- do not recognise how much they could do in-house, relatively inexpensively
- need support in putting staff development more firmly on their agenda
- need help in finding flexible and cost-effective ways of doing this;
- could be helped by HEIs in other material ways

It is also clear that work needs to be undertaken with undergraduates on helping them to manage their own learning and recognise the transferable skills they develop while studying for their degrees. More emphasis on key skills and the changing nature of work needs to be built into undergraduate courses. Undergraduates need more help in writing their CVs and preparing for the realities of work.

3. Graduates need for support and training
Graduates in SMEs need support and training during their first appointments. This service could be provided by the university sector. The Brunel-Link graduates benefited in several ways:

- A link to a university, usually their own university, during their first job. While many graduates survive or find their own networks of support once they start working, for those graduates working in SMEs this can often be harder. If SMEs are to tap into the graduate market successfully, then it may be important to look at the ways of linking them to their alumni services;
- The support and advice from the Brunel-Link team aided the graduates' success in the job. This was coupled with peer support at the Graduate Club that we set up, where they met other graduates in similar positions. Graduates who had been unemployed for some time after leaving university needed particular support and guidance because they often felt they were regarded as second best.

- Access to Lifelong Learning and Continuing Professional Development (CPD): graduates need help in continuing their learning after they leave university. The Brunel-Link scheme helped the graduates to understand the importance of CPD in the context of today's turbulent job market and to see it as part of their work and overall development.

It is worth noting that those graduates who did understand the world of work better, through undertaking structured work placements while undergraduates, were easier to place than those who had not. Experience in part-time work also helped but not so much. This is a clear indication of the importance of continuing undergraduate work placement schemes.

Outcomes and benefits to SMEs
- the recruitment of graduates;
- learning how to recruit graduates;
- assessing and analysing the skills they needed in an employee;
- obtaining access to the graduates
- value for money: receiving these services and benefits inexpensively.

Benefits to graduates
- more positive attitudes towards SMEs;
- opportunities to improve their skills base to meet the needs of the SME sector;
- opportunities to develop a portfolio of skills for employability;
- ability to get a job at the end of the project.

Higher Education Business Partnership
- improved collaboration between SMEs and the higher education sector;
- opportunities to develop shared understanding of each others' needs;
- a model which could be replicated in other contexts.

The Brunel-Link project demonstrated that goodwill and commitment on both sides can help SMEs, graduates and the university itself benefit from a partnership. Brunel-Link will continue at Brunel initially through the Brunel LifeLong Learning System.

Postscript

Ironically the question of getting graduates into SMEs is as important as ever. There are relatively few big businesses left. Gone are the days when they provided lengthy induction courses, high salaries, huge pensions and jobs for life. The Finance sector now offers high risk opportunities, but no security of tenure. Employable young graduates in the private sector like to move around a lot, though this is not always by choice.

SMEs do take on graduates and, guess what, there are complaints that they don't know how to behave at work. Many Higher Education Institutions (HEI's) are setting up Employability Courses as I did at Brunel.

TVEI and EHE both did a lot to prepare young people for the world of work. Unfortunately, over the last twenty years the pressure in schools to be high in the league tables and to meet government targets has seriously eroded the excellent work done previously in schools and universities. So now we have to start again. So why can't we do both? Some places do manage it very well as well as achieving academically. Why can't this be the norm?

BRUNEL LIFELONG LEARNING: WORKING ABROAD

There follows a raft of projects connected with republics which were formally under Russian Control as part of the USSR. Now they are 'economies in transition'.

1. HE-Industry links in Georgia (formerly part of USSR)
EUROPEAN TRAINING FOUNDATION JEP: FEB 1997 - DEC 99 £9,687
AIM: Enabling Tiblisi University to set up HE-Industry links and work placements for graduates and undergraduates. Shared research and consultancy.

Trip to Tiblisi

This was a lovely, very interesting and worthwhile project. We deliberately decided to go to Georgia because we knew of its reputation. Tiblisi is in Georgia formerly part of Russia. Georgia has always been as fiercely independent as possible. It is a beautiful country with high mountains and plains with rich soil and delicious vegetables, fruits and grapes, and absolutely delicious wines. The Georgians are intensely proud of their country. For us, Georgia was an excellent choice. The university had a very good reputation and though inevitably shabby in parts, in good condition. We were looked after very well.

We were also very lucky that the University of Tiblisi had two outstanding members of staff, the Head of the Economics Department, who was doing the 'Preparation for work' and arranging the work placements, and then Erekle, who was in charge of International Relations and who looked after visitors. He made our visits efficient and enjoyable. He spoke excellent English. He had lived in the USA for a while. He was the person we worked with the most closely. The project went on for three years, but of course we visited each year for a week only. Towards the end of the project, they all came to see us at Brunel. They were royally entertained by our Vice Chancellor and we were very happy to see then again.

You will recognise that we were able to link our experience and skills gained from the Brunel Link project into this project. It also used much of my own long experience of guidance and counselling and my work in the Employment Department. My colleague Melanie had also worked in former Russian countries before, which helped with our personal security. Neither of us ever went out alone. When we did go out, we had to be very careful. We did not speak English in public, in case we attracted unwanted attention… or even kidnapping.

I remember the first visit well. Out hotel room was absolutely freezing so we slept fully clothed, including coats and scarves, then piled the covers on top of us. At the end of the corridor, there was an old lady who kept a hot kettle going and would give us a cup of tea and a hot water bottle from time to time. The hotel food was fine, though I did pick up a nasty tummy bug from some yoghourt made from unpasteurised milk just before we left!

The university was a short walk away from our hotel so we were able to see some fine buildings. However, many were inevitably shabby and in need of decorating. Our students were studying economics and several of them were planning to work in a SME after they graduated, or even to set up their own SME. This was an exciting potential possibility now that the Russian regime had gone. With the help of a translator and some miming, we took them through the basics of getting a job. And of course they wrote out their CVs, after some hints about including any information about the experience they already had of the world of work. In fact many of them had already unofficially helped out members of their extended family in their vey small businesses. (It wasn't until I worked in Kyrgystan in 2002 that I found out that most SMEs in these countries employ their relations!). They were all found placements and after yet more briefing, off they went to work experience. The university followed through, reviewed their performance and reported the outcomes to us. Building on this pattern, the university was able to repeat the process and improve the model each time. After the three years, they didn't need any help at all.

The hospitality we received was incredible. Erekle kindly invited us to a party in his council flat. He explained that the council electricity was only turned on for a few hours each day. Sometimes there was neither light, heat, hot water or any way of cooking. To keep your meat fresh you hung it out of the window: the air outside made a perfect deep freeze! Erekle had managed to get hold of a generator, but even this didn't completely solve the problem.

The food we ate was delicious, wonderful fruit and vegetables. And the wine was the best I had ever tasted. Once a year the Economics team took us on an outing and then gave us dinner. I remember going to see the famous caves where people used to live in former times. At the dinners, the convention was that when there was a toast, you had to drink every drop of the wine in your glass and then bang it down on the table upside down. I soon learnt not to take all that much wine. But we all made and received toasts until we were exhausted, and so was the wine! I remember them driving us back through several underground tunnels, as an extra excitement. Their kindness and sense of humour was boundless.

Dinner with the Tiblisi Professor of Economics and his staff, 1997

Other Brunel visits to former Russian states
The Ukraine: LVIV: the Paris of Ukraine

We kept our eyes open and won further bids for short projects in former Russian states. In the Ukraine, we were commissioned to run some short courses to encourage women to set up small businesses. So off we went to LVIV /LVOB, the Paris of the Ukraine. The houses in the centre there were decorated in various delicate colours. They were of course in need of repainting, but it was very obvious what a beautiful and romantic place this city really was. In the courtyard coffee gathering place, we met several poets and artists, one of one of whom insisted in giving me a drawing. We went to the beautiful Opera House which was state subsidised so that that all the people could attend. We made friends, particularly with the women who wanted to practise their English. Although religion was not allowed during the Russian era, the churches now were overflowing, with crowds worshipping outside the churches. There was a strong Polish Roman Catholic influence in this country, where boundaries and ownership had changed many times.

As far the setting up of small businesses was concerned, the most obvious was the sight of a man in the street standing by a box of bananas. Many of the men we met were highly educated electrical engineers, which was the speciality of this town under the Russian regime. So for men and women, thinking up and financing a new small business was not easy task.

Asking the way in Lviv

However, we were reassured and delighted to find that the women who came to our seminars were strong and determined to succeed. They were full of ideas. We discussed legal matters, finance and marketing, with the help of some specialists and did some role play. We left feeling optimistic, even though the task was so hard. Alas, we never heard the end of this story.

With all the trouble in Ukraine today, I can fully understand that the LVIV area is Europe facing: they already were when we were there. They did not like speaking Russian. Lviv is in the west of Ukraine, and leans toward the West. I hope that they are still able to maintain their position.

136,800 Jews massacred in WW2

Estonia: TALLINN

A similar project here with a similar short program and scenario. It all went well. What was different was that the economy for small businesses was already thriving. I went there again in 2005, on one of those Baltic cruises where you visit many countries on the way to St Petersburg: it was flourishing even more. I don't know when these Cruises started, but being on that route will have helped them enormously to get ahead in the early days. The Ukraine was not located on this popular tourist route.

So in the 90s there were already stalls full of handmade good quality souvenirs and clothes. I even bought myself a mock fur lined anorak, because it was so cold. But in addition to the crafts, there were design jewellers, model clothes in the latest fashion, and excellent restaurants, and of course the wonderful architecture and historic buildings.

In retrospect, I really don't think our journey was really necessary, but it was an eye opener and very enjoyable. I have just checked the state of their economy now. It is apparently one of the most savvy and e-wired states in their region, so my impression was well-founded! Or it was until the recent troubles!

Of the three Brunel Projects in former Russian states, the Georgian one was the most enjoyable and satisfying because of the length of the contract, three years. That enabled us to make real differences with tangible targets achieved and a satisfactory end product, and some really good friends.

Brussels with Erekle, 1996

In 1995, I invited Erekle to join me and to contribute with me in speaking at an OECD seminar held in Paris on 'Education in relation to the needs of the labour market.' It went very well and Erekle gave an excellent speech. Alas, we have lost contact since then. But the good news is that in searching through all my papers I have just come across his address.

COMMENT

This was the last Brunel Project abroad, but I made lots more trips to former Russian states later. They are described in a later chapter.

Now we come to the gradual building of Lifelong Learning Systems. Our project in Wembley gave us a great deal of leads on why it was difficult to help train SMEs and why the use of learning technologies would be one way of helping to solve the problem.

From 1996-2002, we gradually raised the money, the skills and the support to develop build and test out a fully operating electronic system for tracking and recording Lifelong Learning, Eventually the final version was an online web-based system which could be reached anywhere in the world and at any time through access to the web. In 1996 that did not seem feasible! However we did it.

By 2000, 2,500 employees in 250 small businesses had learnt all the basic functions of the internet, using the LLS system we had developed. That meant that they would be employable in the 2,000s. Without this training, they could have been unemployable. They were ahead of most employees.

DEVELOPING THE LIFELONG LEARNING SYSTEM 1996-2002

DEVELOPING LIFELONG LEARNING IN WEMBLEY PARK
April 1996- March 2002
Funded by the Brent Regeneration Agency and the Government Office for London **£310,000**

The first year of this project was a feasibility study in which we analysed what the learning needs of the SMEs in this location were. This was before Wembley Park was rebuilt as a world-class football stadium. The area was a very poor one, within a multi-national multi-cultural community. The industrial part consisted of small businesses, some very small and shabby indeed and other new businesses doing well, being innovative and growing fast. It was a tangle of buildings which clearly needed regenerating. Our task at this stage was to interview them and find what kind of training they needed for their staff to help their company grow and become more profitable.

It didn't take long to realise that most of them were not interested in training at all. They did their jobs the way their father did, they didn't really need any training because they did it the way they had always done it. They didn't have any spare money to spend on training, and certainly not from a university. The new companies were keen but had very little spare cash, or time, to spend on training.

So, our attempts to get these businesses to come to Brunel failed. Our steering group pointed out that it was because this was uneconomic, ineffectual, time consuming, failed to use the benefits of the ICT revolution, and reached only very small numbers.

Further in-depth research into the views of individuals and SMEs revealed that they would not go on courses, but that they would be interested in access to learning in their workplace or in learning centres in the community. This led us to devise our over-arching ICT strategy and our aim of developing an online system of logging and tracking learning. Our mission became to reach the people the system doesn't usually reach.

However we soon found that this too was difficult for two different major reasons: cultural attitudes to learning (eg from those who had a bad time at school) and fear of computers. As both these factors began to diminish, we were able to develop even more flexible ways of reaching the unreachable. In the end we were able to customise the access and the provision to the needs of any individual or organisation. This appeared to be the only way to cater for the needs of people who are still reluctant to put time and any other resources into their own continuing learning. The individual was still not entirely driving the system, but considerable progress had been made.

This appeared to be the only way to cater for the needs of people who are still reluctant to put time and any other resources into their own continuing learning. The individual was still not entirely driving the system, but considerable progress had been made.

The Wembley project gave us the feedback we needed to do something radical. We continued working with the Wembley regeneration team until 2002. But to raise enough money to develop and test the system we already had in mind, we needed more money, big money. I put in a bid for the ADAPT ESF fund and other sources of funding and raised an amazing amount. We also linked all our projects. Lifelong Learning Systems was conceived.

Learning to invent new systems and methods

We had been working for some time on the idea of online learning, but of course this was well before the web as we know it today. As the technology progressed, we had to adapt the system we were developing several times. The 2001 version was entirely web-based.

We had always had good relationships with IBM. When I was a civil servant I had taken a three week secondment to IBM to find out all about what they did, how it was developing and potentially altering the way people learnt. Even before that, while I was at Cranford, IBM staff had supervised our sixth form students on the school-to work program. I had also been across to IBM near Heathrow to see the rooms where the great monster mainframe computers were kept. Roll on the laptop! You would never have believed then that it all would become as small as computers are today!

Social Exclusion, Technology and the Learning Society

BRUNEL wins £250,000 award for their work in reducing social exclusion, developing new technologies and contributing to building the Learning Society

In 1996, IBM had heard of our work and invited us to enter a competition they were running across fourteen European Countries. We accepted of course! The six winners were Denmark, France, Ireland, Portugal and **the UK**, namely **the Brunel LLS project**. The prize was £250,000.00 in the form of equipment and consultancy. We were overjoyed to be one of the winners! Now we could make real progress. The computers were equipped with Lotus notes and a range of multimedia materials.

At this stage, we were trying to develop the following features:

- An individual personalised mentoring system
- Self-auditing benchmarking tools,
- A system of logging and rewarding achievements and action planning
- Accees to a range of online education and training programs to suit individual needs.

Our aim was to build the confidence, knowledge and skills of the participants so that they are able to benefit from the new technologies and become skilled people who were employable in the information age.

It was not until after we won, that we realised that IBM was not only trying to help us, but also, understandably, to help their business developments. As promised, IBM seconded one of their most experienced programmers to us for a year. This was very helpful. He patiently but slowly devised the basic structure of the web system. However, initially he wanted to use Lotus Notes. We did not find Lotus Notes easy to use. We found them rather prescriptive. They tied our hands too much. Considerably later, we abandoned them all together and went straight to a web version. We were able to buy computers from IBM for the ADAPT project with some of the prize money. We were and are very grateful to IBM and their staff for all their help.

Postscript

Reading this again, I am surprised that we had made so much progress only a few years after the World Wide Web had reached academics and industries. The Lifelong Learning vision was all there. On the other hand, how chunky and complicated our system was initially. No wonder the take up of this system and all the others being incubated was slow.

Add to this the fact that most people young and old, employers or workers were not computer literate at this stage. (Many still aren't). It is not surprising that these early models didn't sell very well. Many large businesses which had banked on the year 2,000 frenzy and set up elaborate learning online systems. Unfortunately many of them collapsed, closed, and lost a lot of money in the process. The market wasn't convinced and the users still weren't ready.

Two years later we updated our system by making it a web version, but it was still not nimble enough. After I retired from Brunel and set up Lifelong Learning Ltd (I had the copyright by then), it was completely rewritten by my brilliant web designer Matt Dockerty. Alas the market was still not ready and almost single-handed I had neither the ability nor resources to continue. I closed the company in 2007.

No matter, the concepts were and still are being developed and taken up by others. For example, as already mentioned, I was delighted to read in *The Times* that at last several of our best universities, urged on by the Open University, are offering lectures on-line, given by their best academics on the web free of charge! Access and common sense at last! MOOCS **Massive Open Online Courses,** the sharing of the best lectures electronically internationally. The remaining problem is to get universities to exploit their potential fully. The latest development is that that **VOOCs** are now also on their way **Vocational Open Online Courses**!

THE 1996 IBM Competition and seminar
Social exclusion, technology and the learning society
18 June 1996, Salzburg

Before we knew we had won, we had to go to a mega IBM seminar held in Salzburg. The seminar was held in the Schloss Leopoldskron Conference Centre, a magnificent eighteenth century Chateau which overlooked a large lake and the mountains beyond: very *Sound of Music.* I stayed in a magnificent bedroom, with panelled walls and tapestries.

It was an amazing couple of days, networking and comparing notes with the other competitors. In addition, I had been asked to speak at one of the Seminars. It wasn't until I looked at the detailed Programme that I realised that I had been proposed by the European Training Foundation as an expert on training in Central and Eastern Europe! Which was true at the time, but I had never thought of it in that way! (As you will see later!) The topic of the seminar was technology and lifelong learning. We were briefed at the last moment as to what the questions were. (Easier than *Question Time* then!), but questions from the floor were open to anyone. I survived!

One unexpected joy of this conference was to see an old friend, Hywel Ceri Jones who was a member of a dining club I used to attend regularly. He had now become Deputy Director General of the European Commission. In his speech he said:

The European Union is focussed on the importance of a highly skilled and knowledgeable workforce to maintain the competitive edge and the prosperity of the region. This requires a new approach to teaching and learning which will foster a 'Learning Society' capable of adapting to the continuous change, which is the hallmark of the Information Society.

Sounds familiar!

My team were very excited about it all and after we got back we heard that we had won. We were thrilled, the prestige and the money enabled us to move on.

In about 1996, we also met an amazing young entrepreneur called Dominic Marrocco. I had given a talk on our vision in Sheffield and he had approached me afterwards to offer to help us with the design and data-management side of our project. He had set up his company **FIRSTNET** in Leeds. He himself had left school at the first possible stage and then worked in a street market. He taught himself all about computers then became a brilliant businessman, soon building up a business worth millions. He did a great deal to help our project, including making the first web-based version and even better, a thin client version. This latter version can use out of date computers as dumb terminals, through which the very latest materials such as Windows 2000, could be accessed. We then began to collect old computers in order to offer the service to community groups who could not afford to buy new computers.

Thus we could extend access and provision even further, and provide access to logging and learning any where, any time and any how. Using the three versions of the system: stand alone, web and thin client. Learners could work from home, from a learning centre, at work, on their travels, or any combination of these... Today we take this for granted, but then it was revolutionary. Now of course we would simply use our mobiles or ipads /tablets!

To do all this, we needed to raise even more big money. So we went for the ADAPT project. The only snag was that the grant provided only 45% of the costs we had to raise the other 55% ourselves, in cash or in kind. Oh well!

THE ADAPT LOG-IN PROJECT:
The continuing training of people on a typical Contract 1997-2000

ADAPT was an initiative funded by the European Social Fund. In 1997 we won the first tranche of the funding. The project definition said that:

This project will develop the Lifelong Learning System further, so that it can be used to help people at risk of being unemployable, through updating their knowledge and skills and recording their achievements. The prototype will be tested out across the whole of west London through a partnership between the TECS, business links, local authorities, FE colleges and training providers.

IBM is backing the project with matched funding of nearly £1 million. The project uses ICT to build social and economic inclusion in the Learning Society. The system being developed is seen as one of the possible prototypes for the university for Industry. The partnership we built up between all the local relevant bodies did not spring up over night, but came about after a huge amount of work in getting everybody together and to agree. It had always been one of my goals to get local bodies to work together. At last!

FINANCING THE £6,242,930.79 PROJECT!
And raising £3,433,611.84 of this amount ourselves!

When we faced up to the size of the task, I must say that I felt rather weak at the knees. The university itself did not provide any funding in cash, but they also worried about the project, especially as the way of doing the accounting was very strange. The matched funding in cash and in kind tended not to come in until later on in the project. This meant that for a long time, it looked as if the project it was in deficit.

The total funding for the ADAPT project was £6,242,930.79. This sounds wonderful, but the ESF only provided £2,809,318.86 that is 45%. Of the funding, the other 55% has to be found from public funding £1,755,005 (28.1%) and private funding £1,677,616 (26.9%).

Support from the FE colleges was particularly good. The TEC contribution went down because of their demise. The worst job was collecting the beneficiary wage costs. The SMEs had to fill in a form stating the numbers of hour's staff had spent learning and what their hourly cost was. Many companies refused to give us this information, so we could not include them in the return. Nevertheless, by the end of the project, all the targets had been met. Brunel and I heaved a sigh of relief. Nobody ever believed that we could do it.

A huge problem for the project was the fact that all the staff were on temporary contracts. We employed Brunel unemployed graduates and trained them up in the skills of running an ICT system. If they were any good, they left after six months for double the salary! An unexpected side effect, which also fulfilled the aims of the project! We also bought in some experienced staff to do the marketing to the SMEs. My secretary Rita Train and I were the only two people who saw the project through to the end. Rita was brilliant with figures, thank goodness.

How did we fulfil our contract? We struggled for ages finding a course which would solve the problem of making unemployable people employable. Then finally we worked out that from 2,000 onwards many people who could not use a computer and those who were not proficient in the basic computer programs would be at risk of being unemployable. So we started using our old friend ECDL, the European Computer Driving Licence. We were able to deliver this by disc or online. Either way involved using a computer and our system. Some employees just did a few courses others persisted until they got their computer driving licence. We encouraged the bosses to learn too!

WE DID IT! ADAPT project finished on time and on budget

The end result was stunning. Apart from developing the system and serving the FE Colleges, we had worked with 250 small businesses in the West London Region, capturing the learning hours of 2,500 learners and raising 55% of £6.2 million in matched and real funding. This felt like a really useful contribution to the local economy.

Here is a short piece summarising the management process. I wrote it later for an **UACE** Conference, the 'Universities Association for Continuing Education'. **UACE** is now called **UALL:** the Universities'

Association for Lifelong Learning. The change from Continuing Education to Lifelong Learning is now official and permanent, but it is still just as difficult to implement. In many cases, Lifelong Learning is still the 'Cinderella' department.

UACE Conference March 2002: Modernising Local Lifelong Learning
Professor Anne Jones Brunel University
From Conception to Delivery: The Brunel ADAPT project
Making virtual e-learning real

In this paper, Anne Jones briefly describes the work of the Centre for Lifelong Learning at Brunel University which, in 1997, took on the awesome task of developing an e-learning system in partnership with fourteen FE Colleges, delivering it to 250 small and medium enterprises (SMEs) in the west London Region, capturing the learning hours of 2,500 learners and raising 55% of £6.2 million in matched and real funding. She evaluates the outcomes and the impact of the project, drawing on its external evaluation.

The Learning Outcomes/key factors for success fall into four major categories:

1. **E-Project Management**: The key factors for success: tight and focussed management, linked from the beginning to planned outputs and to finance; collection of the data in the format required for final report and final claims; using electronic communications, (not phone, fax or post), meetings and workshops for keeping partners together. Learning e-management techniques. Measuring outputs, outcomes, impact, and ensuring sustainability. Crunching numbers and figures and understanding their meaning. Capturing, learning and getting a helicopter view. Creating and sustaining alliances, networks and mutually beneficial partnerships. Raising money (about £3.4 million) and getting SME participation. Tight-loose, rigorous-warm, strict-flexible, consistent-evolving, focussed-holistic, purposeful-listening: being able to hold on to both ends of the pole.

2. **Change Management: LORCS and ORCs**, locating obstacles to change and overcoming obstacles to change. In particular, technophobia, lack of confidence in using computers, in tutors, in SMEs and in learners; technical fantasy power-games, the ability of technical experts to make everything complicated, incomprehensible and expensive; non-directive counselling as an excuse for avoiding the task; lack of time as an excuse for not beginning to do something new; technical faults as proof that the old methods are best; out-of-date equipment as a reason for not beginning; fear of failure in an unknown world. Overcoming obstacles by persistence and passion, example and support, pushing, pulling and waiting, providing role models, encouraging and recognising success, putting progress chart on the wall, laughing and sharing, showing disapproval of time wasted, team lunches, hand-holding and hand withdrawing, keeping in touch, checking outcomes regularly, hands-on training workshops on site, keeping the vision clear, recognising other people's problems as well as one's own, admitting mistakes, remaining energetic and positive.

3. **Motivating Learners**: Involving the learners in managing their own learning. Reward learning, recording and displaying achievements. Exciting the SME Managers and training the work-based verifiers. Learner management and learner support, essential for e-learning, online learning and work-based learning. Enabling the tutors to let go and yet to remain supportive. Creating a new kind of learning support for the e-age. Finding and training people for this new and demanding role.

4. **E-learning:** the strengths and weaknesses. A tool, not a solution. The need to log and track all kinds of learning, not just online courses. E-learning as an essential precursor of e-commerce. e-HR management e-CRM management and e-management. 'E' remains a tool for working faster and smarter and nothing more. Market trends. Future trends. Hype versus reality.

Lifelong Learning Systems is now designing e-learning solutions for the private and public sector. The LLS e-learning management system logs and tracks, monitors and manages all kinds of learning and also offers over 300 online courses.

Our Business Sponsors and partners included Brunel University, ADAPT ESFg, IBM, NETg, Maxim Training, Plato, ICL, Knowledge Pool, Soft Skills, Blue-U com, NIIT, the Inspiration Group.com, the Technology Colleges Trust and last but not least, Firstnet Services. You will notice that some of these companies no longer exist!

It is a fact that many e-learning companies started up in the late 90s, all of them trying to catch the millennium bubble. There was also an idea around that something horrible was going to happen to computers at the turn of the century/millenium, as the mode of coding/numbering changed. In fact there were no such problems. So another tranche of brand new companies were formed now it was safe to go ahead. Many extravagantly funded companies were set up. They were convinced that e-learning was going to be BIG.

Here is an article I wrote about lifelong learning. I also presented the lecture and a live demonstration at a conference on the South Bank.

Wired Guidance, 1998

Professor Anne Jones was Head of the Continuing Education Department and Director of the Centre for Lifelong Learning at Brunel University from 1990-2000. This article was printed on 10ʰ December 1998 in People Management.

There has been much talk about lifelong learning, but little action so far, according to Anne Jones. She describes how Brunel University and its partners are attempting to deliver it electronically.

LIFELONG LEARNING IS BEGINNING to catch on as an idea, but if you actually want to find some, it's difficult to know where to start. It's particularly hard for full-time employees who can't take advantage of the many courses that are around. Many firms, especially small and medium-sized enterprises (SMEs), are not able or willing to release staff for training off-site, yet they do realise the importance of investing in new skills.

Companies want relevant training that will improve their business performance in a cost-effective way. Individuals want to keep their knowledge and skills up to date so that they can remain employable in an age of rapid technological change. IT skills are particularly crucial. But traditional offering, such as short courses, reach too few people. Something new is needed.

So what is the solution? For some time, Brunel university and its partners have been working together to find a way of meeting the needs of employers and employees in SMEs. Working through a regional partnership with businesses, TECs and Further Education colleges in west London and the Thames Valley (as well as at Fife in Scotland), Brunel's Centre for Lifelong Learning has set up an electronic system designed to reach the individuals to whom formal education and training systems do not usually extend, that is, 80% of the working population.

Our research into the learning needs of SMEs and individuals had shown that 'going on a course' was still seen as an expense rather than an investment. Computers, we found, were being used more for word-processing than as tools for business management. We concluded that a learning system was needed that offered multiple, rather than single solutions, was flexible and provided learning at a pace, place and time to suit the needs of busy people.

The resulting 'lifelong learning system', which links people to the Brunel intranet, goes right into the business or community. Each learner is provided with a computer with the system already installed, and can access the Brunel server via an ordinary telephone line (although most of their course work is done offline). The system will also file data, kept on the server. There are no installation costs. NB: this was one of our early versions before we developed out web-based versions! We abandoned it later when we changed to an online system.

The system gives people a learning log to track their accumulating knowledge and skills; tools to audit their skills and assess their development needs; information about local and national courses; and electronic search facilities for libraries, research papers and data. It also gives access at the workplace to a range of practical courses, business information and advice and training materials.

A particular feature of the system is that it gives online access to 200 IT training courses, which can then be worked on offline in the office, at home, in college, on the train, anywhere. Some of these courses have 24-hour online support. Skills shortages in IT remain acute, as standards of skills required in the workforce are rising all the time. Not enough people find the time or the resources to go on courses, so downloading materials to use offline saves time and money as well as being, for many participants, a more effective way of learning.

All users can obtain advice from a learning account manager or mentor, who may be accessed online, through video conferencing, voice-mail or fax. Each participant uses their learning log to record action plans and achievements. The logging system tracks people's progress and development, helps firms with Investors in People and supports the HR function.

Brunel's system motivates people through recognising success, and it offers a systematic way of improving business performance. Information from the system can also be used for research to inform national policy on learning, since it counts the number of people registering, completing action plans and gaining qualifications.

The potential for such a system, multiplied dozens of times across the nation is huge. Already, several boroughs are exploring the idea of using it as part of their learning strategies. The model has much in common with plans for the university for Industry.

The project is costing £6.8 million to be developed and is substantially backed by the European Social Fund's Adapt Program, which helps people who are at risk of losing their jobs to become more employable. Major industry sponsors include IBM and ICL, and other money is coming from the Higher Education Funding Council and government office of London.

The Centre for Lifelong Learning is now rolling out the system across west London. So far, the response from SMEs and from IPD members is extremely positive. Around eighty businesses are either using the system or in the process of taking it up. The membership target for the millennium is 250.

The reasons why companies are planning to use the facility vary enormously. Among the many users, there are self-employed people re-skilling to get back into employment; a printing company wanting to upgrade its computer system and to know how to use it fully, a manufacturer that needs to build a company skills profile and then make good the skills deficits by retraining employees on-site; and residential home that is using its 'downtime' for staff on night duty to work on customer care CD ROMS, supplemented by group work during the daytime. There is even a professional body that wants to track the professional development of its members. The list is endless.

The challenge now is to meet the requirements of all of these groups quickly and thoroughly. There is a real need for people of all abilities to access learning, recognition, encouragement, support and qualifications-and for SMEs to invest in lifelong learning for sustainability.

COMMENT

That was written in 1998. We were still at the intranet stage which made the system a little more complicated to use. It was still a very good effort, given the date. Later we managed to build a totally online version. That altered everything for the better.

The Institute of IT Training: E-learning seminar, August 2nd 2000
Making e-learning success a reality
Professor Anne Jones Brunel University

I was an active contributor to the 11T (Institute of IT Training) lecture program and magazine. I gave several seminars there. Some companies did in fact use the learning software, but the take-up was very slow. The best ones combined online learning with coaching at work. We had bought a lot of NETG course materials which were excellent and even included accreditation for computer qualifications such as the MCSE. Nobody was interested... even if you gave them to them free. Here is an example of part of an Institute of IT Training Lecture.

In 1995, the Centre for Lifelong Learning was established at Brunel University, with the express aim of promoting lifelong learning. Consumer Research concluded that many businesses, particularly SMEs, do not very often 'go on courses'. So the centre slogan became 'reaching people the system doesn't usually reach', that is 80% of the working population. The obvious means of doing this was to use ICT, Information Communication Technologies: this also helps overcome problems of social exclusion.

Mostly employers were still afraid that training would lead to staff losses rather than business gains. However, many of the employers themselves were not computer literate, let alone confident and able to use ICT to improve business performance. So managers' skills also needed addressing.

In 1997, Brunel bid successfully to the ESFgb ADAPT fund to develop the Logging and Learning System, working in partnership with local FE Colleges, TECs, and Chambers. The Centre for Lifelong Learning developed an electronic Lifelong Learning System which targeted workers in SMEs at risk of losing their jobs. By the end of the project, there were some 250 participating SMEs and some 2500 participating employees. Lifelong Learning Systems, (LLS) was established.

 LLS, now offers each learner a Learning Log, which tracks all kind of learning, training and development. It provides training needs analysis tools, a learning diary, external verification, a bank of learning resources, access to email, discussion groups, newsletters and useful websites and a management information system.

Within LLS, some 300 online courses are already available, mainly on management, IT (desktop and advanced) and key skills. These can be ordered and paid for online. LLS can now be accessed everywhere: in a learning centre, at work, at home or on a laptop! Mentoring, virtual or real, is an option.

It is hard to imagine that in 1995, relatively few SMEs were using computers as any thing more than a typewriter. Then, many SMEs were suspicious of the internet. Since Y2K, the bug, and the advent of free or cheaper internet connections and call charges, the internet has become a real possibility for business development and e-learning. LLS has changed with the times to a web-based delivery system, though the stand-alone system is still available as well

The advantages of e-learning

What are the advantages of e-learning for businesses? First, development of the e-commerce potential: if employees are not competent online, then e-commerce is ruled out. Electronic logging and tracking helps change those personnel files into a living and working tool. Skills gap analysis, succession planning, business planning are all possible. Ensuring that people in the company all have the skills needed to improve business performance, can contribute massively to improved profitability. Furthermore, the employees feel valued because they are extending their skills. There is growing evidence that this builds staff loyalty as well as quality.

What about e-learning online? How does that help businesses to thrive? The first and obvious point is that it saves on the training budget and, used wisely, should provide more for less: one prestigious Company has saved £100 million p.a by practising what it preaches, using online training materials.

The materials themselves often have advantages over short courses. Many people quickly forget what they learn outside the organization, but with e-learning materials, they can be visited time and time again, used for reference or revision when needed on the job. Many online materials do what educators dream about, they test the learner first and then strip out what she or he already understands, knows and can do, so that they only learn what they don't know. The tests are not used negatively, to breed a sense of failure, but positively to help learners practice until they get their optimum score.

Do most people quickly lose interest in online learning? Most people need support, encouragement and recognition if they are to do their best. Making the online learning a key part of the business strategy means planning and organizing the process, structuring the use of the system, following up with recognition for success, ensuring that there is an appropriate mix of self-paced, distance and explorative learning.

Occasional events where course members can meet make all the difference. When they do, even by video-conferencing, they are more likely to be motivated to use the discussion groups and the synchronous and asynchronous online classroom events. And as any trainer knows, peer group support is a very powerful tool in learning.

But the other advantages come from having a holistic system for managing human resources effectively. Skills gap analysis means that the next generation of skilled people can be 'grown' in good time, that company core values and skills can be promulgated effectively. The Database becomes a Management Information System, available on the CEOs 'dashboard' so that the human factors are reviewed regularly along with the other key business information.

LLS is meant to be used as a supplement not a substitute for other kinds of learning: normal classroom, work-based learning, experiential learning, community service, continuing professional development, workshop, formal, and informal learning can all work well in combination with online learning. Through systematically logging and tracking all these kinds of learning in a comprehensive way, LLS supports and reinforces more formal learning. Furthermore, the learning materials can be accessed over a period of lime, so that they can be used for revision and for refreshing know-how.

A key factor in setting up systems in lifelong learning, CPD, HRM etc. is the monitoring of the inputs, outputs and impact overall as the initiative goes along, on consistent criteria. LLS has evolved a 'tight-loose' system which allows for local and central development and monitoring. In addition, the ICT solutions built into the system are capable of being easily and economically adapted as IT solutions improve and get cheaper.

LLS is now getting queries from professional organizations who want to track CPD activity, from Companies large and small who want a Human Resource Management System, from schools and colleges which want to log and manage their students progress, from pursuers of MCI (Management Charter Initiative) and IIP, (Investors in People accreditation) and from geographically scattered organizations, from careers guidance agencies and placement organizations, from local partnerships wanting to track the learning of the whole city or community, and from individuals who want to make sure they have a record of all their achievements to take to their next employer. The possibilities are endless and very exciting... Lifelong in fact!

LEARNERS NEED TO BE AT THE HEART OF THE SYSTEM

This is an article in *Adult Learning*, 2001 written by me for NIACE in 2001(the National Institute for Adult Continuing Education).

What is interesting about this piece is that that it gives examples of some of the smaller but really significant ways in which our ADAPT project helped people.

How lifelong learning has evolved

Lifelong Learning has taken decades to gestate and even now it is taking time for the idea to be understood, made coherent and accessible to adult learners, wherever they may be. In the old days, lifelong learning was described variously as Adult Education, Workers' Educational Association (WEA) classes, continuing education. Continuing Professional Development (CPD), distance learning, correspondence courses, community education, evening classes, training courses, vocational education, on-the-job training and so on. The umbrella name helps, as does the emerging electronic age, to make it seem a realisable vision.

The present movement began in the 80s; when considerable funding was put into such initiatives as the Technical Vocational Education Initiative (TVEI); Enterprise in Higher Education, Compacts, business-education partnerships. All these programs, which I directed, promoted the idea of using ICT to promote lifelong learning. Present government has made it officially part of government policy, with its own Minister, the Learning and Skills Councils (LSCs), the University for Industry (UfI), and many other important and valuable initiatives. Yet more massive funding is going into modernised versions and variants on the Lifelong Learning (LLL) theme. Everyone is talking Lifelong Learning /ICT/widening access and provision, social inclusion, e-learning, online learning, learner support and mentoring, but still progress in turning rhetoric into reality is slow.

Motivation is the key

I left the Employment Department in 1991, in part to do something practical about Lifelong Learning. I was convinced that the learner needed to be central to the process, if it was ever to take off: motivation is the key, and motivation comes through involvement, doing rather than being told. At the same time, there needed to be a system behind the apparent chaos, so that all kinds of learning could be captured, valued and counted towards the national skills treasure chest. The idea of an electronic learning log, which involved the learner, as well as the organisation, seemed to be the answer. The electronic database behind the system would give officials the instant data they needed, at an electronic click, about progress being made, by whom and in what way. At the same time, the learners would feel empowered and proud of their new learning and skills.

At Brunel University, as Professor of Lifelong Learning, I was able to raise enough public and private sector funding to develop these ideas into an electronic Lifelong Learning System. Our £6.2 million ADAPT ESFgb project, run 1998-2000 in partnership with neighbouring Training and Enterprise Councils (TECs) and further education (FE) colleges for some 250 small and medium-sized enterprises (SMEs) and 2,500 adult learners, was particularly helpful in providing the resources to test out these ideas on a big scale. The resulting experience is invaluable in clarifying key issues.

Issues to be addressed

The first issue is that we, as a nation, are still not ready, still not really IT literate or confident, on the scale needed to exploit the advantages of ICT to support the learning age. So the vision of transforming work-based learning so that adults already at work can catch up with the skills they never learned before stalls until e-confidence and e-competence is as commonplace as using a phone/fax, or driving a car.

The second is that not only adult learners but also tutors, mentors and learning managers are also under-confident about new technology a doubt which quickly gets transmitted to the learners.

The third is the question of appropriate learner support, the key to successful e-learning. It is very hard to find people with the right combination of skills. Too often, the technical people are too 'techie', mentors too non-directive, the teachers too didactic. What are needed are people with a miracle combination of facilitating, supporting and technical skills, willing to help the learners solve the problem for themselves.

The fourth, motivating the individual learner. In our project, relatively few individual employees drove their learning forward themselves, even when they were rewarded by a professional certificate. Clearly, neither they nor their SME employers had worked out the savings to be made in time and money by e-learning, nor the value of keeping ongoing records of their learning and skills. The cost of not learning at all was not appreciated!

Nevertheless, we did succeed in getting some 2,500 employees in 250 SMEs logged into the system. The examples of 'making a difference' through the use of the system were heart warming and have encouraged us now to take the system to market.

Here are some real examples of 'making a difference:' brought about by Lifelong Learning Systems

- Enabling a small newsletter publishing micro-business, to move over from an Amstrad to a PC to transform its business through learning to use Word, Excel and the web.
- Retraining in ICT skills the 250 redundant staff of a printing company which had gone out of business, and helping them to get jobs.
- Working with a business with wheelchair bound employees for whom training in IT skills opened up all sorts of opportunities.
- Enabling a hospital to put its entire rather scattered staff through the European Computer Driving Licence (ECDL) to guarantee basic computer literacy as a core competence.
- Providing the system for a national organisation to put 5,000 teachers through their NOP training.
- Enabling a local education authority to log and track the key skills acquired by the pupils through work experience.
- Monitoring and counting the learning skills, and analysing the

characteristics of the learners, in a large, geographically dispersed learning partnership.

- Helping small businesses use the Lifelong Learning System electronic tools to assess how socially responsible their companies are.
- Helping a group of Asian women to use a computer in their own homes, so that they became more confident about going out and gained more skills.
- Providing women's refuge with a system, which they used as a way to a new and better life.
- Equipping a drop-in e-learning centre for young Afro-Caribbean youths who learned skills they did not acquire at school.
- Discreetly providing training in ICT skills for out-of-work middle-aged professionals, who at last acquired the skills they had always previously delegated to a secretary and thus became employable again.

Lifelong Learning Systems became operational as a company in 2001. By now it was entirely online, accessible from anywhere and extremely flexible in its use. LLS provide e-learning solutions for individuals and organisations: learning logs, action plans and online courses. It is much more than an e-learning provider. Most importantly, it can help capture that new learning sklls both for learners and for organisations.

We log and track all kinds of learning: courses, classes, experiential learning and self-directed study, not just online courses. We do not believe that learning should be reduced to sitting in front of a screen. We work to help small organisations which should not be persuaded to invest in a very complex expensive system when something simple and inexpensive is all that is needed in the first place.

Our system is both flexible and simple. It can also be used by adult learners as individuals as well as in a sophisticated way, by organis-ations of any size, for performance management, for linking business strategy to hr strategy and for targeted training plans; In addition, as an electronic personnel system, a communication system, a learning resou-rce, and a management information system. Our five years' experience has taught us that over-elaborate systems can be a waste of time and money Keep it simple and open to adopting new technologies as they emerge.

E-learning is only a tool

E-learning is not a miracle recipe for establishing Lifelong Learning. Within organisations, it needs to be part of a total strategy for improving performance. There needs to be commitment from senior management, the learning has to be planned and managed. The learners themselves need support, encouragement and the reward of external recognition. And the learning needs to be related to the organisation's goals. Then it works brilliantly. Commitment is essential.

E-learning is only a tool, part of a blended solution for human resource development. Most e-learners need a mixture of taught courses, online courses, experiential learning, mentoring, peer group contact, learner management, plus encouragement and recognition, if they are to remain motivated.

Despite all the hype, the predicted growth in the take-up of e-learning has been slow and uneven over the last year. What we have now is pent-up supply, rather than pent-up demand. What people need is not e-learning in isolation but an electronic learning management system which includes e-learning and captures all ways of learning. That way the unmanageable becomes manageable and the learner can be at the heart of the process. Ultimately the learners themselves will be the drivers of the systems. Then lifelong learning will really mean something.

Anne Jones
Founder and Chief Executive Officer, Lifelong Learning Systems Ltd

University Review of the Project: the pressure to keep LLS at Brunel

There were many good reasons why Brunel should keep LLS: to link in with other schools and colleges, continue the various partnerships already established including two nearby Training and Education Councils. Brunel students themselves could have had an ongoing learning log for life.

The university considered embedding and continuing the provision in several ways. The system is seen as having great potential for links with primary and secondary schools as well as with FE Colleges. In addition, Brunel is a member of several nearby Local Authority Learning Partnerships, Hillingdon, Richmond, Hounslow and west London, and a member of two Ufl Hub Partnerships, west London and NW London. Brunel would in all these cases be prepared to offer the technical infrastructure. If the system was robust enough it could be to be turned into a university enterprise, in partnership with other major private and public players and will become self-sustaining. Apparently several bids for funding were put in by Brunel for funding a continuing strategy.

So why didn't it happen? I might have stayed a little longer had I known there was real support and vision for these ideas, other than mine. Nobody had ever discussed these ideas with me. I think the real reason was the one which had always been there: THE STAFF. THE STAFF really didn't see widening access provision and CPD as a very high priority. The priorities were increasing student numbers, the reorganisation and rebuilding program, the pressure of RAE, and the university's own mission to be in the top thirty universities. The staff were already under enormous pressure. The same problem I had had all along!

Externally, the project had an enormous effect nationally, locally and regionally on raising awareness and understanding of the importance of lifelong learning and flexible structures and systems for enabling people and businesses to gain access to the knowledge and skills needed for personal, social and economic development. The added value is that this has enabled these partners to develop their own strategies further and to gain further resources. Externally, the project has been widely disseminated by conferences, launches, presentations and articles.

In the Adapt project itself, the Technology Colleges Trust is using LLS to log and track the IT training of 33,000 teachers over the next three years. Several professional bodies are also interested in the development of a version for tracking the CPD of their members. In other words, the work done can be used in a large number of ways, all of which can help to give wider access and provision to learners. The project has broken new ground and appears to include everything which the Ufl is now developing on a really big scale.

Mission Accomplished...Well not altogether!

I noted the statement above that the university was still not really interested in widening access or CPD, with great interest! So, not surprisingly I hadn't made any impact on those fronts. But I had certainly done a lot for Brunel's reputation and helped people in general to understand the importance of training, development and continuing learning in our ever changing world. That was one of my genuine aims.

So, in spite of all this praise, I wanted a change and a rest, I decided to retire again in 2000 at the age of sixty-five. The Vice Chancellor wanted me to stay on and commercialise LLS (Lifelong Learning Systems) for the university and go on bringing in projects and money. I decided that I had had enough of that. I had done this for ten years and done a lot for Lifelong Learning There were other things I still wanted to do: see more of my family, relax and travel, And to have one last go at getting LLS used at work and in schools. As I wasn't staying at Brunel, I was given the rights and set up a very small business, Lifelong Learning Systems Ltd.

The Vice Chancellor made me an Emeritus Professor in recognition of all the work I had done for Brunel for the previous ten years and in particular all the many thousands of pounds I had brought into the university, without taking any personal bonuses or ever failing to deliver within budget.

An Emeritus Professor has the title for life, but it does not mean you are still on the staff, though you could be involved in projects. I do of course keep in touch with Brunel and attend meetings of Court, Public Lectures and particularly events for small businesses, which are currently thriving.

I probably should have stayed, but I'm glad I didn't. Dominic Morrocco at Firstnet had also offered to fund the business, but in fact I tried to run it more or less single handed and with no funding at all except my own money. This was of course not very sensible! I employed one former colleague to deal with the sale of the online courses. This continued to be very difficult to do. You may remember that no-one took them even when they were free in the project. After two years we gave up the online courses. I ran several quite enjoyable projects for other universities, using the system, but only just covered my costs and salaries. I paid my programmer to do another even better version and we gave the system a really good new look.

We did this just as the announcement of another government initiative; an Enterprise in Schools Project. I also worked one day a week in a secondary school which was willing to test it out for nothing. The Enterprise in Schools Project funded by the DFEE Project had been established to bring back to schools the preparation for the world of work and the development of enterprise skills which I had fostered previously in my schools and in the Employment Department. This was right up my street and could have given me the breakthrough I wanted. However, the enterprise scheme didn't last very long and take up was poor.

I managed to get several schools interested, including the one where I was doing voluntary work. It was there that I found out what the problem was. Ironically by then, most students were extremely good with computers and all the other such devices available. The problem was that the teachers still weren't and they didn't trust the children to work by themselves. They stood over them and the pupils all did what they were told at the same time! The most successful experiment we did was to get the pupils on work experience to keep a WEX diary on the web, to analyse what skills they had learnt and to prepare a summary record of achievement. The students enjoyed that but the teachers saw it as 'more work', not as a better way for the students to learn. Most schools seemed only really interested in improving their score in the league tables. Ah well! Here is a summary of what we offered to schools reasonable price, all online.

Enterprise Track for capturing enterprise education and development

Enterprise Track is a very flexible, well-tested online system for tracking enterprise education and development. It simplifies the task of capturing what the students have learnt in a meaningful way. Each school/college/student inputs the details in their own words and in its own way. Enterprise Track provides: a template for summarising enterprise activities, knowledge, skills, attributes developed by each learner, plus final grades.

- Evidence provided by ten detailed action plans and audit trails
- Structured diary for ongoing student and staff comments, reflection/analysis
- Profile page for photo, summary CV, test results, grades and self-portrait
- Record of achievements for verified, dated logs of experience and skills developed
- An Enterprise Management Audit Tool
- Overview of progress for managers
- What are the advantages of Enterprise Track? It...
- Provides flexible online records, easy to store, to find and to access anywhere
- Provides controlled access to employers, to parents and to teachers, from wherever they are
- Encourages self-managed learning. Improves IT skills, literacy and initiative
- Motivates pupils to do more: they like seeing their achievements online
- Encourages students to reflect on and evaluate their learning
- Includes group marking facility at the touch of a button, accessible from school or home
- Verifies claims for skills, attributes, capabilities by a third party, therefore can be used to support CV's, job applications
- Provides access for the management TEAM to survey progress at any time

I still found it hard to sell and of course there are many other versions of this idea around now. I decided I was wasting my time. So I retired from LLS in 2007 and closed the company which by that time had been overtaken by the 'big boys', though not many of them succeeded either. The market for formal e-learning has still been slow and in some ways it has been taken over by the very latest technology. This means that now, at last, as we had hoped, individuals are able do things their own way, at their own pace and in their own time and place. Pupils are now so nimble with their use of all the technologies that they really don't need to be told by adults what to do. They are well ahead of us.

So that still leaves a big gap for older people to learn to keep up with the world. There is a real need for people of all abilities to be able to access learning, to get recognition for their achievements, encouragement, support and qualifications and for SMEs to invest in lifelong learning for sustainability. Colleges and universities need to help with all of this too.

My social club, Phyllis Court in Henley-on-Thames, runs brilliant computer training and support classes for its members at virtually no extra cost. The secret of our success is that we the members run these classes for ourselves... for details of what happened next go to Chapter 9 Life after work for more detail.

CHAPTER 7: LIFELONG LEARNING IN THE ECONOMIES IN TRANSITION 1990-2007

W HEN I WAS TEN I WANTED TO BE A TEACHER, then I went off the idea. The reason I read modern languages (French and Spanish) at university rather than English, was not in order to become a teacher, but to become a diplomat or an international EC/OECD/UNESCO kind of person. When I actually left university, I still wanted to work in Europe and to travel a lot. I took a comparative education course as part of my PGCE (Post Graduate Certificate in Education). I had, you may remember been Vice President of ULU in my PGCE year, looking after Hungarian refugees and running an international festival. The extra year meant that apart from developing, my leadership and organisational skills, I could work/teach anywhere in the world I happened to be. In the event I finally chose to go into teaching. I was already engaged to be married. A travelling job was out of the question. the travelling could wait until later. You have already read about my travels in Czechoslovakia in 1958. (Chapter 1 page 8) if you want to remind yourself about it! The irony of all this is that between 1991 and 2007 I did an enormous amount of work for OECD, the European Training Foundation, and the British Council. Unfortunately, by then my still fluent French was hardly ever needed. Everybody abroad wanted to practise their English. I did once give a lecture in French to the Chamber of Commerce in Paris and lived to tell the tale!

To give one example of this late development in my career: little did I know that in 2004 I would be asked by OECD to take part in a study and report on secondary education in Bulgaria, Slovenia and Albania! And more, as you will find out very soon.

However I had never expected to have to wait until I was in my sixties and then into my seventies, to do most of my travelling! In the end, I worked in eleven former Russian republics well as some EU countries eg France, Italy and the Netherlands plus the States, Canada, Japan, Korea, Singapore and New Zealand.

It is only when I read through these papers to write this book that I suddenly realised that in those years after I retired from the civil service, I had in effect been working, very part-time, for the OECD, the ETF and the British Council for fifteen years. OECD, the Organisation for Economic Cooperation and Development, based in Paris), the ETF, the European Training Foundation based in Turin and the British Council in London. I have already told you about the work I did at Brunel and thoroughly enjoyed, in Ukraine, Estonia and Georgia (Russia.) Why was I so much in demand?

It was partly because of the new initiatives we had introduced in the Employment Department. We had been working to equip people for the changes in economies and lifestyles which were taking place the world over. The economies in transition, both in main Europe and particularly in the former Russian states, wanted to learn from what Britain had done to support the inevitable changes in level of skills and competencies needed in the future workforce. By coincidence, I have has just read in *The Times* that Europeans are now looking to Britain for examples of how to come out of a recession in 2014! So we still have a reputation for innovation!

One UK idea that OECD wanted to find out about was Education-Business Partnerships, which were beginning to spread across Europe. Here I am in Holland:

OECD: schools and businesses, a new partnership

EINDHOVEN, Holland, May 1992
Paper by Professor Anne Jones, Brunel University UK

LESSONS FROM INTERNATIONAL EXPERIENCE WITH SPECIAL REFERENCE TO THE NETHERLANDS

My comments are based on my international experience over the last few years, first as a Headteacher, then as a senior government official, responsible for TVEI and Education Business Partnerships in the UK, and now as Professor of Continuing Education and International Consultant. My travels have taken me to the States, Canada, Holland, France, Denmark, Germany, Japan, Korea and Singapore.

My first comment is to note a paradox: the East-West divide.

Western countries, in particular the USA and the UK, are promoting education-industry links in general, and EB Partnerships in particular, as a way of improving educational performance. The Pacific Rim countries are not, yet they have, on normal international indices of performance, such as participation rates and exam success, better educational outputs. Why should this be?

In Japan, my questions about education-industry links were regarded as naive and inappropriate. In Korea, there was a total determination to outstrip Japan. In Singapore, education was seen as a way of building strategic competitive advantage. In all these countries, very little energy is spent on active education-industry links at school level.

Why is this? Culture must play a major part, as must stage of economic growth. Perhaps it is harder for the old established industrial nations to invest in the culture change and new equipment needed to remain competitive internationally. But in the Pacific Rim countries, there is an increasingly young population, cheap technology and a growing determination to become creative inventors rather than copycats. In the West, industry is trying to prop up a failing education system: it is a 'deficit model'. In the Pacific Rim countries, investment in education is not to improve education, but rather to increase competitive advantage. Is there anything we might learn from this?

In the West, there is panic about apparently diminishing educational standards. Employer intervention has changed from 'charity' to a desire to 'do something'. This is particularly so in the States, where there are hundreds of short-term piecemeal partnership activities, but not an overall strategy. Partnerships feel good but do they really improve national performance?

In the UK, TVEI (Technical Educational Initiative) offers a thirteen year strategy for making education more relevant to the needs of employers, but the Partnership movement, now part of the strategy of the Training and Enterprise Councils, still has to focus on defining tangible outputs. In Germany the dual-system which has long been the envy of many European countries, is now beginning to be considered too rigid and insufficiently flexible to meet the needs of the

Information Society. The Netherlands, late in developing a national strategy for partnerships may now have the advantage of being able to move more quickly into 'uncluttered' territory.

However, the fact is that most Western countries have not come to terms with the urgency of taking on the new Renaissance that is the Information Age. Strategic goals are set, but these are meaningless if they are not matched by action plans which build step by step from where we are now to where we want to be. Not enough time and skill has been invested in the management of change. Teachers, exhausted by curriculum game-playing and initiative wilt, become resistant to change. In the Pacific Rim, a different set of problems will emerge as those countries move to a new stage of economic growth, and cultural consciousness. But for the moment they are moving forward fast.

Value-added and continuous improvement are now fashionable concepts the world over, but they are easy to talk about and difficult to implement, particularly in education. Continuous education for continuous improvement and life-long learning for life-long earning, such concepts are not built into the mindsets of enough people. However difficult it is, we need now to demonstrate the business advantages of our actions: do education-business partnerships add value? The example of Volvo in Sweden shows this is possible. If we regard education less as a social activity and more as an economic activity, then it becomes easier to measure the gains. But in reaching for national targets, we also have to beware of disenfranchising and rejecting the growing underclass. We need the skills and talents of all our peoples to be enhanced.

Education systems may not yet have come to terms with the demands of the information age and the opportunities for growth offered by a learning society. The 1991 IRDAC Report to the EC stated categorically: 'The information revolution is rendering much previous education and training obsolete or simply irrelevant.'

Knowledge now depreciates at the rate of 7% per year: at Boeing in Seattle a poster proclaims that an engineer is out of date every two years. Communications are now global, instant and real-time. Information and communications technologies offer incredible opportunities for improving the effectiveness of learning. Is this where we should be focusing our efforts?

In the future, brainpower becomes the most important natural resource: the three I's, ideas, imagination and intelligence. Yet at the same time, we need to keep learning in balance so that we develop equally the head, the hands and the heart. Certainly in the UK, there has been too much polarisation between learning basic skills and learning to get on with people. The information age needs people who have ideas and imagination, who are precise and accurate, who can work in teams and solve problems.

Intellectual development, people management, practical skills and creativity, all need to go together. Above all, we need a culture of success not failure, if all our people are to develop their potential.

In the Netherlands, there have been many developments designed to address these issues. The OECD 1991 Review of the Netherlands National Policies for Education summarises the strengths and weaknesses of the Dutch system. The secondary education system which has been divided by religion, by age and by type, is being reformed, since too early vocational specialisation in the lower secondary school 'produces an alarming number of students who have no marketable skills'. The overall drop-out rate in secondary education is 30% high but not higher than other countries, which already have 'comprehensive' secondary education systems. The figures for participants in higher education are amongst the best in Europe. However, according to the OECD Report, academic school students score well on international achievement examinations but are not necessarily trained in the integrative or higher order thinking skills. This may apply equally to Pacific Rim countries.

Comments

Interestingly this chimes in with the PISA 2014 tests on problem solving in which UK did outstandingly well: what I call the TVEI effect.

Not surprisingly, the teaching profession in the Netherlands is suffering from the usual stress which comes from rapid change. Schools have more freedom from central bureaucracy but more demanding output targets. However, there is an encouraging development in education business partnerships at school level. The Rauwenhoff Commission has set up an action plan for 1991-4, for cooperation on vocational education, between employers, trade unions and education: genuine partnership between the social partners. The target is to develop skills and qualifications for the workforce, with the community college as a resource both for school leavers and young workers. The agreement aims to increase the participation rate in secondary education, making education more relevant and responsive to the needs of the learner, and leading to qualifications which are both general and specific.

The evidence from the OECD Report on Education-Business Partnerships is that the fact that these partnership initiatives are backed by national policies and money, will greatly speed the process of change. In building on the strengths of this good start, The Netherlands will want to recognise and reward success, however small, focus efforts on activities which add value, and take small, but positive steps towards national targets.

The lessons for us all are that we need to ensure that our efforts to link education and industry, to build co-operative partnerships within the community, and to realise the potential of all our people, are focused, realistic and add value, to business, to education and to the people themselves.

COMMENT

This was one of my OECD talks and was well received. The aim was to stimulate the Schools into working more closely with employers, to develop the new skills needed in the economy and to implement the Rauwenhoff Commission described above.

I was given a most beautiful set of silver pens engraved and kept in a hand carved wooden box. This was the only time I received such a gift. And I still treasure it today.

THE BRITISH COUNCIL
SEMINAR ON TVET, TECHNICAL AND VOCATIONAL
EDUCATION AND TRAINING   MARCH 1994

Keynote address by Professor Anne Jones Head of the Department of Continuing Education, Brunel University

This is another OECD talk in the UK to educate OECD and members of former Russian states about what the UK had been doing about technical and vocational education.

My contribution divides into three parts: the context, developments in technical and vocational education and training (TVET) and some questions for us to begin to discuss together.

Although I left the Employment Department in 1991, I am still working to promote lifelong learning and continuous improvement through continuous professional development. The key issues for TVET are not the same as they were, even five years ago. When we work in developing countries, we need to ensure that we are not promoting yesterday's solutions for tomorrow's problems. We also need to be sensitively aware of the stage of development and economic growth each country has reached. We have a highly sophisticated system or non-system as someone called it. We need to teach others to fish, not sell them fish. And they may be able to cut out some of the tortuous changes of direction we in the UK have been through. Above all, we need to be customer-focused, not selling our ideas, but helping others to develop and deliver theirs, in the context of their environment.

In the UK, the key question facing us is how to develop higher level skills, how to develop our intellectual capital, now that brainpower is replacing brawn. The added value comes from innovation and creativity, highly sophisticated technical skills, and the 'harder' interpersonal skills such as leadership, team building, decision making, problem solving and conflict resolution. With flatter hierarchies, supervisors are having to learn to be managers, and senior managers are having to reskill themselves in today's context. All need to understand the business they are in as a whole, each needs to be able to manage finance as well as ideas, technology and people. All the competencies are important.

The 'global market' which has now developed, with real-time instant communications the world over, is totally transforming working and learning. The developing countries should be able to leap over the intervening stages and be leading edge in information and communication technologies. This is also making the work of the British Council easier and more efficient. Using distance learning, interactive telecommunication will totally transform the kind of help and advice we can give to developing countries, directly and indirectly.

I define TVET (technical and vocational education and training) as a way of equipping people for work in a rapidly changing highly technological society. In my view, this is a cradle to the grave job. Attitudes are formed very young, and we can not afford to throw away the brainpower and experience of older people. For economic survival, and personal well-being, we need the world over, to develop a learning society in which knowledge workers learn as a matter of routine within their companies. My own experience of travelling through the Pacific Rim countries and parts of the USA confirms that this message is well understood there. In Japan, Korea and Singapore, TVET was not an issue because it was built into the culture.

We have a problem in the UK because many countries turn to us because of our reputation for academic quality. Many countries want to buy into the qualities and the qualifications which made the Empire great. Yet we ourselves have moved on from there, maybe too much, for in going for broad generic skills we have sometimes neglected the technical detail. Both are needed. So we have to beware of colluding with 'academic drift', as the ODA Paper 'Aid to Education in 1993 and beyond,' points out.

What has been happening in TVET in the UK in recent years? Is it exportable? Are elements, ideas, lessons learnt exportable? It all depends. We have a multitude of mechanisms, many of which I initiated and all of which I managed while at the Employment Department. I can only list these briefly:

Mechanisms

1. TVEI: Technical and Vocational Education Initiative
2. WRFE: Work Related Further Education
3. EHE:Enterprise in Higher Education
4. COMPACTS: Guarantees of work for young people, leaving full-time education with specified skills.
5. EBPs: Education Business Partnerships, now working through the TECs (Training and Enterprise Councils)
6. Careers services: new partnerships and pathways
7. TPS: The Teacher Placement Scheme, designed to keep teachers aware of the needs of employers
8. NRA: National Record of Achievement, to be built up over a lifetime
9. National Curriculum: including cross-curricular themes like economic and individual awareness and careers guidance
10. NTETs: National Training and Education Targets for achievement both at foundation level and throughout life.

It is worth saying that the Further Education system is the one which can cope comprehensively with all kinds of learning from basic skills to pre-university work, and all kinds of learner, including women returnees, ethnic minorities and the disabled. FE colleges are now independent and have useful experience of managing their resources entirely themselves.

Qualifications

UK qualifications have been in demand internationally because of their international currency. New qualifications are particularly relevant to TVET, viz. NVQs (National Vocational Qualifications) and GNVQs (General NVQs). The latter have been set up in schools and colleges and include an Advanced level which many students prefer to traditional A-level. Take-up has been unexpectedly high: students like the action-oriented work-related aspects.In all these qualifications, competence is the criterion for success. Input and process have been replaced by output and competence.

Target setting and standards

The move towards setting targets with high standards, with quality assurance built in and output related funding is also important. An 'individual commitment strategy[1] supports individuals who want to get higher level qualifications through a series of devices; career development loans, creches, vouchers, guidance and assessment. Small firms can get training loans. Modern apprenticeships help those young people who have left full-time education. Both HE and FE have become more flexible and responsive to customer need, being willing to provide learning opportunities at a time, pace and place which suit the learner. As the Dearing Report put it:

The country now depends primarily on FE colleges to develop practical employment related education, and offer it conveniently and efficiently *for every applicant, person or employer who needs* it.

The question for us is: what have we in the UK which is relevant to the overseas market? Should the British Council be promoting it? And if so how? What qualifications, consultancy and training can we offer through the British Council?

COMMENT

How things have changed since 1994. I find it staggering to find that nearly every Mechanism to support TVET development has now either disappeared completely or has a diminished role, eg the provision of careers services in every locality has finished, though there are still some around. Their help in schools is greatly missed. They are replaced by the National Careers Service. Some education - business partnerships still exist.

The TECs (Training and Enterprise Councils) were abolished in 2001 and replaced by the Learning and Skills Councils, which were abolished in 2009. The Regional Development Agencies took over but were replaced in 2011 by Local Enterprise Partnerships which are partnerships between local authorities and businesses. They are voluntary. The partners have to bid to establish them. In 2015, there are 39 of them.They have to prepare a strategic economic plan and may bid to government for part of £2 billion fund set up by Nick Clegg. This was the mechanism we used in EBPs COMPACTS, EHE and TVEI I note!

The National Record of Achievement has never materialised, partly because of problems in designing an online system. Cross curricular subjects got somewhat squeezed out of the curriculum for a while in many schools. However subjects like Economic and Health Education are coming back. *Plus ca change*!

It looks like either we didn't get there, or the goal posts have been changed, There is a great increase in the numbers of students going to university and degrees might not be classified as NVQ,s. What is clear from the press NOW is that though we have done well, we have NOT got enough young or old people with a high enough level of skills technical skills for the economy we have now. That's why accessible Lifelong Learning is so important, both for the economy and for our people. And of course the MSC (Manpower Services Commission) which appointed me was abolished, changed its name several times eg the Training Agency and was part of the Employment Department. All this evaporated some time after the TECs were set up.

After the advent of the TECs and then the Learning and Skills Councils and so on… there seems to have been a great deal of confusion about the best way to deliver education and training. Just as well I moved on! The good news is that the coalition government is planning to put some of this right and indeed has already started to do so. Let us hope this is not lost in election fever.

OECD: further work to support the Economies in transition

The Centre for Cooperation with Economies in transition was working with the OECD Directorate for Education, employment, labour and social affairs to help the economies in Central and Eastern Europe. They ran a series of five seminars on higher education. Mine (below) was the third lecture. They wanted the economies in transition to find out as much as possible about the UK systems. I took part in this campaign. There is inevitably some overlap between these two talks.

I presented this next paper to the OECD (Organisation for Economic Cooperation and Development) in Paris (but still in English!)

OECD Conferences

The HE System in the UK:1994. Recent measures to encourage and enable the system to respond to the needs of society and the economy
Professor Anne Jones, Paris 1994

As late as 1987, the Higher Education System in the UK reached only 12-14% of the age cohort. Characteristically, the system was elitist, full-time and highly selective, with a well deserved international reputation for the quality of teaching and research. Relations with industry were good, particularly in terms of sponsorship of Chairs, studentships and research, but higher education did not then see itself primarily as a key contributor to the needs of society and the economy. It was a 'good thing' in itself.

To some extent, this view still prevails, even though HE has now shifted to a 'mass' system with 33% participation rate and growing. An article in the *Higher Education Quarterly (1)* proclaims:

Industry's concern is to make a profit; universities are concerned with open enquiry and intellectual freedom. For more than a decade British government has sought to increase the competitiveness of industry and has initiated many changes in university which it has linked to this policy... if this tendency proceeds unchecked, universities will no longer be able to fulfil their vital role in a free society: the advancement of new and controversial ideas and the education of their students to think critically and autonomously.

Although attitudes have shifted considerably in HE over the last decade, these comments do exemplify the perceptions of some academics.

A contrary view would be that society and the economy needs new ideas and people with the ability to think critically and autonomously, but that this is exactly what the university system is not really achieving. Whichever way you look at this, there is clearly a culture clash here, one which needs a change of mindsets if the best use is to be made of the country's biggest asset, that its brainpower.

In today's and tomorrow's world, intellectual capital becomes our largest natural resource and HEIs have a key role in developing it. The innovation and creativity needed to add value to the economy comes precisely from this stimulation of original, critical and autonomous thinking, and the ability to translate ideas into action through people. All this is the proper domain of the HE system, which itself is potentially the biggest growth industry in the country, particularly if we are ever, as we need to be, to make a reality of life-long learning.

Nevertheless, it is salutary to realise that even in the late eighties, government saw no reason to increase the graduate output, nor to change in any way the nature of that graduate output. Treasury and the (then) Department of Education and Science held firmly to the 12-14% as the maximum participation rate needed!

Arguments in favour were obviously cost, but also fears about loss of quality and over-provision of graduates. It took a lot of pressure from such groups as the Confederation of British Industry (CBI), the Royal society of Arts (RSA), The Council for Industry and Higher Education (CIHE) and indeed industry in general, to persuade government that targets for HE participation should be raised.

It was only in the late eighties that UK realised fully that its graduate output was way behind that of other countries, in particular those in the Pacific Rim, and that in terms of competitiveness, Britain was lagging behind. Porter's seminal work on 'The Competitive Advantage of Nations[2] fuelled the arguments. The targets for participation in HE were raised to 25% with a long-term target of 33% by the year 2000. The target of 33% has in fact been reached this year (1994), six years ahead of time.

However, the arguments were not only about quantity, but also about quality. Employers were vociferous about the lack of skills in graduates, though they took some time to articulate clearly what these skills were. There were two sets of arguments, one to do with lack of specific technical skills (too many arts and humanities graduates), and the other to do with lack of managerial and interpersonal skills.

In a market economy, it is difficult to regulate the number of students in each subject, but the differential grants to HE, more for science and technology, less for arts and humanities, although justified to some extent by higher teaching and laboratory costs, was intended at least in part to 'encourage' greater expansion in the science and technology subjects. Unfortunately, there is still the greatest expansion and over-demand in the arts and humanities areas, and supply shortages/under-demand in science, engineering and technology. The free market has meant that students have exercised their right to choose. There is still a shortage of scientists and engineers, though as jobs become less technically specific and more generic, arts and humanities graduates are demonstrating their ability to retrain to acquire sufficient technological knowledge to manage technological businesses.[3]

In fact government did take seriously the complaint about the lack of 'capability' in the graduate output. It was the Employment Department, not the Department of Education & Science which took the initiative in doing something to improve the 'entrepreneurial' qualities of the educated workforce. The Technical Vocational Education Initiative (TVEI) was set up in 1983 with the aim of influencing young people while they were still at school. I was responsible for it from 1987-1991. By 1997, at a cost of £1 billion, virtually every state School will have participated in a scheme designed to make school students more capable and enterprising, more technologically competent and more highly educated. This was a far sighted initiative which slowly and strategically worked with the secondary education systems to ensure that young people leaving full-time education, at whatever age, are equipped to cope with the demands of a rapidly changing economy, are flexible, capable and keen to go on learning throughout life. These young people are now percolating through the HE system and into work. The increase in participation in HE from 12% in 1987 to 33% in 1994 comes largely from these TVEI graduates. The signs are that they are already more demanding of the HE system itself, since they are by and large not passive, dependent students, but students who realise the importance of taking initiative and taking responsibility for the management of their own learning.

In 1987, the TVEI initiative was followed by **Enterprise in Higher Education** (EHE)[4] a program which was established by the Employment

Department under my direction, and which aimed to equip university graduates for working life. EHE has much in common with TVEI, not only in its aims, but also in its methodology. No higher education institution was required to participate. It was (like TVEI} a voluntary activity for which higher education institutes had to bid, in competition with each other. Despite the initial resistance of the system, and some hostility, there was tremendous competition to participate. Eleven HEIs were accepted in Year 1; currently fifty-eight HEIs have contracted to deliver EHE. Funding, for each institution £1 million over five years, is allocated against a plan with specified targets and outcomes. A key demand is partnership with employers. Each institution interprets the program to meet its own particular context. Thus the free market operates within broad policy guidelines and outcomes which have been agreed. The HEIs are partners in EHE not slaves to it. This combination of targeted policy framework, voluntarily contracted and flexibly interpreted, have been highly effective both with TVEI and even more so with EHE in getting commitment and change in a potentially very resistant cultures.

In the meantime, as participation in higher education has increased[5], various problems have emerged. The demand for HE places has far exceeded government's expectations, so that whereas in 1992-93 universities were rewarded for increasing numbers, in the autumn of 1993 universities were given very strict numbers and a 45% cut in tuition fee levels. They will be penalised in 1994-95 if they either exceed these targets or fail to meet them. Concurrently, the fact that former polytechnics now have university status has caused problems for the new combined admissions system. The merging of the two separate admissions systems has thrown the market for selection into chaos. Whilst previously there were known patterns for selection, this year (1994-95) there is considerable mismatch between student demand for places and places available. Some of the well established universities may have lost out, other capable students may have failed to get places, despite the fact that examination results at Advanced Level have improved both in quantity and quality for the seventh year running. The final picture remains to be seen. The fact is that the 'market' is no longer predictable for either party.

A further emerging problem in the new expanded Higher Education System is that student grants have not been increased for three years and are gradually, in effect, being phased out. The UK has been particularly generous in the past as compared with most European countries, but clearly cannot afford to keep this up in view of the expanded numbers. Many people argue that students should not in any case be subsidised by the state to the extent that they are[6] particularly if their parents are wealthy {student fees but not grants were paid by the state regardless of parental means). A system of student loans is in operation, with the result that many students are in debt.

The UK has always had high retention and low dropout rates. However, there are signs that dropout rates are beginning to rise, and there seem to be two main reasons: financial hardship and difficulties in coping with the academic work. Many students have to take part-time jobs as they study and this may harm their studies. The UK system has not yet totally adjusted to this new kind of student, though the former polytechnics are more used to part-time and students who may need to learn in a more flexible way.

The DFE has taken measures to contain the expansion, and to encourage more flexible provision through the funding mechanisms of the HEFCE[7]. The quality of the British HE system is being fiercely guarded with the establishment of the Quality Assessment Division of the HEFCE, which has the task of ensuring quality standards are monitored through regular assessment. Other measures include extra funding to ease the transition and to allow for 'non formula' funding. Money is also being put into encouraging more 'sub-degree courses (i.e. a qualification towards a degree), more part-time student places and a further sum in preparation for the next HE expansion period in 1997. In 1994-95 the HEFCE will distribute £3,332 million to the 128 HEIs and seventy-five Further Education Colleges providing courses of higher education. £2,641 million is recurrent funding, but it is to be noted that a further £681 million is being offered to compensate institutions for the 45% reduction in tuition fee levels announced in November 1993. As far as the HEIs are concerned, this is cold comfort; yet again the unit of resource has been squeezed and universities will all have to deliver more with less. The HEFCE is the main source of funding for universities. Industry's contribution currently stands at about £350 million p. a.[8], more than most people realise. If HE-Industry partnerships develop as they could and should, the balance between public and private sector funding will also alter over time.

Without doubt, industry itself has realised how important HE is to economic survival. The Confederation of British industry (CBI)[9] has published an important document: 'Thinking Ahead and Ensuring the Expansion of HE for the twenty-first century'. They postulate the need for a 40% graduate population and opportunities for people to be re-educated and trained throughout life if UK is to remain a sustainable economy. They highlight the need to educate those already at work who missed out on qualification the first time around. They criticise the government's stop-go policy on the growth of student numbers in a market economy. They stress that successful companies are innovative and require people with high level knowledge and skills which will enable them continuously to improve their own and their company's performance. Expansion should be determined by levels of demand. The government's retreat from a market orientated approach should be reversed.

However, in encouraging this expansion, the CBI is also demanding more of HE. They want all students to develop the kind of core transferable skills, which EHE is encouraging, that is:

- The ability to learn
- Planning and organising
- Leadership
- Initiative
- Quality
- Analysis of number
- Innovation
- Flexibility

Despite the best efforts of EHE, not all universities or all departments in those universities have accepted the delivery of core skills as part of their role.

However, the HE Quality Council is well aware of the need of universities to change and to develop a more flexible system which is more responsive to the needs of employers and individual learners. The HEQC development project 'Choosing to Change' (1994)(l0) recommends that higher education should move to a system of credit awards so that students can get transferable credits for all their learning and build up qualifications gradually module by module. Although it does not spell it out, clearly a large market for this more flexible approach to higher education will be people at work, all those talented people who have left full-time education and need now to update or upgrade their qualifications. Such proposals are likely to be resisted by the HE system, but for the individual learner and for the economy, they make sense. If and when as seems likely the HEFCE moves to a funding regime that recognises credits rather than full awards, then the shift to a more flexible and customer-focused HE system will come much more quickly. I suspect that the change will meet with initial opposition, but will eventually be adopted.

The HE system in the UK is thus under pressure both from government (more with less) and from employers (more, throughout life). And students themselves are beginning to be a force in the market, being both more demanding and more discerning that hitherto. They are beginning to use their powers of selection better and are more critical of poor learning conditions. They will eventually take their custom elsewhere if they are dissatisfied.

In the meantime, the HE system has entered into various forms of 'partnership schemes' with business/industry. Some of these schemes are individually and locally negotiated. Others are pump-primed by government and, in particular, the DTI. Examples of such schemes are:

1. The Teaching Company Scheme
2. The Integrated Graduate Development Scheme
3. The Engineering Doctorate (EngD).

These all offer opportunities for graduates to do further learning in the context of real work, thus enabling technology transfer to take place. They offer particular opportunities to involve SMEs (small and medium enterprises). In addition, many universities find work placements for undergraduates before they graduate: for example, at Brunel University a four-year degree program includes two six-month work placements and an opportunity to take a diploma in professional development which itself can be counted towards an MEng. These work placements include opportunities for working in other countries.

Some large companies, eg Rover, Ford, Unipart, work very closely with universities and get accreditation for much of the learning developed in-house. There is a danger that if the HE system does not work closely with Industry, then Industry will find a way of giving its own qualifications, without a partnership with HE. The disadvantage of this development would be that both industry and HE would lose out: the cross-fertilisation of ideas and good practice which takes place in a business-education partnership activity gives added value which is much more than the detail of the program itself.

The UK has put more obvious effort into partnerships at school rather than higher education level. The COMPACTS and Education Business Partnership movements, also established by the Employment Department under my direction, have encouraged and made more coherent a range of activities at school level to help education and business work together to equip young people to make the transition to working life. These activities have now been looped into the Training and Enterprise Councils (TECS) which are local employer-led bodies responsible for the skills training in their areas. This is making more sense of the plethora of initiative which were in some senses competing with each other. But it is a glaring omission that most of this 'partnership work' is at lower levels of skill, whereas what UK Ltd needs is the development of higher level skills. In this, higher education is the obvious but so far under-used partner.

However, at least the government has now set targets for education and training. Much encouraged by the CBI, who devised them originally, the government now espouses National Training and Education Targets (NTETS) which are as follows:

Foundation Learning
1. By 1997, 80% of young people to reach NVQ2 (or equivalent).
2. Training and education to NVQ3 (or equivalent) to be available to

all young people who can benefit.
3. By 2000, 50% of young people to reach NVQ3 (or equivalent).
4. Education and Training Provision to develop self-reliance, flexibility and breadth.

Lifetime Learning
1. By 1996, all employees should take part in training or development activities.
2. By 1996, 50% of the work-force to be aiming for NVQs or units towards them.
3. By 2000, 50% of the work-force to be qualified to at least NVQ3 (or equivalent).
4. By 1996, 50% of medium to larger organisations (200 or more employees) to be 'Investors in People'.

COMMENT
Alas these seem to have fallen in by the wayside. The latest figures I have found were for 2002. They are kept in the National Archives in Richmond, London. I suspect that they were never completed.

At last, continuing education and training or lifelong learning is made explicit in policy-makers thinking. However, currently more effort is put into Foundation targets than Lifetime targets. In the Higher Education System, the importance and the potential market of the adult working population has not yet been fully realised nor exploited. In too many universities, Continuing Education is seen as marginal rather than a real source of higher skill development for the nation and appropriate work with high quality students for the universities themselves to undertake.

Universities are currently overwhelmed by the demands of the student population explosion. Despite the demographic decline in the number of eighteen-year-olds, the demand for full-time places is so buoyant, with high demand from students over twenty-one, that the imperative to develop more flexible provision, more suited to people at work, is not strong in the older universities. The new universities (i.e. the former polytechnics) are the leaders in this field.

Government funding policies, employer needs and the demands of the adult learners themselves are likely in the long and medium term to encourage a more flexible responsible Higher Education System, in which people come in and out of learning throughout their lives, building up credits towards a range of qualifications, constantly updating their knowledge so that it remains at the leading edge. To do this well, and retain the quality, which is so important for the nation's competitiveness, partnerships between HE and employers will be essential. In these partnerships, the three players, that is the learner, the employer and the learning provider will need to work out together the best way of delivering, recognising and accrediting that learning. The essence of the partnership is that it benefits all the partners and everybody wins. This is a quite different mode from getting a government grant to prop up an out-of-date system. The key to genuine change and progress is to build together for a better future.

For social regeneration, economic survival, as well as general social well-being, we need to build a Learning Society in which individual and organisations continue to develop their understanding, knowledge and skills to the highest possible level.

Anne Jones, September 1994

Our thanks to OECD for permission to reproduce these speeches.
EC/Phare/OECD (1995), Seminar V: Higher Education Policy for Economies in Transition, National Strategies and Future Dimensions for Regional Co-operation, Bratislava and Slovak Republic, 7-9 September 1994.
http://www.oecd.org/officialdocuments/publicdisplaydocumentpdf/?cot e=OCDE/GD(95)51&docLanguage=En

References

1. M Tasker & D Packham: *Higher Education Quarterly.* Vol 48 No. 3 July 1994. Blackwell
2. Michael Porter: *The Competitive Advantage of Nations.* Macmillian Press 1990
3. Heather Eggins (Ed): *Arts graduates, their skills and their Employment.* Falmer Press 1992

4. EHE: Enterprise in Higher Education: *Education Briefing*, the Employment Department.
5. DFE: *Student Numbers in Higher Education*: Great Britain 1982/8 to 1992/3. Government Statistical Service. August 1994
6. Christopher Ball: *Profitable Learning*. RSA. 1992.
7. HEFCE: *Building on Strength*. Annual Report 1993-4
8. Council for Industry & Higher Education: *Towards a Partnership: the Businesss Contribution to Higher Education* 1991
9. CBI: *Thinking Ahead: Ensuring the Expansion of Higher Education into the 21ˢᵗ century.*
10. HEQC: *Choosing to change: Extending Access Choice and Mobility in HE* June1994

Other Useful Papers

CIHE: *Collaborative Courses in HE, expanding the Partnership with Industry* 1990
IRDAC: *Quality and Relevance. The Challenge to European Education: Unlocking Europe's Human Potential.* March 1994.

Useful Addresses

CBI: The Confederation of British Industry, Centre Point, 103 New Oxford Street, London WC1A 1DU
HEFCE: The Higher Education Funding Council for England Northavon House, Coldharbour Lane Bristol BS16 1GD
RSA: The Royal Society of Arts John Adam Street London, WC1.

COMMENT

Because I was speaking to multilingual Group in Bratislava, Slovakia, I thought it helpful to give them all this extra information in case they needed more. The speech was well received. However, sadly the vision I expressed in my penultimate paragraph did not materialise either then in 1994 and nor even today, twenty years later. We cannot afford to waste so much underdeveloped brainpower. UK can do better and is beginning to prove that it can. Why did we let Adult Education and Training stagnate for so long? Does the Higher Education System still not value capability? The so called e-learning revolution has still not fully arrived. Recently I heard a very distinguished academic explain why MOOCs, (Massive open online courses) for example were so difficult to fit into the way UK degrees were constructed... Maybe the higher education structure needs to be changed radically?

This next OECD Conference was attended by representative of all the former Russian states and most European countries. My job was to be the Rapporteur for the whole conference.

OECD: Centre for Cooperation with Economies in Transition
Directorate for Education, Employment, Labour and Social Affairs

Interaction between Education, Training and the Labour Market, Bled, Slovenia, June 28-29 1995

EDUCATION REFORM IN RELATION TO THE NEEDS OF THE LABOUR MARKET

Rapporteur Professor Anne Jones. Conference Report 1995
The Agenda for Education

Economies in transition face similar problems, even though there are some variations in local context. The broad agenda for education in these economies is to encourage decentralisation, develop more flexible teaching and learning styles and to encourage participation in decision making. Students need to develop management skills and to participate actively rather than passively in learning. Competency based learning systems are developing fast. Education, and in particular life-long learning, is now seen as having a key role in combating unemployment and building economic prosperity and social well-being. There needs to be more investment in people through education and training. 'Blue-print planning' or manpower planning is an outmoded concept, given the fluidity of the economy and the shifts in the labour market. New markets are emerging, but there is a skills gap between the opportunities created by the new technologies and the existing skills supply. Short-term contracts are replacing 'jobs for life'.

The demands of the new economies

This means that adults as well as young people need opportunities to update their skills and knowledge to meet the demands of the new economies. To achieve this, partnership and cooperation between the state and employers is essential. In the United States and the United Kingdom, there are examples of Education-Business Partnerships, both at School and at university level, where students of all ages learn important skills needed in the world of work. These include communication skills, creative skills, problem-solving skills, and the ability to work in teams, inter-personal effectiveness, managerial and entrepreneurial skills.

A Staff Development Program

However, to achieve this, in each case, a massive Staff Development Program has to be put in place. First, the teachers and lecturers have to learn the skills for themselves through practical workshops which give them direct experience of the processes and an opportunity to reflect on their learning. They are then able to work together to adapt the curriculum itself and their teaching methods. In all this, they are helped by close contact with local employers who are able to give feedback and provide case-studies and examples. These are some of the benefits of local partnerships, which reflect local needs. The learners (teachers and students) need to work on the questions and answers for themselves for the learning to be effective. It is not a 'top-down' process. The broader, more flexible curriculum which is emerging is much more responsive to the needs of the individual, the community and industry. It not only helps economic prosperity, but it also helps to equip people to live and work in the rapidly changing society of today and tomorrow.

A culture change

It is relatively easy to introduce reforms without actually changing the fundamental culture: this gives a feeling of making progress, but in fact, may not bring about the culture change which is needed if economies in transition are to make that transition fully. There are three kinds of reform: modernisation, structural reform, and systemic reform. 'Improvements' to existing systems are relatively easy to make, but to meet the real needs of the emerging economies, it is important to re-examine fundamentally the system as a whole and the inter-relatedness of the parts.

Multi-skilling and higher standards

International studies show that the profound shifts in culture being experienced by economies in transition are happening all over the world. Education and training systems worldwide are not adequate at present. 'Narrow' jobs are disappearing, new multi-skilled jobs are emerging. Societies can no longer depend on 25% of the population to produce a stable economy.

Higher level knowledge and skill are needed in the workforce as a whole: that means raising the skills level of the 'forgotten' 50%.

Issues arising from the group discussion

1. The importance of understanding labour market trends

The nature of work itself is changing. In future, there will be less employment and more self-employment. Unemployment will increase for those who have not developed the skills needed in the new, emerging economies. At the same time, there will be vacancies for the most skilled jobs because of the mismatch between supply and demand. 'Jobs for life' are a thing of the past. The numbers of large enterprises are declining, numbers of SME's (small and medium enterprises) are increasing. The effects of new technologies, particularly information and communications technologies have not yet been fully realised. Mobility of labour in a global market means that both migration and immigration effect patterns of employment in unexpected ways. Home working and teleworking offer both threats and opportunities. Demographic trends, in particular the declining number of young people, and the increasing number of old people across Europe as a whole, need also to be taken into account.

2. The need for more guidance and counselling

As new teaching and learning styles are introduced, with more emphasis on empowering the students and teaching them to learn for themselves, so the role of the teacher changes to that of facilitator and mentor. Students need to manage their own learning, to reflect on that learning, to make choices about what to do and how to do it. To do this well, they need support and guidance from their teachers. With the demand for high achievement, some students drop out when the pressures are too great. These students need particularly skilful counselling so that they do not give up. For all students, it is important to recognise and reward progress, however small. The students themselves also need to understand the changing nature of work so that they are equipped for the rapidly changing job market. Their own self-esteem and sense of individual worth will be as important in this as their knowledge and skills.

3. Access to learning and the need for more guidance and counselling

In order to mobilise the latent talent in the adult population, particularly amongst women and the disadvantaged, systems and structures need to be improved further to make it easier for those wishing to return to learning so to do. Support and guidance is needed at the point of re-entry and some specific training in how to learn in new dynamic ways. In this, local partnerships between educators and employers can be very helpful, to ensure that labour market needs are met. Flexible systems built on networks are likely to be appropriate. Information and communications technologies can speed the processes. It is worth noting the success of women returners in setting up small businesses. Adults in the workforce who are already qualified also need access to further education and training, partly to update their previous knowledge and partly to develop their enterprise skills.

4. Certification/Accreditation

Qualifications become more important in a global labour market. Recognition and credit needs to be given for all learning which is relevant to labour market needs, and therefore should include academic qualifications, vocational competencies, the accreditation of prior learning, and a record of achievement. Modular accreditation, that is credit for each unit of learning, helps those who cannot, for whatever reason, take a whole qualification at a time: qualifications can then be built up at a pace that suits the learner's circumstances. Recognition of prior experiential learning helps adults returning to learning build up their credits more quickly. Formal accreditation systems can also be useful in helping to quality assure the work of private training organisations However, whatever systems are put in place, it is vital that the qualifications should be portable and transferable, so that they have currency in the international labour market.

5. The role of government departments

To achieve systemic change, it is very important for the various government departments to work together. If a single government department takes an initiative without this being part of a coordinated governmental strategy, then it may not have the desired effect. For example, sometimes employment department initiatives prevent education departments from changing. There needs to be overall commitment to a strategy and to genuine transformation, not superficial reform.

6. A flexible Higher Education System

The delivery of higher education to the learner needs to be much more flexible and to take account of the needs of the learners and their employers or sponsors. Partnerships between Higher Education Institutions and employers (both public and private sector) can ensure that the curriculum and the teaching methods reflect these needs. Flexible learning systems need to provide the learning at a time, pace and place which suits the learner: for example, this might mean recognising and accrediting on-the-job experience, providing some distance learning materials, offering some workshops on the employers' premises, using inputs and examples from the organisation to make the learning materials more realistic and setting up projects and action research to be done in the work setting. In addition, there is enormous potential for using information and communication technologies to support this kind of learning. There are examples worldwide of universities which have taken the initiative in setting up partnerships with employers. This extra business for the universities has proved to be an important source of revenue and decreased dependency on state funding. Universities can themselves set up small businesses to run short course programs, training consultancy and research.

7. Staff development programmes

To make these shifts in the culture of learning, there need to be sensitive and well thought-out programs of staff development for teachers, lecturers and trainers. They may need to experience the more participatory and inter-active learning methods that they are now being expected to use in their teaching. It is important that they learn these for themselves so that they are not resistant to the changes, but are confident about and committed to the processes. Active participation in workshops, training programs, dialogue with employers, feedback from students, reflection on learning, these are among the methods which can be useful. The best way of developing teaching and learning styles which are participatory, which encourage the learners to take responsibility for the management of their own learning and develop a range of practical transferable skills, is to do this for oneself.

8. Equal opportunities

Equity is an important principle which needs to underpin all developments. Not only is there an obvious need to help women and the physically handicapped to fulfil their potential, but in addition, care needs to be taken to support those with learning difficulties, the late developers and those who are or who may become alienated from the education and training systems and indeed from society, in part because they fear failure or lack confidence. These people need extra help and encouragement so that they themselves are not disenfranchised from society but also have the opportunity to contribute to that society and to feel and to be valued.

9. Small and medium enterprises

Given the enormous growth in the number of SMEs, many of which do not survive very long, there is a need, at local level, to support and strengthen their endeavours. A serious problem is that most SMEs do not have the resources, the systems, the finances or the time to buy into education/training. Yet they do need a lot more support in order to grow their businesses and flourish. This question is one which is universally difficult to solve, but nevertheless needs bearing constantly in mind and urgent action.

10. A Strategy for action

Above all, there is a need at governmental level for a strategic framework which builds long-term strategic change rather than responding to immediate short-term needs. Such a strategic framework needs to be designed in such a way that it can be interpreted flexibly at local level to reflect local needs and circumstances. Both at national and at local levels, partnerships need to be established involving the public sector and the private sector, employers and education/training providers, the voluntary sector and the local community, employees and local people. The learners can be at any age or stage. What is important is that they themselves are able to go on learning and developing, to the benefit of themselves and their families, their community, the local employers and the economy. The purpose of the partnerships at national and local level is to ensure that developments are coherent, flexible, responsive, and effective. Lifelong learning is the key to economic prosperity. We thank OECD for permission to include these papers.

OECD (1995), *Education Reform in Relation to the Needs of the Labour Market*, Bled, Slovenia, June 28-29 1995.
http://www.oecd.org/officialdocuments/publicdisplaydocumentpdf/?cot e=OCDE/GD%2895%29131&docLanguage=En

http://www.oecd.org/officialdocuments/publicdisplaydocumentpdf/?cot e=OCDE/GD(95)51&docLanguage=En

COMMENT

This OECD Conference was attended by representative of all the former Russian states and most European countries. My job was to be the Rapporteur for the whole conference, no mean feat. The economies in transitions are all the countries which were in the USSR and are now Republics in their own right, who have to take responsibility of running their republics themselves.

This was huge task, but as we now know, some former Russian states learnt more quickly than others. Now, twenty years later, most of these economies have made an excellent transition to an efficient and productive economy and can hold their own. Some have joined the European Community. My visit to Lithuania in 2006 to chair a forum on careers guidance revealed a sparkling, clean, smart vibrant place bustling with energy and all the latest 'mod cons'.

The 1995 conference was held in Bled, Slovenia. It was by a

beautiful lake surrounded by the Tatra Mountains. Slovenia itself is one of the most westernised of the former Russian states. The conference attendees were representatives of all the economies in transition. Yes, I did stay on afterwards to explore this beautiful country and take a short break!

OECD Centre for Cooperation with the Economies in Transition

Secondary Education Systems in Phare Countries, 1996

IN 1996, I was invited to help carry out a survey of the state of Secondary Education in three countries, Slovenia, Bulgaria and Albania.

This was a project on regional cooperation in reforming general secondary education in Central and Eastern Countries (CEECs). The aim was to encourage the CEECs to cooperate with each other to establish viable systems and policies in the transitional and post transitional periods.

We worked in small teams of about six people and went on three separate occasions to survey the secondary education systems of **Slovenia, Bulgaria** and **Albania.** The comments below are not the full report but my summary of some of the key points.

Slovenia

Slovenia was the most westernised and modern of the 3 countries. They had already created a new school leaving matriculation ('Matera') examination which was taken after four years of secondary school. It was a bold approach to the setting and the monitoring of national standards. The new Matura is a national external examination which was run for the first time in 1995, on nationally agreed and calibrated standards 'Gimnazia' (grammar schools) comprise 22.5% of the cohort. Technical schools offered a route to either higher professional education or to master craftsman training. Vocational Schools included opportunities to progress to higher professional education, had brought some more teaching resources from the Ministry, and was a catalyst for clarifying international standards across the ability range. Many teachers needed further certification. There was a shortage of foreign language and computer teachers.

Curriculum planning was centralised, leaving little room for local initiatives by a teacher or student. Further new developments were needed: new teaching materials and more cross-curriculum coordination and integration, more in-service training and support for teachers. There was little student choice in the curriculum and limited opportunities for independent study. The new Matura exam and its effects will need to be evaluated. Extensive IT training for teachers was being planned. We were very well looked after,

COMMENT

I personally was very impressed by the Matura in spite of some inevitable teething troubles. It did open up new ways of thinking and learning. It became the school leaving certificate used for further vocational training and entry to university. Over the last twenty years there have been many changes. A National Curriculum Council was set up In Slovenia in 1995. In 2003 two forms of Matera were introduced: the General Matera and the Technical Matera. Today's options for school leavers include the International Baccalaureat!

This time I stayed in Ljubljana, the historic, beautiful capital city. It is a thriving cosmopolitan town which felt quite western and relaxed. Slovenia is a very small country. Within a couple of hours, you can Ski in the Alps and swim in the warm Adriatic Sea. The scenery is stunning. I thoroughly recommend it for a holiday! Henley-on-Thames, where I live has recently partnered with it, the link being rowing!

Bulgaria

The Secondary School system was comprehensive, uniform and under-supported. The standard of the education was generally good. They had falling enrolments. There were four types of secondary education: general, technician, specialist gymnasia, and vocational-technical. There were also some special schools eg for languages, sports and humanities. 98% of lower secondary school continued to upper school. 35% of school graduates went on to higher education. There is a prescribed curriculum of books. Current aims included that the curriculum should be non-ideological, Young people should be educated in a new democratic spirit and be prepared better for life in a changing society. More training in new techniques for teachers needed, for example, group work, project work independent study, project work, student-led discussion and debate. (Sounds like they had read this book!) The former regime did not encourage independent thought or action. In the long-term the high traditional standards may have slowed up the transition to more modern approaches to learning.

Street scene Bulgaria

COMMENT

In Bulgaria, impressive solid old buildings dominated the main towns. Sofia, the capital had some lovely buildings. The atmosphere was more formal. There were also some signs of poverty. We travelled to the countryside schools as well. We were well treated and – yes – I did use my French once! As usual we were very well looked after.

Albania

Eight years of basic free education starting at age six. Absenteeism was a problem 'The Albanian system was under-supported in all standard aspects: money, time students, teachers, buildings, curriculum, materials and equipment, either in terms of shortage and quantity, quality, or efficiency'. The priority is the emergency rehabilitation of facilities. Assessment needs a coherent strategy. There was little teacher in-service training. An equal rights law was being developed in 1994. Resources for learning were limited as were the resources for in-service training. The inflexibility of the highly controlled and centralised system caused some difficulties.

COMMENT

I have one very vivid memory of a visit I made to one Albanian secondary school. Many large windows were broken. Apparently new glass to repair such damage nearly always 'disappeared' on the way to the school. When I asked for a toilet, there was only one that was functioning and the floor was covered in water.

Yet when I went into an English class, I was thrilled to find an excellent lesson in progress. The classroom was bare, with rows of old fashioned desks and one blackboard. Each pupil had a sheet of paper on which there was a description of Trafalgar Square. There followed a lively discussion of the text, all in good English. Next an analysis of the grammar, still all in English. I had not heard such a grasp of English grammar in England for a long time. No doubt the lesson had been carefully prepared in order to impress us. And it did! It must have been very difficult in Albania, all those years of isolation. How did they manage to get such a good English accent without going out of their country?

I did notice that many English speaking Albanians often had a strong American accent. Apparently this came from watching old American films or listening to the radio.

In each of these three countries, we were very well looked after. In Slovenia, especially Ljubljliana the shops were more westernised.

In Albania, there were many fine old buildings, often in need of renovation and some more modern ones, There were also Roman amphitheatres and other ancient buildings. Many of the modern buildings showed neglect or damage: broken windows for example. Signs of poverty too! We still ate well in the restaurants and in the capital, Tirana the fading grand hotels which served afternoon tea.

I found that I could very often largely understand what the officials were saying. I tested this out on myself when the interpreter was translating it all for us. It helped that so much of the 'education jargon' was the same or very similar to the English words. An international language is developing!

My work with the European Training Foundation

The European Training Foundation was founded in1990 and started work in 1994. Based in Turin, its role was to improve vocational training in non-EU countries such as those preparing for EU Accession, middle Europe, the Balkans and former Soviet Union Countries. They offer insight, experience in training and the development of programes to improve lifelong learning, skills amongst migrants, entrepreneurial learning, enterprise skills, employability, in fact most of my special interests! They had in fact funded our Brunel Project in Tiblisi Georgia!

In 1995, they invited me to join them as an expert adviser to the Advisory Forum which comprised experts on education and training from all partner and member states, international organisations and social partners. The advisory forum was divided into four sub-working groups. They were:

1. Decentralisation of vocational education and training systems.
2. The role of the private sector in vocational education and training (VET)
3. Standards in VET
4. Strategies for Continuing Training

I was to be the EU Expert Adviser to group D. We had a preliminary meeting to meet the other chairmen, (all men). Then I was asked to write a paper and to present it in MINSK, in BELARUS in February 1996. There was a problem for me as I was still recovering from an operation. In June 1996 the executive summary and recommendations were discussed. Then in November 1996, there was a further consultation with a wider group of representatives to ensure that the majority of the people consulted were happy with the recommendations for action.

My original paper would have been hard for the representatives of the European economies in transition. Under the previous regimes, they would have had very little freedom of manoeuvre. All were in organisations which were run top down with little room for initiative, leadership, management and human resource development. There was a whole new language to be learnt and then put into practice. So here are the core themes and tasks for the 10-12 June 1996 meeting and the response to my Minsk Paper.

SUBGROUP D: Continuing training
The Role and Responsibilities of key players within continuing training, including management training, government, the employees, the trainers and the learners

The executive summary and recommendations
European Training Foundation 3rd November 1996, Turin

1. Introduction

The subgroup met in Minsk, Belarus in Feb 15-16 1996 under the Chairmanship of Dr A. Sklyar. There was general support for the paper presented by Professor Anne Jones, Expert Adviser to the group. In discussion, the following points were stressed:

- There was no universal solution. Each state was at a different stage of economic and social development and action needed to be tailored to local needs. There was however some common threads in the steps to be taken next.

- The group preferred to say 'government' rather than 'the state', since a new role was being discussed. The aim would be ultimately to have as little government intervention as possible, with decisions and actions taken at regional and local levels. However, it was also generally recognised that in this transitional stage, more government intervention, including some funding, was necessary in order to secure the necessary cultural and operational changes.

- It was unrealistic at this stage to expect employers in the economies in transition to take the strong leading role that they take in continuing training in some established market economies. They are currently in a weak position. They needed help and time to develop an appropriate role, which might in the end be different in some respects from the role in the 'old' market economies.

- It was not appropriate to refer to employers without referring to employees, nor to individuals without referring to their representatives, i.e. professional bodies and trade unions. Thus the scope of these two sections was widened.
- Management Training was not discussed as a separate item but was a thread which went through each section of the report. All the key players needed Management Training and the main question was who should do it since existing trainers and teachers were largely out-of-date.
- It was difficult to get enough examples of developing good practice in the emerging economies. One urgent research task is to build up case-studies of good practice to be shared in future training events. The group made a 'menu' of suggestions for the role of each of the key players and some recommendations for follow-up action to the ETF itself.

2. The role and esponsibilities of government within continuing training

There was general support for the following roles:

1. **Strategic Leadership**: shaping and developing the overall structure, organisation and content of the educational and vocational training systems. This meant, providing a broad policy framework which allowed for initiatives to be taken at a regional and local level to suit local needs and stages of economic and social development. The active intervention of government should diminish over time.
2. **Providing a legislative framework**: to protect and to ensure the rights and responsibilities of all the players.
3. **Quality and standards**: stimulating debate and ensuring that mechanisms exist to monitor and maintain high and consistent quality and standards.
4. **Qualifications**: stimulating debate and ensuring that qualifications have national and international validity. Building bridges between academic and vocational qualifications.

5. **Licensing education and training establishments**: to ensure quality and consistency. Accreditation of approved trainers.

6. **Encouraging partnerships between the key players**: To this end, councils of the Social partners including Officials, employers, Employee representatives and Training Providers could be set up at national regional and local levels.

7. **Extra support to employers, especially SMEs in the interim phases**: such as a levy to which employers and employees contribute to build a training fund or some kind of tax relief to employers and employees for training undertaken. Setting up discussion fora with Business Leaders and Employee representatives to motivate them to participate.

8. **Retraining of state personnel**: cascaded to officials at regional and local levels. Some retraining to be done together with other key players to stimulate mutual understanding and commitment to action.

9. **National, regional and local training targets**: stimulation of debate on desirability of setting training targets.

10. **Research and development**: to encourage an audit of the skills base at national regional and local levels in order to measure progress towards meeting any skill deficit through targeted training.

11. **Management skills for the millenium**: encouraging the development of core management skills across all sectors and levels. Setting a good example by starting with government officials, and then regional and local officers.

12. **Funding**: providing targeted initial short-term funding, matched if possible by European funding, for innovative pilot projects.

13. **The underclass**: ensuring that the underclass and those with special needs are given appropriate extra support, in order to develop their potential and employability.

14. **Individuals and their representatives**: to ensure that their views are heard and their needs understood so that they can play their full part in the social and economic life of their communities. To provide some funding to support individuals' continuing training.

15. **Labour market trends**: measures to raise awareness at national, regional and local levels of the shift from labour market planning to a much more flexible approach to labour market forecasting, in view of the need for multi-skilled flexible workers who are unlikely to be in a job for life.

16. **Social cohesion and community stability through economic growth**: to recognise and appreciate the importance of individual motivation, development and being valued to the wealth, health and happiness of a local community.

2. The role and responsibilities of the private sector: the employers and representatives of employees

1. Training as an investment: to understand that training is an investment, both for the business itself, since it can be shown to improve productivity and business performance, and for the employees who thereby increase and develop their skills and become more employable.

2. Spending on training: to spend money on training as part of the business plan, ideally with contributions from government (national, regional or local) from the business itself and from the individual. Therefore, to set aside part of the annual budget for training, and to lobby for government financial support, particularly in the immediate and short-term. In the longer-term, to help employees build up a training account. To include resources spent on training, including the time of the participants, in company accounts so that the value-added can be calculated.

3. Empowering the employees: in order to stimulate innovation and to develop and use the creativity of the workforce, to give employees more responsibility for the management of projects and opportunities to feed good ideas into the system.

4. Multiskilling the employees: building a multi-skilled workforce, so that employees, whatever their level of formal responsibility, have opportunities for developing and improving their managerial, technical and inter-personal skills. To do some of this training and development on-the-job, through setting up projects, suggesting

new or wider responsibilities, getting employees to recognise that such opportunities increase their long-term chances of remaining employable.

5. Leading and managing change and innovation: self-regulation, by seeing that the leaders and senior managers of enterprises themselves have undertaken quality training in understanding the cultural and technical changes needed and in the managing such changes. Working in partnership with other Business leaders to share experiences and learn from each other. Building cooperative training programs with other business leaders.

6. Linking with education and training providers: taking measures to get to know and understand what is happening in Education and Training at all levels, from school through to university, in order to influence it and make it more relevant to the needs of business and industry. To build partnerships with educators and other Community leaders, and through these, to develop programs of education and training to which all the partners contribute ideas and resources, including opportunities for turning theory into practice, hands-on experience designed to build up skills as well as underpinning knowledge.

7. Setting up internal procedures for employee development: responding to employees' long-term needs by setting up internal mechanisms for the annual review and appraisal of employee performance, the building of individual development plans (owned by the employee) and linked to company training policies; the establishment of management development programs and procedures, in both management theory and practice; the building up of incentives and rewards for capable employees.

8. Using new information and communications technologies to improve business performance: In order to compete in the global market, gradually to buy in leading edge technology and ensure that all staff are trained to use it. To make electronic links with enterprises in other countries, in any part of the world, in order to learn new ideas and get more business. To build opportunities for 'remote 'working and 'remote' learning.

9. Lobbying governments for measures to strengthen Training: working with other employers/employees to get more resources for training initiatives, particularly at the transitional stages of development; to influence government policies, for example, to get government to consider measures to encourage training such as a training levy or tax on both organisations and individuals, so that both had a stake in continuing training and both contributed and benefitted; to feed in views on qualifications and standards.

10. Influencing professional bodies and trade unions: maintaining a dialogue with professional bodies and trade unions to exchange views and build common policies where appropriate.

3. The roles and responsibilities of the training providers within continuing training

It was understood that the training provision could and would come from a variety of sources:

- training providers such as universities, business schools, profess-ional trainers (local and imported), company personnel/training managers;
- practitioners such as business leaders, government officials (national regional or local), successful small businesses;
- practical experience such as managing projects, on-the job training, placements and staff exchanges;
- In a variety of modes, not only short or long courses, accredited or non-accredited, but also in other modes such as distance learning, computer assisted learning, multi-media inter-active CD-Roms, in-house consultancy and work-based projects etc.

It was important for government to see that quality standards were maintained by training providers. However, the free market in training materials which the individual can buy for him/herself is becoming very active and is more difficult to regulate; this can work to the advantage of the individual who can gain access without being dependent on his employer, provided the price is not too high.

The following points were made about roles:

1. Training the trainers: It was generally recognised that most existing trainers in the economies in transition are out-of date and need fundamental retraining, not just on methods, but also on culture and context. They must be retrained. This is the most serious problem for continuing training. Trainers need to be made aware of what is happening elsewhere and to observe and experience if possible training events which used modern participative methods which empowered the learners.

2. Developing flexible programs: Training providers need to develop flexible programs to deliver the learning at a time, pace and place convenient to the learner.

This is particularly important for a learner who works full-time and cannot take time off work, though some employers allow some time off in the day for this. Trainers need also to adjust their teaching styles to suit adults rather than young people. Experienced adults can themselves be a valuable teaching resource. Where possible teaching styles should match the learning style of the individual. Courses should be demand-led, that is responsive to the needs of the market, not merely offering a set product which might be out of touch with current and future demands.

3. Guidance, information and counselling: training providers need to have the resources to provide guidance and advice, so that learners can be helped to choose course appropriate to their needs and level. Students also need guidance on the qualifications structure and which qualifications they can get where. This guidance needs to be linked to realistic advice on job-opportunities. If the training providers are not able to provide all this, they should at least know where such advice can be found and advise accordingly. They also need to provide or know where to find specialist help for students with learning difficulties, who have potential but who might drop out without specialist help.

4. Training providers as businesses: Training providers themselves need to be soundly managed, financially viable, value for money, and not beyond the financialreach of the market. They need business plans and staff development plans, researchand development, marketing, quality assurance and a customer focus just like any other business. They must be prepared to accept external evaluation and quality assurance.

5. Promoting the benefits of training and qualifications: Training providers also have a role in promoting the advantages of training, and particularly training leading to qualifications for the individual and the organisations.

4. The role and responsibilities of individuals and their representatives within continuing training.

It was generally agreed that this was the most neglected role of all the players and one that needed a great deal of strengthening and support. At this stage a Charter of Rights might be more appropriate than a list of responsibilities. The potential role of the professional bodies and Trade Unions, as organisations empowered to represent and to speak up for the individual, is not to be underestimated. However, this still leaves the problem of those people who were not represented by either. The problem of the growing underclass throughout all societies is one which will not go away, but which on the contrary, is liable to grow if predictions about the future of work are to be believed. These individuals cannot be left to fend entirely for themselves. Some intervention from governments will be needed to give extra support to the 20-30% of society who will find it increasingly difficult to find work at all, according to some estimates. It is vital to establish policies and actions which stop this section of society from being excluded from work, if possible.

In as far as the group was able to make recommendations, they follow. They have be phrased two ways, for the group did not feel that most individuals would yet be confident or motivated enough to carry out these roles or tasks without help and encouragement, or indeed, without training. Individuals need some experience of being more assertive, self-reliant, and independent and demanding if they are to learn these skills, yet these are the qualities which they will have to demonstrate if they are to thrive in a world where there are no jobs for life. These are the recommendations:

Individuals should be encouraged to take responsibility:
- for the management of their own learning and careers:
- to seize every opportunity for growth and development
- to seek information and advice about opportunities.
- to show initiative and take extra responsibility in order to improve their life-chances.
- to seek some financial help from their employer or the state to continue their education and training.
- to be self-reliant, rather than depending on the state or their employer for their future well-being.
- Individuals who have succeeded in developing their potential should be encouraged to help others get access to training and self-development opportunities.

Individuals should be encouraged;
- to make action plans with personal goals for achievement.
- to develop multi-skills, including generic management skills.
- to seek further qualifications and maintain a record of achievement.
- Individuals should be encouraged to regard spending on training as an investment in their own future success.
- to press for a national scheme of financial awards/incentives to help adults who want to continue their education and training.

COMMENT
After I read the results of the consultation above, I felt as pleased as I did when I consulted the staff and pupils at my school Cranford! We had buy in. The members consulted suggested and supported these actions, and were therefore more likely to follow them up when they got home. An important point for all change managers!

5. Recommendations to the European Training Foundation
The ETF is strongly encouraged to set up as many of the following

projects/events as possible as a matter of priority: Workshops/joint training events for senior government officials from member countries. Publication of the training exercises used:

1. A 'retraining the trainers' program which could then be cascaded and piloted at regional level. Development of materials which could be published and disseminated.
2. Twinning of officials, training providers with other matched countries.
3. Research to collect case studies of good practice from the economies in transition, to be written up and used in member states.
4. Innovatory pilot projects to be established (perhaps through a bidding process) in member states.
5. Regional training programs in which all the partners work together on the issues in part to train them to work together.
6. Workshops on the desirability of targets at national, regional and local levels.

COMMENT
These were a very good set of ideas, particularly when you take into account the fact that previously in many states; most organisations activities were taken under strict government/managerial control. It is big switch to learn to take leadership, and responsibility, to be flexible and innovative. I regret that I don't know the final outcomes of these processes. Fundamental change always takes longer that you think and it is all too easy to fall back into old ways. But I was very impressed. They had clearly taken the task very seriously and thoroughly.

Some useful quotations for trainers!
The following are some of the quotations which I included in the text of the Paper I originally presented to the conference in Minsk, Belarus. Some of them are to amuse you; others are useful quotations on the subject of training!

1. From *Universal Schools in Pampaedia* by Jan Comenius (Sixteenth century)
Just as the whole world is a school for the whole of the human race,

from the beginning of time until the very end, so the whole of a person's life is a school for every one of us, from the cradle to the grave. It is no longer good enough to say with age, it is too late to begin learning.' We must say: 'Every age is destined for learning, nor is a person given other goals in learning than in life itself.

2. European Commission White Paper on Education and Training 1995

Education and training will increasingly become the main vehicle for self-awareness, belonging, advancement and self-fulfilment Education and training, whether acquired in the formal education system, on the job or in a more informal way, is the key for everyone to controlling their future and their personal development.

3. White Paper by the European Commission 1995

The society of the future will be a learning society... There is no single pattern for all to follow throughout their working lives. Everyone must be able to seize their opportunities for improvement in society and for personal fulfilment, irrespective of their social origin and educational background... The essential aim of education and training has always been personal development and the successful integration of Europeans into society through the sharing of common values, the passing on of cultural heritage and the teaching of self-reliance.

4. Round Table of European industrialists, February 1995

The essential mission of education is to help everybody to develop their own potential and become a complete human being as opposed to a tool at the service of the economy; the acquisition of skills and knowledge should go hand in hand with building up character, broadening outlook and accepting one's responsibility in society.

5. Responsibility for lifetime learning (Dec 1995) UK government

Employers must lie at the heart of all efforts to increase participation in life-time learning. They fund the greatest part of all education and training undertaken by adults. They have the responsibility for making sure that their workforce has the skills needed to meet business objectives.

6. Joe Culkin, Raychem Ltd

If you think training is expensive, try ignorance. Without it you cannot compete or improve. You are dead.

7. Robert Reich

There will be no national products or technologies, no national industries... All that will remain rigid within national borders are the people that comprise a nation. Each nation's primary assets will be its citizen's skills and insights.

8. Caius Petronous AD 66

We trained hard but it seemed that every time we were beginning to form up into teams, we would be reorganised. I was to learn later in life that we tend to meet any new situation by reorganising – and a wonderful method it can be for creating the illusion of progress while producing confusion, inefficiency and demoralisation.

9. Anne Jones 1997

To be employed is to be insecure, to be employable is to be secure.

10. Rosabeth Moss Kanter

There is little power in position as your job can change in a moment. The sustaining power lies in what skills and ideas you have.

11. Anne Jones 1998

The issues are global, the solutions are local.

There were many further meetings of the ETF Advisory Forum and I gave an occasional presentation, for example at the Round Table on Continuing Training: the challenge for the pre-accession process, held in Turin in February 1998. I presented a case study on the state of play and the role of continuing training, the key elements and main functions. In 1996, I was asked to speak about the role of the state and the social partners and so on. I always enjoyed these events.

Then in 1999, I was thrilled to be invited by the ETF to do a project in Kyrgystan which was so successful that it then spread to cover Kahzakstan and Uzbekistan with a final output of a booklet written for employers, especially SMEs. The booklet was called *Human Resource Development, A Practical Guide.*

I still can't believe that I travelled out to these remote places by myself without turning a hair! I was usually met at the airport, (the last person to be met), by a scruffy man with my name on a placard, who took me off in an old car to my hotel or flat! I was not allowed out without an interpreter... that was wise.

I wrote an article on this which was published in *World Link* in 2000. Here it is:

Skills development in Kyrgyzstan, Kazakhstan and Uzbekistan

Anne Jones describes a European Training Foundation project to develop a more business-oriented culture in a former Soviet state.

In December 1999, I went, at the invitation of the European Training Foundation (ETF), to Kyrgyzstan to help train a team of eight social researchers to carry out a survey of the skills and attitudes to training of 200 companies across the whole country. The study was managed by the National Observatory of Krgyzstan; as part of a three-year ETF project designed to support and strengthen Kyrgyz businesses.

In the first year, the aim was to raise awareness amongst employers of the need to retrain and develop the workforce for business success in a competitive world market. By April 2000, the plan was to produce a full skills survey report, a handbook for human resource development and a training tool designed to enable companies to develop in-company training programs for themselves, tailored to their specific needs. Quite a tall order for a newly independent state still in transition from its former status as part of the USSR, and a pretty tall order for me, particularly as I didn't speak Russian, to train the survey team and then to develop an HR manual based on the results.

Luckily, I had already managed to travel and work in a number of such states, Slovenia, Bulgaria, Albania, Estonia, the Ukraine, Belarus and Georgia. This meant that I was culturally attuned to the Russian way of life, which provided an overlay under which the distinctly national characteristics of each state remain.

In Bishkek, capital of Kyrgyzstan, currently Russian is the main language spoken, not the indigenous language, Kyrgyz. Historically, the Kyrgyz were a nomadic people, who originally worked the silk route from nearby China, lived in yurts (tents) and traded silk and horses; they have a strong oral tradition of stories and songs. This is high snow covered mountain country, with deep clear lakes and hardly any flat territory, potentially volcanic, cold in winter, warm in the summer.

There's gold in them there hills, which is being very professionally mined by a Krgyzstan-Canadian venture/project and plenty of water to be turned to hydro-electric power when resources permit. And the potential for tourism, particularly for mountaineers is enormous. The Kyrgyz are already good trading people, tough and enterprising, friendly and caring, even though living conditions are still hard and money is short. In Bishkek, the capital, the housing is mainly state built blocks of flats.

A yurt and horses in the mountains Kazakhstan

So, my first problem was how to train people who only spoke Russian when I only spoke English? Everything was translated but, after a while, I began to understand what they were saying, helped by body language and recognisable international words.

The survey questionnaire was derived from a skills audit of small and medium-sized enterprises (SMEs), devised originally by the UK's

Salford university, to evaluate the way SMEs consider and address the issue of skills need and development within the workforce. With Salford's permission, we translated the survey, removed the explicitly English questions about such topics as national vocational qualifications (NVQs) and made one or two minor adjustments.

My first task was to work with the group, section by section, to make sure that they understood the meaning behind the words. Very often this meant introducing and explaining concepts which were relatively new to the former Russian state. The survey team were mainly social scientists, but a few had worked in business, particularly in banking, and were more familiar with using concepts such as quality, customer care and just-in-time, so they were able to add examples to my words. The concepts of key skills and of multi-skilling took longer to get across. The employers we spoke to later reinforced the view that multi-skilling was becoming more important in an emerging enterprise economy and was hard to find in a society which formerly had prided itself on very highly skilled specialist technical expertise.

Role play

In the training sessions for the survey team, we did a lot of role play: for example as the researcher in discussion with the reluctant employer, who was refusing to take part, demanding an explanation of why to bother, worrying about confidentiality, asking the meaning of the new words and ideas in the questionnaire, refusing to give details about the existing training programs. Then we did a complete run-through of the face-to-face interview, with each person trying out the role of interviewer and interviewee, the preliminary patter and the post-interview reassurance. By the time I left, the team were confident about the skills survey, but apprehensive about the employers' reactions. They need not have worried. They were well received, mainly by the managing director. Access was easier than anticipated and the refusal rate was low.

The first findings of the survey were both interesting and encouraging:

- 200 employers from all over Kyrgyzstan had taken part in the survey

- Of these 141 were private enterprises
- 80% of companies were introducing qualify improvements and 71% were introducing new services
- 76% saw price and quality as key determinants of competitiveness
- In these companies full-time staff numbers had reduced by 1,200 in the past year and by 8,932 over the last five years
- Labour supply exceeded demand: 73% said they had no problem finding staff
- Skills shortages were mainly at senior manager and middle manager level
- There was sometimes a skills mismatch at this level; there were many highly qualified professionals who need now to widen their skills to meet the demands of the market economy
- Overall, 28.5% of employees were computer literate with marked sectoral differences. Highest computer literacy was in banking and finance, 74.2%; media 43.1% and communication 39.2%
- 59% had trained staff to use new equipment
- and recognised the importance of investing in training and development.

Narynbek who managed the project in Kyrgyzstan

At a conference in February to present the initial results, the employers mentioned the lack of entrepreneurial qualities in many highly qualified graduates and the problems of motivating long-serving staff to retrain in these skills. It sounded quite familiar!

Technical expertise, a great strength in the workforce, was no longer enough; management and social skills, such as good communication, self-presentation, team working, motivation, flexibility, showing initiative and responsibility, were needed as well. The employers preferred company-based training: less expensive and targeted towards company needs.

In April, Karen Richter, a European expert from Eastern Germany, who does speak Russian, ran a course, using the training tool she developed to enable companies to devise their own training and development programs. Employers were invited to send a key member of staff to participate. The aim was to enable companies to customise the training tool and use it to meet their own specific needs.

Empower and equip

In the meantime, the HRM guide is being developed, with some difficulty. The aim is for the European expert (that's me!) to be advisory, but the problem is finding enough Kyrgyistan people with the skills and experience to be the main authors. At a distance, the language problems loom larger because there is no body language to add to the words. We've already changed the title from 'manual' to 'handbook' or 'guide', as there's absolutely no point in attempting anything too comprehensive. The KISS (keep it simple, stupid!) principle has to prevail, though then we may stand accused of doing something superficial and lightweight, compared with traditional Russian tomes of rules and regulations about personnel practice. And as for other resources, such as books, training videos and online interactive courses, these are difficult to find, let alone at the right price for a country at this stage of economic development and growth. And they do want to do it for themselves and not be preached at by American/English 'experts'.

The overall aim of the project is to empower and equip the employers rather than impose western methods on them. Encouragingly, there does seem to be a move towards realising that a new way of working is needed. As one employer said at the end of the conference: 'When I arrived, I was thinking about the skills needed now. As a result of this discussion, I am now thinking about the skills needed in the future as well.'

A seminar and tea in Kazakhstan

Postscript

I wrote this when I was still Director of the Centre for Lifelong Learning at Brunel University. I retired in 2000. I was then asked by the ETF to do the same training first in Kazakhstan and later in Uzbekistan. In both cases it went well. Both these countries are, like Krygystan, land locked, originally nomadic, and part of the famous Silk Road. Kazakhstan is the largest landlocked country in the world. Tashkent, the capital of Uzbekistan is fascinating, still with beautiful Hotels redolent of the thirties when it was a very fashionable resort for Westerners. As for the golden gate of Samarkand, first it wasn't golden, neither was it particularly lovely, But the beautiful squares, mosques, mauseleums, with their wonderful tiles and mosaic clad walls in delicate blues, more than made up for this.

I had several adventures during this period. The scariest was when I had to get back from Tashkent to Bishkek, the capital of Kyrgyzstan for a meeting with the team responsible for the new HRD booklet we were working on. The quickest way was to go by car. My Russian driver pointed out that we were likely to be stopped by the border control. Apparently, they sometimes abducted westerners for ransom. Luckily we arrived without any such incidents!

Horse riding in Kazakhstan

The first version of the HRD guide had been a disaster. My Krgyz colleagues had tried to make it very scholarly by quoting from traditional Russian text books. My job was to wean them from this style at the same time as getting it to do it themselves. I was, as usual, living in a block of flats, up a stone staircase into a warm and comfy apartment. I was not allowed out by myself without a Russian speaking guide, as this was potentially dangerous. So I was taken out for meals or the team brought food in for our working lunch and my supper. At the end of a further week's stay, we agreed the final text. As I was putting away the Russian laptop which contained the manuscript, I suddenly realised that the choices for closing down were in Russian and I couldn't remember or work out which was 'close'. After an agonising twenty minutes I pressed the button. YES it was saved!

In 2001, the document was published: *Human Resource Development, A Practical Guide.* It was given out to SMEs over a wide area. To celebrate the completion of the three projects and the publication of the booklet a huge conference, with representatives of all the economies in transition was held at Issyk-Kul, a wonderful resort in Kyrzgyzstan, the 10th largest lake in the world, backed by the Northern Tian Shan Mountains. Fabulous! The HR Guide was launched to all the three participating countries and disseminated to all the countries in that region. My thanks to the National Observatory of Kyrzgyzstan, and the European Training Foundation, particularly Arjen Dej who supervised me.

A seminar on human resource development in Uzbekistan

In these projects, I was once again humbled by the friendliness and the hospitality of my Hosts, Salaries were very low and even Doctors only earned about $5 a month. Many people had to do two jobs to make ends meet, yet when they insisted in inviting you around for a meal, they produced colourful plates piled high with delicious food.

COMMENT

This was a really worthwhile project with good solid outcomes. I was especially grateful to Arjen Deij country desk in those three countries and Narynbek Djunushev who led the Kygys part of the project, for their help and support.

This next piece is chronologically my last excursion into the former Russian states.

Mountains near Lake Issyk-Kul

The development of lifelong guidance in Lithuania 2006

In 2006, the British Council invited me to join a short study group in Lithuania. I was then selected to be the Rapporteur. We met in Vilnius which was a smart, bustling and thriving town in which the ancient buildings looked clean and cared for and shops looked modern and fashionable. The river gave it added charm.

The group include representatives of half-dozen or so EU countries. We were impressed with what we saw, the university was particularly impressive. There were a large number of computers, so that students could benefit from the Information age.

The group attending was a little frustrated as they really wanted to share information about their own systems. Their commitment to lifelong guidance was very strong. They also stressed the importance of mentoring, and distinguishing between information advice and guidance. CPD for guidance workers was important, as were good communications between all sectors.

These features were found strongly in Lithuania and in some of the participating states. Lithuania had benefited from starting later and sometimes improving on longer established practices of other European states. The group was impressed with Lithuania's progress after a late entry into this field.

We found: Quality materials in different formats including multimedia, rapid development of forward-looking systems based on research into existing European tools which were sometimes taken them further by the enthusiastic and high calibre personnel involved in delivery and development of systems across the nation. The active players shared the ambition to make the vision the reality in the near future and the goal of giving more people access.

Quality standards were not yet in place everywhere. Careers guidance was not always fully integrated into education programs in schools, VET & HE. The system is not sufficiently connected with the rapidly changing workplace environment. Guidance needs to have a multi-lingual and inter-cultural dimension to help the social inclusion of migrants and to help overcome historical conflicts between minorities.

Across Europe, there is a need for careers guidance to implement: the harmonization of qualifications, a legal framework for the profession, international competence standards and quality standards for the services, professional training entitlement, access to lifetime and life-wide careers guidance for all age groups, as a guiding principle for all Europe. At the moment access to adult guidance is limited. More exchange of good practice in integrating guidance across the school and VET curriculum is needed. Training in careers guidance should be part of teacher in-service training.

This was a most valuable study group from which we all learnt a lot and found that we largely shared the same vision. We thanked Lithuania for its warm welcome and their progress in establishing modern guidance systems.

COMMENT

This was the last of my formal visits to the economies in transition. By then I was already in my mid seventies and extremely busy in my local community, in theory I was starting to slow down... really?

Conference in Dartington Hall in 1985

This is an extract from a talk given by Anne Jones, thirty years ago, about the danger and the potential development of fanatical religious extremism.

We are at the beginning of the end of advanced industrial societies and the beginning of societies that may have to be invented. This statement reflects accurately where we stand now as a society, indeed as a world: on the threshold, of something unknown. In a different way, Renaissance man and woman must have felt like this too. The challenges to advanced industrial societies are economic, political, social and spiritual. At the moment the spiritual element, that is anything to do with the soul, the imagination, the expressive, intuitive, emotional side of ourselves, and the strictly spiritual in the more religious sense, is very largely underplayed.

I sense that there is a quest, amongst the young especially, for spiritual meaning. In a life which could be seen as full of meaningless actions, the quest is for meaning of any kind. I note the deep feelings and passions evoked by the Rushdie's books. There is a danger that the world could swing too far the other way. However, people may need to cling to rigid truths in order to make themselves feel safer in an uncertain world. The strength and the power of the Muslims should not be underestimated. The extremism of the East-West religious clash is potentially very serious. The resurgence of all this emotion and passion is partially about our deep need for balance in the individual person, in the group, in society, and in the world as a whole. When life becomes too materialistic then spiritual things begin to assert themselves. There is a danger that the world could swing too far the other way: Fanatical religious extremism would not be the answer either.

Thirty years later, we know it is not. And there is no simple solution.

CHAPTER 8: LIFELONG LEARNING IN THE ANTIPODES 1993 AND 1995

Education's role in an effective society NZ PPTA Principals' Conference Auckland, July 1993

Professor Anne Jones, Head of Continuing Education
BRUNEL UNIVERSITY, UK sponsored by the British Council

IT IS BOTH AN HONOUR AND A PLEASURE for me to be here today. I've always wanted to visit New Zealand ever since I was a very small girl reading *Alice in Wonderland*, who herself wanted to come to the Antipodes. And in any case I am a born pioneer (Aries) and as such, can resist anything except temptation. It took just one phone call from one of your dearly beloved brethren to hook me.

Now I am here, I am even more impressed than I ever expected to be: not only because of the beautiful scenery, the incredible hospitality, the wonderful spirituality of yesterday's opening ceremony, and the amazing singing and dancing, but because this is the first international conference I've ever attended where three major speakers on one day were all women! I know it's the Centenary of women's rights, but I trust that this is more than a Centenary gesture. My opinion is that women have skills which are particularly suited to leadership and management in today's and tomorrows turbulent times. If you have recognised that here, then you are on to a winning streak!

The title of the conference begs as many questions as it answers, but I cannot resist putting in my pennyworth. I sincerely believe that teachers have both the ability and the power to transform society from being a set of meaningless statistics into something rich and strange, a set of meaningful and life enhancing experiences, which add value, not in terms of a price tag, but in terms of the quality of life. It is very easy in the panic which affects society today to spend all one's time rearranging the deck chairs on the Titanic, to build a society in which people know the price of everything and understand the value of nothing. Education has the power to reverse this but a power which it too often neither dares nor knows how to use.

It seems to me that we have all been experiencing a series of step changes: step changes, not sea changes. There doesn't seem to be much real difference in the fundamental way education works and that's partly the problem: a lot of incremental, cosmetic changes and not enough real change. What's needed is revolution not evolution, a paradigm shift, not a system change, in fact the shift from teaching to learning. Underlying this is confusion about what makes society, education and people effective: an absence of a coherent framework and beliefs against which to set new actions. Various people have postulated a tension or conflict between human needs and economic needs. I don't see these as alternatives, but as complementary.

Meeting the individual's need for growth and development, the community's need for meaning and society's need for a sound economic base, these seem to me to be three sides of a triangle, all of which are interdependent and equally essential the one to the other. But there does need to be a vision: 'where there is no vision the people perish.' Anomie replaces 'communitas', selfishness and self-centredness replace humanity, economic sterility replaces economic prosperity.

In the United Kingdom we've been suffering from the 'Eeyore syndrome' for some time. You remember Eeyore, the prophet of doom and gloom. So people have been moving the deck chairs about at an ever more frequent rate of knots. Not only that: certain defeatism has led to pronouncements about the United Kingdom being near the bottom of every league table ever invented. I think this is meant to stir us into action. On international standards, both within the OECD and Pacific Rim countries, it appears that the UK has relatively poor exam results, a low staying on rate at sixteen, low participation in higher education, and low standards of literacy and numeracy. Or so it is said. And not only that, it also appears that the only reason that the United Kingdom is not competitive economically is because the education system has failed. Does it sound familiar? Is it true?

The fact is that it is **not** true. The 'outputs' of education in the United Kingdom have improved dramatically in the last five years.

Perhaps it is a secret weapon we're not letting anyone else know about. You will not be surprised to know that teachers have found it depressing to be blamed for the economic problems of society when in fact they have worked hard to achieve higher standards and succeeded.

In 1987, 47% of sixteen-year-olds stayed on at school. In 1993 the figure is nearer 80%. In 1987 12% of the age cohort went on to higher education. In 1993 the figure is nearer 30%. Examination results have improved in real terms every year but unfortunately so have the skills and knowledge required in the workplace. We do still need to achieve higher standards, but that is primarily because of the mismatch between the skills we traditionally have and the new higher level requirements of the workplace. In the future there will be very little work for unskilled people. We need to raise the educational achievements of all our people, not only our school leavers, but of the whole population.

In the last few years, there have been dramatic changes in the UK education system. Many national education bodies have either been abolished or reformed totally. There have been three Secretaries of State of what is now no longer the DES but the DFE: Department for Education and each has modified the National Curriculum first introduced in 1988. The Parents' Charter has brought about league tables for exam results and, in theory, greater parental choice. Local management of schools is well established (and largely appreciated by Heads), though opting out to be Grant Maintained is still slow to happen.

The National Curriculum Council and the Schools' Examination and Assessment Council have been abolished and replaced by one united Council, which is what we had originally. HMI have been replaced by OFSTED (the equivalent of ERO) with newly trained registered inspectors who have to tender for contracts for inspection. Attempts to introduce testing procedures at fourteen on a national scale this summer (1993) failed: teachers unions refusal to take part were upheld in the High Court on the grounds of overload. Headteachers in the NAHT took the unprecedented action of booing the Secretary of State at their annual conference.

Teacher training is under severe threat. The move is to make it largely school-based, and those university departments running post-graduate courses are now at risk of closure. The CNAA (Council for National Academic Awards) have been abolished. The UFC and the PCFC have been abolished and replaced by the new HEFCE (Higher Education Funding Council) to reflect the fact that the polytechnics now have university status.

TECS (Training and Enterprise Councils), primarily employer councils are now responsible for seeing that NETTS (National Education and Training Targets) are achieved in each locality. There is a move towards output related pay, certainly for vocational qualifications, where money comes only if the student trainees pass their exams.

In schools, GCSE course work is being cut down drastically and GNVQs (General National Vocational Qualifications) are being introduced as a way of bridging the academic vocational divide. National Records of Achievement replace local records of achievement and the NRA becomes the portfolio which the school leaver takes with him/herself through a life of continuing education and training.

Acronyms abound, and most people – parents, employers and even teachers claim that they are very confused. Certainly it is very difficult to keep up with all the changes and the man or woman in the street may unwittingly still be using out of date terms and concepts.

Headteachers are finding it difficult to steer a course through these changes, though on the whole they relish their new-found powers of financial management. Like you, they complain about overload and chaos. However, the fact of the matter is that out of chaos and the void there came light. I believe we are not yet out of the chaos and indeed we may never be, in this turbulent world of ours, but I do believe there is enough light to generate hope. We need now to learn to thrive on chaos. School leaders have the potential to use their power, positively and constructively, to transform what could be mere bureaucracy into learning opportunities which build confidence, hope, competence and flexibility. However, too many of us see chaos as a threat rather than opportunity. It is no good doing a Canute, trying to turn back the tide. We need to learn to ride the waves, to use their energy, to enjoy them, to turn them to our advantage.

Once you have learnt how to do it, managing discontinuous change in a turbulent and variable environment is as exciting as sailing a boat or paddling a Maori war canoe. You can change tack according to the prevailing external conditions, but you know where you are going, and you get there.

In Tom Peters book *Thriving on Chaos*, he quotes Barbara Tuchman who postulates that there are three aspects of folly:

1. Being oblivious to the growing disaffection of your constituents
2. The primacy of self-aggrandisement, getting too big for your boots
3. The illusion of invulnerable status. I think we all recognise these three signs that someone or something is about to be toppled!

It's worth pondering on this statement. Does your country really need you? The ultimate organisational structure could be the clover leaf: one third only of staff with employed status, one third of teachers on short-term and specific contracts, and the other third consisting of contracted-out non-teaching staff. I am not suggesting this will happen. I am merely suggesting that anything could happen and we should not extrapolate from the present in imagining the future. Be prepared for anything! The only way to cope with this kind of scenario is to be proactive rather than reactive. Ostriches will no longer survive. Dinosaurs will adapt or die. I would suggest the following armoury which might help Principals to prepare themselves and their communities for this unknown future. These are just a few of my ideas. You will have others and more:

Strategic management skills: essential in rapidly changing times.

Ansoff's definition of strategic management is 'a systematic approach to the positioning and relating of the organisation to its environment in a way which will assure its continued success and make it free from surprises.' I find this useful, particularly in the emphasis it gives to being sensitive to the environment and what is going to happen next. In my study of Heads, most of them looked inwards only relatively few looked outwards across the boundary.

A framework of values and beliefs: These have to be genuine: 'to thine own self be true.' For me, they need to be based on equity and justice, equal respect, belief in the potential of every human being, wherever they are at, to go on learning and the importance of releasing and using that potential if we are to achieve personal, community and societal well-being.

The importance of relating education to the world of work: Not in a narrow skills-based way, but as part of providing a realistic context through which people are motivated to learn, equipping people to cope with the demands of adult and working life.

Education of the head, the hands and the heart: Too many people talk as if these were alternatives. To me, they are all essential and need to be kept in balance. It is not an either/or curriculum. To these, I would add the capacity to pause and reflect on experience as a way of learning. Only by reflecting on experience can we understand how much we already know.

Empowering the learner, not being afraid to share power, that is knowledge, skills and understanding others: with staff, with pupils, with the community. Encouraging passive dependence and conformity stifles growth and true learning.

Encouraging life-long learning: That means seeing initial education as a beginning, not an end in itself. It means seeing school leaving qualifications, not as terminal events, but as milestones on the way to a lifetime of continuing learning for continuous improvement. It means recognising that people learn unevenly throughout their lives and some people don't fit in to the school time span. It also means recognising that these days qualifications rapidly become out of date and that we all need to relearn and retrain.

Sticking to the knitting: Not taking on all the ills of society, but building a learning community with learning as its main objective. Setting limits: knowing the boundary on which you work and doing that well. Looking across the boundary and being alert for what is on the horizon.

Open and flexible learning: Helping teachers to understand the importance of a more flexible approach to learning, so that people can learn at a time, pace and place that suits their needs; using modern technology to help in this. Supporting classroom teachers in their efforts to make the transition from teaching to learning.

A world society: What is clear is that we can no longer afford to think and behave as separate nations. Ours is now a world society, a global economy. We need to think globally and to think locally at the same time. The heightened awareness of ethnic communities the world over, as we become more global, is very striking. We need to be aware that European countries have shrinking populations and a workforce which is aging and largely uneducated. Pacific Rim countries have growing populations which are being well educated and trained to high standards of achievement and use modern information and communications technologies to the full. We cannot compete with this unless we do develop our intellectual capital to the full. Yet knowledge depreciates at the rate of 7% a year as the use of personal computers increases exponentially. The greatest source of untapped ability lies in our adult populations.

In the information society we are now entering, we need to remember that the key skills are: Evaluation and analysis; critical thinking; problem solving; the organisation and retrieval of information; synthesis; application of knowledge to new areas; creativity; making decisions with incomplete information.

Communication skills in many modes: Are we sure that we are equipping our students with these skills? A recent report from the European Round Table of Industrialists stated: 'The information revolution is rendering much previous education and training obsolete or simply irrelevant'. It is our job to make sure they are wrong, to make meaning out of chaos and to equip our people young and old to use their ideas their imagination and their intelligence to build an effective society in which the people can flourish.

My two NZ grandchildren, Ben & Alice in 2013

COMMENT

On this trip, I was looked after incredibly well by Alon and Audrey Shaw. We became friends for life. I came to New Zealand again in 1995, this time to Wellington, to give a talk on the future of work at the Harkness Employment Conference. In 2001 my son Christopher married a New Zealand girl, Sarah whom he met in England. They now live in Devonport, Auckland where I now have two delightful grandchildren, Ben and Alice, so now I go every year to see them and the Shaws.

The Harkness Employment Conference Wellington New Zealand, May 1995
TECHNOLOGY AND EMPLOYMENT

The following paper was originally prepared for the EU in 1992 by David Stevenson of HRD International and Professor Anne Jones, Brunel University, UK. In 1996, this paper was published in a book called Employment and the future of work *by the Institute of Policy Studies in New Zealand, where it was presented along with a further paper on Education and Training by Professor Anne Jones.*

KEEPING EUROPE COMPETITIVE: the key role of information and communications technologies, education and training.

Overview

The explosion of developments in information and communications technologies is opening up opportunities for dramatic improvements in the efficiency of European community industries and services. Such improvements could increase productivity, profitability and opportunities for employment for EC members. Thus, the EC could improve its share of the world market at the same time as improving the social and economic conditions of its workforce.

However, the urgency of action cannot be over-stated. The EC's main competitors, in North America, Japan and the Far East, are equally aware of these opportunities. They are also, in some ways, better positioned to take advantage of them. If the EC is slower than its competitors to react, then the competitive battle will have been lost.

The costs of not taking urgent action are serious: the EC loses a big share of a key and fast developing market, locks itself into a 'low skills job market' loses an important source of wealth generation and increases unemployment. The evidence for this has already been well-documented in research, much of it done on behalf of the Commission. What is needed now is action, and fast.

The key to success lies not so much in the technology itself, which exists in abundance and becomes daily cheaper, but in people and their capacity to use ICT in all aspects of their work, from the strategic to the routine. To increase the capability of the workforce requires more education and training, both initial and continuing. However, current education and training methods themselves massively underutilise ICT. As a result, they are largely obsolescent and relatively inefficient, preparing people for an out of date market through old fashioned methods. ICT can give added-value and increase the productivity of a more focussed education and training process. Multinational organisations can more easily tap into the leading edge global markets and methods, but the majority of the small and medium sized enterprises which make up 80% of the EC's employers, are caught in this particular 'skills gap' trap.

To get out of this double bind, the EC needs now to find and develop examples of good practice, where ICT has itself been used in education and training to develop programmes of learning which enable people at all levels of an organisation, to use ICT as an effective value-adding tool for increasing productivity and the EC1 s share of the world market.

1. The speed of change

The IBM PC was launched as recently as August 1981. Yet by the year 2000, there will be £100 million personal computers in use in Europe alone. The transeuropean network will enable member states to communicate, not only with each other, but also globally. The convergence between computer, broadcasting and telecommunications makes microprocessor technology the all-pervading link which affects everybody, whether at work or at leisure. The EC's own conference on social aspects of ICT, in October 1991, provided conclusive research evidence showing that almost every sector of industry would be constrained and would lose, both on productivity and market share, if ICT was not diffused more rapidly into working practices. This loss of market would have serious knock-on effects on the employment prospects and quality of life of the people of Europe.

2. Productivity gains

It has been estimated that a more rapid diffusion of ICT could, by the year 2000, bring an increase of 10% in the European GPD and a fall of consumer prices of 5%. Greater productivity brings more real income, with which to generate further developments. In such a thriving economy, the quality and standard of life improves. A major growth industry could be education and training itself, which could massively increase its productivity if only it exploited the potential of ICT fully. ICT could lower the unit cost of education and training at the same time as increasing the output. Whereas in the past, arguments about the cost of equipment were valid, now costs have dropped and continue to drop: costs halve every eighteen months.

3. People power

However, there is no point in having vast and inexpensive computer power if the people power does not match it. Ultimately, winning the battle in the world market depends on the ability of people to use the equipment they have to the best advantage. Low level and routine manual and clerical operations are now best done by machines. People have opportunities to use their cognitive skills more fully and to be more creative. This also adds value to the EC's GDP. Intellectual capital itself becomes an economic resource which the EC cannot afford either to squander, or to leave under-developed. The problem, however, is how to develop it on a big enough scale and quickly enough. ICT can help with this.

4. Intellectual capital

Europe has an aging workforce: in the year 2000, more people in Europe retire than join the workforce. Yet in other countries, this is not so. In the Pacific Rim in particular, there is a young and growing population which is being highly trained: a competitive combination of highly skilled but relatively inexpensive labour. The only way that Europe's static and aging population can compete with this is to 'add value to its intellectual power'. The highest level skills need to be developed initially. Knowledge and skills need to be continuously updated, throughout life: continuous development for continuous improvement.

5. The knowledge explosion

World knowledge is set to double over this decade, yet current knowledge now depreciates at a compound rate of 7% a year. Thus, even that percentage of Europe's existing workforce which does have high level skills and qualifications will rapidly become out of date without an extensive programme of continuing education and constant updating.

6. The latent pool of ability

Further, it has to be remembered that 70-80% of the workforce in the year 2,000 have already left full-time education and training. The majority of this group are both intellectually underdeveloped and technically under-qualified. In addition, they are also likely to need enhanced management and interpersonal skills. Developing and harnessing the potential of these people, for ICT, through ICT is essential, if the EC is to maintain its position in the world market.

7. The throughput from higher education

Across EC member countries, numbers staying on and participating in Further and Higher education have increased significantly, though insufficient numbers of scientists, technologists and engineers are coming forward. It is worth noting that in Europe, the share of engineers on higher education courses fell by half during the last twenty years at a time of growing opportunity in world markets. However, the increase in the participation rate brings its own problems. Partly because Higher Education Institutions themselves have not yet been fully through the ICT revolution, HEIs under considerable pressure with these increased numbers. The irony is that it is ICT which will both ease the pressure on HE staff and reduce unit costs, thus increasing capacity and productivity. It could be added that HEI's need to get into this market, in part to assure their own futures, and in part to ensure that their teaching is appropriate.

8. Perceptions of the link between education and competitive advantage

Enormous strides have been made in improving education systems and in helping them understand better their role in preparing people for adult and working life. However, even amongst policy-makers, there is too often a split between education for life and education for work. 'There is a lack of adequate awareness of the importance of education and training as a strategic weapon in Europe's competitiveness.'

The European Round Table of Industrialists has particularly noted that European universities have been slow to enter the Continuing Education market, even though it is through the re-education and training of the existing workforce that the main hope of maintaining any competitive advantage lies. It still does not appear to be part of the 'mindset' of the educators that they can make a critical contribution to the economic success of Member states, and therefore to the well being of the people. Neither are they sufficiently aware that all too often, employers regard their contribution as out of date. 'The information revolution is rendering much previous education and training obsolete or simply irrelevant.' (IRDAC Report 1991) Open and distance learning, for example, too often becomes absorbed into education as a way of improving it for its own sake, rather than as a way of investing in economic success.

9. Management of change: the role of higher education

It would appear that all organisations, including HEI's, need massive support in understanding, introducing and managing the changes in ways of working which are now upon us. All these changes require learning: learning and understanding why such changes are necessary, learning how to cope with them and how to manage and incorporate them. HEIs could have an incredible role in helping to bring about these learning gains. Not enough are yet seizing the opportunity of so doing.

10. Partnerships between employers and HEIs

Despite the many measures introduced by the EC, designed to encourage partnerships which connect education with the needs of the economy, there is scope for much faster and further development of this concept into practical action. It is difficult for any organisation, large or small, to keep up with the speed of technological change. Shared working between employers and HEIs might help both parties keep up with leading edge knowledge, developments and practices. The shortage of engineers has already been mentioned. There is growing evidence that if enough of the senior members of a management team understand the strategic and operational implications of the technology well enough, then the shortfall in the numbers of technologists becomes less critical. This is an important concept which not only helps with problems of labour supply, but also with the problems of small and medium enterprises.

11. Employers responses

European employers are aware, some more acutely than others that Europe's productivity is already falling behind that of its competitors. Lack of people with appropriate managerial and technical skills is more of a problem than lack of equipment. A real breakthrough would come if the EC made more effective use of its existing investment in technology. This is only possible through know how.

12. Linking education, training and ICT

Nevertheless, not enough employers are aware of the strategic advantages ICT could bring if it were properly used, both as a business tool and as a training tool: both aspects, if well focussed to that end, increase productivity. Senior managers do not appear to have made this link sufficiently. When training is brought in it tends to be biased towards the acquisition of relatively low level skills for the individual, at the expense of senior level strategic understanding. Both are needed.

Not enough employers have yet fully exploited the advantages of the connective technologies', expressed in such developments as computer integrated manufacturing, networking, electronic data interchange and electronic mail. These integrated systems work most effectively if the people in the system understand the whole process and work as a team.

13. New organisational patterns

Neither have employers fully recognised the organisational benefits of ICT. In an organisation which has integrated ICT into its working practices, everybody can contribute to the strategic thinking and improved operational plans. As organisations become flatter and less hierarchical, as people work more and more in autonomous teams, as real time interaction between geographically dispersed team members becomes a fact of daily life, so organisational structures need to reflect these changes. For these benefits to be realised, training in the management of change is essential, starting at the top with the Chief Executive. However, gaining the commitment and using the creativity of the whole workforce is essential if organisations are to move more highly value added products. Small businesses have a great deal to gain from these trends, provided they can be appropriately supported.

POSTSCRIPT

Twenty years later, it seems amazing that we were struggling so much to embrace and use to the full the benefits (and discover the problems) to do with a fully functioning global instant real time communication systems which now reach out to the whole world. It seemed to take until 2,000 to get faster take-up but it wasn't really until the second millennium that worldwide communication by every means was accessible to rich and poor, young and old alike the world over.

This is a total transformation of the way ICT is used, not always for the better.

Europe has now entered a period of serious problems to do with unemployment, financial crises plus great instability and regime changes in parts or Europe and the Middle and Far East.

The Harkness Conference Wellington New Zealand Curriculum and Curriculum Process for a Changing World and an Uncertain Future by Anne Jones

Professor Anne Jones first delivered this paper at the Harkness Conference in Wellington 1n 1995. In 1996, it was published in a book called Employment and the future of work *by the Institute of Policy studies in New Zealand. The paper itself was written by her in 1994 and published in 1995 as Chapter 7 in a book called:*

Bringing Learning to Life, edited by David C. A. Bradshaw, The Falmer Press, 1995. She has now re-edited the text and changed the title to *Bringing Lifelong Learning to Life*.

BRINGING LIFELONG LEARNING TO LIFE 1995

Plus ça change, plus c'est la même chose. We sometimes speak and write as if we were the first generation to meet and tackle unprecedented change, or to debate endlessly the appropriate balance between knowledge skills and attributes. Not much remains of my degree in Modern Languages, long past its sell-by date, but what is seared on my brain is the simple truth of Montaigne's (1580) sixteenth century words: *Je préfère une tête bien faite* à *une tête bien pleine.* Too often the quest for knowledge, even now, becomes the quest for facts, stuffed into the computer-like head, until the brain seizes up, loses its creativity and innovative thoughts, and its sharp cutting edge. Too often the quest for certainty in an uncertain world, where the whole order of things is about to be transformed into something rich and strange, itself puts a block and a damper on the creative and imaginative acceptance of that emerging new order. Too often we have not learnt to ride the waves of change, and enjoy them, but rather we try to hold back the tide. In doing this, we also too often neglect the inner core of our own being, which is what will really give us the strength, not only to survive, but more importantly to thrive in the next phase of human existence.

As Montaigne put it: *Connais-toi toi-meme*. That is the only certainty from which we can venture into the unknown. The last few years have brought seismic world change: collapse of cultures, economies, political and religious orthodoxies, giants turned into pygmies, enemies into friends, world powers into third world powers, poor economies into world-class economies, ill-educated nations into knowledge-driven nations, top nations into third-rate nations. In the new 'borderless world' (Ohmae, 1990), businesses are run on a global scale in real time, with a workforce which could be anywhere in the world: for example, most of the paperwork and number crunching for British bankers is now done in northern India. Yet, simultaneously, as work becomes more global, local cultures become more important, and people cling more tightly to their ethnic roots. What we are experiencing is not cosmetic or superficial: it is a transformation just as great as the Renaissance, the Industrial Revolution, or before that, the decline and fall of various world empires. And the process continues, as Thurow's (1993) survey of current trends and their consequences demonstrates with graphic realism. My view is that the world is once more in the chrysalis stage and what will eventually emerge will be totally different from what preceded it. Whoever would have thought that butterflies could develop out of caterpillars?

Against this changing background, the debate about the curriculum seems out of proportion. Furthermore, the assumptions behind the debate are often based on outmoded concepts of what makes a good education. The concept of Britain as a learning society has not really caught on. The motto for success used to be 99% perspiration, 1% inspiration. In truth, what we need now in our workforce is more like 50:50. Yet current trends in education too often reflect the pint-pot, well made head, remember and regurgitate model of education, and the more the panic about 'standards' increases, the more education is pushed back into rote learning, counting and testing. Just as we need to release the creative energy, imagination and ideas of our people, if we are to survive economically, we appear to be reducing learning to league tables, standard scores and testing to destruction. And despite mutterings about lifelong learning and releasing the potential of all our people, most of the systems and structures still reinforce the idea that education is something you take in a great lump between the ages of 5-16, or if you are lucky, 5-21.

This is what I call the 'boa constrictor' model of education, swallowed in one gulp, not very well digested and fairly rapidly eliminated. Much more appropriate in today's climate would be a 'slow release' model, something like that which can now be produced in fertilizers, soap powders or cold cures; the kind of education which is provided at a time, stage, place and in a style which is appropriate to the learner's needs. Furthermore, in the new 'New World', the learner will be the driver of the learning, which may not necessarily be provided by the education system, but will come, as it always in fact has come, from a variety of sources. The real curriculum is the whole of life. The trick will be to help people to understand, to record that which they have learnt, and to get it verified if need be.

So, *revenons à nos moutons*, as Rabelais (1533) said as he wandered from his original theme. The debate about the balance between knowledge, skills and attributes takes many forms: know that, versus know how; content versus process; learning how, versus deep learning; rote learning, versus action learning. What I have observed over nearly forty years in education is that balance is rarely ever reached. The pendulum swings backwards and forwards, from one extreme to another. When I was a young school counsellor, I recall the words of a very distinguished HMI (school inspector), who said that he never took trends in Education very seriously: if you stayed where you were, the fashion would eventually swing back towards you. He was describing the kind of natural oscillation between the two poles of most human behaviour, and is reflected in individual as well as corporate behaviour. In my lifetime, the education system has constantly rearranged the deckchairs and tacked from side to side, but it has not fundamentally changed. As T S Eliot (1954) put it:

Where is the life we have lost in living? Where is the wisdom we have lost in knowledge? Where is the knowledge we have lost in information?

That is, until now. In my youth, the emphasis was on inputs: filling people up with knowledge, teaching them well 'Learn 'em', as Rat said in *Wind in the Willows*. Then in the 1960s and 1970s came the idea that the process was all important 'it ain't what you do, but the way that you do it'. The predominant idea was that learning how to learn was the most important function of the education system. Now the emphasis is on outputs what it is that the person knows, understands and can do as a result of the educational process. And now there is the concept of impact, what is left after the process has finished and the outputs have been counted. Is there anything there at all, or has the boa constrictor fodder merely gone in one end and out the other? Has any real value been added to this person? Or are they merely just as intelligent or slow as they were at the beginning. Even more sophisticated is the concept of intellectual capital. Has the intellectual capacity of this person been extended, has their practical capability been increased, has their understanding been deepened and attitudes broadened? What are they doing with this capital: counting it, using it, making it grow, or keeping it 'under the bed'?

No-one really knows the answer to these questions. Although there is a lifelong quest here for educational researchers more than enough work to keep them busy for ever valid conclusions on a grand and enduring scale will never be reached since the ball-game, the context and the goal posts are swinging around endlessly. By the time megatrends have been measured, the object of the research will have disappeared or altered beyond recognition.

This point was particularly brought home to me when I was

responsible for education programmes within the Department of Employment. One of these, the Technical and Vocational Education Initiative (TVEI), was probably one of the most researched initiatives of all time. Thousands of pounds were spent on research which was, by the time it finally came out, looking at issues which were no longer of prime interest. More disturbingly, there was no conclusive evidence as to whether or not the initiative had been successful. Those of us who were closely connected with it were convinced that its net effect was even greater than the sum of its parts but we would say that wouldn't we? The plain truth is that it is almost impossible to disentangle what causes what in this multi-faceted fast-moving world. It reminds me of those sparkling crystal cut balls which used to hang in the middle of dance halls, whirling endlessly and catching the light in a myriad of different ways. Measuring learning accurately is like trying to catch a falling star. But you still recognize it if you see it.

Swings and roundabouts

The various curriculum movements over the last fifty years illustrate what I have been saying. What follows is a gross exaggeration, with notable exceptions, but the general trends were definitely there. The products of the 1944 Education Act were largely brought up on a knowledge driven curriculum, except that it was not knowledge driven so much as fact driven. In those days, I was really good at remembering miscellaneous facts about Britain: Kings and Queens, major towns, big battles and rivers. But it was only when I learnt to drive that I realized how hopeless my actual sense of geography was. Poems and times-tables were chanted in class. In the air-raid shelters too, where there was hardly any vision, let alone visual aids, we chanted, recited, quizzed, repeated and sang our way through the day, trying hard to remember what we were told and repeat it when asked. And even though I could do mental arithmetic then at the speed of light, ever since I left school. I cannot even remember those times-tables which I used to rehearse and manipulate with such confidence. Learning by rote didn't really work then and it works even less well now when there is too much to remember. We do not seem to have registered that knowledge now depreciates at the rate of 7% a year, and therefore 'know how' becomes more important than 'know what'. I was, I think, saved by going to a rather unusual secondary school (Harrow Weald Grammar) which was way ahead-of-its-time in getting facts into perspective, and in giving its pupils considerable responsibility for the management of their own learning. But that was not the norm.

So in the 1960s, 1970s and 1980s, came rebellion against the curriculum of the 1930s, 1940s and 1950s: what was the point of all these facts if people did not know how to use them, how to apply their knowledge, how to think for themselves? Emphasis began to switch to the process of learning getting pupils to manage their own learning, use initiative, research and find out for themselves, work in teams, make presentations, interview each other and even 'real people'. Along with this set of ideas which only took hold slowly and patchily, was the idea of pastoral care and the development of the whole person.

The rebellion was not only against what was too often a narrow, passive curriculum, but also against the suppression of the individual. The telling, controlling, testing culture of rote learning had encouraged passive dependency and conformity in pupils. For some pupils, those who found learning difficult, it had also induced a feeling of fear and failure, a reject label which did nothing to inspire and motivate them and a lot to switch them off education for the rest of their lives. So as an antidote to all this, and as the comprehensive school movement took hold, there developed a new emphasis in schools (which had always been present in the best of the previous schools) in building a 'caring community' in which the needs of each pupil were addressed. There sprang up systems of pastoral care, individual counselling and guidance, and extra support for those with learning difficulties. The pastoral care systems began to rival and even dominate the academic systems (Jones, 1984). Many schools began to take on all the problems of society, and the role of teacher became blurred with that of social worker. Teaching methods changed with a growing emphasis on mixed ability, group work, investigative work and a cooperative rather than a competitive culture. Everyone was to be valued equally, at least in theory.

The thrust behind this movement (of which I was part) was admirable. Its aim was to counterbalance the over rigid and sometimes negative systems of the past, and to release the potential of all pupils. The Newsom Report, *Half our Future* (Ministry of Education, 1963) stressed the 'waste of talent' for the nation if we did not nurture and develop all our pupils. The down side of this era was that it went too far. The swing to 'caring' began to detract from the quest for achievement. For some reason, we seemed as a nation to find it difficult to combine high academic standards and high standards of personal development. The swing from one extreme to another was too great.

But even this pastoral/academic split was not the whole problem. There was also the neglect of capability, which is the ability to translate theory into practice, to take an idea and implement it, to design, produce and to use the end product to good effect. What we really needed to develop was head, hands and heart, a kind of three-legged stool, in balance and stable, and able to withstand considerable pressure. Developing the intellect and the emotions is all very well, but practical ability counts too. So we still had a two-legged, rather than a three-legged stool, and the result was lopsided.

In the early 1980s, the RSA's education for capability movement did a great deal to put this right, and certainly brought the problem into public consciousness. My Cantor lecture at the RSA in 1985 (Jones, 1985) emphasized this point first-hand. Progress has been made with the result that today's curriculum outcomes are couched in terms of what the learner knows, understands and can do. This is an enormous breakthrough. I like to think that a paper I wrote with colleagues for the Secondary Heads Association in 1983 also helped to bring about this shift in emphasis. In *A View from the Bridge* SHA (Secondary Heads Association) we defined desirable areas of learning; added economic literacy, computer literacy and technological literacy; and advocated a modular structure; a role for schools in continuing education; lifelong learning; a negotiated curriculum; records of achievement and action planning; prevocational education (bridging the academic/vocational divide); and opportunities for people to manage their own learning and thereby become more mature.

During the 1970s and 1980s the emphasis on process to balance the previous emphasis on content was welcomed, but it put insufficient emphasis on outcomes and ultimately the process became an end in itself. Process in this sense is quite different from 'process re-engineering' which is a way of using the process to improve the outcomes continuously. On the contrary, in schools and colleges of the 1970s and early 1980s, process too often appeared to take away from achievement, hence the panic now about standards.

International Competition

The stunning findings from my visit in 1990 on behalf of the Department of Employment to the USA Canada, Japan, Korea and Singapore are reported on pages 222-8 Chapter 5 The Civil Servant, study trip to the USA and Far East 1990 (and vice versa).

They showed that we were behind the Pacific Rim countries in developing the kind if skilled workforce needed in the technological age to come.

In the meantime, the Pacific Rim countries, with their high achievement rates in compulsory and post-compulsory education still put a great emphasis on knowledge, but it is not always sufficiently acknowledged that their students are also capable and good with people. In the UK we need to keep head, hands and heart in better balance. In most cases, this now means putting more emphasis on 'head'. Knowledge workers will be almost the only workers of the future. We need every ounce of brainpower we can develop if we are to remain 'world class' and competitive as a nation.

The good news is that TVEI still holds up as a bold national strategy with all the right components. Maybe we should be even bolder about stressing the importance of achieving high standards of success in exams, especially maths, science, technology, IT and languages. But we are absolutely right to stress as well as much as we do the 'person' and 'task management' skills. None of the other countries put as much stress as we do neither on these nor on links with industry. So these additional factors could be our trump card. If we could pull off the trick of continuing to achieve an increased participation rate in post-16 (relevant and appropriate) education, and better exam results, we could still rule the world.

But this will not happen if working practices in industry do not change. TVEI Pupils will want to go to work in places where their skills and capabilities are used otherwise they will become disaffected and frustrated. We are preparing our future workforce but are we preparing our workplaces?

The 'future shock' is fundamental not cosmetic, in most cases a change of organizational culture, management styles, working practices, and education and training provision, value systems and human relation-ships. Incremental changes will not be sufficient. Only those companies that take a strategic view which they follow-up with action will survive in the competitive global economy which is already with us. In other countries, companies are tackling these issues with a precision and determination. If they have not done so already, islands of integration will suddenly snap into fully integrated systems. What are we going to do, now, to overcome our apparent competitive disadvantage in the world market? Jones (1990).

Looking back it seems to me that we had taught our pupils about the information technology revolution but we had not systematically taught them how to take part in it. That may be because we, the adults, were not then sufficiently confident at using these new technologies. Most of our young people have taught themselves and now surpass their elders in competence and capability. Nevertheless, the fact remains that our targets for school leavers still do not include explicit competence in information and communication technologies (ICT). Contrast this with, the example of Singapore, admittedly a small country, but one where all school leavers are technically proficient in ICT, and where a programme of adult IT literacy ensures, at government expense, that all managers are ICT trained. What was also disturbing to note from this visit was that there was a marked difference in approach to education and economic success between the West and the Pacific Rim countries. In the United States and the UK in particular there was, and still is, a great emphasis on education-business partnerships: a great deal of energy and time spent on getting the two 'sides' to talk to each other and understand each other better.

In the Pacific Rim this was deemed to be unnecessary. The pervading culture included an agreed implicit assumption that economic survival depended on being competitive on a world scale. There was no need to muddle up and confuse the roles of education and industry; everybody accepted that economic success depended absolutely on each sector developing the potential of its people to the utmost. As Pascale and Athos, (1985) put it: 'the core of management is precisely this art of mobilizing and pulling together the intelligent resources of all employees of the entire firm'. And this task has been ruthlessly pursued with a great deal of apparent success. We might feel that 'all-round' development has been neglected at the expense of high-tech performance, but we may be wrong even about that. If we do not take this competition seriously we are in danger of deluding ourselves. It used to be said that the USA fostered individual brilliance and collective mediocrity, whereas Japan fostered individual mediocrity and collective brilliance. Whatever the truth of this, in the UK we certainly need to target both individual and collective brilliance.

The fact remains that the Pacific Rim countries are pushing, and successfully, for ever higher standards of academic achievement, albeit on rather narrower indices than we have been pursuing in the West. This fact is reflected in the numbers now staying in education to eighteen and/or completing higher education. This would not in itself constitute such a threat to the UK economy if it were not combined with other factors. In the UK we have a rapidly ageing workforce, and in Europe in the year 2,000 more people will retire than will join the labour market. We also have an expensive and relatively unskilled workforce. In the Pacific Rim countries, conversely, there is a growth in numbers of young people, who themselves are well educated and highly skilled. These countries therefore have a growing number of highly competent skilled workers, who are relatively cheap to employ. So, in thinking about the curriculum for a changing world and uncertain future, we have to take account of the international competition, and to do this on a number of dimensions. To maintain and re-secure our leading edge, we need to think and act very fast. We certainly cannot afford to waste the talent locked up and under-developed in our existing workforce.

Organizational Changes

If this set of factors were not enough, we need also to examine the changing nature of organizations, the effects this is having on people and the kind of curriculum they will need if they are to survive in this uncertain future. Just as Britain does not yet truly have a learning culture, so some organizations are not yet truly learning organizations. Senge (1990) defines a learning organization as one where people continually expand their capacity to create the results they fully deserve. This requires a change of mindset even more complicated than organizational reshuffling, if the creativity of all members of the organization is to be released. As Einstein said:

I never discovered anything with my rational mind.

My observation is that a large number of organizations now know about and talk about the kind of dramatic changes that are taking place in organizations, but very few of them have actually worked out the implications of these changes, or what they should be doing now if they are to sustain their businesses. Comfortable lip-service is paid to flatter hierarchies, delayering the organization, even the concept of the learning organization, but little changes fundamentally, even when the flattening and delayering actually takes place. The shape of the organization might change, but the assumptions on which it works do not, so nothing really changes. If organizations are unable to manage this transition from caterpillars to butterflies (or whatever else emerges) for themselves, then they may have to break down completely in order for a new kind of organization to emerge, one which is more appropriate to this brave new world.

How will individual learner-workers fare in this anomic environment? I do not have the answers, though they may be simpler than we imagine: it is easy to become overwhelmed by complexity. In any case, people have to work out for themselves the answer which is appropriate in their circumstances. However, the trends are very clear, and are borne out by an in-depth series of interviews which we in the Brunel Management Programme (based at Brunel University) have undertaken. The organizational trends noted were hardly surprising, and only confirm the predictions of the organizational analysts such as

Handy (1994). Universally reported were the following trends:

- Smaller organisations, dramatically smaller, with a growing trend for setting up devolved autonomous units or cost centres, each of which has to be self-sufficient.
- Flatter hierarchies, with several tiers of management stripped out.
- Focus on customer care, for sustained growth.
- Partnerships with suppliers.
- Strategic alliances with other former rivals.
- Great hope pinned on business process re-engineering.
- Continuous change on a global scale as a permanent backcloth.
- Shift from management to facilitative leadership.
- Focus on continuous learning and self-development.
- Collaborative team working to retain competitive leading edge.

Devolvement to autonomous sub-units requires a whole new order of integrative mechanisms: who has the picture of the whole? Is this now irrelevant? The stripping out of layers of hierarchy may have gone too far: have the right people been moved out? Senior managers may no longer be used for implementing decisions rather than taking them: workers will need a lot of support to develop their 'management skills'. The 'core' business may now be too lean: is there sufficient experienced manpower around to carry the remaining core business? The question of how to build in appropriate continuous development in a changing context, and particularly without an organization to belong to, may be difficult. New role models and working practices will need to be developed. *Quis custodiet ipsos custodes?* How will individuals sustain their learning or get support for their learning? They will not be able to depend on their large organization to pay, and even if they regroup into small organizations, they may find them-selves under too much pressure for survival to make time or resources available for formal learning.

The fact is that in the future lifelong learning will no longer (even if it ever did) come from lifelong employment. This is not necessarily a bad thing though it does raise enormous questions about who pays. Expensive management training courses will not be in the reach of most individuals. However, my own view is that lifelong learning will become more of a reality when people depend less on their employing organization and more on their own initiative to ensure their own continuous professional development. If learning pays, who will pay in the future? Certainly not the large organization of yesteryear: such organizations will rarely exist and, instead, we are likely to move to cooperative self-help learning organizations. Perhaps those people who work alone or in very small organizations will get their support and professional sustenance from professional bodies who should, along with careers guidance workers, assume much more importance.

The Handy Report (1989) postulated a 'clover-leaf' organization, with a third employed, a third subcontracted as needed and a third providing services to the core, has come upon us with a vengeance; in some cases the 'hard core' third may be hard pressed to cover all that is needed for basic survival. Too lean and mean could mean extinction. But the corollary of all this is that organizations as we have known them are breaking down completely. It could be that at least two thirds of the working population in the future will be self-employed. What curriculum prepares people to cope with this?

At first, the idea of self-employment is seductive; people in control of their own lives, selling their services and skills in the market place, only working as much as they choose. Originally, many of the people taking and developing this 'option' did so voluntarily. Many of them were well-established experts in middle years who perhaps had taken an early retirement. They could immediately be subcontracted back by their previous employer amongst others. This first generation of peripheral suppliers to the hard core quite often had paid off their mortgages, had seen their children through their education into independence, and maybe even had a small pension to cushion them through leaner times, or allow them to take a holiday from time to time. So far so good!

But then other factors came into play. First, the market for independent consultants or very small companies began to get overcrowded. Those lucky enough to secure contracts began to take on more and more work, because they soon discovered that if they said they were unavailable, for whatever reason, the work would go to someone else. Those who started up later began to find that it was very hard to get a foothold in this precarious and very unstable market: but at least these older people were not destitute if the work did not come, though their morale and self-esteem may have suffered. But what has prepared these successful and less successful consultants for this pressurized life in which there is very little time to stand and think? Their own core of inner strength, motivation and intellectual capital will be their main resource, and even this will need sustenance and replenishment.

So much for the older generation of experienced company workers now working alone or in small groups! What about the younger generation? I am thinking here particularly of the very many highly educated people who have heeded the advice of adults and taken degrees, masters, even doctorates in an attempt to make sure they are qualified for high level work in this new knowledge based high-tech world. Many have taken further postgraduate qualifications, in part because they could not get work and, in part, in the sometimes erroneous belief that this will get them a job. The overall increase in the numbers of qualified graduates in the last few years has been phenomenal: in 1987 when I joined the Employment Department, some 12-14% of the age cohort obtained degrees. Now the figure is approaching 30% and some would argue that it ought to be 50%. The CBI (1994) has come out with a target of 40% by the year 2,000 as a minimum. It sees higher education as 'a prime source of highly skilled people, a key contributor to a dynamic economy and central to the future competitiveness of UK businesses. I agree, but there are transitional difficulties.

This group of highly qualified young people now face at least two sets of major problems. First, they may have degrees but it does not follow from that they are capable people with marketable sets of skills, despite the efforts of the Enterprise in Higher Education Initiative, which I set up in 1987 on behalf of the Employment Department. The flight into 'higher degrees' may in fact have handicapped, not enhanced, their employability in the short-term.

But a much more serious problem is that there is not much employment to be had, particularly at the higher level: this is still a hard fact to swallow, considering the fact that there are still skills shortages in some high level jobs. But, never mind, these highly qualified young people can surely, set up their own small businesses, or work as consultants/servicers of the remaining small core organizations? Or can they?

My observation is that in the long-term it will pay to be a graduate, and my views are shared by Sir Christopher Ball (1992). But in the short-term the going for these young people is extremely tough. If they are self-employed at this stage in their lives, then all too often (as we know from Maslow's hierarchy of needs, (1970), they do not have sufficient basic security from which to develop their full potential. What is missing for them? Unlike the older generation of self-employed entrepreneurs, this younger generation lacks many 'benefits' of employment: for example, pensions, holidays, sick leave, relative security of tenure, maternity/paternity leave. No work, even for a few weeks or months, means no money. And this vicious circle means that it becomes very risky to buy a house, have a family, take out a personal pension plan, or take a holiday. And certainly there is neither the time nor the money to buy into the formal education system.

Obviously some people do very well, but for all too many life becomes a series of short-term contracts, with all the insecurity which goes with that life style. It becomes impossible to turn down an opportunity for work in order to take a much-needed holiday. It is a treadmill. Sometimes such people's insecurity is also exploited: wages may be relatively low and long hours can be demanded. If people do not like the conditions under which they work, then they do not have to be kept on. There are plenty of other people ready to take up the contract. These conditions are not conducive either to learning, or to the release of creativity or full potential.

But this is not all. Not only do these people not have any of their basic needs for security met, they are also isolated. They do not belong to an organization, and though they may well have some support through professional organizations, through their peer group or through some social/sports activity, basically they are not going to get the benefits, which many of us have taken for granted in the past, of belonging to an organization. Such benefits include companionship, stimulus, cheap meals, challenges, use of shared amenities, training, fun, and even something to complain about! (Remember Elliott Jacques seminal work on the organization as a defence against anxiety, 1955) Yes, we all know that organizations create their own set of problems, such as inertia, bureaucracy, power games, paralysis by analysis, but for many people working virtually alone can be very lonely and very time consuming. Having to do all your filing, book-keeping, marketing and reprographics becomes tedious and inimical to creativity. Yet, in this scenario, it is not always possible to employ others to do this.

In addition, people who have not worked in organizations may also find they are constantly re-inventing wheels for themselves. This can be stimulating and exhilarating, but it is a slow process. It is almost as if organizations now had to re-invent themselves *ab initio*. Re-engineering the organization with a vengeance! It is probably this complete recreation of the concept of organization which is needed in the long term, organizations based on different assumptions from those which now hold sway. But the transition, the chrysalis stage, can be worrying. Most people feel very insecure when they cannot see the light at the end of the tunnel or the butterfly emerging from the chrysalis. You can see why networking has become so important.

Yet even more frightening is the fact that I have been discussing here the plight of the highly educated. What will happen to those people who have not had the advantage of an extended education? How will they cope in a jobless world? How will they cope particularly if they have already been labelled as educational failures? To build a permanent under-class is a recipe for disaster. My feeling is that this trend cannot continue indefinitely and that eventually totally new forms of organization will emerge. Then the whole cycle may well repeat itself though my hope would be that the organizations of the future would be based on an entirely different premise from the power and line cultures of the past.

So, back to the question: what kind of curriculum will help people of all kinds and levels of intelligence to survive and thrive in this very uncertain world? Current national concerns, not surprisingly, are about raising standards of achievement, meeting national training and education targets, catching up with our world neighbours, particularly those in the Pacific Rim. 'Learn 'em harder and harder': with an implicit assumption that 'failing' can be eradicated by better, tougher teaching. If only it were as simple. Some people respond to carrots, others to sticks, but most people need recognition, confidence, and some kind of security if they are to learn optimally. We forget this at our peril. These 'human factors' apply regardless of brainpower or background. Whatever systems we introduce to improve our collective performance, we need to ensure that they enable everyone to learn more, better and faster, and to be able to apply that learning to improved performance. We need also to enable that learning to continue through life, to be recognized and celebrated, to be put to the benefit of the nation, the community and the people themselves. These are not only in themselves beneficial, but also motivating factors.

In the emerging new world, the individual rather than the organization becomes the mover, the provider and the pusher of learning opportunities. The role of education and training systems changes from teacher to facilitator, supporter, counsellor; peer group stimulus and support grows in importance; educational institutions will be increasingly customer-focused if they are to remain in business. People, not organizations, will be the paymasters, and mostly they will neither want nor be able to pay very much. They will move back into 'self-help' groups where learning resources rather than large organizations are used to bring about intellectual and personal growth. Individuals who want to get on will be addicted to learning, but they will want that learning to be accessible, flexible and good value for money. They will not pay for poor teaching or time serving.

Whatever kind of curriculum will cope with all this? It could be that the idea of a curriculum is itself out of date. Think of all those years anguishing about what should be in the national curriculum. The concepts of transferable core skills, still being pursued in the new national curriculum, are also included in the CBI requirements for graduates for the twenty-first century (CBI, 1994). They include personal and interpersonal skills, communication, information technology, application of number, problem solving, and modern language competence. These skills were originally piloted through TVEI (1983-1994) and then extended to Enterprise in Higher Education: it is good to see that they have survived all the chopping and changing. However, it seems to me that a new order of core skills is beginning to emerge, not to supplant or replace those former core skills but to add to them some overarching qualities that the learner-worker of the future will need to develop. These are the development of intellectual curiosity, the motivation to do better, the confidence to admit learning needs, the determination to find out more, the will to share joy and pain with others, the ability to translate ideas into practicality.

How do we learn all that? Not entirely from our parents and upbringing, though these are key factors: more needs to be done to help parents with this very important role and the RSA project, Parents in a Learning Society (1994), is one small but significant step towards this. Most of us do not learn from being in a passive and totally dependent culture; the breakdown of large organizations may well help to shake people out of this childlike dependency into mature adulthood. People learn when they take responsibility for the management of their own learning, a fact well recognized by the FORD EDAP scheme and the Rover Learning Business: in both of these companies the employees themselves decide what additional learning they want to undertake. They are clearly 'learning organizations' which fit well with the vision for human resource development propagated in a Eurotechnet publication (1993):

In the learning organization, the process of learning is permanent not intermittent, holistic not segmented, problem centred, context related and includes all members of the enterprise. The learning organization brings the strategy, structure and culture of the enterprise itself into a learning system. Management development is transformed into a self-learning self-management process. The transformation of the whole system for greater competitiveness is the goal!

This is the kind of approach we need to apply to creating a learning society in which lifelong learning becomes a reality. There are encouraging signs that this is beginning to be understood. An ESRC document (1994) setting up a £2 million budget for research into The Learning Society makes the same point:

While the need to create a 'learning society' is becoming widely recognized, the tremendous increase in learning required for a labour process based on conscious involvement and a society of citizens active in their working and democratic lives to a learning organization does not just mean more training, the whole organization culture has to change.

In other words, a paradigm shift from training to learning, and learning for all. My own concern is whether present mechanisms to enable people who have left full-time education to continue to be lifelong learners really exist. However, the emphasis in the White Paper on Competitiveness (DTI, 1994) on incentives and mechanisms to enable mature people to return to learning is encouraging. A whole section on lifetime learning promotes career development for all, tax relief and Investors in People: whilst for schools there is a new general diploma, vocational courses, a vastly improved budget for careers guidance, and modern apprenticeships. The extension of the idea of Learning Credits bodes well. There is, however, a long way to go before every adult in the country actively and consciously feels that they are a 'learner'.

When I was responsible for TVEI, I took great care to build the concept of continuous learning for continuous improvement into our thinking. When we thought and spoke about the curriculum, we were not focusing entirely on the secondary school curriculum but had lifelong learning in mind. The kind of requirements of the curriculum which we were providing is summarized in this speech:

- Giving young people opportunities to continue in further and higher education
- Ensuring that all young people are equipped to cope with change
- Increasing the number of people who are successful learners and therefore want to go on learning throughout life

- Bridging the academic-vocational divide
- Building a more flexible and responsive education system
- Using modern technologies in the classroom so that they more readily mirror the realities of life after school (Jones 1990)

Motivation, a sense of direction, recognition of success module by module, a record of achievement, these are vital ingredients for effective learning. So the curriculum of the here and now and of the immediate future needs to be tough on technical detail, tender on suitability to individual needs, demanding of each person one further step in growth, rejecting of tell and sell, and strong on do-it-yourself. As managers in industry are now shifting to become leaders and facilitators, so teachers at whatever stage or age need to become facilitators, learning supporters, providers of guidance and counselling, builders of confidence and demanders of higher standards. The shape of things to come is still impossible to determine: 'that is of no importance', as le Petit Prince said to the Flower (St Exupery, 1945). The principles of a learning person, a learning community and a learning society have never changed. And that is where the stability and the continuity comes from in this uncertain world of ours.

Postscript:

This was written in 1995, way before global internet communication was established. Apart from the disenfranchised, who are not connected, People now are learning all the time, even the disconnected, but they don't always realise it. So the next question is so what? Do we control this in an orderly fashion or just let it be?

References

BALL, C. (1992) *Profitable Learning*, London, RSA.

BRUNEL MANAGEMENT PROGRAMME (1994) *Organisational Trends*, unpublished

CBI (1994) *Thinking Ahead: Ensuring the Expansion of Higher Education into the 21st century*, London, CBI.

DTI (1994) *Competitiveness: Helping Business to Win*, London, HMSO.

ELIOT T.S. (1954 edition) *Chorus 1 from the Rock*, London, Faber &

Faber

EMPL0YMENT DEPARTMENT (1987) *The Enterprise in Higher Education Initiative,* London, HMSO.

ESRC (1994) *The Learning Society: Knowledge and Skills for Employment.*

EXUPERY, A. de (1945) *Le Petit Prince*, London, Heinemann

GRAHAME, K. (1908) *The Wind in the Willows*, London, Methuen.

HANDY, C. (1994) *The Empty Raincoat*, London, Hutchinson.

HANDY, C. (1989) *The Age of Unreason*, London, century Hutchinson.

JACQUES, E. (1955) *Social Systems as a Defence against Persecutomy and Depressive Anxiety in new Directions in Psychoanalyses*, London, Tavistock.

JONES, A. (1984) *Counselling Adolescents: School & After*, London, Kogan Page

JONES, A. (1985) *Tomorrow's schools: open or closed?*, RSA Cantor Lecture.

JONES, A. (1990) *Key features of USA and Far Eastern study tour,* unpublished report to the Employment Department.

JONES, A. (1990) *Future agenda*, Address to Imtec International Conference, Oxford.

MASLOW, A.H. (1970) *Motivation and Personality*, New York, Harper & Row.

Ministry of Education (1963) *Half Our Future*, London, HMSO (The Newsom Report).

MONTAIGNE, M. de (1953 edition) *Essais*, Paris, Editions Gamier.

OHMAE, K. (1990) *The Borderless World*, New York, Harper Business.

PASCALS, R.T. and ATHOS, A.G. (1985) *The Art of Japanese Management*, London, Penguin.

RABELAIS, F. (1955 edition) *Gargantua & Pantaguel*, London, Penguin Classics.

RSA (1994) *Parents in a Learning Society*, London, RSA.

Secondary Heads Association (1983) *A View from the Bridge*.

JONES (1987) *Leadership for Tomorrow's Schools*, Oxford, Blackwell.

SENGE, P. (1990) *The Fifth Discipline*. London, Doubleday.

CHAPTER 9: Life after Work 2000-

2000 onwards: Retired at last.

What I had not realised was that I would soon be as busy as ever and that this would include quite lot of work... Surely I could have predicted that? It was however good to take more time out to enjoy my island house more and to see my children and my rapidly growing number of grandchildren, and my friends, old and new.

It was in 2000 that I was first asked to write this book, and it has taken fourteen years for me to agree! My publisher has been very patient.

Retirement in Henley

Once I really stopped 'work' a whole new life opened up for me. The first step was to confirm that yes I really did want to make Henley my retirement home. The answer was yes! I had always wanted to live in Henley, at least since before the M4 or the M40 were built. We used to go through the middle of Henley on our way to have lunch with my parents in Bampton (now Downton's village!) or on the way to our cottage in Wales. This was before the one way system, so I was able to admire the church, the Tudor and Georgian houses and of course, the river and the scenery.

When I was young, our family used to come to Henley or Winter Hill to hire a punt and picnic on a deserted island. I remember looking enviously at the houses built on the river bank, with green lawns sloping down to the river. It was only when in 1984 I bought a house on Rod Eyot Island that it all came back to me. Yes, Henley was where I wanted to retire! I was Head of Cranford then, (Exit 4 on the M4) so in the school holidays I could easily go back to school to check on what was happening. I could also read books, write books, entertain friends, old and new, go to the Kenton Theatre, (no cinema yet), row around the island every day in a small dinghy and generally relax. So in a sense my true retirement began long ago.

You may have noticed that all my jobs were full-on. In all of them I got home late and then worked all evening until the small hours. This is when my brain is at its most active and clear and there is silence apart from the water birds. I actually prefer to work at night,

When I finally retired from Brunel in 2000, I was still very busy doing a range of very interesting jobs, most of which were not paid. So again though I have never really stopped working, I have also had lots of mini-retirements. I have had a fascinating time doing exactly what I like. Between 1993 and 2000 the Cabinet Office invited me to be an occasional member of the Final Selection Board for the civil service, mainly the potential high flyers who were going to end up in the Foreign Office, or eventually become Permanent Secretaries or at least Under-Secretaries. I found that very interesting work and wondered how ever had I managed to become an Under-Secretary in one bold step!

Between 1995 and 2003, I was an occasional independent lay Chairman for the south-east Regional NHS. My job was to Chair the Complaints Panel reviews and decisions. This was a difficult and sometimes stressful task, but well worth doing.

In 2004, I was fortunate to be invited to become a governor of the Abbey School, Reading. The Abbey is a highly successful private school for girls from 3-19, which was led in my time as governor by an outstanding and inspiring Head, Barbara Stanley. I became the governor responsible for human resources, a task which became harder every year, as rules and regulations became more and more demanding, as did being prepared for an inspection at any moment. Part of my job was the annual review of the Head's (and the school's) progress in achieving the targets set for each year. All I can say is that the school improved dramatically every year, with outstanding results and pupils who were confident and capable as well as fully prepared for their future lives. The staff were brilliant at bringing out the best in each pupil. It was a privilege to serve there. I retired from the Board in 2012. How different that school is from Malvern Girls College in the fifties. What a transformation! Hope **The Education Roundabout** stays put at that point of excellence for a while.

When I was working full time I hardly ever read a book for pleasure, except on holiday. I was fortunate in my retirement to be invited to join a Book Club run by a group of highly intelligent women. We meet once a month to this day. That has been wonderful, lifelong learning for me at last! Next I joined The Ramblers, which I enjoyed. It was a great introduction to the local area as well as healthy and good company. Alas, my left knee began to play up at this stage, and I found it difficult to keep up with the others, especially in the Cotswold Hills. Then I joined the local gym, but found that difficult too and didn't keep up with anything except the monthly fee! ...all the time I was working, I had had no physical exercise at all except gentle walking. It's a miracle I am as fit as I am.

In 2004, I joined the Reading Branch of the Chartered Management Institute (I had been made a Fellow). I rapidly became Chairman and the attendance at our lecture meetings improved but after four years I had had enough, it was too much like work.

I hadn't found anything that totally inspired me until I joined the Henley Choral Society. I used to sing in the school choir and I had joined the Malvern Choral Society when I was teaching there. I hadn't sung for over fifty, years and both my voice and my sight reading skills were decidedly rusty. Fortunately HCS does not audition new members so I got in.

It turned out that the choir was having a low patch as such organisations do from time to time. Nobody wanted to be Chairman and there was a risk that the choir would have ceased. A good friend of mine suddenly got up at a meeting and said 'Anne is good at that kind of thing'. The rest is history: I became Chairman of the Henley Choral Society in 2005. Then our Musical Director resigned. This is where my experience of recruiting and appointing came in. We advertised on the web and got seventy applications. I cheekily phoned the Royal Academy and asked the head of choral direction if there were any good candidates coming out of the Choral Direction Course that year. He said 'try Will Dawes.' There were five other excellent candidates on the final shortlist. Will Dawes was unanimously chosen by our members as our musical director. The choir immediately began to flourish and grow, to the extent that we really needed to buy proper staged seating for 100 singers, something I managed to organise for the choir. We now have yet another outstanding young musical director, Ben Goodson. I stood down from being Chairman in 2008 and now I am at last thoroughly enjoying being an irresponsible member of the choir, who is still learning to sing great works.

I joined Phyllis Court Club around 2001. I was asked to speak about LLS (Lifelong Learning Systems) at Probus. I was immediately co-opted onto the Probus Committee as speaker secretary for four years and then became Chairman. I really enjoyed every minute of Probus. Why? It's another lifelong learning activity. The talks are so interesting that members are re-energised by them.

In 2009 I was elected to PCC Council and given the responsibility of being the link between Council and the interest groups. I like to think that I am the Council member FOR the interest groups. This is no mean task. There are now over thirty activities which members can take part in. My job is to keep the IGs and the PCC Council happy. It seems to be working. For me, it's like being a mini-Head with thirty Heads of Departments, all of whom have great amount of automomy and responsibility for what they manage. In all the thirty interest groups, the members are all learning something new each time they meet, as well as having a lot of fun and many friends. So as far as I'm concerned it's another lifelong learning activity for them and me.

Anne Jones at Phyllis Court Club with Katherine Grainger MBE gold medalist at the London Olympics

During the Olympic year, I was also asked by Council to run some Olympic events for the club as well as my work with the interest groups. We ran thirteen trips to London to view the new Olympic Stadium and the East End, which was equally fascinating. We also ran six dinners to which we invited all the Olympic rowing medallists or would-be medallists. They mingled with the members and we followed their progress with great interest. We also collected for a charity, Headstart, based in Henley and raised £6000.

At a special Olympic rowing champions dinner at Phyllis Court Club Naomi Riches (2nd from right) won a gold medal in the Paralympics mixed fours.

I have never given up on my personal mission: Encouraging and supporting lifelong learning, making a difference and being useful, helping others and even now encouraging the idea of community schools.

The sudden death of my daughter Katy has left us all shattered, but we know she would have wanted us to carry on with our various missions. I am blessed that my other children, Christopher and Becky are thriving and doing well. My seven grandchildren likewise, and I am very proud of them all. My brothers David and Michael likewise.

My five grandchildren who live in England on holiday in Mexico, 2007
Left to right: Sarah, Huw, Alex, Freddie and Harry

Monaco, our island cottage on the Thames in Henley,
set out for our annual family party

Our 2012 family party including members who had come from New Zealand and Malawi to be there